THE RECORDS OF THE NATION

This book has been issued as
Extra Volume 2
to subscribers to the British Record Society

The British Record Society acknowledges with gratitude
a grant from the Aurelius Trust

THE RECORDS OF THE NATION

The Public Record Office 1838–1988

The British Record Society 1888–1988

EDITED BY

G.H. Martin and Peter Spufford

THE BOYDELL PRESS

THE BRITISH RECORD SOCIETY

First published 1990 by The Boydell Press, Woodbridge

The Boydell Press is an imprint of Boydell & Brewer Ltd
PO Box 9, Woodbridge, Suffolk IP12 3DF
and of Boydell & Brewer Inc.
PO Box 41026, Rochester, NY 14604, USA

ISBN 0 85115 538 3

British Library Cataloguing in Publication Data
The Records of the nation : the Public Record Office, 1838–1988 : the British Record Society, 1888–1988.
1. Great Britain. Public records, history
I. Martin, G. H. (Geoffrey Haward) II. Spufford, Peter
942
ISBN 0–85115–538–3

Library of Congress Cataloging-in-Publication Data
The Records of the nation : the Public Record Office, 1838–1988, the British Record Society, 1888–1988 / edited by G. H. Martin and Peter Spufford.
p. cm.
Includes rev. papers from a conference held in London, Aug. 8–10, 1988.
Includes bibliographical references.
ISBN 0–85115–538–3 (alk. paper)
1. Great Britain. Public Record Office – History – Congresses. 2. British Record Society – History – Congresses. 3. Probate records – Great Britain – Congresses. I. Martin, G. H. (Geoffrey Haward), 1928– . II. Spufford, Peter.
CD1043.3.R43 1990
354.410071'46–dc20 90–33864

This publication is printed on acid-free paper

Printed and bound in Great Britain by
Woolnough Bookbinding Ltd, Irthlingborough, Northants

CONTENTS

PREFACE

The year 1988 marked the one hundred and fiftieth anniversary of the foundation of the Public Record Office, and the centenary of the British Record Society. It was decided to celebrate that happy conjunction with an historical conference in London, which was opened by the Lord Chancellor, Lord Mackay of Clashfern, in the Hall of the Inner Temple on 8 August, and closed with a dinner presided over by Lord Bancroft, as President of the Friends of the Public Record Office, on 10 August. The present volume contains revised texts of papers and addresses delivered at the conference, with an additional paper, (no.17) on the incidence of wills surviving from the early modern period. As editors we have taken the opportunity to select which papers to print, and to alter some of the papers quite considerably from the oral form in which they were delivered. We have allowed some contributors to amplify their papers, whilst at the same time truncating others. We hope that the resulting volume addresses a number of themes in a significant way.

Just as the conference celebrated two institutions, the one a public office concerned with the multifarious business of acquiring, assessing and safeguarding the Public Records, and the other a private association devoted to enlarging and enhancing public knowledge of them, so this volume seeks to address the two broad themes, of preservation and use, in a way useful to all who are interested in archives. The first fifteen papers discuss various aspects of the Public Record Office's holdings as a whole, whilst the last six are focussed upon the present concern of the British Record Society with probate records.

The papers on the public records have been arranged in two sections. The first is concerned with the history and development of the Public Record Office itself, whilst the second addresses a problem of the greatest importance to every reader, that of access to records by way of calendars and indexes. In other words how users of every kind can judge what evidence they may be able to find. Those two sections are followed by two papers representing the interests of two major groups of present readers.

The probate record section offers some new approaches to wills, inventories and probate accounts, including the first fruits of a number of lines of research being pursued by younger scholars in the field of social history. It is of particular interest to those working in early modern English history, the period for which at present probate records have most to contribute to historical studies. It has been suggested that the papers on probate records might be developed and reprinted together as a manual at a later date.

The editors, as the then Keeper of Public Records and as Chairman of the British Record Society, would like to take this opportunity of expressing their thanks to all those who made the conference such a success. They are especially grateful to the Lord Chancellor for agreeing to open the proceedings and address the first session.

The smooth succession of the meetings, often in parallel sessions, was a striking tribute to the work of Miss Stella Colwell who bore the burden of the months of preparation for the conference, and managed to show at the same time a remarkable attention to the details of organisation and the needs of individuals. At the conference her skill and experience in conference organisation bore visible fruit.

The conference would not have been possible without a substantial and timely loan made by the Aurelius Trust to cover preparatory outgoings before any fees from delegates came in. The Trustees have since most generously converted that loan into a grant towards the expense of this publication. The Editors would therefore like to express their warmest thanks to Dr Marc Fitch and the Trustees. The Society's bankers, Barclays, also provided welcome assistance in the financial arrangements for the conference.

The editors are also grateful to the treasurer and Masters of the Bench of the Honourable Society of the Inner Temple for making the Inner Temple Hall, the Arbitration Room and the Parliament Chamber available for the conference, and to Jean Morris, Deputy Sub-Treasurer, for her help and advice, and her staff for their ready assistance.

All members of the conference would wish to thank the Public Record Office itself for inviting them to its birthday party in Chancery Lane, and its staff for arranging an evening tour of the Office at Kew.

From the British Record Society Carolyn Busfield and Patric Dickinson, the Honorary Treasurer and Secretary of the Society respectively, gave great help in running the conference. Mrs Busfield spent a very considerable amount of time dealing most effectively with the financial details of the conference organisation, whilst Patric Dickinson and his fellow members of the Bar Theatrical Society provided an appropriate and much appreciated evening's entertainment.

From the Public Record Office John Walford, who provided liason with the Office at Kew, Nicholas and Jane Cox, Elizabeth Hallam and the Keeper's secretary, Mrs Patricia Marron, all gave valuable assistance before and during the proceedings.

Amongst others David Bedford Groom, Susan Lumas, and, especially Vicky Clements, gave timely help, whilst Andrea Duncan was not only actively involved in preparing for the conference, but also in launching the Friends of the Public Record Office whose association was launched on 9 August. We thank them all for their generous expenditure of time and energy.

G.H. *Martin* — *Peter Spufford*
Wimbledon — *Cambridge*

OPENING ADDRESS BY THE LORD CHANCELLOR

The Right Hon. The Lord Mackay of Clashfern

I am honoured to be able to speak to you this morning both because this is such a memorable double birthday and because I stand before such a very distinguished audience. There can rarely have been a greater concentration of expertise in the field of British archives sitting together in a single place. So I hope you will accept these few words from a relative newcomer on a subject where antiquity rightly counts for so much.

We are here to celebrate two very significant anniversaries in the history of the preservation and publication of our national archival heritage: the one hundred and fiftieth anniversary of the Public Record Office and the centenary of the British Record Society.

Although we are today commemorating just 150 years of the records of the nation, the tradition of preserving our public records is a long one. Domesday Book has been carefully safeguarded for nine centuries. The systematic creation and preservation of records by the Exchequer and Chancery goes back some eight hundred years. And record repositories were established by the end of the thirteenth century in the Tower of London, the Exchequer at Westminster and in the House of Converts (*Domus Conversorum*), which was founded near the New Temple in 1232 for Jews who had converted to Christianity. The last of these repositories was used for the storage of the rolls of Chancery, and from there, their custodian took his title of Keeper or Master of the Rolls and the site its later name of the Rolls Estate.

Centuries of freedom from foreign invasion and only minimal disruption from rebellion and civil war left the contents of those repositories virtually undisturbed. Their location to the east and west of the City of London even protected them from the Great Fire. Thus, gradually their custodians began to develop archival principles and practices, which were rudimentary but which formed the basis for the comprehensive and professional techniques of today.

Nevertheless, by the end of the eighteenth century the quantity of public records had grown beyond the capacity of the main repositories and it was estimated that there were some sixty places in London housing public records. According to the report of the Record Commissioners for the period 1800 to 1807, many of these records were 'unarranged, undescribed and unascertained, . . . many of them . . . exposed to erasure, alienation and embezzlement and . . . lodged in buildings incommodious and insecure'. Concern over the chaos which threatened and the risk at which the records were being put led to a lengthy campaign by a group of far-sighted individuals to establish a central records repository. The campaigners included Henry Cole, later to be Prince Albert's *alter ego* in planning the Great Exhibition of 1851 and, perhaps more significantly, the inventor of the Christmas card, Sir

Francis Palgrave, then Keeper of the Records in the Chapter House, Westminster, and, most crucially, Henry Bickersteth, who had taken the title of Baron Langdale on his appointment as Master of the Rolls in January 1836.

The outcome of their efforts was 'An Act for keeping safely the Public Records', which received the royal assent on 14 August 1838. That Act brought public records into the custody or charge and superintendence of the Master of the Rolls; it established the Public Record Office and provided for the appointment of a Deputy Keeper of the Records to be 'Chief Record Keeper' under the Master of the Rolls. Over the next thirteen years Lord Langdale and Sir Francis Palgrave, whom he had appointed as first Deputy Keeper, laboured to create the Public Record Office. They faced the problem of integrating into a single institution men (there were, of course, no women on the establishment at that time) of varying temperaments and ambitions, working at four separate locations: the Rolls Estate; the Chapter House, Westminster; Carlton Ride (the old riding school of Carlton House, where Cole had become Assistant Keeper); and the Tower of London (where Thomas Duffy Hardy, who had in the past come to blows with Palgrave, was Assistant Keeper – he was later to succeed him as Deputy Keeper).

But perhaps the hardest task which faced Langdale and Palgrave – and one with which we are not unfamiliar today – was to persuade the Treasury to give effect to that section of the Act which required it 'to provide such suitable and proper or additional Building or Buildings as may be requested for the Reception and Safe Custody of all the Public Records which . . . shall be in the custody of the Master of the Rolls'. Lord Langdale had already given the Rolls Estate to the nation to be the site for a new record repository. The Treasury however favoured the use of the Victoria Tower in the new Houses of Parliament which were just at that time rising again from the ashes of the terrible fire of 1834. The Victoria Tower, of course, subsequently became the home of Parliament's own records.

Not until 1849 was agreement reached on the use of the Rolls site and Sir James Pennethorne commissioned to proceed with his plans for what was to be the first stage of the present Public Record Office building in Chancery Lane. The new repository was specially designed to provide secure conditions for preserving the public records, but I am eager to point out that it was not, as is sometimes said, the first such building in Britain: as a Scot I must enter a prior claim for Robert Adam's Register House in Edinburgh, completed in 1789, which is now the headquarters of the Scottish Record Office.

By the time work started on the new repository Lord Langdale was dead and it was his successor, Sir John (later Lord) Romilly, who was to preside over its opening and the removal of the records there from the surviving ancient repositories. He was also to round off the efforts of his predecessor in securing recognition of the role of the Public Record Office as the repository for departmental papers as well as legal records. The 1838 Act applied specifically only to the records of a list of named courts. Provision was made for other bodies to be added, and one or two departments had already deposited records in the Office by 1852, when an Order in Council regularised these arrangements. Even so the State Paper Office, which housed the papers of the Secretaries of State from Tudor times onwards, remained an entirely separate institution until 1854. Only then did it become a branch of the Public Record Office, thus ending Palgrave's fears that the State Papers might be deposited in the Department of Manuscripts of the British Museum. Thus at last the Public Record Office was clearly established as the national repository for all public records.

That other great area of archival work, that of publishing transcripts or calendars of the public records, and thus making them available to a wider audience and facilitating research in them, antedates the establishment of the Public Record Office. In the eighteenth century editions of Domesday Book and the Rolls of Parliament had been published officially, and much pioneering work on English and Scottish records had been undertaken between 1800 and 1837 by successive Record Commissions, which had employed as editors, among others, Palgrave, Cole, Hardy, and the Rev. Joseph Hunter (another of the original Assistant Keepers of the Public Record Office).

Given this continuity of personnel, the Public Record Office saw one of its initial tasks as being to round off the work of the Commissions before it embarked in the later 1850s on the first of its own monumental series of calendars, the *Calendar of State Papers*. But then, as now, the volume of the records and the limited resources of the Office meant that much of the work of publishing public records had to be left to the initiative of local and specialist record-publishing societies.

Among the latter the British Record Society's *Index Library* stands out in terms both of quality and quantity. The first of its volumes, a calendar of Northamptonshire and Rutland wills, was published in 1888 and in the following year the first two of many volumes relating to records in the Public Record Office appeared: a calendar of Chancery Proceedings for the reign of Charles I and an index of names to royalist composition papers. The founder of the Index Library and the compiler of those, and many others of its early volumes, was William Phillimore, record scholar, genealogist, advocate of local record offices, and instigator of several other record publishing societies. His early energy and initiative has led over the intervening century to the publication by the Society of an average of a volume a year. In the course of this endeavour a wide range of public records in the Public Record Office and elsewhere has been made more accessible to users, and in particular to family historians, whose cause the Society fostered long before the subject attracted the mass following of recent years. Without the Society's series of basic calendars and indexes the search for one's roots would be even more speculative and hazardous than it undoubtedly still is.

In congratulating the Public Record Office and the British Record Society on their anniversaries I also lay claim to a small share in the celebrations, because just over thirty years ago, on 23 July 1958, a new Public Records Act received the royal assent. This brought to an end one hundred and twenty years during which the Master of the Rolls had directed the Public Record Office and had custody of the public records. In his place the Lord Chancellor was made responsible for the care and preservation of public records for the Public Record Office, and the custody of the records in it under his direction.

In that role of Minister responsible for the care and preservation of public records the Lord Chancellor may be something of a parvenu, but as a creator of public records he can claim a pedigree which stretches back almost eight hundred years to 1199. In that year Hubert Walter was appointed Chancellor of England. A versatile man, he had earlier accompanied Richard Coeur de Lion on his Crusade to the Holy Land and had been his chief negotiator with Saladin. After Richard's capture he was, with the Queen Mother, the prime mover in raising the £100,000 that was required for ransoming the King. In 1195 he issued an edict requiring every man above the age of fifteen to take an oath for the maintenance of the public peace, before knights appointed for the purpose in every shire. From this sprang the offices, first of Conservators, and later of the Justices of the Peace themselves, whose appointments are, like that of all my predecessors, an important part of my work as Lord Chancellor. But more relevant to today's celebrations, it was Hubert Walter who instituted those great series of rolls of Chancery, recording royal grants and instructions issued under the Great Seal which form the core of our understanding of medieval administration. The longest lived, if not quite the earliest, is the series of Patent Rolls, which opens with two letters patent dated 23 September 1201 in favour of Robert de Turnham, Seneschal of Poitou and Gascony, and continues to the present day, albeit in a somewhat different format.

Until very recently the Patent Roll was engrossed in manuscript on parchment by a scribe in the Royal Courts of Justice. This process was slow and laborious. It has recently been replaced by a technological revolution that has taken place in the Crown Office in Chancery under which, by electronic means and a laser printer, three documents are produced as part of a co-ordinated operation. These are the Warrant that is submitted to Her Majesty for signature, the Letters Patent themselves that are produced in accordance with that Warrant, and finally the entries for the Patent Roll. The latter are produced on individual sheets which are then bound up into volumes in book form, there usually being one or two for each regnal year. I am glad to say, however, that they continue firmly to be referred to as 'The Patent Roll'.

Hubert Walter was unusual in one respect which I very much hope not to follow. He paid a visit to Canterbury to be with those who were responsible for maintaining the records there (I mean of course the monks), and expressed the warmest interest in their welfare, as I do in you who are here today. Unfortunately, however, he promised to 'stay with them longer than usual' – and amply fulfilled that promise by dying and being buried in their midst.

Over the next three days you will consider many aspects, past, present and future, of the selection, preservation and use of public records, and I am especially pleased to see that although much of the focus is on the Public Record Office, public records in local places of deposit are not to be neglected. For instance, tomorrow is devoted, for those who choose that option, to the study of probate records. A significant innovation of the 1958 Act was the bringing within its ambit of public records of local interest which it is neither practicable nor desirable to take into the Public Record Office. For such records the Lord Chancellor has been given powers to appoint as places of deposit local record offices and other institutions which have suitable facilities for their safe-keeping and preservation, and for their inspection by the public. About one-fifth of all public records selected for preservation are now held in such places of deposit, and I welcome this opportunity to pay tribute to their custodians and to recognise the debt owed to them by users of such records, among which pre-1857 probate records figure so prominently.

The deposit of Public Records in local offices under the Public Records Act 1958 has greatly enriched our archival heritage, and connections with the local repositories have been strongly developed through the work of the Public Record Office's Liaison Officer, whose role has transcended the formal bounds of inspection, and has extended to valuable professional exchanges with local archivists. At present the Public Record Office's relations with the archival profession as a whole in this country are closer than ever before.

The Public Record Office has also played a full part in both the work of the Society of Archivists and in the newly-formed Commonwealth Archivists' Association.

Despite these welcome developments I know that it is a matter of concern to all those whose work is involved in the field of records that we lack a fully effective system for co-ordinating our national archives, both central and local. I myself would welcome such a system, while recognising that there would be financial and other implications, and that many of these would fall to others than me to decide on. I do feel very strongly, however, that despite the great strides that the Public Record Office and those responsible for local record offices have together made in recent years, the lack of a system which could co-ordinate the work on an overall basis – particularly in respect of finding aids – is a real drawback. We have, countrywide, what must be easily the richest collection of records in the world, but we have much more work to do before its potential is fully realised. I hope therefore that, in years to come, it will prove possible to develop and extend the work that has already been done by many devoted people throughout the country.

There is one other event which I should like to commemorate and to which I am sure many of you will wish to add your own tributes, both formally and informally. This conference marks one of the last official functions of Dr Geoffrey Martin as Keeper of Public Records. It is a fitting finale for one who, after a formidable career as an academic historian, which included among numerous other distinctions being Professor of History and Pro-Vice-Chancellor at Leicester University, took on the considerable burden of Keeper of the nation's records enthusiastically and conscientiously. He will be particularly remembered for the imaginative way in which he planned and carried through the exhibition in 1986 which commemorated Domesday Book. We wish him well in his retirement.

And it seems fitting also to congratulate Michael Roper on his appointment as the new Keeper of Public Records with effect from 1 October. I am entirely confident that he will continue to build on the excellent traditions of record-keeping so ably maintained by Dr Martin.

The nature and contents of the public records have changed frequently over the past nine centuries, but perhaps never so rapidly as they are changing at present, and one wonders what Langdale and Palgrave would think of the present Public

Record Office (especially its Kew building) and what Phillimore would make of the current family history boom.

But one wonders also how they, or we, would feel if we returned in fifty or even in twenty-five years' time. New means of transmission, recording, and retrieval are being developed so fast that systems can become antiquated almost as soon as they are developed. The speed with which vast amounts of information can be processed now is quite simply staggering, though when, if ever, we will reach the celebrated paperless society remains a matter of speculation.

I certainly have a strong suspicion that it will be some considerable time before Government departments, my own included, dispense entirely with the familiar, tangible ministerial brief. Nevertheless, now and in the future, the Public Record Office, local record offices and record societies face a stirring challenge. The task of tracking information and records, of collating them and finally of preserving them for posterity becomes ever more complex.

The Public Record Office, in keeping with its popular conception, keeps a watchful and steadfast gaze on the past. But, like Janus, it must, and does, look to the future too. And I know that the Office is in the forefront of the race to develop means to manage the records of the future.

Whatever media may be used to preserve and publish the public records of the twenty-first century, I am sure that the Public Record Office and the British Record Society will continue to have vital roles to play, though I suspect that if we were to come back at the occasion of their three-hundredth and two hundredth and fiftieth anniversaries, respectively, we might find it difficult to comprehend those roles.

I congratulate the Office and the Society on their anniversaries. I wish each well as it starts on a new era of its history, and I wish you all an enjoyable and fruitful celebratory conference.

THE HISTORY AND DEVELOPMENT OF THE PUBLIC RECORD OFFICE

1. The International Role of the Public Record Office

Michael Roper Keeper of Public Records

From its very beginnings the work of the Public Record Office has had an international dimension, although the nature and extent of its international role has varied over the years. Five strands, overlapping each other chronologically and not necessarily mutually exclusive, can be traced: the use of records in the PRO by readers from overseas; the publication by the PRO of records in foreign archives relevant to English and British history; the copying for overseas archives and libraries of records in the PRO relevant to their national histories; the provision of professional and technical advice by the PRO and its staff to overseas archives and archivists; and the drawing by the PRO on the experience and expertise of the international archival community.

Access by foreign scholars to British public records antedates the establishment of the Public Record Office itself. A team of French scholars transcribed records in the Tower in the eighteenth century. Foreign scholars also had access to the State Paper Office. A register recording permits to inspect state papers there, which starts in 1800 and continues until 1877, fifteen years after the State Paper Office had been absorbed into the PRO, shows Mr Lorenz, the Hessian Ambassador, consulting and copying treaties with Hesse Cassel in 1809, the first of many foreign readers of the state papers, including a certain Professor Ranke, who had permission in 1865 to examine papers relating to Prussia and the German States in the reign of William III.[1] Meanwhile, in 1851 fees for 'literary searches' in the public records had been abolished, but formal permission to undertake such searches had to be sought, and, of course, applications were recorded. The first overseas reader whose name appears in the register was H. G. Somerby of the United States, who visited the Office fourteen times in 1852, consulting 234 subsidy rolls, a recusant roll and eight inquisitions in the course of his research into the genealogical history of New England. A noted Danish antiquary, J. J. A. Worsaae, who applied three days after Somerby, appears never to have visited the Office, perhaps because he had discovered in time that there was little there relevant to his research into the connection between Denmark and Ireland.[2]

The number of foreign readers in the PRO has increased dramatically since

1 PRO 6/325.
2 PRO 35/1.

Somerby was their sole representative. By 1948 one hundred out of 570 reader's tickets issued were for foreign students, by 1962 224 out of 1,800.[3] Now it is estimated that about a quarter of the readers in the PRO (and over twelve thousand reader's tickets were issued last year) are from overseas, mainly from North America, Australia and Europe, but also, and increasingly, from other parts of the world.[4] Many of those present-day readers are descendants of emigrants and are researching their family history, others are studying the history of their own country, but not all fall into these two categories: scholars from North America and Australia are just as likely to be researching in British history, and we have even been visited by Japanese and Soviet historians whose interest has been in life in a medieval English village.

Towards the end of his Deputy Keepership Sir Francis Palgrave, having rounded off the publications work of the Record Commission, began to put together the first planned programme of PRO publications. This was based around the state papers, and it was thought desirable to complement the calendars of those records by parallel work in sources for English history, especially of the Tudor period, in foreign archives. The first volume of the *Calendar of Letters, Despatches and State Papers, relating to the Negotiations between England and Spain, preserved in the Archives of Simancas, and elsewhere*, edited by Gustave Bergenroth, was published in 1862, to be followed in 1864 by the first volume of Rawdon Brown's *Calendar of State Papers and Manuscripts relating to English Affairs existing in the Archives and Collections of Venice and other Libraries of Northern Italy*. Those two series were to be supplemented later in the century by a series of calendars of documents relating to British and Irish affairs preserved in the Vatican. Isolated volumes were also published calendaring documents in France (edited by none other than J. H. Round) and Milan, and some foreign material was included in the *Calendar of Letters and Papers, Foreign and Domestic, Henry VIII*. This research in foreign archives continued spasmodically between the Wars, and publication dragged on until 1961 (indeed the *Calendar of Papal Letters* still continues but under the auspices of the Irish Manuscripts Commission), but work of this kind no longer figures in the PRO's list of priorities.[5]

Nor, unlike many other national archives, did the PRO revive its interest in extraneous sources when the advent of photography and microfilming made the copying of such sources relatively straightforward. We have always had more than enough to handle with the large volume of accessions from departments and courts, and have no cause to devote resources to the acquisition of non-public records. Consequently only a handful of photographs and microfilms of documents in over-

[3] *110th Report of the Deputy Keeper of Public Records* (for 1948), p. 7; *Third Report of the Keeper of Public Records* (for 1961), p.1; these and the intervening reports are the only ones specifically recording the number of foreign students who obtained reader's tickets.

[4] *25th Report of the Keeper of Public Records* (for 1983), p. 2.

[5] Many of the transcripts from which the calendars were compiled are now in PRO 31. A collection of material acquired by Rawdon Brown for the Venetian calendar and bequeathed by him to the Office constitutes the class PRO 30/25. For a list of the calendars see *British National Archives*, Government Publications Sectional List 24 (1984), pp. 27–29.

seas archives is held, mainly in the classes PRO 22 and PRO 28, and the only significant collection is the official United Kingdom series of microfilms and prints of the German Foreign Ministry archives. They were produced after the Second World War by the German War Documents Project set up by the British and American governments, joined subsequently by the French, to film, study and publish German records relating to the origins of the War. They are now in GFM classes.

If the interest which the PRO has taken in extraneous sources has been limited, the same cannot be said about the interest of overseas archives and similar institutions in sources in the PRO bearing on the histories of their own countries. First in the field was the Public Archives (now National Archives) of Canada, which began a programme of transcription of records in the PRO in the late nineteenth century.[6] During the First World War the Canadian government installed a photostat camera in the PRO, mainly for the work of its military history section based there, but also for copying historic documents. This latter work continued when the machine was transferred to the PRO after the War, to become the foundation of the PRO's present Reprographics Department.[7] A second machine was introduced for the benefit of the Library of Congress of the USA in 1929.[8] In 1941 a microfilm camera was installed by University Microfilms Inc, on behalf of the American Council of Learned Societies, financed by the Rockefeller Foundation and sponsored by the Library of Congress, with the dual purpose of providing security copies of documents which were at risk because of the War in Europe and establishing in the United States a research collection of sources for American history in the United Kingdom.[9] In 1948 two further microfilm cameras were introduced, a second camera for the Library of Congress and the other, proposed in 1939 but delayed by the War, for a joint project by the National Library of Australia in Canberra and the Mitchell Library in Sydney.[10] The Canadians also switched to microfilm. The London office of the National Archives of Canada and the Australian Joint Copying Project, now covering several other Australian institutions, still continue their work in British archives, although the sources in the PRO have been now largely exhausted, but the Library of Congress project has come to an end. The consequential reduction in the demands for microfilm from those long established customers has been more than compensated for by the business which the PRO's Reprographics Department does with other national archives and libraries, which have in recent years included institutions in Burma, Hong Kong, Kenya, Malaysia, Qatar, Singapore, Sri Lanka

6 Public Archives of Canada, *General Inventory of Manuscripts*, Vol. 2 (Ottawa, 1976), p.15.

7 *Guide to the Public Records. Part I. Introductory* (HMSO, 1949), pp. 55–56.

8 *91st Report of the Deputy Keeper of Public Records* (for 1929), p. 3. A proposal in March 1929 by the Library of Congress to introduce a portable microfilm camera does not appear to have been followed up: PRO 1/96, Pt 1, f. 236.

9 PRO 1/314, 394; *103rd Report of the Deputy Keeper of Public Records* (for 1941), p.1. A list of the records filmed was published: C. K. Born, *British Manuscripts Project* (Library of Congress, Washington DC, 1955).

10 PRO 1/273, 652; *110th Report of the Deputy Keeper of Public Records* (for 1948), p. 6.

and Zimbabwe. One particular international institution which has become a major customer for PRO microfilms is the Genealogical Society of Utah.

Because the PRO is required to recover the full cost of its reprographic service and has no interest in microfilm exchange, it has not always been easy for overseas institutions to find funds to acquire PRO microfilm, but several have been able to finance significant programmes from their own resources or with the assistance of Unesco and other international aid agencies. In the case of the Soviet Union an ingenious solution has been to establish the British Academic Committee for Liaison with Soviet Archives (BALSA), on which the PRO and other interests are represented. This acts as an intermediary in ordering microfilm from Soviet archives on behalf of UK institutions and scholars, charging them at PRO rates for those copies and applying the income received to the purchase for Soviet archival institutions of a corresponding number of copies of documents in the PRO. The Committee acts similarly as an intermediary in the exchange of archival publications, co-operates in the joint publication of documents on Anglo-Russian history and smooths the path of UK scholars seeking access to Soviet archives.

Another area of international dissemination of information is in the field of exhibitions. It is permissible under the 1958 Public Records Act for the Keeper of Public Records to lend documents for temporary commemorative exhibitions outside the PRO, and recently notable documents from the PRO have been made available to a wider audience at exhibitions in Vancouver, New York, Washington and Berlin. Such loans are not made lightly: the PRO has to be assured that environmental, lighting and security conditions meet stringent standards; an officer of the PRO has to accompany the document to and from the exhibition and only he (or she) can place the document in or remove it from its case; all the expenses, including the provision of a security photograph or microfilm, insurance, transport and the cost of any necessary prior conservation work and mounting, have to be borne by the exhibition or its sponsors.

Overseas interest in the PRO is not confined to the records which it holds. The professional and technical expertise which we have developed over the past one hundred and fifty years is also in great demand, and many members of PRO staff have gone overseas to pass on that expertise, while even more overseas archivists have come to the PRO to learn from us.

This aspect of the PRO's international role is largely a post-Second World War development; indeed the War itself may have provided the impetus. From February 1944 to July 1945 Hilary Jenkinson, then the Principal Assistant Keeper of the PRO, was seconded to work in the War Office with the Adviser on Monuments and Fine Arts, Sir Leonard Wooley, as Adviser on Archives. In this role he was concerned with the protection of continental archives, providing guidelines for the occupying Allied forces on the handling of enemy records, which he drafted in the widest possible terms to afford protection not only to 'historical' records but to all archives, including modern and current records, and visiting from time to time the appropriate sections of the Control Commissions in Italy, Germany and Austria. Two assistant keepers, Roger Ellis (later Secretary of the Historical Manuscripts Commission) and Humphrey Brooke (later Secretary of the Royal Academy) and a former temporary assistant in the Office, H. E. Bell (later Tutor and Librarian of New College, Oxford), were seconded from their army units for service as Archives Officers with the Monuments, Fine Arts, and Archives Sub-Commission in Italy, where under Jenkinson's guidance they were able to minimise the destruction of Italian archives and to afford such protection to the records as was feasible in a war zone. Later, Ellis and Brooke moved on to Germany and Austria respectively for similar duties.[11]

As the War ended and the Allies took on the administration of Germany and Austria, the PRO lent E. C. Matthews to head the Archives Section of the British Element of the Control Commission for Germany, where he was assisted by H. A. (Johnny) Johnston, also of the PRO, on secondment from the Royal Air Force; another member of the PRO staff, Russell Farmer, was seconded from his army unit to head the Archives Section of the British Element of the Control Commission for Austria.[12]

Maybe his wartime experiences had stimulated Jenkinson's increasing interest in the wider archival community; certainly having become Deputy Keeper in 1947 he was then in a stronger position to follow through his natural Napoleonic inclinations. Already before the War he had, through the Colonial Office, assembled information on archives in the colonies for an abortive second volume of the *Guide International des Archives* (of which more later). This interest he revived and developed in 1946, prompting the Colonial Office to circulate in 1948 a memorandum by himself on the keeping of archives and a questionnaire enquiring into the state of those in each colony.[13] One outcome of this enquiry was an invitation to Jenkinson (by now Sir Hilary) to undertake an advisory mission in Jamaica in February 1950.[14] This was the first such mission outside Europe undertaken by anyone from the PRO, but since then there can be hardly a country or territory of the Commonwealth, not to mention non-Commonwealth Third World countries, which has not received a consultancy visit by a PRO expert. Most such visits have been short-term and advisory, but Jeffery Ede's mission to establish an archive service in Tanganyika (as it then was) lasted a year; Daphne Gifford spent two years working on the records of the Falkland Islands; and Russell Farmer, after his retirement, spent several years in Iran.

The mirror image of that export of expertise has been a steady stream of archivists, records managers, librarians and others concerned with the preservation and dissemination of information to the PRO to see how we do things. Last year we

11 PRO 30/75/42–46 (Jenkinson Papers); WO 220/596; H. E. Bell, 'Archivist itinerant: Jenkinson in wartime Italy' in *Essays in Memory of Sir Hilary Jenkinson*, ed. A. E. J. Hollaender (Chichester, 1962), pp.167–177; *106th Report of the Deputy Keeper of Public Records* (for 1944), p.1; *107th Report of the Deputy Keeper of Public Records* (for 1945), p.1.

12 *106th Report of the Deputy Keeper of Public Records* (for 1944), p.1; *107th Report of the Deputy Keeper of Public Records* (for 1945), p.1.

13 PRO 30/75/7: H. Dawe, Colonial Office, to Jenkinson, 17 August 1934; PRO 1/738, 783, 867.

14 PRO 1/1056; PRO 30/75/49; C. V. Black, 'Jenkinson and Jamaica', *Essays in Memory of Sir Hilary Jenkinson*, pp.153–166.

received professional visits by archivists and members of related professions from twenty-four countries.[15] Such visitors have ranged from junior archivists from Commonwealth countries on study visits, often linked to the archives course at the School of Library, Archive, and Information Studies of University College London (where their teachers will have included members of the PRO staff) to senior archivists from all over the world, often accompanied by architects or computer specialists, hoping to learn from our experience in planning and operating the new building at Kew, still of interest over ten years after its opening and despite its air-conditioning problems, and in the application of computers to archival work. At present international interest is being directed especially to our pilot project to test the optical digital data disk as a storage medium for a machine-readable data archive.

The exchange of professional experience and expertise has not been entirely a one-way process. The PRO has also been able to learn from archives and archivists of other countries. In the very early days of the Office Sir Francis Palgrave cited the French École des Chartes as a model for the study of palaeography when making proposals for a system of examinations for the clerks and assistant keepers of the PRO, proposals which were not acceptable to Lord Langdale and came to nothing.[16] Over half a century later, following visits to study archives in Belgium, France and the Netherlands, the Royal Commission on Public Records in its report of 1912, while concluding that the 'continental system of "Archive economy" deserves the careful attention of our own authorities', made only one recommendation specifically based upon those studies, namely that the PRO should learn from the systematic training of foreign archivists by establishing a system whereby successful candidates for appointment to the Office should undergo a special training and pass an examination in technical subjects before being confirmed in their appointments.[17] This recommendation has never been implemented, or at least not in respect of the examination.

The Royal Commission drew attention to the seminal Dutch archival manual of Muller, Feith and Fruin, first published in 1898 and already in 1912 translated into a number of other European languages, but not into English. It was not to be translated into English until 1940, and then in America not Britain. However, Jenkinson was aware of its existence and cited it from the French translation of 1910 in his own *Manual of archive administration.*

The Royal Commission also noted that an International Congress of Archivists and Librarians had been held in 1910 as part of the Brussels international exhibition. Although no permanent international organisation of archivists emerged from it, that meeting is usually regarded as the starting point of the history of international archival co-operation. Its impact on the PRO was nil. S. R. Scargill-Bird,

15 *29th Report of the Keeper of Public Records* (for 1987), p.18.

16 Information provided by my colleague J. D. Cantwell, who mentions it in his forthcoming history of the Public Record Office.

17 *First Report of the Royal Commission on Public Records*, Vol.1, Part I [Cd 6361] (1912), pp. 38–40, 49; Part II [Cd 6395] (1912), Appendix IX.

Secretary of the PRO, acknowledging a telephone invitation from the Board of Trade to be represented at it, wrote that 'this Office partakes so little of the nature of a Public Library that it is very doubtful whether any advantage could possibly accrue from such a course', and after consulting with the Deputy Keeper, Sir Henry Maxwell Lyte, declined to send a representative.[18] The PRO maintained its distance from the international archival community throughout the inter-war period, playing no part in the activities of the Archives Commission of the International Committee for Historical Science apart from responding with rather bad grace to its questionnaires. In 1931 C. S. B. Buckland, one of the Assistant Keepers, after commenting scathingly on one questionnaire from the Commission, minuted: 'Discourage the dreary Nabholz [the Swiss secretary of the Commission] and his dubious colleagues'.[19] However, Hilary Jenkinson had taken part, clearly extra-officially, in a meeting in Paris in January 1928 of a committee of experts on the conservation of manuscripts and published materials held under the auspices of the International Institution for Intellectual Co-operation of the League of Nations (a forerunner of Unesco).[20] He also collaborated, again apparently extra-officially, in another venture of the IIIC, the *Guide International des Archives*; indeed in correspondence with H. Bonnet, the Director of the IIIC, he claimed that the *Guide* had been his own idea.[21] The first volume, covering Europe, appeared in 1934, but plans to extend and update it, with Jenkinson providing information on archives in the colonies, were brought to nothing by the War.

Only after the Second World War did the PRO begin to appreciate the benefits which it could gain from official participation in the international archival community. In 1953, in his valedictory report as Deputy Keeper, Jenkinson recorded the first flowering of internationalism within the PRO:[22]

> I represented this Country on a Committee which in 1948 under the auspices of UNESCO (but reviving a pre-War project) drafted proposals for an *International Council on Archives*: and was one of its first Vice-Presidents. Since then there have been Conferences and Committee Meetings at the Hague and in Paris which I and some other Members of the Staff attended and to which we made some contribution; the Executive Committee of the Council has met once, by my invitation, at the Public Record Office; and on my ceasing to be a Member of this Committee I have been succeeded by the present Principal Assistant Keeper [i.e. D. L. (later Sir David) Evans]. There is no doubt that Archive Science has now reached a stage where international co-operation is both possible and valuable; as we have ourselves independently proved in connection with our Publications and with the exchange of Microphotographs. The more formal arrangement of periodical Conferences, a Journal and the like unquestionably

18 PRO 1/75: drafts, S. R. Scargill-Bird to Board of Trade, 7 February and 8 March 1910.

19 PRO 1/99: miscellaneous, minute by C. S. B. Buckland, 20 April 1931.

20 PRO 30/75/7; there is no trace of Jenkinson's participation in this meeting in the official correspondence of the Office in PRO 1.

21 PRO 30/75/7: Jenkinson to H. Bonnet, Director IIIC, 29 June 1934.

22 *115th Report of the Deputy Keeper of Public Records* (for 1953), p.10.

> have value: though some of our Colleagues in other Countries would appear to have more time to devote to such activities than is available, unfortunately, in our own case.

Participation by the PRO in the work of the International Council on Archives has continued, and perhaps more time has been made available for such activities. There has usually been a PRO representative on the Executive Committee and two Keepers, Jeffery Ede and Freddie Mabbs, served as Vice-President and President respectively. There has been a PRO presence at each of the quadrennial International Congresses on Archives and annual International Archival Round Table Conferences; we hosted a Round Table Conference in 1965 and the Congress of 1980, which was attended by more than a thousand archivists and accompanying persons from eighty countries. Representatives of the Office have also contributed to and benefited from the work of ICA's technical committees, especially those concerned with automation and reprography. Outside those formal ICA activities the Office has benefited also from study visits to overseas archives and from participation in a wide range of overseas conferences, seminars, symposia, and workshops.

Jenkinson felt that archival science had, by 1953, 'reached a stage where international co-operation (was) both possible and valuable'. Thirty-five years on, in an age of rapidly advancing technology, with all that that implies for the creation, preservation and use of archives, and for the management of archival institutions generally, international co-operation has become essential if each country is not to waste its resources re-inventing its own archival wheels. Involvement in the international archival community is no longer an optional extra, a mere opportunity for 'cultural tourism'; it is a vital necessity for the PRO, just as much as for the national archives of Vanuatu.

2. The Public Records in 1988

G.H. Martin Keeper of Public Records 1982–88

As an historical archive, the Public Records today are what the Public Record Office has made of them since 1838. Over the past hundred and fifty years the ancient and many of the modern records of the Crown have been gathered together and made available for daily uses of which their remoter custodians, and perhaps even some of their more recent begetters, could hardly have dreamed. In the process they have been carted, examined, sorted, cleaned, repaired, listed, boxed, and shelved; some, though not yet enough, have been edited and published. All have been assimilated to the purposes of the Office established to receive them, without losing the departmental character and connexions which give them their historical importance. The Lord Chancellor has said something of the work of his medieval predecessors and their clerks which established the professional keeping of, as distinct from the business of generating, the documents which record the daily acts of government from the twelfth century onwards,[1] and my colleagues will speak about the ways in which the records have been housed, and about the work that is entailed in acquiring and caring for records today. My own part is to celebrate the assembly of this distinguished company, and my sense of good fortune in being Keeper at this historic and propitious moment, by looking briefly at the development of the Office and its services over the first century-and-a-half of its existence.

The passing of the Public Record Office Act of 1838, 1 & 2 Vict.c.94, was a significant episode in the history of British archives and therefore in the study of history in this country. It marked, however, the end of a phase quite as distinctly as any new beginning. The ancient records of the Crown were distributed at that time amongst more than fifty repositories in and about London, including the Tower, the buildings on the Rolls Estate in Chancery Lane, and the Chapter House at Westminster. The means of best securing them and of enabling their study had been a subject of parliamentary and public discussion since 1799, through the agency of a Select Committee and six successive Royal Commissions, whilst for almost a century before that public funds had been applied to the publication of records in the form of Thomas Rymer's *Foedera* (1704–35),[2] the *Rotuli Parliamentorum* (1767–1777), and most recently *Domesday Book* (1783), which was reissued in a new edition, one that is still valuable, in 1816. The protracted reform of the Exchequer

1 see above p. 1.
2 See also below pp. 90–1.

begun in 1786 and the catastrophic burning of the Palace of Westminster in 1834, which so narrowly spared Domesday Book and the other documents in the Chapter House, each served to emphasise the unique character of the oldest records and the dangers to which they were exposed. The last of the Record Commissions lapsed amid recrimination and controversy in 1837, but the public mind had been prepared by debate, and by the extensive publication of texts, for the expense of establishing a new repository, and a new means of safe-keeping, for the Public Records.

What was done in 1838 marked both a departure and a very English continuation of existing practice. The Act established a new department of government, a benison which has become a good deal more common since that time, but it did not abate the long-established notion of departmental ownership, behind which lay the notion of what we should call ministerial ownership, of the records. It vested responsibility for the care of the records in the Master of the Rolls, the senior Chancery judge whose predecessors had long kept the records of Chancery, many of them in and around Rolls House and the Rolls Chapel. At the same time it prescribed the means by which the records were to be secured without providing the means by which they could be safely housed, and it transpired that the Treasury, always anxious to afford the public purse the protection of a deliberate procedure, wished to consider the matter further. In the meantime, however, the Master of the Rolls, Lord Langdale, who was strongly supportive of his new charge, appointed the most able and far-sighted of the existing custodians, Sir Francis Palgrave, who had kept the records in the Chapter House, as his Deputy Keeper. The first of the Deputy Keeper's annual reports, published in 1840, records the opening stages of a ten-year struggle both to acquire and store records and at the same time to persuade the Treasury that nothing truly useful could be done until there was a new building on the Rolls Estate.[3] Lord Langdale, who had originally provided an impetus to the Act by granting the Estate as a site for the Office, was dead by the time that the foundation stone of the new repository was laid, in May 1851, but he was succeeded by Lord Romilly, who proved an equally stalwart champion of the records. The building, designed by Sir James Pennethorne, was an example of Victorian pragmatism at its very best, its decorative style well shaped to the requirements of a secure, fire-proof, and naturally-lit structure in which readers and records, though not then their custodial staff, could be decently accommodated. It was opened to the public in 1856, but it was already clear that it was not large enough and a new campaign had to be mounted for an extension. The events of the Crimean War brought pressure from the Board of Ordnance to remove the remaining Chancery records from the Tower. The War Office was engaged in reforms that produced the first modern files of departmental papers as well as more effective action in the field, and the price included a substantial displacement of older archives. Current administrative practice was impinging on the Office for the first time. Further congestion at Chancery Lane was then promised by a decision to pull down the State Paper Office in St James's, and transfer the accumulated papers of the former Secretaries of State

[3] See also below pp. 39–41 for the Chancery Lane buildings themselves.

to the Public Record Office. The transfer was something for which Palgrave had fought; he died in 1861, having at the last also seen Domesday Book removed from the Chapter House to its present home, and having by a characteristically bold decision committed it to be photographed by the Ordnance Survey: a further reminder, if we needed one, of the nineteenth-century mind's ready response to technological change.

Palgrave's intuitive sense of archival practice, which owed something to his own experience but nothing to any kind of instruction, also told him from the beginning that modern administrative papers were of the same concern to the archivist, and ultimately to the historian, as the oldest material in his care. We owe the preservation of the records of the Decennial Census to his vigilance in the 1840s, and an informal scheme of transferring papers to the Public Record Office from other departments of government was begun in his time, though on a smaller scale and of a more rudimentary kind than he had originally wished to see.

His successor, Sir Thomas Duffus Hardy, who had hoped for the Deputy Keepership in 1838, hated Palgrave with a loathing that extended far beyond the tomb, and had no desire to be seen in accord with him over anything. He found himself beset by the problems posed by modern papers, but his own particular interest and expertise was in record editing and publishing, which Palgrave had not seen as a matter of the first urgency. During his term of office Hardy made his own substantial contribution to the Rolls Series, the *Descriptive catalogue of materials relating to the history of Great Britain and Ireland* (1862–71), and he was also much concerned with editorial policies and with the establishment and early operations of the Royal Commission on Historical Manuscripts. Both the Rolls Series and the Commission were by definition concerned with records other than the Public Records, and valuable as both were to the wider study of history and the nation's awareness of its historical resources, they did represent some diversion of the Deputy Keeper's energies. Nevertheless one of the best times for doing things is when the opportunity presents itself, and the most that we ought to say is that Hardy might have found equally challenging work in the archives of later periods of history. As it was the Office's accommodation was substantially increased in his time, with an eastern extension begun in 1863 and completed in 1871, and the last years of his deputy-keepership produced a new Act, the Public Record Office Act 1877, 40 & 41 Vict. c.55, which addressed the accumulation of obsolete and obsolescent departmental records.

The Act regularized the existing scheme for disposing of papers for which departments saw no further use, and although that may sound some distance removed from the reverential awe that preserved Domesday Book, it must have seemed, and really was, the only way forward at the time. It remains, in a more refined form, the principle upon which records management is conducted today.[4] A departmental committee was set up to authorize the destruction of material, and substantial quantities were cleared away. It must be said that although the committee's decisions were often sweeping, and that in retrospect, from a stance which is at once the

4 For current practice, see below, chapter 5, pp. 49–6.

historian's strength and weakness, many have seemed to be indefensible, the volume of the material was alarmingly great, and continually growing. Administrative needs were no less pressing than at any other time, whilst the disparaging view of the recent past to which we are all prone extended even further back in the nineteenth century than it does today. It was not until after the First World War that history was called in to elucidate, or perhaps exorcise, living memory. Hardy was succeeded in 1878 by his brother William, like him a product of Henry Petrie's training in the old record office in the Tower of London, but a man of lesser energy and talent. William Hardy recruited or accepted two outstanding assistant keepers, Charles Trice Martin and Hubert Hall, but his term of office was not a dramatic one. He was followed upon his death in 1886 by a markedly different character, Henry Maxwell Lyte, then 37 years old: the first graduate to hold the Deputy Keepership, the first, and for years to come the only history graduate in the Office, and one whose previous experience of the public service was confined to some recent work as an inspector for the Historical Manuscripts Commission. The appointment was an inspired one, for Maxwell Lyte's manifest self-assurance rested upon a high degree of academic and adminstrative competence. He gave the Office a character and sense of purpose that lasted into our own time, and is by no means yet a spent force.

Maxwell Lyte found the Office half a century old, with its own routines, and its original object accomplished in the secure custody of the ancient records. He thought it time for a new direction, and sought to promote the scholarly uses of the records. He also had an eye to practicalities, however, and his earliest acts included the installation of electric lighting and the first lift in the Office. He was deeply dissatisfied with what the Rolls Series had become, and took steps to end it, and to promote in its place the series of calendars and lists that have diffused knowledge not only of the nature but also of the contents of the Public Records all over the world.[5] To those who use the records it has always seemed so desirable to have an index to them all that the want of one can only be attributed to the irresolution or perversity of their custodians. To those who daily have the uncounted millions of documents under their eyes the usefulness of the exercise, which could exclude any other activity whatever, is a good deal less compelling. Within particular categories, however, it can be abundantly justified, and the availability of the new calendars of the Chancery rolls, which appeared from 1894 onwards, opened a whole new phase of English historical studies.

As the electric light proclaimed, the scholarly work of the Office, which now seems wholly characteristic of Maxwell Lyte's time, was only one of the matters of which he applied his energy. Chancery Lane took on its present shape by the building of the west street front in 1892–95, and then, at the expense of the Rolls Chapel, one of the most interesting monuments of London's legal enclave, the westward extension of the repository in 1899–1900. The new premises were dignified, even awe-inspiring, but they included a museum, with a permanent display of

[5] See also below pp. 93–4.

records, which acknowledged the interest of a wider public than the privileged world of learned readers.

In 1910 the sessions of the Royal Commission on the Public Records allowed the Deputy Keeper to expound his view of the Office and its accomplishments, and although he was not content with all its recommendations, the Commission's reports remain the most explicit and comprehensive survey that we have of British archival practice. The Reports appeared, however, in 1912, 1914, and 1920, and their dates mark off some of the ominous themes of our own day. By the time the Commissioners were assembled the Public Record Office was handsomely complete, but once again it was also full, and had to be supplemented by temporary storage. There were, however, greater trials to come. The war that began in 1914 was an agent of cataclysmic change, amidst which the archivist might be forgiven for distinguishing a prodigious increase in the use of paper as something of lasting consequence. The power of the industrial state, realised between 1916 and 1918 beyond any previous imagining, required a correspondingly great administrative effort to marshal and sustain it. Amongst the things that would never be the same again after the war were the relatively modest level of governmental activity that had sufficed to sustain daily life before 1914, and the relatively modest acreage of paper that had sufficed to record it.

When the crisis was over the nation discarded its weapons more readily than its typewriters. It might have been better to have kept both, but in the event some of the typists found further employment on the official and other formal histories of the great conflict. Not only were there more records to assimilate than ever before, there was also a wider curiosity about them. The habit of inquiry had burgeoned with the social sciences, and historical research itself moved towards contemporary experience. Maxwell Lyte retired in 1926, at the respectable age of 78. He had always responded decisively to the demands of his post, and it is no disparagement of his successors to say that the Office continued in his image to the Second World War and even beyond. In his later years he continuously developed the programme of publication and scholarly enterprise that he had initiated, and in the course of it promoted, in M.S. Giuseppi's *Guide to the Public Records* (1923–4), the first effective introduction to the riches of the Office's holdings. The work required close attention from its readers, but then application to the records assumed a scholarly commitment in itself.

The relative shortness of the interval between the First and Second World Wars muffled the effect of the crisis which now faced the Public Record Office. It was plain that more space was needed, but the time was not one for large building programmes, and the increasing use of the records by the public could reasonably be contained by minor adjustments. The onset of the war then brought new preoccupations, but postponed the reckoning only to increase its cost. The civil and industrial exertions of the second war exceeded those of the first by a handsome margin, and again greatly accelerated the pace of technical change. Like almost everthing else in the country, the Office in 1945 was in serious need of constructive investment at a time when resources of all kinds were at a premium. In one sense, and by a merciful dispensation, the problems look more formidable in retrospect than they did at the time, but the business of controlling paper was both fundamental and the most daunting. That it also affected every department of government did not make its resolution any easier. However, the Grigg committee weighed the matter in 1952–3, and its recommendations, which formed the basis of the Public Records Act in 1958, have served the Office and its users ever since.

With the fifty-year rule of 1958, which was almost immediately modified to allow the release of material from World War I, and then amended in 1967 to become the thirty-year rule, the archival back-log of something more than a century was cleared, and a consistent flow of material established.[6] The problem of accommodation had still to be solved, however, and by the time that it could be addressed its terms were widely different from those of the past. The second great change that the twentieth century has worked on archives, and probably a matter of more consequence than their mere bulk, is in their readership. It is likely that as many readers will consult the records during the rest of the present year as used them over the whole of the nineteenth century, and their demands not only on the academic expertise of the Office but also upon its technical resources will match those of any decade before 1950. Those were the considerations that shaped the building at Kew, which has now been open for more than ten years.[7] In another ten it will be full, but in that respect at least it has done better than Chancery Lane, which was filled up regularly all the time that it was a-building.

Kew has depended on the computer for its operation since it was opened, and only the computer can now keep pace with the accumulation of records. The extension of automated ordering to Chancery Lane in 1985 has left the means of reference there unchanged for the moment, but takes us towards an integrated system of requisitioning. In the meantime machine-readable records present themselves daily for machines and others to read. The continuing and still-growing public interest in the records, the constant refinement of academic enquiry, and the elaboration of the technology of communications all promise a lively time for records and their keepers over the next hundred and fifty years. It is a measure of the keenness with which the Public Record Office and its users look to those developments that we have come here to celebrate not only what is past but also the prospect before us.

6 See also below, chapter 8, pp. 75–86.
7 See also below, pp. 41–2, for the Kew building.

3. Nine Centuries of Keeping the Public Records[1]

Elizabeth M. Hallam Assistant Keeper of Public Records

In his *Compendium of Records*, written around 1600, Arthur Agarde, Deputy Chamberlain of the Exchequer and the father of modern archival practice, wrote that: 'There is a four fold hurt that by negligence may bring wrack to records, that is to say: fire, water, rats and mice, misplacing. Which may be prevented, so far forth as man's wit may do (because all things are vain and perish daily) by a fourfold diligence and care to be had about them. There followeth yet a last danger worse than some of the former, that is even plain taking of them away'.[2]

For many years one of the most memorable exhibits in the Public Record Office Museum consisted of fragments of writ files, solidified into unrecognisable lumps, with the skeletons of dead rats which had been impacted into them.[3] These striking relics reflected neglect in the eighteenth and early nineteenth century when the art of record keeping was at its nadir, and are a telling illustration of what happens when Agarde's archival enemies rule unchecked. It should not however be thought that archival history is one long sad tale of decay. The picture is more cyclical – there were periods of sortation, experimentation, and innovation: the later twelfth century, the early fourteenth century, Elizabeth I's reign, the decades after the passing of the 1838 Act.

Moreover even at times of the greatest laxity, concern for the archives of state has not entirely died, as witnessed by the committees of both Lords and Commons which investigated the state of record keeping in the early eighteenth century; or the Record Commissions which sat a century later and whose work prefigured the passing of the Act which the Conference has celebrated. Despite all the problems and vicissitudes, nine centuries of record keeping have preserved for England the

[1] I would like to thank Dr T. Chalmers, Miss M. M. Condon, and Dr D. Crook for valuable discussions on various aspects of archival history. Further debts are recorded in the footnotes below. Part of the research for this paper was undertaken during the preparation of (1) E. M. Hallam and M. Roper, 'The capital and the records of the nation', *London Journal*, IV (1978), pp. 73–94, and of (2) an as yet unpublished illustrated history of the Public Record Office and its predecessor archives.

[2] IND 1/17126 (with copies in IND 1/17128, British Library Lansd. MS 127 and Harl. MS 94); printed in part in F. Palgrave, ed., *The Antient Kalendars and Inventories of the Exchequer*, 2 vols (1836), II, 311–35.

[3] E 163/24/31.

richest national archive in the world. Moreover, no matter how badly the bulk of the records have been treated, a select group amongst them has always been viewed with respect. This includes treaties with foreign powers, and a few key records of the central administration. The greatest honour of all – even reverence – has been paid to Domesday Book, with which this survey of nine centuries of record keeping begins.

Record keeping in the middle ages

Domesday Book, our earliest public record to survive, is a survey of landholding and tax liability whose scope was to remain unequalled until the nineteenth century. Even while it was being compiled, in the late 1080s, it began to acquire mythic properties which it has never lost, and its rôle as a national icon has long surpassed its more practical uses as a legal record and as a historical source.[4] Many factors, including the detail and sophistication of Domesday and the speed with which it was compiled, suggest that there were already in existence records of geld assessment and landholding, stretching back into the Anglo-Saxon past, upon which the Conqueror's administrators were able to draw while compiling the survey.[5]

Such of these records as the Old English kings preserved centrally would presumably have been kept in their main treasury, with their treasure and jewels, in the castle at Winchester, the Anglo-Saxon 'capital'.[6] Winchester continued to house the treasury of the Norman kings, and Domesday Book was placed there after its completion and was used to solve issues of taxation and tenure. From about 1100 it was known as the 'Book of Winchester' or the 'Document of Winchester': the familiar Domesday title was not in general use until about a century after its completion.[7]

Domesday, however, presented a fixed and immutable picture of English landholding and geld assessment in the late 1080s, and as the Conqueror's sons granted out royal and confiscated lands it became increasingly out of date. In about 1110, a new and more narrowly financial type of record, annually updatable, was devised probably by Roger, bishop of Salisbury and his associates. This was the pipe roll, which formed a record of the sheriff's accounts after their audit at the Exchequer.[8] Behind the pipe rolls – the first surviving example dates from 1129–30 – lay a rapidly expanding bureaucracy: a recent calculation suggests that Henry I's clerks produced as many as 4,500 writs each year, of which only 1% has survived.[9]

4 E. M. Hallam, *Domesday Book through Nine Centuries* (1986).

5 For one recent view see M. Chibnall, *Anglo-Norman England, 1066–1166* (Oxford, 1986), pp.106–114, and compare M. T. Clanchy, *From Memory to Written Record* (1979), pp. 12–17.

6 F. Barlow, ed., *Winchester in the Early Middle Ages* (Oxford, 1976), pp. 303–4.

7 *Domesday Book through Nine Centuries*, pp. 35, 39–40.

8 J. Green, *The Government of England under Henry I* (Cambridge, 1986), p. 41.

9 *From Memory to Written Record*, p. 42.

Interestingly, about the same proportion of modern departmental records is today selected for permanent preservation.

Henry I's scribes were clearly industrious – in 1130, for example, only four were at work disseminating the royal commands. Some royal clerks would have travelled with the king, while others would have been situated more permanently at Winchester, where the pipe rolls and their subsidiary documents would have joined Domesday and Henry I's coronation charter in the Treasury. Even under Henry I the records had their custodians, for a treatise on the abacus written by Thurkill, a royal clerk, in about 1117, is addressed to his friend and colleague 'Simon of the rolls', the title referring perhaps to the pipe rolls.[10]

Despite the disruptions of Stephen's reign the royal chancery continued to function. His successor, Henry II, was from the beginning of his reign able to use the Exchequer financial machine to collect his revenues and to settle backlogs. However, in their ruthless pursuit of efficiency Henry's officials created more records than they could conveniently use and became bogged down in their own system. One contemporary, Richard Fitzneal, describes the unfortunate initiative of Richard of Ilchester, whose duty it was both to stop the Treasurer from falling asleep and to supervise the making of the rolls. This keen bureaucrat began to keep a roll recording the writs of summons to sheriffs as a double check on debts, but it created so much confusion that it had to be discontinued.[11]

In Henry II's reign, as earlier, the 'royal archive' was at Winchester. In 1155 a papal bull and an emerald ring were placed there, and in 1164 a record copy of the notorious Constitutions of Clarendon – all by royal orders.[12] But Henry was one of the most itinerant of all our kings, and he increasingly required many of his records to be placed in great chests, known as the 'arks' or 'hutches' of the treasury, and carried in his baggage train for ease of reference. According to Richard Fitzneal these documents included Domesday Book, the pipe rolls and numerous charters and writs: a pipe roll entry of 1169–70 records a payment for the movement of the great chests with their regalia, rolls and tallies.[13] Henry's successors continued this practice. In 1215 some of King John's treasure chests, containing jewels, relics and the Exchequer rolls, were left at Reading Abbey on his travels,[14] and it is fortunate for posterity that the unhappy accident to the royal baggage train in the Wash in the following year did not include items such as Domesday Book.

As the records proliferated, it became impractical to carry them all around with

10 *From Memory to Written Record*, p.133; *The Government of England*, pp. 30–31: other treasuries were located in major abbeys and castles throughout the country. On 'Simon of the rolls', see C. H. Haskins, 'The abacus and the king's curia', *English Historical Review*, XXVII (1912), pp.101–6.

11 *Domesday Book through Nine Centuries*, p. 41; *From Memory to Written Record*, p. 47 and notes.

12 *Ibid.*, pp. 48, 133; *Dialogus de Scaccario and Constitutio Domus Regis*, ed. C. Johnson (Oxford, 1950), pp. 27, 74–75.

13 This is following the interpretation in *From Memory to Written Record*, pp.133–34; and see also *Pipe Roll 16 Henry II*, Pipe Roll Society, vol. XV (1892), p.126.

14 *From Memory to Written Record*, p.134; *Rotuli Litterarum Patentium*, ed. T. D. Hardy, I (1835), p.145.

the king. By 1200 London and Westminster had already eclipsed Winchester as the hub of the royal administration and courts, and it was here that the records were in the main stored. The Exchequer – the king's financial office – already had its own system of keeping and referring to its past records, and this idea was extended into other related areas by Hubert Walter, archbishop of Canterbury. As the chief justiciar from 1193 to 1198, he arranged for the third copy of final concords, the feet of fines, to be returned to and preserved in the Treasury, together with the estreat of issues of the eyre[15] – although it was not until the middle of the thirteenth century that the same principle was successfully applied to the eyre rolls. In Edward I's reign the limit of legal memory was moved forward from Henry II's coronation to Richard I's coronation in 1189, for processes in which the Crown used writs of common form as opposed to prerogative writs. Such updating had hitherto been standard practice, but, significantly, despite public opinion and political pressure from parliament, was never to be repeated, presumably because common law records stretch back that far. Since 1275, 1189 has remained the limit of legal memory.[16]

As King John's Chancellor, from 1199 to 1205, Hubert Walter extended the same principle to the records of Chancery. In 1199, 1200 and 1201 he instituted series of rolls, recording respectively royal charters, letters close and letters patent; the latter two have continued into this century.[17] At the same time he re-organised the Chancery personnel: the Chancellor, at the head, was assisted by the vice-chancellor who had charge of the Great Seal, and by a protonotary who supervised the writing of royal documents. Beneath them was a growing host of officials, clerks and other factotums, who by 1215 included William Cucuel, who was keeper of the Chancery Rolls, and an un-named 'portjoye' or sergeant of the rolls of Chancery, whose task it was to arrange the carriage of these records from one place on the royal itinerary to another.[18]

The royal wardrobe, which ministered to the sovereign's personal needs, had by John's reign also developed its own accounting procedures and records. In addition it gained responsibility for keeping leagues and treaties, which were carried with it on its travels: in 1213 the wardrobe archives occupied four large chests. Its earliest surviving accounts date from the 1220s, by which time it had begun to deposit some of its own records in the New Temple and elsewhere.[19]

The apparent logic of Angevin administrative structures was not reflected in the choice of places where the archives were kept. Records were made the responsibility

15 *From Memory to Written Record*, pp. 48–9, 122–23; D. Crook, *Records of the General Eyre* (1982), p.12.

16 *From Memory to Written Record*, p.123; *Domesday Book through Nine Centuries*, p. 95; T. F. T. Plucknett, A *Concise History of the Common Laws*, 5th edn (1966), p. 719 (my thanks to Dr W. M. Ormrod for the last reference).

17 *From Memory to Written Record*, p. 49; *Guide to the Contents of the Public Record Office, Part I* (1963), pp.16–18, 22–24.

18 P. Chaplais, *English Royal Documents, King John – Henry VI, 1199–1461* (Oxford, 1971), pp. 20–21; *From Memory to Written Record*, pp.134–5.

19 T. F. Tout, *Chapters in the Administrative History of Medieval England*, I (Manchester 1920), pp.164–9, 193–8.

of individual officials who stored them where they could, and no single centre was established. This was a precedent which was in future to cause much damage to the records, and which, even since 1838, has never been broken for any length of time.

Religious houses had for many centuries acted as safe deposit boxes for treasure, jewels and documents, both public and private, and several of those in the vicinity of London, including the New Temple and St Bartholomew's Smithfield,[20] housed royal records at various times throughout the middle ages. From the thirteenth century the most important was Westminster Abbey, which served as the English coronation church and principal royal mausoleum, and lay directly next to the palace of Westminster where the Exchequer had its headquarters. The Chapel of the Pyx and the undercroft of the Chapter House were both places of deposit for royal records thoughout the middle ages, although a daring burglary carried out by Richard of Pudlicote in 1303 – perhaps with the connivance of the monks – caused a temporary loss of enthusiasm on the part of the royal officials for entrusting their muniments to the abbot.[21] At a local level, too, religious houses had custody of royal records and treasure: a later list of ecclesiastics and others having control of the keys to royal treasure chests in different counties contains a preponderance of friars. One was the Dominican Robert de Humbleton, who supervised one chest in his own house at Beverley, and another at Kingston-upon-Hull.[22]

Locating records might in these circumstances be a tricky business. For example, writs of *certiorari*, issued by Chancery and ordering earlier records to be searched for information, are addressed initially to the treasurer and chamberlains of the Exchequer or to the sheriffs or justices in the shires, whose officials then sent the requests to the appropriate record keepers for searches to be made. Returns on the writs and other sources show that many such searches were successful, but this was not always the case. In 1276 the prior of Holy Trinity Aldgate was able to prove, from evidence in the Chancery rolls of Henry III, that he had been authorized to close a road – an example of the way in which monastic houses kept a careful note of any royal privileges.[23] Four years earlier, in 1272, the prior of Christ Church Canterbury, the cathedral priory, had exhibited letters patent of Henry III at the papal *curia* in Rome in a lawsuit, but Henry III wrote to Pope Gregory X insisting that, as they were not enrolled in his registers, they were undoubtly forged. His clerks had been lax in this case, for the letters are in fact enrolled on the 1265 patent roll, and the prior had been caught by bureaucratic inefficiency.[24]

It was the constant expansion of the royal archives that produced problems of

20 A. Sandys, 'The financial and military importance of the London Temple', *Essays in Medieval History Presented to T. F. Tout*, ed. A. G. Little and F. M. Powicke (1925), pp.147–62; below, note 37.

21 T. F. Tout, 'A medieval burglary', *Bulletin of the John Rylands Library*, II (1914–15), pp. 348–69.

22 E 163/8/15; *From Memory to Written Record*, pp.136–38.

23 For Chancery *recorda* files (now largely re-assembled), see C 260; and for examples relating to the Domesday Book, see *Domesday Book through Nine Centuries*, Appendix I, pp.199–209; *From Memory to Written Record*, pp.139–41.

24 *From Memory to Written Record*, pp. 49, 139–41.

this kind, and the solutions devised mark a breakthrough in archival practices. The Treasury of Receipt led the way when in about 1282 a calendar and compilation of earlier diplomatic documents was begun; it was completed in two volumes – the *Liber* A and the *Liber B* – in about 1292. For ease of reference the documents were arranged according to the country to which they related and the transcripts were then carefully checked against the originals.[25] Similar summaries of wardrobe book and rolls were initiated in 1302.[26]

At first the king had evidently been unaware of what his record-keepers were doing, for in 1291, seeking historical evidence to support his claims to the overlordship of Scotland, he turned first to the monasteries, which provided extracts from their chronicles, before having an unsatisfactory search made in the rolls of Chancery.[27] However, six years later, in 1297, Edward went straight to the treasurer and barons of the Exchequer to search the records in the Treasury and elsewhere for treaties made three years earlier with the king of Germany and the archbishop of Cologne;[28] and in 1300 a vaguer but more comprehensive order was given to search the rolls and remembrances of the Exchequer concerning the king's rights in Scotland.[29] On the more domestic level, in the same warrant Edward's officials were required to collect information about royal forest rights; the result, which included extracts from Domesday Book, were collected from the Exchequer at York in May 1300.[30]

A second major development in archival practices took place in the reign of Edward II, with a great array and sortation of the Exchequer records. One impetus to this was probably the dissolution of the Templars in 1312, which deprived the king of some of his most important record keepers at one blow. The presses ordered for the White Tower at the Tower of London in the same year were perhaps intended to house some of the displaced documents. The sortation can also be seen as one part of a programme to streamline the workings of the Exchequer, primarily for fiscal reasons.[31] Confusion evidently reigned in the financial archives, for in 1319 an ordinance for the reform of the household included the comment that storage of the Exchequer records was highly deficient: people other than Exchequer clerks had been allowed to handle them and all too often they could not be found at all.

The task of remedying these problems fell to Walter Stapledon, bishop of Exeter,

25 G. P. Cuttino, *English Diplomatic Administration, 1259–1339*, 2nd edn (Oxford, 1971), pp.113–15.

26 *From Memory to Written Record*, p.124.; E. B. Fryde, ed., *Book of Prests of the King's Wardrobe for 1294–5* (1962), pp. 229–30.

27 *From Memory to Written Record*, pp.123–24.

28 M. Prestwich, ed., *Documents illustrating the crisis of 1297–98 in England*, Camden 4th ser., XXIV (1980), pp. 4, 80.

28 *From Memory to Written Record*, p.124; *Calendar of Chancery Warrants, 1244–1326* (1927), p.120.

30 *Ibid.*; *Domesday Book through Nine Centuries*, p. 66 and App. III, p. 211.

31 *From Memory to Written Record*, pp.135–6; E 101/469/16; M. Buck, *Politics, Finance and the Church in the Reign of Edward II: Walter Stapeldon, Treasurer of England* (Cambridge, 1983), esp. pp.168–9 (my thanks to Dr W. M. Ormrod for discussion of the sortation).

who, on his appointment as Treasurer in 1320, almost immediately ordered that an 'array' of Exchequer records should take place at the White Tower in the Tower of London. More new aumbries were ordered and then from August 1320 to January 1322 the records, which had been gathered at the Tower, were sorted out by more than a dozen clerks. The Exchequer records were brought by river from Westminster and returned there after they had been dealt with, but a number of legal records remained at the Tower thereafter.[32] At the same time calendars were made of records relating to royal rights in Gascony, of other diplomatic documents of a more general nature, of estreat rolls, and of documents relating to forfeited 'contrariant' lands, continuing and building upon work begun in the Wardrobe treasury by Elias de Jonestone in 1318.[33]

For much of the fourteenth century the Tower of London continued as a major Exchequer record office and jewel store; and it also began to house Chancery records, including the rolls. In 1360 space was needed in the White Tower for the imprisoned King John of France, and a number of records were moved to the Wakefield Tower: these two record treasuries continued in use mainly for Chancery records until the nineteenth century.[34]

By the end of the fifteenth century the Tower had passed its heyday as the principal Chancery record office, a function taken over by the Rolls Chapel in Chancery Lane. The chapel was founded by Henry III in 1232 as part of the *domus conversorum*, a religious house for Jews who had taken the Christian faith, but within a century it was better known as an important repository for recent Chancery records. At first only a staging point for the documents, by 1500 it had ceased to transfer anything of importance to the Tower, despite continuing attempts by the Tower record keepers to obtain what they felt was due to them.[35]

The legal records were rather less well organised and preserved than those of Chancery and Exchequer. Until 1257 plea rolls were normally retained by the justices who created them, and although the requirement that these vital records should be handed over to the Exchequer at the end of the justice's term of office was often observed, this was not invariably the case.[36] In the fourteenth century the King's Bench plea rolls were divided between the Tower of London and Westminster, and those of the Common Pleas had one main treasury at St Bartholomew's, Smithfield. In 1384 four writ files produced by the prior for legal proceedings were found to be damaged, and he was instructed to repair the roof of his muniment room

32 Galbraith, 'The Tower as an Exchequer record office', in *Essays to Tout*, pp. 231–47, esp. pp. 231–34.

33 *Ibid.*, pp. 236–38; Buck, p.169; E. M. Hallam, 'The Tower of London as a record office', *Archives*, XIV (1979), 3–10, esp. pp. 4–5.

34 *Ibid.*, pp. 5–6.

35 H. C. Maxwell-Lyte, *Historical Notes on the Use of the Great Seal of England* (1926), pp. 8–10; R. B. Wernham, 'The public records in the sixteenth and seventeenth centuries', in L. Fox, ed., *English Historical Scholarship in the Sixteenth and Seventeenth Centuries* (1956), pp.11–30, esp. pp.16–18.

36 *Records of the General Eyre*, p.12. Legislation in Henry IV's reign required them to be delivered 2 years after completion: Statute 11 Henry IV cap. 3.

to prevent water from getting into the chests again. Despite such drawbacks the records remained there until 1461 when they were transferred to the Tower.[37] Another cache of Common Pleas records was kept in a place known as 'hell', situated beneath Westminster Hall, which was fitted out for the records in 1351, and later gave its name to a tavern in the vicinity.[38]

During the fourteenth century the Exchequer record keepers became increasingly powerful and their domain at Westminster better organised. At the Treasury of Receipt, the deputy chamberlains emerged as the principal custodians of the records, with responsibility for making searches and copies as well as safeguarding the records in their charge.[39] As earlier, their documents were kept at the Treasury of Receipt and in the Abbey, according to a carefully devised system.

In the treasuries above the Receipt, and in the Chapel of the Pyx, the records were stored in chests – in part to meet the continuing need of portability, and in part for security from rats and mice – although time-honoured tradition seems to have played its part in this practice as well. Thus great chests bound with iron, and massive coffers almost invariably secured with three keys, were the basic storage units. One chest, known as the 'trial of the Pyx' chest and made in the early fourteenth century, probably shortly after the Pudlicote burglary, is an example. Similar chests, probably contemporary and of analogous design, are still extant at the abbey above the cloisters and in the Chapel of the Pyx.[40]

Inside these massive chests were smaller chests, such as a fine oak coffer in four separate sections each with its own lock. It was made in 1255 and has been carefully preserved. Other smaller coffers, of a type often described as pixes in the documents, have also survived.[41] Less ornamental, but very practical, were hampers of woven twigs; only one example is now extant in the Public Record Office,[42] but they were so commonly used that they gave their name to the hanaper, the office which levied fees for the sealing of letters. Within the hampers were fine white leather pouches, which closed like a Victorian lady's reticule.[43] They were clearly labelled with their contents for ease of reference, and they kept the parchments inside, usually accounts, in an excellent state of preservation. Examples of such pouches made of canvas have also survived, their contents described by parchment strips sewn to

[37] *Calendar of Close Rolls, 1381–85*, p. 428; G. O. Sayles, ed., *Select Cases in the Court of King's Bench under Edward I*, Selden Society, LV (1936), pp. cxxiii–iv; M. Hastings, *The Court of Common Pleas in Fifteenth Century England* (New York, 1947), p.142.

[38] E 101/471/6; *The Court of Common Pleas*, pp.143–4.

[39] J. C. Sainty, *Officers of the Exchequer*, List and Index Society, spec. ser., XVIII (1983), pp.164–5; *Domesday Book through Nine Centuries*, pp. 55–6.

[40] *Early Chests in Wood and Iron*, Public Record Office Museum Pamphlets, VII (1974), p. 4. My thanks to Dr Richard Mortimer, Keeper of the Muniments at Westminster Abbey, for showing me the chests at Westminster.

[41] *Early Chests*, pp. 3–4. Another smaller example survives from the later middle ages. Exquisitely decorated with iron filigree work, it may have been a jewel chest (SR 67/12/8). Another example, dating from around 1500 (SR 67/11/1a), is a tooled leather treaty box. Its protuberance on the top was clearly intended to house a great seal in its case.

[42] SR 67/11/4.

[43] Numerous pouches of this kind are preserved in E 101.

them. Other records, such as charters bearing larger seals, were placed in skippets of wood or metal, again clearly labelled with their contents. The Public Record Office holds a collection dating from the thirteenth to the sixteenth centuries, some of very fine workmanship.[44] Another way of storing records was in canvas bags hanging on nails,[45] but none are known to have been preserved.

Although relatively few great chests now survive, in the middle ages there must have been many hundreds of them in the Treasury and in other repositories. In the Tower of London record presses had been used as an alternative from the early fourteenth century, but at Westminster they seem still to have been regarded as something of a novelty even in the sixteenth. Some great oak aumbry doors, made for the Exchequer in Mary's reign, bear a finely gilded 'guilloche' design, with the proud inscription that in 1555 William Paulet, Marquis of Winchester, caused this place and the rest of this office to be fitted out with presses for keeping pells of receipt, warrants and so forth.[46]

Smaller cupboards for rolls – an example from the pipe office is drawn in Madox's *History of the Exchequer*[47] – and larger shelves or presses[48] subsequently became the normal way to store records. Nevertheless the Deputy Chamberlains and their clerks at the Receipt, with characteristic conservatism, continued to use chests for some items into the nineteenth century. An amusing item in the papers of Peter le Neve, Deputy Chamberlain from 1684 to 1712, describes a bitter quarrel he had in 1708 with the tally writer's clerk over seating arrangements at the Exchequer in the Tally Court, during the course of which the custody of keys to the record chests became one matter at issue.[49] A century later, in 1807, a survey of the Chapter House records, carried out for the Record Commission, showed that almost all the records were now stored in presses and cupboards, but that in the basement there still remained a number of record chests containing particularly valuable items. An example was chest number seven, holding treaties, papal bulls, and the foundation indentures of Henry VII's chantries and chapels.[50]

In the later middle ages even Exchequer books, like the rolls, seem to have been stored and transported in chests. Domesday Book, as a particularly precious codex, was probably packed flat, but others may have been stored upside down and lifted out by the flaps of their strong leather chemise bindings. Some lost their skirts in the eighteenth century for better storage, and many other surviving bindings of this

44 SR 67/12/9; e.g. E 36/26/36–7.

45 E. M. Hallam, 'Annotations in Domesday Book since 1100', *Domesday Book Studies*, ed. A. Williams and R. W. H. Erskine (1987), pp.136–50, esp. p.142; E 31/2/1, f. Ev; below, note 76.

46 *Early Chests*, p. 2.

47 T. Madox, *The History and Antiquities of the Exchequer* (1712), *Discreptatio Epistolaris*, p. 64.

48 For diagrams of the contents of presses in the State Paper Office, see E. M. Hallam, 'Problems with record keeping in early eighteenth century London', *Journal of the Society of Archivists*, VI (1979), pp. 219–26 and plates.

49 SP 46/139, pt. 1; *Domesday Book through Nine Centuries*, pp.127–30.

50 OBS 1/692, ff. 9v–10. The chest is now in the Library at Westminster Abbey.

kind have been ripped, presumably as the result of rough treatment. In one case a leather strap was fitted to enable the book to be lifted more easily.[51] Celebrated volumes were given names such as the Red Book of the Exchequer or the Black Book of the Exchequer, and early surviving bindings were in fact dyed in these colours.[52] The chemise bound books were also coloured red and green to distinguish them one from another.[53]

Finding the right items amongst the ever-growing tide of royal records was as much a problem in the middle ages as now, and an ingenious solution based on pictograms was devised in the Wardrobe and later adopted and elaborated in the Treasury of Receipt.[54] The *Liber B*, one of two registers of diplomatic documents completed in about 1292, tells us that, for example, treaties and other records relating to Aragon were kept in a red coffer decorated with the sign of jousting knights; and that Gascon records were signified by the sign of grapes being pressed.[55] Memoranda books of the Exchequer, recording the arrival and exact storage places of a variety of documents, show how the system worked from Edward III's to Henry VIII's reign.[56] Thus in 1366, letters patent of Edward, prince of Wales, were placed in the room above the Receipt in a hamper in a small chest with three locks bearing the sign of a lion. Four years later, letters of the king of Scotland were placed in a hamper in a chest in the muniment room at the Receipt under the sign of an axe. Later the hamper was put, with other memoranda of Scotland, in a coffer decorated with painting, and standing within the great coffer in St Stephen's Chapel.[57]

A particularly fine example of these painted chests is one made in about 1360 and used to house the records of the Treaty of Calais, the ratification of the Treaty of Brétigny. It is beautifully decorated on the front with the shields of John de Buckingham and others, unidentified but probably French. On the lid are the shields of Richard FitzAlan, earl of Arundel, of Old France, of the Black Prince – and one which is now obliterated.[58]

Although increasingly capital letters and full written titles replaced these pictorial *signa* as the means of identifying documents, symbols continued to be used for several centuries. The Chancery Treaty Rolls of the late fifteenth century had their covers crudely ornamented with signs depicting guns, together with Roman numerals signifying their regnal years.[59] As late as the 1730s, pictorial labels were used to

[51] E.g. E 164/9 (chemise binding); E 166/3 (chemise binding with strap). I am grateful to Mr F. Bearman of the Conservation Department, Public Record Office, for his information about chemise bindings.

[52] E.g. E 164/2 (Red Book).

[53] E 164/11.

[54] *From Memory to Written Record*, pp.142–3; the idea may have originated with earlier chroniclers Ralph of Diceto and Matthew Paris.

[55] E 36/276, ff. 71, 10.

[56] Printed in *Antient Kalendars*, I, 156–299, II, 1–240, III, 1–97.

[57] E 36/273, ff. 2, 6.

[58] E 30/153 case; *Early Chests*, pp. 2–3.

[59] E.g. C 76/178 cover.

mark Common Pleas writ files. Each of the five signs – a heart, a ladder, a crow, a buckle and a bell – denoted a geographical area of the country.[60]

In the Tower of London and the Treasury of Receipt archival practices remained unchanged for centuries and precedent was followed as closely as possible: thus in 1708 Peter le Neve, while involved in his trivial and irascible dispute over seating arrangements at the table in the Treasury of Receipt record office in Tally Court, harked back to the reign of Henry II, more than five centuries before, for justification.[61] Pipe rolls, enormous membranes sewed at the head, and Chancery rolls, smaller membranes joined at the head and foot, were highly impractical ways of recording information, yet no serious attempts were made to change the ways in which they were made up. Like the creaking machinery of Exchequer and Chancery which created them, they remained triumphantly immutable from the twelfth century into the modern period.

Record keeping from 1500 to the present day

Already by 1500 the medieval system of record keeping was giving way at the seams. At Westminster the Remembrancers, the Clerk of the Pells and the Auditor of the Receipt were all retaining their own records rather than transferring them to the Treasury of Receipt: and the new courts created in the sixteenth century to cope with the expansion of government business – Star Chamber, Requests, Augmentations, Wards and Liveries, First Fruits and Tenths – all did the same. Although they were brought under Exchequer control around 1560 many of their records suffered considerable neglect in subsequent centuries. They were not included in the new record repository provided when the Exchequer buildings were remodelled in the 1570s.[62]

Nor did the passage of time improve matters at Westminster: some horrifying stories emerge in the report of a House of Lords Committee set up in the early eighteenth century to investigate the state of record keeping. For example, in 1709 the records of the Court of Wards were found to be in a house adjoining that of the royal fishmonger in Fish Yard, near to Westminster Hall. The royal fishmonger, we are told, did as he pleased with the records, which were perishing rapidly. The records of King's Bench were not far off, but equally under threat. They were stored above a place which had formerly been a cook's shop, but was by 1709 partly a wash house and partly a stable 'which is a very Improper situation for records of such consequence.' By 1711 some attempts had been made to rescue both sets of records and the fishmonger's house was being organised as a record repository.[63]

Another problematical record store at Westminster was the Chapter House,

60 SR 16/89; *Reports from Committees of the House of Commons*, I, 511.
61 SP 46/139, pt. 1.
62 E. Green, 'The management of Exchequer records in the 1560s', *Journal of the Society of Archivists*, V (1974), pp. 25–30.
63 *Journals of the House of Lords*, XXI, 135; XXVIII, 715–17; T1/133, f.103; *History of the King's Works*, V, *1660–1782*, ed. H. M. Colvin and others (1976), p. 425.

where in 1709 King's Bench and Common Pleas records were lying in piles on the damp ground, and where 'the bills, answers etc. of the Star Chamber have lain many years in a great heap, undigested, without any covering from dust or security from rats or mice.'[64] Considerable sums of money were spent on improvements, yet by 1740 the roof had to be shored up; and in 1751 it collapsed altogether.[65] It was reconstructed specifically as a record office, and as such was much to impress the Record Commission officials who visited it in 1800. Its later restorer, Giles Gilbert Scott, was far more critical: 'seldom', he wrote in 1863, 'do we see a noble work of art reduced to such a wreck. It was made over to the tender mercies of some barbarian, who fitted it up for the records with studious regard for concealment or destruction of its architectural beauties.'[66]

The Tower of London was by the sixteenth century a record office in gradual decline. Despite concerted efforts on the part of its keepers, and the issue of a number of royal warrants to them, it failed to obtain the Chancery rolls from Richard III's reign onwards, which remained at the Rolls Chapel, whilst transfers of other records, such as Chancery bills and answers, were limited and spasmodic. Fees for searches fell away, and in 1674, while the keeper and his deputy were away, one of the clerks forged several records, to the consternation, disgrace, and near dismissal of Thomas Ryley, the deputy. 'O great cheate and forgery', he wrote sadly in his register of searches.[67]

Worse still, the Tower records were under constant threat from the Ordnance Office's store of gunpowder kept in the basement of the White Tower. Additional stores, such as wooden wheelbarrows, added to the potential fire hazard. The Board was first asked to move the explosives in 1620, to no avail. When upbraided on the matter in 1718 its officials replied that there was little cause for concern, since the number of barrels had been reduced in number from 12,000 to between sixty and seventy. In 1832 the Record Commissioners again asked for the gunpowder to be removed, the Board riposting that the records should go instead.[68] A major fire, caused by arson, did eventually break out in the White Tower in 1885, but by this time the records had been evacuated.[69]

The Tower's rival storehouse for Chancery records, the Rolls Chapel, was equally a prey to neglect and decay in the seventeenth and eighteenth centuries. In 1717 the House of Converts was pulled down and replaced with the Palladian style Rolls House, which was designed by Colin Campbell and cost some £5,000 to build.[70] As the principal residence of the Master of the Rolls it was kept in a reasonable state of repair, and in 1818 was expensively refitted to suit the grandiose

64 'Problems with record keeping', p. 221.

65 *History of the King's Works*, V, 415.

66 G. G. Scott, *Gleanings from Westminster Abbey*, 2nd edn (1863), p. 40.

67 OBS 1/672, ff.109–112; 'Tower of London', p. 7.

68 *Ibid*, p. 8; SP 14/116, no. 5; House of Lords Record Office, Main Papers, Original papers laid before the Committees (1717–20), paper laid on 5 and 7 Feb. 1718/19.

69 WO 94/58/22; WO 94/66/1–2.

70 *History of the King's Works*, V, 537–39; *Reports from Committees of the House of Commons*, I, 519–23.

tastes of Sir Thomas Plumer.[71] Some charming pencil sketches made in the early nineteenth century give an idea of what the interior looked like.[72]

There were, however, continuing complaints about the fabric of the Rolls Chapel nearby, which in the 1770s was in so bad a state of repair that the documents were in danger of decaying altogether.[73] When in 1833 the Record Commissioners visited it, they commented that 'it exhibits a most remarkable specimen of the extremest economy of space, the very seats of the Chapel being in fact cases for the records. On the ground are the Patent Rolls, in a spot so dark that no one can see to read any one there, and a candle is not properly allowed. They can be removed, therefore, only by guess matured into habit.'[74]

Meanwhile the old structures of record keeping, both physical and administrative, had since the sixteenth century had new demands placed upon them. A new kind of record user, the enthusiastic antiquarian, visited the record offices ever more frequently in search of genealogical and antiquarian material – despite the size of the fees for searches and copies when he got there.[75] An early example is George Owen, of Henllys in Pembrokeshire, who in 1589 arrived at the Exchequer hoping to find out about the lordship of Cemaes, and who wrote about his experiences. He consulted, he says, 'the Book of Domesday, which remaineth with Mr Agard and Mr Fenton in the Cellars office,' but 'the book is very ancient and hard to be read and whoso findeth any things must pay for the copy of every line iiij. d and it must be exemplified in the self same correctness as it is written in the book, which is strange and hard for any man to read whether you find [anything] or not'. He was also shown 'divers records particular for Wales . . . and a great canvas bag full of records for South Wales wherein were bundles endorsed "com. Pembroek, Cardigan, Carmarthen", which I am promised to have the perusal of.'[76]

The scale of the fees levied from searchers continued to be a source of complaint for many centuries. Thus in his *Observations on the State of Historical Literature*, published in 1830, Sir Nicholas Harris Nicholas fulminated that the mountainous charges were a major impediment to historical research. At the Tower, for example, 'no individual can inspect a document which is confessedly the property of the public, and for the conservation of which the public is taxed, without paying the sum of *sixteen shillings and eight pence*, of which sum ten shillings is for making the search, as it is termed, and six shillings and eight pence for one of the clerks rising from his chair, walking a few yards, and opening a roll . . . The expense of a mere transcript of a *public record*, from a *public office*, the keeper of which receives £500

71 *History of the King's Works*, VI, *1782–1851*, ed. J. M. Crook and others (1973), pp. 476–77; *Reports from Committees of the House of Commons*, I, 446, 520–21.

72 PRO 30/88/1, nos 11–13.

73 *Journals of the House of Commons*, XXXIII, 791; XL, 388, 419; *History of the King's Works*, V, 359.

74 C. P. Cooper, ed., *Proceedings of His Majesty's Commissioners on the Public Records, June 1832 – Aug. 1833* (1833), p. 283.

75 M. McKisack, *Medieval History in the Tudor Age* (Oxford, 1971), pp. 93–4.

76 *Domesday Book through Nine Centuries*, p.115.

per annum from the *public* . . . , amounts altogether to very nearly as much as is paid for an *original article* in a popular publication.'[77]

The picture of 'reader services' from the sixteenth to the nineteenth centuries is not one of total and unremitting gloom. A number of the record keepers gave excellent advice for the fees they were paid. Arthur Agarde, Deputy Chamberlain at the Exchequer from 1570 to 1615, brought to his office a scholarly and archival dimension which it had not had before. He worked carefully on the records in his care, sorting, calendaring, annotating and listing them; and he compiled a catalogue of the records in the four treasuries in the Exchequer which was an invaluable guide for searchers. His expertise was widely recognised and valued by the antiquarian community of his day, and he mixed on equal terms with such noted politicians and book collectors as Sir Robert Cotton.[78] Agarde was not alone in his attempts to methodize the records and to aid research. William Lambarde, at the Tower of London, crowned a distinguished career as an antiquarian and record keeper by writing a *Pandect*, or guide to records in the Tower of London, which he presented to Queen Elizabeth I on her visit in 1601. Similar work was taking place in other record offices too, among them the Corporation of London and the City of Exeter archives.[79]

Many of Agarde's successors in the Exchequer looked back to his example, as, for example, the already mentioned bombastic and quarrelsome herald and antiquarian, Peter le Neve (Deputy Chamberlain from 1684 to 1712), and his more conscientious but equally argumentative colleague, John Lowe. In the intervals between their disputes both men sorted and indexed the Treasury of Receipt records, and helped Thomas Rymer to select records for the first edition of his *Foedera*, a project funded by the public purse.[80] Another major and official government publication, a transcript of the parliament rolls, was at first, in the late 1760s, actively hindered by Henry Rooke, Deputy Keeper of the records at the Tower, who impugned the expertise of its editors and refused them access to the records. Much later work was carried out by a future keeper of the Tower records, Thomas Astle;[81] and at the Chapter House in Westminster, Abraham Farley, Deputy Chamberlain and later Keeper of the Records, made a superb transcript of Domesday Book, issued in printed form in 1783, which remains the definitive edition to this day.[82]

Another major archival development of the sixteenth century was the creation of the State Paper Office. Arising from the need of the sovereign to have a private

77 N. H. Nicholas, *Observations on the State of Historical Literature* (1830), pp. 50–51.

78 E. M. Hallam, 'Arthur Agarde and Domesday Book' (forthcoming); *Medieval History in the Tudor Age*, pp. 77–83.

79 'Arthur Agarde and Domesday Book'; P. Cain, 'Robert Smith and the reform of the archives of the city of London', *London Journal*, XIII (1987–8), pp. 3–16. I am grateful to Mr Cain for discussion about sixteenth century archival practices.

80 'Annotations in Domesday Book', pp.146–8; SP 46/139, pt I.

81 M. M. Condon and E. M. Hallam, 'The publication of the Public Records in the eighteenth century', *Journal of the Society of Archivists*, VII (1984), pp. 348–88, esp. pp. 363–370.

82 *Ibid.*, pp. 376–383; *Domesday Book through Nine Centuries*, pp.133–140.

library of domestic and foreign papers, its access restricted to the Crown's servants, it began informally in the 1580s under the aegis of Thomas Wilson. In 1610 his nephew, also named Thomas Wilson, was formally constituted joint keeper by James I.[83] In 1619 the expanding collection was taken from the Palace of Whitehall into the Holbein Gate, missing by only a matter of weeks the fire that devastated much of the area, including the rooms from which they had been removed. For several subsequent decades the papers, and the privy council registers which joined them, were a prey to neglect and to embezzlement, John Milton being a major offender in the latter respect.[84]

When in 1704 the House of Lords Committee investigating the state of record keeping visited the Office, it heard a dismal tale from the keeper, John Tucker. His predecessors had so neglected the Holbein Gate, he told them, that on his own appointment he had been obliged to install new windows and doors to prevent damp from damaging the records. Despite his efforts the premises were still ramshackle and overcrowded.[85]

At the same time Tucker produced several diagrams of the layout of the papers at the Holbein Gate. He also came up with a scheme for arranging his records in presses labelled with letters: A would stand for ecclesiastical documents, B for the Council, C for the Secretaries of State, D for the Treasury, and so on.[86] He proposed various remedies which evidently impressed the lords, for not only did they arrange for repairs to the Holbein Gate, they also called in Sir Christopher Wren, as Surveyor General of the King's Works, to fit out the Middle Treasury Gallery for some of the papers.[87] The Holbein Gate was saved from destruction in 1718 through the intervention of Sir John Vanburgh, but by the 1750s it had become highly delapidated once more, and prior to its demolition in 1759 the room containing the Privy Council registers had to be broken open with a sledgehammer.[88]

Some of the State Papers next found their way into a house in New Scotland Yard, which was liable to flooding at high tide, others to another residence in Great George Street which 1828 subsided altogether. It was then decided that a purpose built State Paper Office was required, and a competition was held, from which Sir John Soane emerged as the winner. His design was completed in 1834 and cost almost £24,000; and yet it was to be demolished only 28 years later, in 1862, to make way for the Foreign Office.[89]

The work of the Record Commissions and the consequence of the 1838 Act have been described elsewhere in this volume,[90] and I will consider them here only

83 SP 45/20, nos 12, 14; F. S. Thomas, *A History of the State Paper Office* (1849), pp. 8–9.
84 'Problems with record keeping', p. 223.
85 *Ibid.*, pp. 223–4.
86 *Ibid.*, pp. 224–5.
87 *Ibid.*, pp. 225–6.
88 *Ibid.*, p. 226; *History of the King's Works*, V, 303–4; T 64/309, f. 23; SP 45/21, no.122; WORK 6/17, f.188.
89 *History of the King's Works*, VI, 567–70; T 64/309, following f. 49; OBS 1/682–3.
90 Above, p. 24 ff; and below, *passim*.

in so far as they affected the physical custody of the records. Despite the good intentions of the progenitors of the Public Records Act, and the extent to which public concern had been aroused for the state of the national archives, the problems of the record repositories were not solved overnight: it was not until 1851 that work on the Public Record Office in Chancery Lane began. Meanwhile the existing record offices at the Tower of London, the Chapter House and Rolls Chapel and Rolls House – joined later by the State Paper Office – functioned under their assistant keepers working to Sir Francis Palgrave, the first Deputy Keeper.[91]

Particular problems arose for the records dislodged by redevelopment following the fire at the palace of Westminster in 1832. Some were taken to the Royal Mews at Charing Cross: then, removed in the teeth of considerable resistance to make room for the National Gallery, they were taken to the old riding school at Carlton House, known as Carlton Ride, where they were placed in the custody of Joseph Hunter and Henry Cole.[92]

In his memoirs Cole gives a vivid description of the later removal of the King's Bench records from Westminster to Carlton Ride. They were, he says 'strewn all over the floor of the roof of the Augmentations Office. It was necessary to mount a ladder to get access to this apartment, the roof was nearly dark, and an area of about 25 feet by 20 was piled up from two to three feet high with documents, all in confusion. You could not step without sinking among them. The mass was thickly coated with soot, dust and dirt.'[93] The many talented Cole was determined to try to make up for centuries of neglect, the results of which he graphically portrayed in a water colour painting, now in the Victoria and Albert Museum.[94] He therefore made great efforts to sort and organise the documents in his charge. Carlton Ride was fitted out with record presses, painted red for the Common Pleas records and blue for the Exchequer ones. Prince Albert made a visitation in 1842 and was apparently much impressed with Cole's work – a portent for their future collaboration on the Great Exhibitions.[95]

The great defect of Carlton Ride was that as a predominantly wooden structure, it posed a great fire risk. In 1843 a wash-house chimney smouldered and almost broke out in flames, and Cole and Hunter recorded their fears to Palgrave. Cole drew up a plan of the Ride to demonstrate the problems, but he was anxious that the fire watchman should not have access to the Treasury – what we would call the Safe Room – at the ride, which contained, he thought, 'the most valuable assemblage of records in the world': feet of fines, *curia regis* rolls, pipe rolls and memoranda rolls.

91 'The capital and the records of the nation', pp. 78–9.

92 D. Crook, 'The Rev. Joseph Hunter and the Public Records', *Transactions of the Hunter Archeological Society*, XII (1983), pp.1–15; *Second Report of the Deputy Keeper of Public Records*, pp.14–15; *Third Report of the Deputy Keeper of Public Records*, pp. 20–25.

93 *Fifty Years of Public Work of Sir Henry Cole*, KCB, 2 vols (1884), I, 15–20.

94 Dating from 1836, the painting is held by the Department of Prints and Drawings at the Victoria and Albert Museum.

95 *Fifty Years of Public Work*, pp. 23–4.

This record office was the first to be evacuated, in 1856–7 when the first stages of the new building at Chancery Lane neared completion.[96]

The delay in starting the new office was caused by considerable disagreements as to the best site. In 1837, on the suggestion of Lord Langdale, the Rolls Estate was vested in the Crown, and the Office of Works was empowered to build a record office there, for which a proposal was produced in 1840 by Thomas Chawner. Unfortunately, the houses of Parliament were in the course of reconstruction during the 1840s – a project so ambitious and glamorous that all other schemes were eclipsed. The Treasury proposed the use of the Victoria Tower for the records, unrealistically forecasting that its space would prove sufficient for the records for several centuries. But Palgrave managed to show that this accommodation was inadequate, and in 1846 attention shifted back to the Rolls Estate.[97]

James Pennethorne, an architect associated with major schemes for metropolitan improvements, next produced an ambitious plan to remodel the entire area round Chancery Lane. At the hub was a lavishly ornamented Elizabethan style record office, its dimensions carefully worked out in consultation with Henry Cole.[98] The expense of this proposal led to a postponement of two years; and to a more limited budget, which Pennethorne was to accept only with reservations. Years later he wrote that 'in those days we foresaw the necessity for a large library, for large searching rooms etc. etc.; all these things were washed away by economy, and will hereafter have to be provided at greater cost and with less convenience' – prophetic words indeed.[99]

Nevertheless, as requested, Pennethorne then came up with a more limited and utilitarian scheme for a record office to be built in stages. On the advice of James Braidwood, superintendent of the London Fire Brigade, and of Cole, security from fire was given the highest priority in the design: the building was to have a stone facing but to be supported on iron girders. It was to be a series of cell-like rooms, each a fireproof unit, with slate shelves for storing the records. However, Pennethorne did not abandon all pretensions to creating a building magnificent as well as functional, as a dramatic plan for the central clock tower, including a monstrous clock, well demonstrates, but regrettably it was never constructed, nor was another proposal for a library and office, reminiscent of an Oxford College.[100]

The first block of what the foundation stone calls the 'treasure house' of the national records was begun in 1851, and was completed in 1858 at the cost of

96 PRO 1/7, 30 November 1842; *First Report of the Royal Commission on the Public Records* (1912), App. III, pp. 26–28.

97 R. H. Ellis, 'The building of the Public Record Office', in A. E. J. Hollaender, ed., *Essays in Memory of Sir Hilary Jenkinson* (1962), pp. 9–30, esp. pp. 9–15; G. Tyacke, 'The Public Record Office to 1870', chapter from *Sir James Pennethorne, Architect and Urban Planner*, unpublished Ph.D. thesis, University of London (1987), pp. 3–4. I am grateful to Dr Tyacke for the valuable information contained therein.

98 *Ibid.*, pp. 4–6.

99 *Ibid.*, p.10; PRO 8/4, f. 41.

100 WORK 30/2655.

£77,000.[101] The Chapter House, Carlton Ride and the Tower were cleared, but it soon became clear that the space was woefully inadequate. The never ending tide of incoming documents, swollen by the departmental records and the State Papers, was diverted into some 'old, dark, ill-ventilated, rickety' houses on the Chancery Lane side of Rolls Yard.[102] From the mid-1850s Palgrave had been pressing an unwilling Treasury for an extension of the Office, but it was not until 1862 that Pennethorne was finally commissioned to draw up plans for the East Wing. This was built in two stages, finished respectively in 1868 and 1871, and including the Long Room (alias the Legal Search Room) and the Round Room (alias the Literary Search Room), probably inspired by Smirke's reading room at the British Museum.[103]

Sir Henry Cole wrote in his memoirs: 'Standing at the corner of Fetter Lane, on the north side of Fleet Street, may now be seen a fireproof stone building full of windows, as strongly built as a fortress: it has an architectural expression full of truth, originality and of its purpose, which is highly creditable to the common sense of its architect, James Pennethorne.'[104] Yet Pennethorne's work did not meet with universal approval. J. S. Brewer commented in 1851: 'externally the new building has not much to recommend it on the score of artistic beauty. To which of the recognised styles of architecture it ought to be referred would puzzle Mr. Ruskin himself to determine. Its pinched buttresses, its quadrangular windows . . ., the absence of all ease and freedom in its meagre ornaments and narrow proportions, reveal the mechanical graces of official Gothic.'[105]

For two decades after the completion of Pennethorne's record office subsequent Deputy Keepers made strong protests about the decay of the adjacent houses in Chancery Lane used for record storage, and asked for their replacement by another new block. Finally in 1890 Sir John Taylor was asked to produce a suitable design, which was built between 1892 and 1895. *The Times* welcomed the transformation of Chancery Lane and removal of the old houses which disfigured it.[106]

In order to complete the building Rolls House had also to be demolished – an operation completed without too much public opposition. The Rolls Chapel was more of a problem. Out of alignment with the new building, it was evidently considered by Taylor, by the Deputy Keeper, Sir Henry Maxwell-Lyte, and by the Office of Works to be little more than an inconvenient fire hazard. During the course of building the final block of the record office the chapel was demolished, to the ire of a public to which anything even vaguely medieval was sacrosanct. Lord

101 'The Public Record Office to 1870', p.17; *History of the King's Works*, VI, 474–5; 'The building of the Public Record Office', p. 2.
102 'The capital and the records of the nation', p. 79; 'The building of the Public Record Office', pp. 22–26; for photographs of the houses see PRO 8/23.
103 'The Public Record Office to 1870', pp.19–20.
104 *Fifty Years of Public Work*, I, 32; MPD 177/7, a watercolour by Pennethorne, shows the same idealised approach to the building.
105 J. S. Brewer, *English Studies* (1881), p. 2 (my thanks to Dr Tyacke for this reference); 'The Public Record Office to 1870', pp.17–18.
106 'The building of the Public Record Office', pp. 24–5; WORK 12/66/11.

Archibald Campbell fulminated in *The Times* about the 'destruction and desecration' going on the Chancery Lane.'[107] The glass and monuments were preserved and were incorporated into the museum which was built on the site, and which was opened in 1902.

This as it happened was the end of building at Chancery Lane. In 1914 a substantial south wing was planned, but it was never constructed, and between the wars additional accommodation was found for modern accruals at Cambridge and Canterbury gaols.

During both wars provincial repositories were opened for many of the records. Belvoir Castle and Shepton Mallet prison were two of the main sites in use for records evacuated from London during the Second World War – on the same principle as children. The documents returned to London in 1945–6, and many were housed in deep shelters in Fetter Lane, Goodge Street, Camden Town and other stations. These were subsequently replaced as overflow record stores by a site at Ashridge, in use from 1950 to 1978, and another at Hayes, Middlesex, which still remains our third record office, occupied largely by as yet unaccessioned departmental records under the supervision of the generating departments.[108]

The Public Records Act 1958 and the introduction of the thirty year rule in 1967 brought yet further pressure on existing storage places; and the growth of historical research in the 1960s brought greater urgency to the need for better search room facilities. Temporary accommodation was found at the Land Registry building in Portugal Street – which still contains part of the Conservation Department – but the problem was finally deemed too great for the Rolls Estate. In 1969 the decision was taken to build a new office for the departmental records on a riverside site, off Ruskin Avenue, Kew, already in the Crown's possession. Plans were drawn up jointly by the Public Record Office and the Ministry of Public Buildings and Works and in 1973 Taylor Woodrow began its work of construction.[109]

The Public Record Office Kew was a new and radical solution to old problems of storing records in safety and producing them for readers with ease. Special design features were included to preclude the danger of flooding from the river and to create a controlled atmosphere where the documents could be stored at a constant temperature and humidity. Thus the office is raised on a podium and is heated and ventilated by an air-conditioning system. The documents are shelved in large segmented open-plan storage areas, the risk from fire being minimised by special smoke detectors and strong fire-proof doors. The requisitioning system, making use of the computer technology available in the 1970s, broke new ground and has been widely admired and imitated.[110]

107 'The building of the Public Record Office', pp. 26–30; WORK 12/66/11; WORK 12/67/2; W. J. Hardy, 'The Rolls Chapel', *Middlesex and Hertfordshire Notes and Queries*, II (1896), 49–68; *Fifty-Seventh Report of the Deputy Keeper of Public Records*, App., pp.19–47.

108 'The capital and the records of the nation', pp. 80–88.

109 *Ibid.*, pp. 88–90.

110 N. G. Cox, 'The new Public Record Office at Kew', *Archivum*, XXXI (1986), pp.133–42.

The Kew Building – seen by many as a blueprint for the future – brought a temporary respite in the battle to house the incoming records. Yet with accessions running at about a mile a year its seventy miles of shelving are now nearly full – and plans have to be made for the future. Let us hope that the lessons of the past may provide us all with some guidance.

4. THE FUTURE OF THE PUBLIC RECORDS

G.H. Martin Keeper of Public Records 1982–88

The purpose of an anniversary conference is to celebrate what has been accomplished by reviewing and commending the past. That achieved, it is quite natural that we should then look to the future, and in considering it express the hope that we shall all do as well as we have done already, and if anything rather better. That is indeed my hope, and a lively one. The Public Record Office and the British Record Society have been usefully busy for a long time, and there is every reason to think that their usefulness will not only continue but increase. When it comes to saying in what ways that usefulness will manifest itself, however, I find that my confidence, though strong, cannot extend to certainty, and that despite the title of my paper I do not wish in a conventional sense to say anything about future developments at all.

There are two particular reasons for that avowal, and although either might suffice I am very willing to confess them both. The first and more obvious is that the policy of the Public Record Office at any time is the policy of Her Majesty's Government of the day, as it is applied by the Keeper. I could tell readily enough what my successor's immediate problems are likely to be, but it is hardly for me to do that, and the more so because he will resolve them so resourcefully and ingeniously that they may well not appear as problems at all. The second reason is equally cogent, and it has a wider application: I have studied history and my fellow historians for some time, and whilst I would not wish to say that history has no predictive value whatever, I do believe that historians make notably unreliable prophets. They may not really be more undependable in that respect than other people, but having set the past to rights they are often under a temptation to say a closing word about how things are likely to go along hereafter, and usually it would be a very good thing if they were to resist it.

Futurology is a new-fangled expression, but the guessing-game that it describes has been popular for some time. The pace of technical change over the last two hundred years has made it seem safe to predict that there will be further changes, and that they will tend in the same directions. The notion is broadly true, and yet there is nothing easier to distinguish and date than such a prediction, because it is always, and in retrospect most obtrusively, rooted in the conditions and preoccupations of its own day. Nothing is more redolent of the 1890s than a *Punch* cartoon of that time depicting the future uses of the gas telephone or the aeronautical bicycle.

In the event it is almost invariably not the change itself that matters, but its literally unpredictable consequences. The daily habits and assumptions that the telephone has engendered have taken us far from the far-from-simple fact that we can talk to almost anyone over any distance. We may not even now be able to take account of them all, yet the telephone has been with us for a century. With all which in mind, and the future before us, let us look by way of illustration at the fortunes of the Office over the years that are past, and see what a conscientiously reflective prophet might have made of them at the time.

The history of the Public Record Office as we have sketched it here falls fairly neatly into three fifty-year periods. In the first its staff were concerned to bring the ancient records of the Crown into secure premises and to arrange them in such order that they could be readily retrieved and studied further. In the second the Office developed the expertise which it had acquired in the first period, and in the process became a notable centre of scholarship. In both periods the assimilation of modern records had effectively to be postponed. During the third period the Office has largely discharged the accumulation of archival problems which it inherited from the first two, and has also come to terms with various technological innovations, some of which have been positively helpful to it whilst others seem to promise further complications. It has also moved from serving hundreds to serving hundreds of thousands of readers. How far might it have been possible to predict the course of events in each period? What indications of the future does the present ever show? In 1838 Queen Victoria had begun her reign, but had scarcely had time to declare its character. The great innovation of the time, the railway, was a little over a decade old, but most cross-country travel was still by coach, and the towns were, and would long remain, almost as full of horses as they were of people. The penny post had not yet appeared, but there were a few miles of electric telegraph in the fields between Paddington and West Drayton. Railway enthusiasts could foresee a time when the iron network would be national and complete, but if they also foresaw excursion trains, Parliamentaries, workmens' returns, and milk trains or even newspaper trains they kept their thoughts to themselves. The issues of the day, amongst which the Corn Laws had for the moment displaced cholera and the Poor Law, were enough in themselves.

The unremitting growth of London had been a source of wonder and concern for centuries, but there were islands of dusty repose even at the centre. The Rolls Estate, a medieval liberty straddling the boundary of the City, was one of them. We are fortunate to have its atmosphere evoked for us by Dickens and Trollope. Alice Vavasour's father suffered his weekly martyrdom in a dingy office nearby, and *Bleak House* breathes the country air of Lincoln's Inn Fields in the summertime as well as the winter fogs of New Court and Chancery Lane. In any season it was a surprising setting for a new-minted department of government, though one in which the mouldering parchment from the floor of the Chapter House at Westminster might feel instantly at home. It was also unmistakably part of that London which was not so much the capital of the country, as the place where the courts had been held ever since King John agreed in 1215 that Common Pleas should not follow his person, but should be heard in one place. Gathered in Rolls House and the tumbledown tenements surrounding it, Sir Francis Palgrave and his new colleagues were very conscious of the antiquity and the bulk and the vulnerability of the records in their care. They had to wait almost twenty years for a new building, and in all that time their daily task was to impose order upon the cartloads of documents that they received, and the greatest danger to what they held was perceived to be from fire. When eventually the new repository was built in the 1850s it was therefore made massively secure and ingeniously fireproof. It was well-contrived in other ways, but it was also too small, and neither of its subsequent extensions was on a large enough scale to keep pace with the accumulation of records. The new accessions were still mainly of ancient material, and although Palgrave had a clear-headed notion of what might or ought to be done with modern records he was not able to pursue it in the face of the other and more pressing problems of the day. At the same time the uses to which the records might be put were hardly clear. Public interest in them was largely a matter of personal and professional inquiries, that is to say largely a matter of legal searches. Literary searches, which we should now describe as academic work, were freed from charges in 1852, but even at that time there was practically no academic profession to pursue them. History had only recently made its appearance at the universities, of which there were still only four, and it was far from producing a cadre of researchers whose demands would shape custodial policies. If it was difficult in 1838 to predict the size of the building required to house the older records, it would certainly have taken extraordinary acumen to see what might be done with them. And to have foreseen the world of which the Record Office would be part by 1888, in which substantially more than half the population lived in towns, in which the railways had brought the greater part of that population within a day's journey of London, and in which the Post Office with its telegraph wires and Anthony Trollope's iron letter-boxes had enabled an exchange of messages within a day, again almost everywhere, would have required a talent altogether beyond both that time and our own. A national institution in 1888 was a creature of quite another kind from a national institution in 1838.

That was, however, the setting of Maxwell Lyte's early keepership, and he showed himself responsive to it not only by installing electric light (the D.C. system favoured by the City of London coexisted with Westminster's A.C. for several decades), but also by cultivating the academic community that was now ready to take an interest in the riches of the Office. The cheapness of printing and, alas, of wood-pulp paper made it possible to multiply and diffuse the means of detailed reference to the records in a manner that would have been wildly extravagant half-a-century before. It was still not clear what part modern records might play in serious academic inquiry, but the role of the early material was now very evident. There were other opportunities that were less readily perceived. The typewriter brought women into the commercial world, but not as yet into the Public Record Office, and despite the rapid refinement of photography the handwritten certified copy, a nostalgic relic of the days of official perquisites, effortlessly held its own.

We can readily see, as contemporaries could not, much greater changes looming. The radical building campaign of the 1890s, which removed the last vestiges of the old Rolls Estate, made no significant difference to the accommodation available for records, which was probably the Office's most urgent need. What is more, although Victoria's life and reign had a decade to run their aftermath was a short one. In 1888 the First World War was only a volunteer's lifetime away, and the Second rather less than a pensioner's. It would hardly seem reasonable now to have expected Maxwell Lyte and his learned colleagues to foresee the convulsions through which most of them were to live, and still less to do anything about them, yet we not uncommonly seek to impose such burdens upon ourselves.

So powered flight and the insurance stamp, social surveys and cinematic photography, which have all left their marks upon the Office and its records, came about in short order, and were then followed by an appallingly destructive war. The war brought bewildering changes amidst its unaccustomed dangers and inconveniences. Staff disappeared, some of them to die in action, and those who were left wrestled with a world in which almost everything was disconcerting and surprising. Under the threat of aerial bombardment Domesday Book and other prized material was sent away to quieter parts of the country. The Office's out-store at Canterbury proved an enduring institution, but the mass of paper accumulated in the new departments of government, from the Air Ministry to the Ministry of War Transport, surpassed the output of many previous centuries.

When peace returned for a while, and it seems now to have been a poignantly short while, the measured discussion of the older records resumed in a strange new setting. The world of motor traffic and wireless broadcasting was also one of the official and semi-official histories of the war, which brought recent records under public scrutiny, in however discreet a fashion, more rapidly than ever before. However, academic readers for the most part remained intent on the remoter past, and the 1930s, though full of incident, were not a time for enlarging repositories and reading-rooms, and devising new means of reference for an unquantifiable future demand. The future itself was ominously uncertain. The Office celebrated its centenary in 1938, but within a year the staff were again preparing to disperse the records to places safer than the capital, in which the government expected to face casualties numbering hundreds of thousands within weeks of the outbreak of war.

In the event the precautions against air raids proved, for almost a year, a greater hazard than missiles from the sky. When London was drawn into battle the Office escaped all but superficial damage, and all through the war daily life called more often for patience and contrivance than for active heroism. But all those qualities made their own demands on paper, and the paper that had sustained the state in its exertions between 1914 and 1919 was as nothing to what it consumed between 1939 and 1945. On this occasion, too, the greatly enlarged apparatus of government was carried over into the peace to manage the reconstruction of society. That something would have to be done about the archives of the modern state was plain enough, but what it might be, and when, was less obvious. There were few indications, too, in the years immediately following the war, that in the second half of the twentieth century academic and other professional searchers would be greatly outnumbered by readers whose previous experience had been gained in public libraries. What the Office might become was a matter for speculation; what it was now was a matter of daily concern. For the moment, and for several years, the most pressing business was the restoration of services, and even some expansion of them, within the straitened means of the post-war economy.

Once again the Office seemed to have changed less than the world around it. The legal profession is not addicted to novelty for its own sake, but there were women working in neighbouring firms in some numbers. The Office moved more deliberately, and despite having employed Dame Mary Smieton in the days of her youth it waited some inexplicable decades before repeating the experiment. There were, to be sure, typewriters amongst the inkwells (perhaps Jack Cantwell will tell us to what cultural horizon the Office pencil-sharpeners belong) but as late as 1950 it would have been easier to predict that one day, perhaps even in Our Time, there would be women in all grades, and that in that atmosphere of licence men might go in their shirtsleeves, than that typewriters would soon have memories, and that electrostatic copiers would print positives, and that even Principal Assistant Keepers would not expect to find hardware at an ironmonger's. In the meantime there were vacuum tubes to speed the flow of requisition slips, and another lift.

In the 1950s, however, the Grigg Committee scaled the Himalaya of departmental paper, and took a searching view of the landscape from the top. The reorganisation of the Office, and the consequent provisions of the Public Records Act of 1958, provided the means with which we are managing the last quarter of the twentieth century. For good reasons it is more profitable to devise and refine administrative practice than it is to guess where technology might take us. Although the reprographic work of the Office has expanded greatly over the last four decades, we are not using microfilm in the ways in which the 1940s supposed we should use it. And in more recent years we have noticed that paperless offices can produce a good deal of paper.

The commanding events of the years since 1945 have occurred on an even larger stage than the generous scope of our present conference. They are firstly the world-wide growth of population, which for good or ill has enlarged the scale of almost all human activities, and secondly the fulminating inflation of currencies that has accompanied it. In those societies in which subsistence is not the first and last concern, provision for leisure makes irresistible demands upon the economy, some of which take subtle forms. The disruption of family life by the restless movement of industrial society has interrupted the natural flow of family lore at the same time as the state has offered the means of restoring it by research. Record offices provide neither bread nor circuses, and even in temperate climes they are less numerous than swimming pools, but in terms of their established functions they have now become places of formidable public resort.

In our recent experience the most important result of techological change has probably been the revolution in travel. It is the universal growth in numbers of readers quite as much as the growing bulk of records that has made current technology available to archivists, and the readers continue to come. Whether they recognise it or not, even the most harassed of them travel more freely than the most leisured of eighteenth-century clergymen. In the coming half-century, however, it may be that the technology that now serves the reader in the Public Record Office and elsewhere will be turned to make facsimiles of documents available at a distance. The means is already available, but at the moment its application would cost more than a return ticket from Saltburn-on-Sea, or even a moderate bargain negotiated in Tempe, Arizona. The Office is now storing machine-readable records on optical disc, but while the thirty-year rule obtains we know that it will take in more paper than tapes for at least thirty years. We also know that the first ten instalments of that paper will more than fill the repository at Kew. Kew was designed for the rapid retrieval of documents, and its methods have been successfully extended to the more variegated and unwieldy holdings at Chancery Lane. When the next stage of the repository is built it will be to the same general specifications, but it is not difficult to imagine the automatic retrieval of documents being practised within our own lifetimes. That is precisely the point, however, at which observation gives way to speculation, and that in turn is a signal that it is time for me to stop. After one hundred and fifty years of keeping the Public Records, the Public Record Office is busier today than it has ever been. It can also claim, with all modesty, to be a more popular institution than it has ever been, and that is a truly refreshing thought for a statutory body. Heartened, in this company, both by the occasion and by our deliberations, I shall close not with a prophecy but with a confident hope: that whatever developments the future may hold, the Public Record Office will continue to offer the world the means of studying them.

5. SAMPLING AND SELECTION: CURRENT POLICIES

K. J. Smith Principal, Public Record Office

The title of this session requires, perhaps, a few words of explanation. In records management, the terms sampling and selection increasingly have the same connotation. Until quite recently, sampling always referred to case papers – records of individuals, particular places, etc. – and selection to general subject and policy papers. Two developments, however, have served to blur the distinction.

Firstly, there is the increase in modern public records, an increase that has corresponded closely to the increase in human population since the nineteenth century. That population increase has made necessary an expansion of governmental activity, and that expansion has had as one of its concomitants a tremendous increase in record production. As modern technology has come to be applied to the production of records, their growth has been in a geometric rather than an arithmetic ratio. Selection of general subject papers has, therefore, decreased somewhat – at least in the way envisaged by the Grigg Report in 1954[1] – and a good deal of sampling of policy papers is now carried out. Many events and issues, for example, emerge only from records that have been sampled to illustrate the machinery and organisation of government.

Secondly, the trend of research away from the study of administrative history to the study of social history continues unabated. Ironically, public record appraisers – essentially Inspecting Officers of the Public Record Office in conjunction with Departmental Record Officers – are beginning to select case papers rather than sample them. This has certainly happened within the last few years – an example is a class of unemployment returns of the old Ministry of Labour which is now in the Public Record Office as LAB 85 – and I see this trend continuing.

So what is the current position on appraisal – which is what I shall call sampling and selection? In the United Kingdom the principle has been followed since 1958 that appraisal should be delegated to the originating departments. It is a principle that was expounded in the writings of Sir Hilary Jenkinson, who considered that neither archivists nor researchers should be involved in the appraisal process.

> . . . for an administrative body to destroy what it no longer needs is a matter entirely within its competence and an action which future ages

1 Report of the Committee on Departmental Records, HMSO, Cmd. 9163.

(even though they may find reasons to deplore it) cannot possibly criticise as illegitimate or as affecting the status of the remaining archives . . .[2]

The point that he was trying to make, I believe, was that appraisal should be impartial, that the historical record should reflect the tendencies and spirit of the administration of the day and not those of the academic researchers of the time.

But surely the appraisal process requires a particular knowledge, one that represents the interest of research to the world of administration and the needs of administration to the world of research. The recognition of such knowledge, however, is still not paramount, although it is making some inroads into current techniques of appraisal. Proponents of the traditional method of appraisal will not necessarily hold up Jenkinson as their guiding light, but they may point to outside forces which they cannot control. These forces consist mainly of the lack of resources. Records managers and archive administrators are at the lower rung of recognisable professions. In government departments they are among the first to go when the Treasury hones its staff-cutting axe.

This somewhat negative outlook of the profession is going to change and a number of new initiatives are beginning to emerge. In a novel way, the problem is being approached from the other end, from the standpoint of the managers of current information.

What has been so daunting to records appraisers in the last decade or so, apart from the bulk of the records, has been the complete confusion, not to say shambles, of files and papers that are coming through for review. It takes a PRO Inspecting Officer an inordinate amount of time to understand the muddle before he/she can begin to work on forming a valid judgement on the value of documents. Now, however, administrators are being exhorted to manage their current records in such a way that will not only lead to the preservation of better material and a less complicated appraisal process, but also to a better control of that resource which is most important to them and without which management itself could not function – namely information. As part of the initiatives a series of leaflets is being issued to departmental record officers and records managers, and it is hoped that many more organisations, both in the UK and abroad, might learn from the new steps that are being taken. Information is only valuable if it is accessible. If the information that management wants is surrounded by rubbish that should have been consigned to the bin as soon as action on it was completed, it cannot easily be reached. Decision-making suffers and management suffers.

Two major points have emerged from these initiatives. Firstly, it is clear that a large amount of the records in government need not have been created in the first place, and this includes the proliferation of copies. The photocopier is the worst machine ever invented as far as the records appraiser is concerned. Secondly, many more records than at present can be assigned pre-determined periods of retention in

2 Hilary Jenkinson, *Manual of Archive Administration*, Percy Lund, Humphries and Co., 1965 (2nd edition), p.149.

order to take them out of the review process and thus save a great deal of time. I shall say more about the use of disposal schedules later.

So, with these new initiatives and the gradual recognition of a special knowledge required for records appraisal, there seems to be a new belief that an administrative body, be it a government department, local authority, or whatever, is perhaps *not* wholly competent, as Jenkinson suggested, to decide what of its records are of historical value. In addition, social history transcends departmental boundaries and records appraisers cannot judge the true value of a collection of records in isolation.

Whilst a number of interested parties may take part in the appraisal process, final decisions on sampling and/or selection would generally rest with one individual. That individual is a particular breed. He/she must be well-versed in records management techniques and archive administration principles; must be aware of the course and details of modern history; must be in touch with both trends and methodology of research; and must, above all, be a communicator.

Appraisal of records should not be based on intuition or arbitrary suppositions of value. It should be based instead on thorough analyses of documentation bearing on the matter to which the records pertain. Analysis should always be the essence of records appraisal.

Current trends show a greater understanding of the value of disposal schedules, and consequently they are used more widely. In simple terms a disposal schedule is a list of files or series of files for which pre-determined destruction or retention dates can be agreed between a records manager and the creating agency. Their use obviates the need to conduct a file by file examination to determine disposal.

An excessive retention of records is proving expensive in staff, time, space, and equipment. The use of schedules helps to:

- save space by removing from the office records no longer required or no longer in current use;
- save time by reducing the volume of records which must be searched for information;
- avoid additional cost for the purchase of storage equipment;
- promote efficient control over records – if the least valuable of the records can be identified, then the management of the more important records improves;
- identify the valuable records for archival preservation.

The kinds of papers that would appear on disposal schedules and thus be destroyed after a relatively short period of time are those which are likely to be unregistered – not part of a formal file classification system – and would include such records as invoices, orders for stationery and equipment, vehicle logs, daily sick records, etc.

The percentage of documents that can be destroyed by means of disposal schedules will depend to a large extent on the nature of the work of the organisation concerned, but generally record appraisers are looking for a figure somewhere in the region of 40 per cent.

In some countries there are two types of schedule: a General Records Schedule, compiled and maintained by a central organisation (such as the National Archives) and covering records common to all departments and agencies (usually called 'housekeeping' records); and secondly a Departmental Disposal Schedule, compiled and maintained by individual organisations and covering records peculiar to them.

Canada, for example, is well-advanced in the use of these two types of schedule, so much so that most of the operations in compiling and monitoring them are now computerised. In the United Kingdom, however, each organisation tends to have its own schedule, and there is no standard format. The result is a rather disjointed system of appraisal of the relatively valueless records, especially of those common to most organisations. The Data Protection Act 1984 has had some effect on the compilation of schedules of records, but that relates, of course, only to information held on automatic processing equipment.

The appraisal of records which might have a longer term value than those on disposal schedules is, as I mentioned before, still carried out in accordance with the Grigg Report of 1954, that is, the responsibility falls largely upon departments, albeit with the expert guidance of Inspecting Officers from the Public Record Office. Indeed, the principle was reiterated by the Committee on Modern Public Records (Wilson Committee) in 1981.[3] In essence the principle continues that policy of disposal which is determined by the needs of the originators of the records and the known and anticipated requirements of other potential users. I think that the order of these determinants is noteworthy.

The appraisal of general subject and policy files continues to follow set lines. The PRO Manual of Records Administration[4] lays down general criteria and gives examples of the types of papers that are likely to be preserved:

1. Papers relating to the origins of the department, its organisation, staffing, functions, and procedures, including office notices, directories, and organisation charts.
2. Annual and other major departmental reports – although some are published it is usually convenient to preserve a records set for use in conjunction with other departmental records.
3. Principal policy papers relating to the preparation of legislation; and
4. Those relating to the implementation or interpretation of policy; for example those which reflect major changes in policy throw significant light on the main functions and programmes of a department.
5. Record sets of minutes and circulated papers of major departmental bodies, such as committees and advisory councils.
6. Papers relating to significant accomplishments of departments, as well as
7. Those relating to obsolete activities or to abortive plans.
8. Papers cited in, or noted as consulted in the preparation of, official histories.
9. Papers relating to rights and obligations of, or against, the Crown.

[3] Modern Public Records: Selection and Access, HMSO, Cmnd. 8204.

[4] A Manual of Records Administration, PRO (Records Administration Division), 1982.

10. Papers relating to notable events and *causes célèbres* or other events which gave rise to contemporary interest or controversy.
11. Developments or trends in political, social, and economic history.
12. Records of the more important aspects of scientific, technological, or medical research and development.
13. And finally, papers containing information of significant regional or local interest on which it is unlikely that evidence will be locally available.

Some recent developments in the Records Administration Division of the PRO have taken this list a little further by widening the advice given to departmental record officers and record reviewers. Firstly, records for review are now more clearly divided into three categories:

(a) *Policy Papers*, e.g. records of major departmental bodies; bill papers; submissions to Ministers; records relating to the formulation, implementation, and interpretation of legislation.
(b) *Administrative Papers*, e.g. records relating to the origins, organisation, staffing, functions, and procedures of a department; manuals and instructions; planning of activities; reports.
(c) *Case Papers*, sometimes referred to as particular instance papers, e.g. benefit claims; grants files; licensing authorisations; permits; survey returns.

Secondly, information about the *context* in which a particular policy was conceived is considered essential to reviewers and users if they are to make sense of the records. Why was the record created in the first place? How was it used and by whom? If these questions cannot be answered, the value of any judgements on the long term importance of the record is likely to be impaired.

In the late 1950s T. R. Schellenberg, a former Director of Archival Management in the United States National Archives, expounded a theory of records appraisal which viewed the values in public records as of two main kinds – primary and secondary – primary being for the originating agency itself, and secondary for other agencies and private users. He further considered that the secondary aspect could be ascertained most easily if records were considered in relation to two kinds of value:

(a) the *evidence* they contain of the organisation and functioning of the body that produced them; and
(b) the *information* they contain on persons, corporate bodies, places, conditions, etc., with which the body dealt.

Generally these secondary values have received closer scrutiny today, in particular the second, the informational value. Records management is developing into information management and, as mentioned earlier, informational values are now considered more closely in current historical research. So how has Schellenberg's theory been adopted, if at all, to present day requirements of records appraisal?

Public and other records are created to accomplish the purposes for which an organisation has been created – legal, administrative, fiscal, or operating. Those are the primary values. The appraiser considers the procedural significance and functional character of the record when it has ceased to be of current use.

Each record has a function (which is usually reflected in its title); it may:

(a) authorise or direct action;
(b) document, or provide a statement of, information;
(c) explain and inform.

So the first decision to be made is whether the record is of continuing use for the conduct of the organisation's business. Public and other records, however, are preserved in archival institutions because they have values which exist long after they cease to be of current use and, as Schellenberg envisaged, these secondary values are split into evidential and informational.

Evidential value is predominant in policy papers and administrative papers, and in judging the evidence, the appraiser seeks to explain the activities of the creating organisation by preserving records of policy decisions, records which reflect the functions of the organisations, and records which are representative of a significant range of institutional or individual activities. Informational value is predominant in case papers. It is this particular aspect of records appraisal that is receiving more attention at present than all others put together – largely for the reasons I outlined earlier, and mainly the continued interest in quantitative historical research.

Informational characteristics are derived from the factual data that the records contain about persons, corporate bodies, events, problems, conditions, etc. They can be evaluated on the basis of:

(a) the uniqueness of the record;
(b) the information it contains;
(c) the importance of the content.

The informational needs of genealogists, historians, economists, sociologists, demographers, *et al.*, have to be taken into account by the records appraiser.

Case papers in government are generally very large collections of files or papers, and the dilemma for the appraiser is to reconcile the demand for preservation from researchers with the capacity for storage of such large collections. Some indication of their size can be seen from the following examples:

National Insurance Contribution Sheets	55,000,000
War Pensions Awards Files	3,500,000
Supplementary Benefit Claims	4,000,000 per year

and, of course, there are hundreds of other examples.

Before examining current methods of appraisal of these collections, it is worth noting one major difficulty. On many occasions the records are of long term administrative use, usually far beyond the normal access period given by governments. For example, many of the war pensions awards files, although over forty years old, are still active. As long as individual ex-servicemen are alive, their papers are required by the body administering their pension.

Personal files of civil and public servants are also required long after people retire, usually because there are questions of superannuation to be resolved. This category of records presents special problems in that the information on the file that is required for long-term use forms such a small proportion of the file itself, and yet the whole file is kept. This means that a disproportionate amount of storage space is being provided for the information.

As we saw earlier, when applying the test of informational value, there are three aspects to consider.

(a) *Uniqueness*

The term uniqueness means that the information contained in particular records is not to be found in other documentary sources *in as complete and as usable form*. Information is obviously unique if it cannot be found elsewhere. But information in public records is seldom completely unique, for generally such records relate to matters that are also dealt with in other documentary sources, and the information they contain may be similar or approximately similar to that contained in other sources. In applying the test of uniqueness, an appraiser brings into review all other sources of information on the matter under consideration. These sources encompass materials produced outside as well as within the organisation. The material produced outside may be published or unpublished; it may consist of private manuscripts, newspapers, or books. Uniqueness also includes the matter of duplication. Records can be duplicated from one administrative level to another and within an organisation several copies of a particular record might exist.

(b) *Content*

The degree to which the information is concentrated in the records may be in one of three ways:

(i) Few facts are presented about many persons, events, etc. (*extensive*).
(ii) Many facts are presented about a few persons, events, etc. (*intensive*).
(iii) Many facts are presented about various matters (*diverse*).

For example, census schedules and passenger lists may be said to provide extensive information in that each schedule or list pertains to many people. Pensions files may be said to provide intensive information in that each file covers one person and gives a great deal of detail. And reports of consular or diplomatic agents would contain information on diverse matters. Content might also include the physical condition of the records as well as the information within them. Physical condition is important, for if the records are to be preserved in an archival institution, they should be in a form that will enable people other than those who created them to use them without difficulty and without resort to expensive mechanical or electronic equipment.

(c) *Importance*

> In applying the test of importance, the appraiser is in the realm of the imponderable. Who can say definitely if a given body of records is important, and for what purpose, and for whom?

Nevertheless, the appraiser takes into account the actual research methods of various groups of people and the likelihood that they would under ordinary circumstances make effective use of archival material. By and large, the feeling is that the scholar can usually rely on the overwhelming mass of published material on recent day-to-day social and economic matters, but, while the appraiser might normally give priority to the needs of the historian and the social scientist, he also preserves records of vital interest to the genealogist and the student of local history. He does not, however, preserve records for very unlikely users, such as persons in highly specialised technical and scientific fields, who do not use records extensively in the normal exercise of their professions and are not likely to use archival material relating to them.

Research values are normally derived from the importance of information in aggregates of records, not from information in single records. Documents are collectively significant if the information they contain is useful for studies of social, economic, and political matters, as distinct from matters relating to individual persons or things.

Records relating to persons or things may, of course, have an individual research value. Normally the more important a person is, the more important is the record relating to him/her. Such records might also have associational value because of their association with heroes, dramatic episodes, or places where significant events took place.

In selecting records for their informational value, two separate courses are available.

(a) To select complete those series of records that represent concentrations of information, such as census schedules, where single documents provide extensive information in a concentrated form.
(b) To select a limited number of documents that are representative of the whole.

Because of the bulk of these records, there are few that will be selected as a complete collection. Census records are an obvious exception, because they are useful to a particular, fairly large, group of researchers. When it comes to selecting a limited number of documents from a collection – or sampling, as it is usually called – there are three methods which can be followed:

(a) Special selection
(b) Random sampling
(c) Systematic sampling

(a) *Special selection*

This is a method that has little true archival merit and may also be of uncertain value for research purposes. Nevertheless, there are occasions when it is adopted with some justice. The method simply means the selection from a relatively ephemeral series of papers of one or more specimens to illustrate administrative practice at a particular date. The resultant sample represents a very limited historical or other use since it can only be cited as an indicator and in no way can it be used for comparative or statistical study.

Special selection is often applied to personal files, where those of eminent persons may be selected for their intrinsic value only.

(b) *Random sampling*

This method implies that every unit in a series has an equal chance of representing that series, and in this context it is necessary to use a random number table – a list of numbers normally generated by computer and checked in a number of different ways to ensure that they are as random as possible. The table is applied to file reference numbers and documents are selected accordingly.

(c) *Systematic sampling*

This is the usual method for selection of particular instance papers and it is carried out at various degrees of complexity. The most simple way is to decide on the size of the sample required and to select every 5th, 10th, 50th, 100th, or nth file from the series. In a collection of regional papers, the system might be to select records for one particular year from region A, for the following year from region B, and so on, in a continuous cycle. In a series with annual cycles, the files from every 10th year might be taken as the sample. In an alphabetical series, all the files with a particular initial letter might be selected for particular years.

Whatever selection system is used will depend very much on the characteristics of the whole collection, and, to a certain extent, on the size of the sample required. For researchers the problem with systematic sampling is that it depends on a subjective decision of the criteria to be used. Although academic historians are being increasingly consulted before these decisions are made, this sampling method remains the one least favoured by them.

Although the scholar can very often rely on the mass of published literature for information on social and economic developments, it can be argued that the existence of published conclusions drawn from a collection of particular instance papers is not in itself a valid reason for destroying the raw data. Such data can be used for further research purposes, other than those for which it was originally compiled. In addition, published abstracts often give rise to false, or at least contentious, conclusions which are not supported by original data.

Such large collections of papers take up an inordinate amount of space and the feeling is still current that as many of them as possible must be destroyed. The argument against that, of course, is that researchers are being deprived of valuable sources of study.

A number of solutions to these problems have been suggested, including:

(a) that the collections be microfilmed, the film preserved, and the original documents destroyed. The main argument against this is one of the prohibitive cost involved in filming.
(b) that collections not selected for permanent preservation be kept in an intermediate repository and made available to researchers for a specified period, say between five and ten years, so that they can carry out any research on them. After that period they would be destroyed.
(c) that collections not considered worthy of permanent preservation in the national archives be offered to other historical institutes and associations, including those privately owned.

Before leaving this subject, I should say a little about the appraisal of machine-readable records. The main elements involved in the appraisal of computer records are essentially no different from those involved in dealing with paper records. But because of their format and because of the technical problems involved in handling them, certain special considerations have been brought into play.

Because of the extreme compactness with which data can be stored in machine-readable form, large collections of information can be considered for permanent preservation in their entirety. But, despite the savings in costs of physical storage, there is a high technical cost and a high cost in skilled manpower involved in the maintenance and preservation of such records. These include the necessity to convert the several different types of systems to a common, archival, medium.

The main criteria that are currently borne in mind when appraising machine-readable records are that:

(a) The informational content of the records should be high.
(b) The information available in the records should not also be available from conventional records in an acceptable form.
(c) The information should not be aggregated to any significant degree.
(d) The information should be susceptible to analysis for purposes beyond that for which it was originally collected.
(e) Accompanying documentation must be sufficient for full and proper understanding of the data.

Another medium that has received a great deal of attention in the past and is still considered from time to time is microfilm. A number of government departments, anxious to reduce their storage costs, see microfilm as a substitute for paper not only for semi-active records but also for active records. The saving of storage space, however, is not enough on its own to justify a policy of filming documents, destroying them, and keeping microfilm as a substitute. Although it is sometimes suggested that it is cost-effective, no costing exercise that has been carried out has yet confirmed that. From the point of view of appraisal and review, splicing, or refilming to eliminate parts of film not selected or subject to extended closure because of sensitivity, would lead to a very protracted, if not impossible, exercise.

To finish off the session, I should like to say a little about current trends in the management of information as a resource, a subject that, as we have seen, directly affects sampling and selecting. Many departments in the Civil Service are seeking to improve their management of information, stimulated by the ever-increasing volume, the costs of storage and retrieval, the pressures on resources, the burdens on industry, and, by no means least, the opportunities provided by developments in information technology.

Information management is now seen as the hub of four previously distinct functions: records management, libraries, archives, and information technology. A strategy has been suggested which will embrace these functions, analyse and identify the information needs (based on a department's aims and objectives), define policies and objectives for information, and make the necessary arrangements for the continuous management of the information resource.

Quite apart from the data which is held and processed in computer systems, 2,000,000 files are opened each year by departments, some 1,500 shelf-miles of non-current paper records are held by departments, and about 500 shelf-miles of paper records are in regular use. The size of the problem is there for all to see.

The long-term benefit derived from thinking of information as a resource which is essential for the work of a department is also plain to see, and the new information strategy, coupled with the records management initiatives, will go a long way towards an improved appraisal procedure.

In short current trends in sampling and selection are moving slowly in the right direction.

6. Government Record Keeping: A Tale from the Department of Employment

R.J.R. Lorimer Departmental Record Officer, Department of Employment

I have been asked to talk about government record keeping, with particular reference to the Department of Employment and my own responsibilities for the records of the nation there, as Chief Registrar and Departmental Record Officer, accountable to the Lord Chancellor through the Keeper of Public Records.

My appointment, in 1980, to the posts of Chief Registrar and Departmental Record Officer to the Department of Employment, upon transfer from the Manpower Services Commission, continued a well-tested practice of placing a senior officer with detailed knowledge of the Department gained at local, regional, and headquarters offices, at both operational management and policy decision levels, into those combined posts. My predecessor, Richard Billing, spent ten years learning the job, and that will be my own term of office and practice by the time of my retirement in February 1990.

As Chief Registrar and Departmental Record Officer I am responsible for
(1) the care of all papers from the time they are created or first received in the Department until they are disposed of;
(2) consultation with the nominated reviewing officers, to decide which papers need to be retained for departmental purposes after their first review;
(3) deciding, jointly with the Inspecting Officer from the Public Record Office, which papers at the second review should be destroyed, transferred to the Public Record Office for permanent preservation, or exceptionally retained in the Department for administrative purposes for a further period;
(4) devising registration systems which will ensure adequate classification of papers and the smooth operation of the reviewing procedure;
(5) controlling and knowing the whereabouts of all papers in the Department, whether registered or unregistered; and
(6) obtaining, particularly from unregistered documents, samples of case papers (Particular Instance Papers) for preservation by the Public Record Office.

Most major departments in the Civil Service are seeking to improve their management of information, stimulated by the ever-increasing volume, the costs or storage and retrieval, the pressures on resources, the burdens on industry and, by no means least, the opportunities provided by the development of Information Technology.

Quite *apart* from the data which is held and processed in computer systems, *two million* files are opened each year by departments (there are times when one thinks they are *all* raised in the Department of Employment), some 1,500 miles of non-current paper records are held by departments and about 500 miles of paper records are in regular use. Even in quite small departments regular and unremitting effort has to be devoted to making good use of information. The factors which press departments to focus attention on information are:

— staff at all levels throughout government devote an enormous amount of time and effort to handling information in all of its forms;

— information is seen to be central to most of the tasks carried out by government and improvements in its availability, accuracy, timeliness and quality might therefore be expected to contribute significantly to the effectiveness of the Civil Service;

— that, notwithstanding its importance, information is an ill-understood resource, the management of which is not normally seen to be part of the day-to-day responsibilities of Civil Servants;

— the volume and complexity of the information with which Civil Servants deal is, by observation, growing rapidly through the wider use of information technology (computing and telecommunications), the growing number of paper records and the general increase in the volume of information in society as a whole;

— the pervasive nature of more recent developments in information technology highlight the need to be able to identify more clearly than in the past key departmental information and information systems; and

— that few tools are currently available to enable Civil Servants to gain an insight into their needs for information or the cost-effectiveness of the information which they currently collect, create, use or store.

As departments will find, there are significant benefits to be gained from devoting time and energy to the more efficient and effective use of information. A major Treasury report, *Management of Information as a Resource*, about how departments take forward information handling at the macro level is currently being considered at the highest levels of management in the Civil Service. Where will Chief Registrars and Departmental Record Officers fit into such an esoteric exercise?

The role of most registries is subservient and their approach mechanistic; they provide storage and retrieval of filed information when not in use and their staff has no detailed knowledge of the information contained within the file, its application or its worth to others. Additionally, there is also likely to be much information that never finds its way on to an official file. Registries undertake reviews of older files, in consultation with Nominated Reviewing Officers, to see if the files, or some of the information in them, should be retained – but this is usually long after the information would have been of current use. Any attempt to manage information as a resource requires an input of resources – human and financial – and an enhanced registry is one approach to achieving at least two of the information management objectives, namely:

— to ensure that the organisation has appropriate mechanisms in place to keep under review its information holdings against its requirements and, where necessary, to dispose of information which is no longer needed;

— to ensure that appropriate storage, retrieval and communications mechanisms are in place to allow information to be moved from its source to the point of need in the most cost-effective manner.

However, within the context of the development of Management Information as a Resource a number of micro actions have been introduced. In the late 1970s the Department of Employment's Registry and Reviewing staff totalled thirty-five, which allowed for the provision of an in-depth subject cross-referencing index and a high percentage success, at minimum staff time cost, in finding files containing information required by a multiplicity of clients. Cutbacks in public expenditure meant reduced staffing levels and a consequential diminution of the service that could be provided – the subservient and mechanistic approach already referred to. Bearing in mind that *all the information* is logged away at least once and its retrieval placed great strain on inadequate staffing resources the only solution was to develop a computerised system for managing file retrieval and the storage of information. This involved consultations with twelve major suppliers of programmed registry systems, testing their proposals and equipment (mainly *in situ* but also at their premises) which provided considerable hands-on experience to our own staff who had no prior experience in computer operating. The McDonnell Douglas system was finally selected from the exceptionally good final tenders and the system has also been installed in the Northern Ireland Civil Service. There are many benefits to be gained from the introduction of a computerised registry system:

— identifying subject areas on which information is being collected and who is collecting it;

— identifying where specific information is held;

— identifying the response to major initiatives by interrelated policy branches; and the

— development of value-for-money initiatives, particularly in relation to space savings.

Other initiatives in hand are:

— the development of close links and active involvement with our Regional registries, with Cabinet Office, with other government departments through the Special Interest Group chaired by the Department of Trade and Industry, with the PRO, the Records Management Society of Great Britain and other archival bodies;

— the preparation and issue of a Statement of Policy on custody, preservation and disposal of records in the Department of Employment, and

— the preparation and issue of a Disposal Schedule agreed and regularly updated with all commands and Branches in the Department of Employment.

A more detailed list, set out in my Annual Report, covers staff training, raising the profile of Registry, Newsletters and Advice Notes to regions. To return to computerisation for a moment – the initial realised benefits of a computerised registry have been:

— reduced clerical/typing input when a file is raised;

— reduced time in dealing with markings/tracings through the storage of readily accessible information relating to file title (and unlimited cross-referencing), its movement and frequency of use;

— speeded up closure/review/destruction process in the light of decisions made during the active life of the file;

— a facility to review *low* activity files after closure to facilitate transfer to Hayes Repository (or other area) where immediate retrieval is not required;

— the development of performance indicators/output measures year by year (or day by day if required);

— the provision of listings of files due for first or second review which Nominated Reviewing Officers may see before receiving a file for review (an instant decision might be made to discontinue review action if file is no longer required);

— and, assisted forward planning by providing information on the number of files due for review which identifies space required for intermediate storage.

Incidentally, the original purpose of preparing an annual report to my Director of Establishments, copied to the PRO, the Cabinet Office, the Department of Employment Group and other government departments was to record the year's achievements, to set objectives, to provide an *aide-mémoire* to succeeding Departmental Record Officers and also for use as an on-the-job training guide for all Registry and Reviewing staff. Additionally, it lets Nominated Reviewing Officers know how their work fits into the scheme of things and also that it is appreciated.

I should like to end with a personal reminiscence. One of the benefits of the job has been working in a prestige office in Whitehall and visiting many offices in glorious surroundings; but records material does turn up in some peculiar and unexpected places. For example, it was in the Bakery Ovens at the Orphanage School, Watford, (now located in Surrey as the Reed School) that I came across a collection of major statistical records relating to unemployed, vacancies notified and vacancies filled by age, sex, industrial and occupational classification. These ledger records related to every local employment office in Great Britain on a monthly basis from 1920 through to 1940. The 1958 Disposal Schedule showed that these records should have been destroyed (they are support material to published figures) and here we come up against the first of two major management styles:

management by assumption, which is closely followed by the second management style currently in vogue – that of dynamic ignorance!

It is interesting to note from an entry in a particular instance paper found with the ledgers that in 1926, 1932 and 1934 *adjustments* were being made to the unemployment figures –

Nothing changes – it has all been done before!

7. Preservation and Conservation: Will our Public Records Survive Another 150 Years

Timothy R. Padfield Head of Conservation, Public Record Office

As an assistant keeper of public records, and perhaps even more so in my present post as Head of Conservation, I could be said to be involved with the preservation of the past. Indeed, the main purpose of this conference is to celebrate an event which took place 150 years in the past. However, the past is all very well, but just at present I am more interested in looking at the past in terms of its future. It is rewarding to look back, but 150 years ago the founders of the Office were looking not backwards but forwards, and it is thanks to their foresight that we have a Public Record Office today. I am keen that in another 150 years there will still be some public records for people to use and enjoy.

In 150 years time there is no doubt that the world, and human life, will have changed. Try to imagine what it might be like in August 2138. I do not suppose there will be any cars, just rockets; no houses, just spaceships; and no work as we know it now for many because computers will do it: milk the cows or process your mortgage. In such a world one might suppose that people will have lots of leisure time. So what will they do with it? Go jogging across the Sea of Tranquillity? Tend the flowers in the space capsule's greenhouse? Watch TV, short, I anticipate, for telepathyvision? Read?

I do not suppose it will be all that easy to find things to read in our conventional sense. Old-fashioned books, archaic handwritten letters, minutes and reports, or clumsy maps with writing on might well not be all that common. After all, we already have speaking books, video telephones are just round the corner, and Phillips are busily marketing a navigation system for cars which tells you where to go without recourse to maps. In such a world, musty, dusty, old-fashioned libraries and record offices, if they survive at all, will be havens where those with a mind to do so will still be able to exercise their intellects without the intervention of machines.

In the environment I am imagining, books will be just as much under threat as documents, but I am not a librarian. I am concerned with the documents, and I have to ask the question: will there be any left to read? I can all too easily envisage the day when a computer will be able to beam the data from a book into its own memory and process it; if the book or the document is falling to bits anyway, what will be the point of preserving the original?

On the other hand, in the heady days of August 2138, cost will no doubt still be a factor in one form or another. If we can show the Committee on the Redundancy of Public and other Records that a lot of time and money has been spent on those originals, that they really are worth keeping and that they are in a condition to survive a further 150 years or more, a decision might be made in their favour. There are other reasons, of course, for preserving, or as it might be for not preserving, the originals, but on the whole they are not the concern of the Conservation Department. They tend to be involved with more abstract concepts such as archival integrity; conservation is involved with a more practical question. Will the documents, in their original form, survive and be usable?

When the Office was established there was no way in which it could be anticipated that documents would one day be so numerous as they are now, nor that they would present such problems for preservation. The very creation of a record office had solved the principal preservation problem by bringing documents together securely in a virtually fireproof environment. Now there are different problems, beyond the scope of our predecessors, and it is up to us to try to find a way to cope with them.

So what are the problems facing the preservation of the public records? I have identified eight; there are of course others, but these seemed to be the ones which presented the greatest obstacles.

(i) The composition of the documents themselves

As a presenter for the BBC's *Timewatch* programme recently put it, a lot of paper contains the seeds of its own destruction. The subject of acid paper, as it is generally termed, has taken over the minds of many people in the library world to such an extent that at no meeting or conference at which preservation is discussed can the subject be escaped. It is not surprising, since acid paper is present in huge numbers of books all over the world. Thankfully it is not such an overwhelming problem in record offices, which contain documents most of which do not consist of the poorest quality papers. It is still a serious problem though. Many of the most vulnerable documents in the Public Record Office are among those most recently received. Paper of the 1940s and 1950s, the years of shortage and rationing, was not made with preservation but with economy in mind. From the same years, too, come early photocopying processes, with heat sensitive materials which are nearing the end of their lives, and samples of unsuccesful attempts to find a stable and safe film base to succeed the inflammable nitrate stock.

Librarians are working hard to persuade publishers to convert to 'permanent paper' for their books, and to persuade paper makers to manufacture it. It would not help us now but it would be a great benefit to the archivists and conservators of the future if offices too would adopt this paper so that the files they create have a better chance of survival. Permanent paper is promoted by the British Library, and even has an ANSI (American National Standards Institute) standard to itself. It is becoming fairly widely used in the United States but is not so common in Britain; indeed, so far only one of the archival journals in Britain, *Archives*, is printed on permanent paper. What hope, then, for records?

Paper has been the principal record medium for the last few hundred years, but its dominance is now being threatened. The impact of machine readable record storage has not so far reached beyond the office to the repository, but computer records are on the way and, thankfully the Public Record Office has responded appropriately. Unfortunately, though, the long term storage medium selected for computer data, the optical disc, is a relatively recent development. I am sure it is ideal from the point of view of the computer staff, but no firm information on its long term stability will be available from PRO sponsored studies for ten years or so. The National Archives and Records Administration (NARA) in the United States is seeking to promote the development of archival standards, for the manufacture, use and storage of optical discs, but nothing is likely to be published by them on the subject for some time. The time is going to come when a sizable archive of material in this format will exist. If there are problems with its preservation it would be as well to be aware of them sooner rather than later.

(ii) Bulk

It is generally estimated that on average the Public Record Office takes in records to fill a mile of shelving each year. That is a lot of documents. At present, we have no useful information on the physical state of those documents when they arrive, but it is known for certain that by no means all of them are in pristine condition. There are a few reliable indicators. At present, for example, space is having to be found in the repository at Kew for some 40,000 maps from Valuation Offices round the country. From the quantities seen so far, some 10 per cent of them are in a condition of 'needing attention', and many of those are sufficiently bad to justify being marked 'unfit for production'.

Accruals of records are adding to the bulk, but there is already plenty of material in the Office which is crying out for attention: with 80 miles or so of it, there is bound to be. Once again though there is only very scanty information on the general condition of the records. We might get some idea of the likely scale of the problem from looking abroad. In the States, NARA has carried out, to the best of its ability, a survey of its 500-odd miles of records. It estimated that there are in the order of 3,000 million sheets of paper on those shelves and that over one sixth, or about 530 million sheets, are at risk of losing some information value. Mercifully, our problems are not on that scale, but then our funding is not on their scale either. If one sixth of our holdings is at risk, we have a lot of work to do: that would be over 13 miles of records.

(iii) Handling

One of the statutory functions of the Public Record Office, and there would be little point in its existence if it were not, is to make the records available to the public. The Keeper also has the duty to provide for copies of documents to be made. The effect of these functions on the records, unfortunately, is in direct conflict with the very first duty assigned to the Keeper, 'to take all practicable steps for the preservation of the records under his charge'.

The production of documents from the repository causes damage, less at Kew than at Chancery Lane because the majority of items are boxed and the working conditions are better. At Chancery Lane, there are plenty of bulky, heavy documents stored in cramped little strongrooms with spiral stairs up to the mezzanine floor. Coupled with that, the staff are under pressure to produce documents for readers in the shortest reasonable time, so small wonder that in their haste they cause some damage.

Other staff are responsible for producing copies. They are expected to get a good image every time, so volumes have to be opened hard to expose the gutter, and often also have to be turned over to lie on a photocopying machine. Once again there is pressure to work briskly because the sale of films brings in money. It would certainly help, although it would probably slow down the filming, to use some of the new equipment available to produce photocopies from a face-up document. Should income really be our first consideration?

Then there are the readers. Their primary concern is the information content of the document, although there are some who appreciate the item as well. Hasty turning of pages causes tears and weakness; leaning on the item causes folds, the breakdown of volumes, and the loss of ink from the surface of parchment; heavy handling of fragile papers leads to the loss of small fragments. Yet documents are historic artefacts as well as information-carrying media. One would not consider maltreating one of the terracotta warriors from Xian in China, so why do people maltreat documents?

(iv) Time

The treatment of a document by conservation staff is a slow process not, on the whole, susceptible to mechanised techniques. Work is currently in progress on the repair of a small class, 30 boxes, of papers relating to Loyalist claims for losses in East Florida during the American War of Independence. A high proportion of the class was unfit as a result of partial immersion in floodwater and sewage in the basement of Somerset House: the papers were either congealed together in a solid lump, or had fallen to pieces scattered in the box. One conservator has been piecing the documents together and up to six laminators, using the process closest to full mechanisation which is currently available to us, have been painstakingly plugging the gaps and making them up into pages again. The task has so far taken two years and at least another year will be taken up completing the lamination: all for 30 boxes.

Then what is one to think of the parchment Plea Rolls from the Court of Common Pleas? There are over 4,000 of them, many in a parlous state, and it has been estimated that a conservator working by hand (there is no other way, in this country, at present) would take five years to complete a single roll.

(v) Motivation

If you were a portrait painter you would no doubt derive enjoyment and a sense of achievement from your work. On being presented, though, with the task of painting separate portraits of all 650 members of Parliament, I am inclined to think your enthusiasm would flag a little.

It is the same for conservators. They feel, justifiably, a tremendous pride in their work, but like everyone else their enthusiasm will flag when faced with a repetitive and seemingly endless task. The sense of achievement on completing the binding of a volume or the repair of a file of parchment bills is dulled by the knowledge that dozens, even hundreds, more remain to be done.

It is possible to vary the diet, of course, by changing from one class of records to another: it is all work which needs to be done. That does not get the work finished on the large class from which we have shied away, though.

(vi) Distraction

The long-established method of alleviating conservators' boredom, practised for them generously by other departments, is to treat Conservation as the odd-job department. Mounting notices, framing pictures, laying out *Proscript* (the house journal), even mending broken sandals, are thought to be all in a day's work. I am far from being convinced that they ought to be. Conservators have spent four and a half years being trained at considerable expense; if we need an odd-job man who needs minimal training, or a layout artist with an appropriate computer program, we should employ them to do the work and spare the conservators to get on with their own.

The biggest distraction of all from normal work is officially sanctioned. The preparation of documents for exhibition takes an alarming amount of time. During the present year, the two conservators who repair seals have all but forgotten what a seal looks like, so busy have they been on the Office's own museum and loans to the Glorious Revolution and Armada exhibitions. What makes matters worse is that many of the documents exhibited would have had no call for any conservation attention, or would have been low on the list of priorities, in the normal course of events. All being well, this problem will be alleviated in the next year of so by the appointment of extra staff, but it will not go away completely.

(vii) Will

Archivists woke up to the need for conservation decades before librarians, but they are too inclined now to rest on their laurels. There can be no doubt that libraries are now far more active in this field, and are doing far more to bring the subject to public attention and thus to raise extra funds, than record offices. To a large extent archive conservation has been allowed to become a backwater and it is not hard to understand why. The demands of the public are vociferous and incessant; any failure on the part of Search Department, Repository, or Reprographic is quickly noted. In contrast, delays in conservation work rarely have any direct impact on readers, and, of course, on those occasions when they have, resources are simply redirected to the solution of the immediate problem regardless of any other preservation-related priorities.

The rest of the time record offices, including the PRO, have been content, on the whole, to allow Conservation to tick along. It is all too easy to take no particular notice of output: to take it all for granted. With the impetus given by librarians, times are perhaps changing, but still all too slowly. Conservation is a serious matter; if it is ignored the readers will have cause to complain and yet there could very well be little we can do about it.

(viii) Cash and staff

It is clear that in the area of conservation, as in precious few others, not everything can be solved by a massive injection of cash. On the other hand I am not going to say that more money would not help. Large capital injections, however, would not be the answer. There are a few expensive machines one could buy to make particular tasks possible or quicker, but conservation remains primarily a craft skill, and that means long term money for extra staff and materials.

In the area of staff, HM Treasury willing, some action is now being taken, though the numbers involved will not make a large dent in the task before us. The British Library and other trustee institutions have serious difficulties of their own, no doubt, but they do at least have the liberty to raise funds for particular projects and to use those funds in any particular way such as to pay for extra staff for the purpose. The Public Record Office operates on the same terms as other departments of government, and must cut its coat from the public cloth.

In discussing those problems I have suggested a few solutions, though they would not necessarily be easy to implement. There are a few other large-scale answers to preservation problems which ought to be mentioned.

(a) Mass treatment

Several national libraries round the world are looking for mass-treatment processes for their degrading and fragile books which would bring the cost and time involved in dealing with a single volume down to acceptable levels. For several years, the National Library of Canada has been operating a mass deacidification process, and the Library of Congress is funding research into a different method of treatment. In Britain, the British Library is working with the University of Surrey on a process to restore the strength of degraded paper by subjecting it to gamma irradiation.

In some respects those processes are appealing for record offices, since they overcome the difficulties posed by bulk and time. They are all costly to establish and run, however, and only the Wei T'o deacidification process as used in Canada is beyond the experimental stage. Moreover, documents are not so homogeneous as books: they contain not only paper but varying quantities of photographs, photocopies and at times textiles; even when they are entirely of paper, they contain a variety of types from different sources; and many of the writing inks used have far less stability than the printing ink in books. To leaf through every file and remove unsuitable materials before treatment would be undesirable, and would do away with much of the advantage of a mass treatment.

It will be necessary to keep an eye on mass-treatment processes, but at present they seem to have little to offer to the record office.

(b) Revised selection

It would appal an archival purist, no doubt, but one way to reduce our growing problem would be to introduce the condition of the records as one of the criteria for the selection or rejection of material for permanent preservation. It could not be the principal factor of course, but if a reviewer were in doubt about whether to preserve something, it would be a most helpful pointer.

Given the scale of the task already before us, what prospect do large quantities of unfit new accessions have of being conserved in the near future, if ever at all? If one accepts that they are unlikely to be repaired, why waste valuable storage space for them? The purpose of preserving documents is to make them available to the public, but that purpose is hardly fulfilled by having them on the shelf in a condition which renders them unusable.

(c) Conservation microfilming

The production to readers of microfilm or microfiche as a substitute for the original documents is the most popular method of reducing the wear on the document. The initial filming has to be carried out carefully to prevent damage, but once completed it should not need to be repeated, and the original can be stored in a secure and stable environment which could even be on a remote, and thus less costly, site. Even with that solution though there are difficulties.

The first appears to be competition. There is a tremendous demand for film copies of documents, and the sale of them brings in revenue. The Treasury relishes any operation which is a source of revenue, and looks to get out of it as much as possible. Conservation filming does not get much of a look in. We keep the negatives of all films sold of course, but the selection of documents has had no reference to any order of priorities which we might have laid down since it is carried out by the person placing the order. In addition, only rarely does a commercial order cover a complete class of records, and it is impractical and undesirable to regard film of part of a class as conservation film.

The other difficulty relates to the status of the original documents once filming is complete. The National Archives in Washington has accepted that documents with no intrinsic value, that is where the information is of value but the nature and form of the document is not, can in many cases be destroyed after filming. That is not a view I should subscribe to readily, for several reasons. One is the assumption implicit in the policy that what is regarded as true now will always be true. Who is to say that in 150 years time, the original form even of modern documents will not be as important as their information content, for some reason which we do not yet understand? Moreover, who is it who is taking this decision? Certainly not the descendant of the person who wrote the letter or the paper historian who is interested in the type of paper used by government departments in 1984. There are objections too to microfilm as the only medium for storing and reading the information. Extra equipment is required for its use which might not in all cases be available or acceptable. Also, it has not been around all that long. Next year will, in its turn, be the 150th anniversary of the announcements of the discovery of photography, but the two types of film base currently in use have been around for only forty years or so. By contrast, paper has been with us for centuries. I have yet to be convinced that film stock can challenge paper for permanence, whatever the results of accelerated aging tests.

There will be difficulties with any of the solutions which might be proposed to the problems I have discussed. That does not mean they should be discarded, but that they should be used appropriately. If those solutions, or others to replace them, are not implemented all the work of selecting documents for permanent preservation will be barren. Conservation must be given higher priority and a higher profile, within the Public Record Office and outside. We should make a wider public aware of the plight of our records, make them eager to help and make it possible for them to do so. At the same time, the long-term future of the records, which we hope will be valuable to generations of readers, must be given priority at least equal to the demands of the present generation. Without such long-sightedness, the choice for the records will parallel that before one of the great figures of galactic exploration, Marvin the paranoid android:

> Do you want me to sit in a corner and rust, or just fall apart where I'm standing?

8. THE THIRTY-YEAR RULE AND FREEDOM OF INFORMATION: ACCESS TO GOVERNMENT RECORDS

Nicholas Cox Principal Assistant Keeper of Public Records

My purpose here, in discussing freedom of information in relation to the public records, is to examine the background to the arrangements that have existed for giving access to government records, and in particular the origins of the 'fifty-year rule'. The thirty-year rule itself is of course still not thirty years old, and the Cabinet, Treasury and other departmental papers covering the discussion of the change are not available to me, although there is quite a lot in published official sources. In reviewing the present practice, I shall say something about what the arrangements are now and how they have changed, and then make some brief comments about the relationship between the concept of freedom of information and the operations of the Public Records Acts.

I am assuming that most people here know already that the legal basis for the work of the Public Record Office is provided by the Public Records Act of 1958, and the amending Act of 1967, which brought the normal restriction on public access down to 30 years. The detailed arrangements for selecting and transferring public records from the courts and from government departments are not provided for in the Public Records Acts, but follow the recommendations of the committee on departmental records, the Grigg committee, which reported in 1954,[1] and which led to the passing of the 1958 Act. A committee on legal records, the Denning committee, reported in 1966.[2]

Before the 1958 Act came into force there was no legal right of access to government records in this country. That is not to say that government records were not being made available: they were, through the publication of Official Histories and official collections of documents, and in the PRO too, of course. But it was only at the individual departments' discretion that their records should be available in the PRO, and down to which dates, and those dates were by no means all the same.

In the mid 1950s, the records of the Admiralty, the Colonial Office, the Foreign Office, the Ministry of Health (that is to say the records of the Poor Law and Local

1 *Committee on departmental records: Report*, Cmd 9163, London, 1954.
2 *Report of the committee on legal records*, Cmnd 3084, London, 1966.

Government Boards), the Privy Council Office, the Ordnance Office, the Ministry of Transport (with the Board of Trade records that it had inherited), the Treasury, and the War Office could all be seen down to 1902. The records of the Board of Trade and the Paymaster General's Office could not be seen after 1885. The Home Office papers were available down to 1878, although they were proposing to open non-sensitive papers down to 1900. Some departments' records were not available at all, such as those of the Inland Revenue, except for the eighteenth-century Apprenticeship Registers (IR 1), and those of the Treasury Solicitor, except for the West New Jersey Society records, which had been in his custody (TS 12). And there was still the question of the records of the Cabinet Office, only established in 1916, but holding the records of the Committee of Imperial Defence back to 1902. None of those had ever been transferred to the PRO, and there was certainly no public access to any of them that had not been published as part of the programme of Official Histories, or otherwise allowed to be made available under specific authority.

The general arrangement was that every ten, or perhaps twenty years, the date at which a department's records became available would be moved forward, so that new papers were made accessible in quite large tranches, but at intervals. As a matter of interest, I wonder how many people here could guess which department proposed in July 1939 (when the open date was still 1885) that its records should be open down to 1901 – a 38 year rule, at least initially – and suggested that all other departments should do the same, and which department stalled the suggestion, at least long enough for the outbreak of the war to put the proposal beyond consideration. I will ask again at the end of what I have to say, and then tell you.

Apart from the confidentiality in which any organisation may need to conduct its business, there are as well three constitutional principles of British government which have led to government records not being made generally available until the passage of some period of years. The first, which relates particularly to the records of the Cabinet, is the principle of collective Cabinet responsibility, which requires that differences of opinion between ministers should not become apparent, and that individual opinions on government policy should not be attributable to individual members of the Cabinet, either during the life of the administration or after it. The second is the principle that individual ministers are responsible to Parliament for the actions of their departments, which requires that the advice that their officials offer them should be confidential and should not be attributable. The third is related, and concerns the political impartiality of the civil service. If confidence in that is to be maintained, then likewise the advice of officials needs to be given in confidence.

Discussions of those questions in relation to making government records available were being carried on before the Grigg committee was appointed in 1952. In the Cabinet Office, in January 1947, William (the future Sir William, and later Lord) Armstrong proposed to Sir Norman Brook, the Cabinet secretary, that Cabinet records should be transferred to the PRO to be made available when they were fifty years old.

He did not believe that the current situation, in which the records were to be kept in the Cabinet Office for ever, and in perpetual secrecy, would in the long term be tenable. And he wrote,

> It is difficult to see how the *permanent* secrecy of the proceedings of former Cabinets can be regarded as an essential feature of the constitution, as has sometimes been claimed.

Sir Norman agreed, and began drafting a submission to Attlee, after holding a meeting on 24 January with Sir Cyril Flower, the deputy keeper of public records. He was cautious enough to say 'not less than fifty years' in what he wrote. Even so, it is clear that the proposal could not have been well received, and there is a note on the file that it would be left over 'until a more auspicious moment'.[3] I have not been able to find anything relating to it in the briefs to the prime minister, or in the Prime Minister's Office papers.

These proposals concerned Cabinet records, and those of a long way back. On the question of identifying individual civil servants in the publication of the Official Histories of the Second World War, Sir Norman was not prepared to be so free. In discussions in 1950 and 1951 he reiterated the instructions that Sir Edward Bridges had given in 1942 as his predecessor, that no attributions of the expressions of opinion or the giving of advice by civil servants were to be made.[4]

When the Grigg committee was appointed in 1952, it was the process of handling and selecting government records that was uppermost in the minds of the Chancellor of the Exchequer and the Master of the Rolls, who set the committee up between them. The question of public access to selected records was not mentioned in the committee's terms of reference. Although the committee ended up by recommending a fifty-year rule, it is interesting to note that there is no mention of the question anywhere in the committee's minutes, until they had the draft report, with that recommendation, before them at their twenty-first meeting on 28 January 1954, only four months before they signed the report.[5] And all that is minuted there is a comment by Professor (now Sir John) Habakkuk, that fifty years would disappoint the diplomatic historians, who wanted Foreign Office records open down to 1914. The committee's secretary, Kenneth (now Sir Kenneth) Clucas said that he had sent a copy of the draft to E. J. Passant, the Foreign Office librarian, and would raise the point specifically with him. Passant replied that fifty years would indeed not be welcome to British and other historians, and that he would personally have preferred forty years. But fifty years it remained.

What had happened was that on 24 April 1953 Sir James Grigg, the committee's chairman, had been to see Sir Norman Brook, who had resurrected his ideas of 1947. He told Grigg that he wanted to hand over Cabinet and CID papers to the PRO for them to be made available after 50 years. He thought that other departments ought not to make their records available earlier than this, because they would then have to strip off Cabinet material from their files, before they could

3 CAB 21/1649.
4 CAB 103/522.
5 T 222/610.

transfer them to the PRO. Grigg was delighted to be told this, and wrote to Clucas that,

> This means that PRO will have a series of documents it has never had before, an unrivalled source of information, & one which entitles us to be a good deal less careful of the historical criterion in sorting departmental records.[6]

Whether everyone would agree with his final comment is another matter.

When the committee's report was submitted in May 1954, it proposed a limit of fifty years after raising the questions of collective Cabinet responsibility and the responsibility of individual ministers to Parliament for their own departments. The original draft of this section of the Report had added, 'The anonymity of civil servants must also be preserved', but Brook had commented that he did not believe it to be relevant to Cabinet records, and that sentence was taken out. It was not raised in the proposed extension of fifty years to all departmental records.[7]

In that context the committee made one further point about public access. They believed that if records became available in less than fifty years, the 'unselfconsciousness' of the papers would be likely to be impaired, if officials knew that what they wrote would be generally available during their own lifetimes. Clucas had minuted to Grigg in March 1954 that there would 'be a lot of opposition from officials to any idea that records should be opened after less than fifty years'. Incidentally he added that,

> I find the Foreign Office attitude on this difficult to understand, unless it be that they are all exhibitionists in any case, and therefore do not mind having what they wrote made open to public inspection during their lifetime.[8]

From a home civil servant's point of view, there was something in this. In the early 1950s, hardly anyone outside political, official, or higher journalistic circles would have known who the permanent secretaries of departments were, and even fewer would have recognised them by sight. It was ministers who propounded government policy, and their officials kept well out of sight. The conduct of diplomatic affairs was quite different. His or Her Majesty's ambassadors were well known in the capitals of the countries to which they were accredited. It was they who were the mouthpieces of the British government, and they could not have been worried about being identified. Also the Foreign Office was anxious that the British point of view on international questions was made known as soon as it diplomatically could be. Clucas had returned from a posting from the Ministry of Labour to the British embassy in Cairo to become the committee's secretary, and perhaps spoke from experience of the tone of diplomatic life.

The comments of a retired Treasury official may be of interest here. He is

6 T 222/541, undated notes by Grigg for Clucas.

7 Grigg *Report*, paras 145–155.

8 T 222/615, Clucas to Grigg, 13 March 1954.

reported to have said in a radio talk in 1977 that if he had known that what he wrote at work would be made public, it would have been of a higher quality. I have not been able to find out who he was, and his comments may perhaps be well known.[9]

What is more interesting is what happened after the Report was submitted. Sir Norman Brook, secretary of the Cabinet, was perfectly happy with the fifty-year proposal for Cabinet records – in fact he had suggested it, as we have seen. Sir Edward Bridges, now permanent secretary of the Treasury and head of the home civil service, was certainly not happy at all.

Sir Norman had produced a paper for Cabinet on the change,[10] and Bridges had to brief his minister, Rab Butler, the Chancellor of the Exchequer – and one of the two commissioners of the Report – on it. Although Sir Edward admitted that it was clear that Cabinet records would be thrown open to the public ultimately, and that there was 'a lot to be said for the 50-year period proposed', he went on to attack fifty years as 'too close on the heels of living experience to be altogether comfortable'. It was, he said, not a matter of logical argument, but 'of the psychology of confidence'. His instinct was 'to play safe'. If sixty years looked 'silly, I would prefer to start with 75'. If after a while seventy-five years seemed too long, it could easily be reduced, but it 'would be the devil and all to increase the figure', once fifty years had been made the rule. He admitted that all this was 'hunch', and that ministers might 'take a less cautious view'. But he enlisted the views of his colleague Sir Thomas Padmore, who he said had independently arrived at the same conclusions.[11] Rab, typically, but maybe not so enigmatically, circled 'hunch' in red, and underlined 'a less cautious view'.

The Cabinet considered Brook's paper on 3 March 1955,[12] but put off making a decision on the question of access, thereby leaving all the Grigg committee's recommendations also in abeyance. The delay allowed the fight against the access proposal to continue. Sir Alexander Johnston, of the Treasury, suggested that ministers were being persuaded to consent to fifty years under the impression that a close scrutiny was to be given to records, paper by paper, to see that what was disclosed was fit for the public gaze, whereas the Grigg committee had not intended such a scrutiny.[13] The committee had indeed suggested that a department might give notice that it did not wish the rule to apply to a particular class of its own records.[14]

Sir Thomas Padmore was more farsighted. He minuted to Bridges on 25 October 1955 that, if some Cabinet minutes were segregated out for ten or even twenty years,

> I should expect the process to focus an unhealthy amount of attention on them when they were released. What is more, I should expect the Govern-

9 James Michael, *The politics of secrecy*, (Harmondsworth), 1982, p. 78.
10 CAB 129/70, C(54)265.
11 T 222/800, 6 August 1954.
12 CAB 128/28, CC(55)20.
13 T 222/801, 24 October 1955.
14 Grigg *Report*, para. 154.

> ment of the day to be a good deal pestered to explain its reasons for withholding them – and these might be very marginal and uncomfortable to talk about. I should therefore think it better that a firm decision should be taken either to withhold the whole of the Cabinet records as a class for longer than the normal fifty years; or, because a great deal of other departmental material which is just as full as the Cabinet records will have been disclosed, to take the risk of making the lot available after fifty years. If such a decision were to be taken there could still be a saving for any very occasional minutes or papers which were peculiarly embarrassing.

Four days later he minuted again that he did not believe that Cabinet ministers had the leisure, under the pressure of the business in Cabinet, to worry about what the world would think in fifty years' time. But,

> I am in the position of having still a certain instinctive feeling that fifty years is a bit on the short side. When I try to rationalize it . . . I make very little progress.

Since no Cabinet records would be available under a fifty-year rule until the late 1960s, he suggested deferring a decision, and recommending to Ministers not to include the Cabinet records in any decision they took on Grigg. Bridges agreed, and was prepared for Cabinet papers or Cabinet material to appear on released departmental papers, even though the Cabinet records themselves were not available.[15]

As is apparent now, the Cabinet decided to proceed with the Public Records Bill, but to follow the advice to defer a decision on the Cabinet's own records. When the Bill came before Parliament, it contained the proposal that fifty years should be the general period for all departmental records. Although amendments were put down to reduce the period to forty years, there was no serious opposition, and on 1 January 1959 the 'fifty-year rule' became law. It was only on 2 July 1959, seven months later, that the prime minister announced, in a written answer in the Commons, that the Cabinet had decided that Cabinet and Committee of Imperial Defence records should be treated in the same way as departmental records under the new Act.[16]

The new legal arrangements for making records available, by which new material became open automatically at the start of each new year, depending on its date, were almost unprecedented in this country, although three departments had recently been exercising them independently. The new system was referred to by some of the PRO's staff as the 'creeping barrage': it was not entirely welcome to them, partly because of the extra annual work it was (correctly) thought it would entail, and partly because 'ragged' file keeping by departments would produce inconsistencies in the dates at which individual files in series would become accessible.[17]

It is one small indication of the astonishingly rapid swing during the early 1960s

15 T 222/801.

16 House of Commons, *Official Report*, Written Answers, 2 July 1959, columns 62–63.

17 See PRO 1/1445, memorandum of D. B. Wardle, July 1954, and PRO 1/1589, R. H. Ellis to D. L. Evans, 22 March 1955.

in general public and official attitudes to almost everything that had been held essential to the national well-being in the mid 1950s, that proposals were being made for the reduction to thirty years of this fifty year rule within a few years of its inception.

In 1963 the Advisory Council on Public Records, itself a creation of the 1958 Act, investigated the extent to which departments were exercising their powers to allow access, to serious scholars, under section 5(4), to records under fifty years old. The proportion of requests from scholars which were granted varied considerably from department to department, the Council stated in its report for 1963. Departments appeared much more likely to give access to papers relating to individual actions or occurrences, than to those touching matters of high policy. The fifty-year rule was being strictly applied by the Cabinet Office to its own records.[18]

During the following year the Advisory Council conducted an inquiry into the operation of the fifty year rule. In its Report for 1964 it referred to growing criticism of the fifty year period, and to the pressure from academics for thirty years. They pointed out that the fact that some other countries were by then more liberal than Britain in allowing access to records, meant that the British point of view was usually missing from what was being written about international questions.

The Council reported that its eleven members *all* thought fifty years too long. We may note that the members of the Council included Professor Habakkuk, Mr Justice Buckley and Sir Goronwy Edwards, who had served on the Grigg committee. More importantly they had included since March 1964 Lord Normanbrook, now retired from the post of Cabinet secretary that he had held during the earlier part of this story. *Most* of the Council's members thought that thirty years was too short a period. They recommended to the lord chancellor, the minister now responsible under the 1958 Act for public records, that fifty years should come down to forty, and also that more liberal access should be given to records under forty years old.[19]

The Council repeated its recommendations in its Report for 1965, and expressed disappointment that nothing had been done.[20] However early in 1966 the Government announced that all records down to the end of 1922 would be opened forthwith. It also stated that it was in consultation with the other parties on an amendment to the Public Records Act.[21]

On 9 March 1966, the day before the 1964 Parliament was dissolved, the prime minister, Harold Wilson, announced that the government wished to see a thirty-year rule, despite the Advisory Council's recommendation of forty years, but that, although he had the consent of the leader of the Liberal party, he had not obtained that of the leader of the Opposition.[22] The former prime minister has said subsequently that he threatened at this stage to put the proposal for thirty years into his

18 *Fifth report of the Advisory Council on Public Records*, PRO 43/126, para. 6.
19 *Sixth report*, PRO 43/127, para. 4 and Appendix.
20 *Seventh report*, PRO 43/128, para. 5.
21 House of Commons, *Official Report*, 10 February 1966, columns 614–615.
22 House of Commons, *Official Report*, 9 March 1966, columns 561–563.

party's manifesto for the 1966 election, which he, and most other people, had little doubt by early March 1966 he would win decisively.[23] It was not put in, but at any rate he announced in the Commons on 10 August of the same year, having won the election, that a Bill was to be introduced to effect the change, and that the change now had general support.[24] Whether or not the legislative change would have been made, if the result of the 1964 and 1966 general elections had been different, there is no way of telling. But the Public Records Act of 1967, which provides for the thirty-year rule, came into force on the first of January 1968.

Since 1968 there has been no general legislative change in the availability of government records. However, at the beginning of 1972, in accordance with an announcement made by the government in 1969,[25] the records of the period of the Second World War, down to the end of the wartime government for Prime Minister's Office and Cabinet records, and to the end of 1945, and in some cases later, for departmental records, were made available in one go.

The Public Records Acts now lay down that public records in the PRO shall not be made available for public inspection until the expiration of the period of thirty years since their creation, but that the Lord Chancellor may prescribe a longer or shorter period, with the approval, or at the request, of the minister or other person. . . primarily concerned, for the time being. The Acts do say 'shall not': there is a presumption against disclosure before that time has expired, unless the records were already available before transfer.

The Acts also specify that records whose disclosure would involve a breach of good faith on the part of the government, or of persons who obtained the information contained in them, should not be disclosed, and also saves the Keeper of Public Records from having to make available any records covered by a list of statutes set out in schedule II of the 1958 Act, which prohibit disclosure of information, or any other statutes which prohibit disclosure.

When he introduced the new Public Records Bill in the House of Lords in 1967, the then Lord Chancellor, Lord Gardiner, referred to the categories of records for which he and his predecessors had prescribed closure periods of longer than fifty years. He said that they were,

> first those containing information about individuals whose disclosure would cause distress or embarrassment to living persons or their immediate descendants (such as criminal or prison records, records of courts martial, records of suspected persons, and certain police records): secondly those containing information obtained under pledge of confidence, such as the Census and various individual returns used in publishing statistical compilations: thirdly, certain papers relating to Irish affairs: fourthly certain exceptionally sensitive papers which affect the security of the State. In

23 Harold Wilson, *The Labour government 1964–1970, a personal record*, (London), 1971, pp. 203–204.

24 House of Commons, *Official Report*, 10 August 1966, columns 1706–1708.

25 House of Commons, *Official Report*, 18 December 1969, Written Answers, columns 412–413.

addition certain papers, the ownership of which is shared with 'old' Commonwealth countries, cannot be released until all the Governments concerned have given their consent.[26]

On the recommendation of the Advisory Council on Public Records in 1970, the Lord Chancellor later set out the categories of records for which he would approve applications for closure for longer than thirty years. They were very similar to the categorisation just described. They were,

(1) Exceptionally sensitive papers, the disclosure of which would be contrary to the public interest whether on security or other grounds (including the need to safeguard the Revenue);
(2) Documents containing information supplied in confidence, the disclosure of which would of might constitute a breach of good faith;
(3) Documents containing information about individuals, the disclosure of which would cause distress or embarrassment to living persons or their immediate descendants.[27]

In 1978 a new committee was set up by the Lord Chancellor, under the chairmanship of the late Sir Duncan Wilson, to review the arrangements for the selection of records for permanent preservation and for subsequent public access to them. The committee discussed at some length the operation of the 'thirty-year rule', which they preferred to call a 'norm', but did not feel able, under their terms of reference, to go so far as to recommend any change. But they did suggest that the power to open records earlier than after thirty years should be used much more widely.[28] And they commented that 'embarrassment' in the third criterion above was too broad a ground for closure.

Following the Report of the Wilson committee the wording of the third category was changed to 'cause distress to or endanger living persons'.[29] The Lord Chancellor gives his approval to changes in the thirty-year rule for specific records, or categories of records, by instruments, which are made publicly available,[30] scheduling the records concerned.

The Public Records Acts also permit records more than thirty years old to be retained in departments, with the lord chancellor's approval, for administrative or other special reasons. Under Section 3(4) of the 1958 Act 'blanket' approvals have been given for the retention of records concerned with intelligence and security, and with civil and home defence planning, and of those dealing with defence uses of atomic energy. These are simply unavailable. Other blanket approvals for reten-

26 House of Lords, *Official Report*, 11 May 1967, column 1657.

27 *Twelfth Report of the Advisory Council*, PRO 43/133, para. 11.

28 *Modern public records: selection and access: report of a committee appointed by the lord chancellor*, Cmnd 8204, London, 1981, paras 160–237.

29 *Modern public records: the government response to the report of the Wilson committee*, Cmnd 8531, London, 1982, paras 26–27.

30 They are available in the PRO search rooms, and also in PRO 51.

tion have been given for civil servants' personal files, which need to be kept by departments for periods after their active life. The approvals by the lord chancellor for these retentions are subject to reconsideration after stated periods.

There are other records, which are retained by their departments under section 3(4), which are still needed for current administration, but which can be made available. Many records of the state museums and galleries are included in this category, as are the records of the Parliamentary Counsel. Some have been retained to give more time for them to be processed for transfer, as were the records of the British Element of the Control Commission for Germany. Those particular records have now been transferred and made available, under the normal arrangements.

Few people are going to be entirely satisfied with a system which provides for the withholding of records relating to them. I do not know whether you remember the public controversy there was about the information that was asked for in the 1971 census and its confidentiality. But I do know that a very angry searcher arrived in the PRO demanding to have access to it (and not to his own record either), and complained that he could not get it, at the beginning of 1972. The state collects, or compiles, such a variety of information on individuals and organisations for its current purposes, and is known to do so – and needs to do so as well – that the conflict between privacy and openness is always bound to be a live question. But I must not be thought to imply in saying so, that questions of personal sensitivity are always those that most exercise the minds of those who want greater access to recent official records.

Which brings us on to the question of Freedom of Information, which I am supposed to be talking about, as well as the thirty year rule. I have not much to say, partly because the question of FOI is the business of others and not of the PRO (the Public Records Acts are sometimes regarded as surrogate Freedom of Information legislation, which they are not), and also because the whole question is under discussion following the publication of the recent White Paper, and public comment on those questions is not for a civil servant. But it is a question which has worried, and perhaps still worries, archivists, from a purely professional point of view.

The purpose of current legislation in this country governing public records is the selection and preservation of records which are worthy of permanent preservation, and for their eventual availability to public inspection. It does not give public availability a higher priority than preservation. As the present deputy keeper of public records (whose appointment as keeper from October 1988 was announced at the opening of this conference by the lord chancellor) stated at a research workshop on open government in 1986,

> If sensitive records cannot be given appropriate protection against premature disclosure then the risk that vital records will not be created or, if created, will not be preserved, is increased, to the long term detriment of historical research. Weighed in that balance, it is surely better that there should be a system for protecting sensitive records for as long as their sensitivity continues, and even that those responsible for administering

> that system should err rather on the side of caution, than that such records should be suppressed irregularly.[31]

Public records held in the Public Record Office, which are unavailable to public inspection for longer than thirty years, including the very large body of census records, closed for 100 years, amount to about 1% of its holdings. Records, approval for whose retention in their departments of origin has been given, amount to the equivalent of around 1 or 2% of its current holdings (in 1988, about 87 miles).

> In time, every record which is now subject to extended closure, or selected for preservation but retained in its department of origin, will become open to inspection . . . This is not to argue against freedom of information legislation. In this respect public records legislation should be neutral. If this neutrality is recognised, FOI legislation need not adversely affect the operations of the PRO or impose an undue burden opon it. Nor, conversely need public records legislation conflict with FOI legislation.[32]

The call for 'freedom of information' seems to cover a number of different concerns. It covers a general desire for 'open government', for administration to be carried on more publicly, maybe for more information to be given out, rather than papers. It also covers a desire to see government records made available much earlier – what Peter Hennessy has called the 'ten-minute rule'. And, perhaps just as important, it covers the desire for access to information on environmental and health and safety questions – what one might call the Ralph Nader categories of information: again, perhaps, a request for facts rather than necessarily for records. I do not see that any of these points should need to concern public archivists *professionally*, so long as it is the current custodians of the records who have the obligation to make them available.

Archivists have also been anxious that records might have to be transferred much earlier, before the historical criterion for selection can be exercised properly in perspective, and also that they might find themselves having to preserve many more records, than would not otherwise have been selected. But the fact that records might have been made available to enquirers in the past, seems no reason for them to *have* to be preserved in perpetuity, unless their subject is such that they should be kept anyway. If I had been allowed access to files about me held by a government department, or to papers concerning something other than myself, I certainly would not expect that simply because access had been given to them, they acquired permanent historical value. If access were to be obtained to very recent government papers, I would not expect that they should be kept for ever in an archive, unless their subject merited it. That seems the crucial question.

The PRO has, anyway, been in receipt of current documents from one government department, stating its point of view on questions of policy, for the last ten years. Following the issue of the 'Croham directive', a circular letter from the

31 M. Roper, 'Access to public records', *Open government*, ed. R. A. Chapman and M. Hunt, London, (1987), p. 89.

32 *Ibid*, pp. 88–89.

permanent secretary of the Civil Service Department in July 1977 to the administrative heads of other departments on disclosure of official information, the Foreign and Commonwealth Office has made available two series of papers, Foreign Policy Documents and Background Briefs, which can be seen in a variety of institutions on their issue. The copies of those documents passed to the PRO are available on FO 972 and FO 973 as soon as they are transferred.

In 1981 the Wilson committee commented that freedom of information legislation 'would clearly undermine completely the principle of the 30-year norm'.[33] It does not seem as clear now that this is so, as it was to them then, for the reasons just outlined. And since their report was published the Australians have passed both a Freedom of Information Act, and also an Archives Act, which provides for a general thirty-year access period. As they have done in other professional matters, Australian archivists may have something to teach their colleagues here.

'At some point of time, the secrets of one period must become the common learning of another.' I leave you with that statement, not of any pressure group for Freedom of Information, but from the Report of the committee of privy counsellors on ministerial memoirs in 1976.[34] Or perhaps I am not leaving you, but your and my descendants. And is that not what archives are all about?

Earlier on I said that I would tell you about the department that proposed a 1901 rule in 1939. On 4 July 1939 Sir Stephen Gaselee, the Foreign Office librarian, and keeper of its papers, suggested that the open period for Foreign Office records should be extended to 1901. You would not guess from the contents of this particular file,[35] that this country was about to go to war with Germany, although there was worry expressed that the opening of the records to 1901 would make available material which the Germans would use against us on the question of the South African War.

However Sir Alexander Cadogan, the Foreign Office's permanent under secretary, agreed almost immediately with Gaselee. And so a letter was sent on 14 July to the PRO asking the deputy keeper to obtain the consent of all departments to opening their records down to the same date. I am afraid that it was the reply of the Public Record Office on 8 August, which said that the work of altering all the lists of records, and of moving the new ones up from Canterbury, where they were held, and providing accommodation for them, might take three years, which temporarily scotched the proposal. In the meantime the events of only a few weeks later put a stop to it for almost a decade.

I should add that I do know from our own records, and from talking to former colleagues, that the real reason why the PRO answered as it did, was that the staff were almost entirely occupied at the time in packing the records into containers to be evacuated from London, out of the way of the coming bombs.

33 Wilson *Report*, para. 217.

34 *Report of the committee of privy counsellors on ministerial memoirs*, Cmnd 6386, London, 1976, para. 82.

35 FO 370/588, L4826, L5773/4826/402.

CALENDARS AND INDEXES

9. PUBLIC RECORD OFFICE PUBLICATION: PAST PERFORMANCE AND FUTURE PROSPECTS

J.B. Post Principal Assistant Keeper of Public Records

This paper will dwell on the past: not to adopt a complacent attitude towards the mighty labours of colleagues and predecessors, but to explore the purposes which have produced such an astonishing range and scale of works. Any frequenter of large reference libraries can testify to the thick serried bindings of the PRO and its predecessors, from the irregular folios of the record commissions, through the familiar shelves of *Letters and Papers . . . Henry VIII*, past the countless plump calendars of Patent Rolls and Close Rolls and State Papers Venetian, to the sturdy and (mostly) well-thumbed handbooks of recent years. This solid evidence of past endeavours, so familiar and so widely used for so many purposes over the years and the generations, distracts attention from the intentions of those who initiated these vast and notable projects. For the genealogist whose ancestor witnessed a treaty, the publication of that treaty is self-evidently justified; for the demographic historian using the calendars of Inquisitions Post Mortem to establish the ages at which medieval women matured to childbearing, the primarily statistical uses of such calendars is axiomatic. We see our own purposes reflected in the reference works we use, and a different sort of reflection is needed to infer the more general character of policies towards publication.

The origins of modern archival publishing in this country can be traced in the early stages of modern historical scholarship in the seventeenth century, when historians like William Dugdale set new standards of detailed archival research and systematic synthesis.[1] Dugdale was not unique in his time, but his *Antiquities of Warwickshire* (1656) set local history firmly in its evidential context, while works such as his *Monasticon Anglicanum* (completed in 1673) ranged more widely and yet with the same attention to detail. There arose – not only in England but elsewhere in Europe as well – the idea of publishing careful and critical editions of historical documents, comparable to the long-established editorial traditions for chroniclers and other ancient authors, in order to serve a school of history which understood the more nearly objective value of contemporary administrative documentation.

1 See generally D. Hay, *Annalists and Historians: Western Historiography from the Eighth to the Eighteenth Centuries* (London, 1977), chapters 7 and 8, and, more particularly, D. C. Douglas, *English Scholars* (London, 1939), throughout.

The first large-scale archival publication in England was funded (albeit sparsely and tardily) by central government.[2] Thomas Rymer, the historiographer royal, painstakingly assembled -- mainly from the scattered forbears of the PRO, but also from other collections and archives – an elaborate and eclectic work know briefly as *Foedera*, whose publication began in 1704. *Foedera* contained, primarily, treaties and other diplomatic agreements, and royal and other correspondence and papers relating to international affairs, but Rymer's net was cast very widely indeed, and in consequence *Foedera* included the texts of large numbers of documents whose bearing upon the conduct of diplomatic business was slight but whose value for the political and administrative history of England was substantial. That this value was recognised can be deduced from the production of a second edition, not long after the first, and from the (largely unfulfilled) project to produce a much enlarged and extended edition, a project which occupied much of the attention of Thomas Duffus Hardy when deputy keeper of public records in the 1860s.[3]

Rymer's *Foedera* was not only a first of its kind; it was scholarly and systematic in a way which makes it useful as a work of reference today because of its accessibility and reliability in areas where it has not been superseded. It reflected, however, two concepts, or two approaches, which were creditable and defensible in their day but which have bedevilled schemes for archival publications subsequently – not, perhaps, still troublesome, but part of the past which is better remembered as a lesson than as an example. One was the idea that real history is about the political and constitutional doings of the great, and that any incidental references to smaller fry are just accidents, of use to the genealogist alone. *Foedera*, by its very theme, dwelt upon the doings of the great; but in this respect it elicited emulation, quite inappropriately, in textbooks and collections of 'select' documents well into the twentieth century. (Interestingly, an assistant keeper of public records, A. E. Bland, collaborated in the first published selection of documents for economic history.)

Foedera's second underlying principle was that of 'select documents': printing texts of whole treaties, but also picking and choosing entries from rolls and registers and archives on the basis of the editor's perception of their value to the project in hand. This is a perfectly intelligible principle for a historiographer royal – indeed, it is a perfectly intelligible principle for any historian, and is one of the operations essential to the preparation of any work of historical synthesis. Moreover the publication of representative selections of texts, judiciously chosen and scrupulously edited, has an important part to play in education and in academic studies: many collections, from the 'Jackdaw' facsimiles to Martin Gilbert's massive editions of Churchilliana, are self-evidently constructive and well conceived for their particu-

2 M. M. Condon and E. M. Hallam, 'Government printing of the public records in the eighteenth century', *Journal of the Society of Archivists*, 7(6) (1984), especially 349–59.

3 For all material events and personalities, see J. D. Cantwell, *The Public Record Office 1838–1958* (HMSO, forthcoming). Other details can be found in the annual reports of the deputy keepers (from 1959, of the keepers) of public records, published as parliamentary papers. Full details of all Record Commission, Rolls Series, and PRO publications up to 1984 are in *British National Archives* (HMSO, sectional list 24), last published in 1984; for subsequent publications the keepers' reports must be consulted.

lar ends. What went wrong with this approach in the context of Rymer's *Foedera* was the development of assumptions that the archivist could and should be the arbiter of all texts and entries that were worth publishing. Again the name of Thomas Duffus Hardy must be invoked, for he – who should have known better – was writing, as late as 1869, that it would be possible to supplement *Foedera* with 'a brief but complete calendar of all authentic documents . . . necessary for the verification and illustration of the political, ecclesiastical, civil, and military history of Great Britain'.[4] That he should have devoted years of effort, and his considerable abilities, to such a gargantuan aned quixotic enterprise, when countless millions of documents remained neglected, unsorted, and inaccessible, is a fair basis for judging both Hardy's own preoccupations and, more generally, a cast of mind which affected the character of archival priorities for a long while.

The same cast of mind characterised one of the PRO's most notable and most widely respected publishing ventures, *Letters and Papers . . . Henry VIII*. This mighty project was pursued continuously for more than seventy years, during which it had only three editors (one of whom, James Gairdner, spent fifty-five of his sixty-seven years in the PRO on this one publication). Now *Letters and Papers . . . Henry VIII* is a classic piece of sustained scholarship, and its utility to generations of scholars in a heavily-worked field cannot be overstated – indeed, it is conceivable that its very existence has encouraged a disproportionate volume of studies in this area; yet the narrowness it bred in its votaries was typical of the PRO in this era. At one time, in the 1860s, Gairdner was set to work on some of the vast collections of unidentified and unlisted miscellanea. He was frank about his system: 'the object of my search was . . . to select . . . such papers as . . . might seem important . . . for the calendar of Henry VIII'.[5] In other words, (as anyone who has used the State Papers classes for the period will testify), the idea of selecting texts for a publication became translated into the idea of using a subjective criterion for the arrangement of the records. It is even possible that the survival of the records depended in some cases upon their utility for this project; in later years it was said that the first editor, Brewer, used to sort documents into four piles – Henry VIII, Not Henry VIII, Trash, and Rubbish – and at least one sighting of a document marked 'Trash' has been recorded.[6]

It would be unfair to imply that all the early archival publications were noble, narrow, and selective. Some were cheapskate, diffuse, and undiscriminating; some were dull but worthy. Into the 'dull but worthy' category fall many of the publications of the record commissions. Between 1800 and 1837 there were six successive commissions charged with setting in order the administration of the national records, which at that time were divided between numerous repositories, with different administrations, different traditions, and highly variable standards of preservation, conservation, and reader access. These commissions did very little to further a

4 *Rymer's Foedera: Syllabus in English, with Index*, ed. T. D. Hardy, I (London, 1869), cxi.

5 *Appendices to the First Report of the Royal Commission on the Public Records* . . ., volume I(III), Cd 6396 (1912), 67.

6 C. Johnson, 'The Public Record Office', in *Studies Presented to Sir Hilary Jenkinson* C.B.E., LL.D., F.S.A., ed. J. C. Davies (London, 1957), 179.

coherent policy for the management of the public records, but they did indulge in publications – possibly as an easy but highly visible suggestion that they were doing something to justify their existence. Many of the publications were hastily edited versions of editorial material already to hand, and these materials, by being pressed into a service for which they were never intended, changed the character of record publication. What had happened, over the years and generations, was that custodians of the records had prepared for themselves finding-aids of various kinds to the most commonly used records, and these finding-aids tended to consist of rough-and-ready abstracts of series of documents – Patent Rolls, Inquisitions Post Mortem, and so on – sufficient to allow these custodians (who normally carried out the searches themselves) to identify relevant entries. They were archivists' working notes rather than anything more polished or comprehensive, but they were voluminous and they were easily prepared for the press. In the event these publications failed, and quite rightly, to convince central government that the record commissions were a suitable means to the end in view; but they did do something else. They had begun their lives as in-house finding-aids for the experienced archivist, but in their apotheosis they became, whether or not they merited the role, published substitutes for the documents themselves. Scholars who were remote from London, or who baulked at the fees and conditions of the repositories, or who could not be bothered to search, or, indeed, who needed only a trifle of information which happened to be set forth clearly in the published version, came to refer to the published 'calendars' as though to primary sources. Thus, almost by accident, the modern notion of the use of a calendar was developed upon the basis of texts which had been drafted for no such purpose.

The development was fitful and erratic. At the State Paper Office – which did not become part of the Public Record Office until the 1850s – the idea of publishing series of records in full was already well established, with the preparation and publication, begun in the 1830s, of Henry VIII's correspondence; and yet it was later decided that the calendars prepared to facilitate the identification of materials for these transcripts should themselves be published, as they were from 1856 onwards. Thus the processes which the Record Commissioners had instituted for medieval records were repeated, complete with tactical errors, for records of the early modern period. The Tudor specialist of the mid nineteenth century was faced with the enormous luxury of published transcripts of extensive material up to the death of Henry VIII, followed by the barest rough list from Edward VI onwards.

Meanwhile, however, the modern notion of a class list in a standard published format was developing in the appendixes to the deputy keepers' annual reports. The deputy keepers' reports from the 1850s to the 1880s were almost invariably overshadowed by these appendixes, which carried (as they do today) tabular information about the transactions of the PRO in its various capacities, but which already carried full-length class lists, and sometimes many in a single year. Here can be seen the arrival of a clear idea of a primary list: presented in an order corresponding to the arrangement of the documents; containing enough housekeeping information to identify the documents uniquely for requisitioning purposes; containing enough information about the content of the documents to indicate to the searcher (or at least to the patient and experienced searcher) which might be, and which might not be, useful to the research in hand; and, finally, making no pretence of substituting for the documents themselves. True, not all of these appendixes fulfil all these aims; some are decidedly better than others, while the standardisation of format went, certainly, far beyond the vagaries of the manuscript lists in the reading rooms, but did not exactly adopt any real consistency of typography and layout.

It was Henry Maxwell Lyte, coming to the PRO as a relatively young deputy keeper in 1886, who finally arbitrated on lists and calendars in their now familiar forms. He did four things with PRO publications which have stood for almost exactly a hundred years. First, he detached the publication of lists from the back of the deputy keeper's report and established a series of Lists and Indexes, which provided separately conceived and separately titled volumes for the lists and indexes of different classes. Second, he appropriated the name, if not the notion, of the calendar. Although the loose use of the term 'kalendar' to mean any list or register is medieval in origin, the State Paper Office term was closely defined as meaning the listing or cataloguing of documents in strict chronological order, whether or not that order represented the internal arrangement of a document, or of a group of documents, or of a whole class; in practice the forcible arrangement of the State Papers into a chronological scheme meant that calendar and class tended to follow the same sequence, but this was not invariable. Maxwell Lyte, however, used the term 'calendar' to indicate the full summary of a document or of a series of documents in the order of arrangement – which, for such things as entries on a Chancery roll, might be very far from a calendar sequence. Third, he adopted the principle – broadly true of some of the State Paper calendars, quite untrue for many others – that a calendar should convey for ordinary purposes all the information which was in the original document, and thus in general substitute for it for the purposes of historical research. Fourth, he inaugurated calendars on these principles for the major series of medieval records – Patent Rolls, Close Rolls, Fine Rolls, Inquisitions Post Mortem, 'Curia Regis' Rolls – with a view to providing a readily accessible core of dated information about people and events which could then be used to aid the identification and arrangement of the vast mass of miscellanea still unsorted.

For many people, especially for medievalists, the text and calendar series revivified or initiated by Maxwell Lyte represent the finest traditions of archival publication in England. Volume after massive volume, they embody countless years of scholarly labour and they have served countless years of scholarly research. While, inevitably, the quality is variable (it is worth checking the prefaces in order to become familiar with the idiosyncracies of their many editors), the standards were generally much higher than in previous publications, and the rate of productivity was astonishing.

This renewed emphasis on publication had its effect upon other PRO work. There arose in the PRO – it is difficult to document precisely, but it was burgeoning before Maxwell Lyte's time and reached full flower in his later years – the idea that work for publication was somehow of a higher order than other types of work; it was called 'literary work', and it carried a kudos which did not attach to mundane archival tasks. Thus, to caricature (but not unduly): an assistant keeper of the highest training and abilities might be set to edit a volume of Latin transcripts; a competent but less exalted colleague might be set to calendar a series of common-form documents; but the work of identifying, arranging, and listing unsorted miscellanea was left to those whose talents were thought to be markedly inferior to those of their fellows. Thus the lofty but, in terms of service to the records, secondary work of publishing documents which were already in a satisfactory order was given to the most able, whereas the dirty, thankless, and obscure business of tracing the provenance and context of a myriad scattered miscellanea – surely a task of primary importance, as well as one demanding omniscient precision in the archivist – was entrusted to the weaker and less professional. To this extent the PRO's high standards of publication, and the snobbish cachet associated with it, positively distracted attention, and diverted resources, from the basic duty of making the records available to readers by identification, sorting, listing, and the other routine but fascinating chores of a record repository.

This does not mean that the less exalted forms of finding-aid were wholly neglected. Most notable, perhaps, most exasperating, most readily outmoded, and (frequently) most difficult to obtain have been the various guides. Private endeavour produced handbooks for students of the public records before ever the PRO existed, but official guides were also produced: Thomas's *Handbook* in 1853, Scargill-Bird's *Guide* (three editions, 1891 to 1908), Giuseppi's *Guide* in 1923–4, and the ostensibly authorless *Guide to the contents of the Public Record Office* of 1963–8. Each in its day was, and was meant to be, the serious student's introduction to the PRO and its records, the means by which the range of materials was set forth in as readily digested a form as could be managed, and by which the searcher could gain some approximate guidance towards the lists and indexes which would further a quest. Every record repository should have a guide; not all have them; and few need guides as complex, and as promptly rendered obsolete, as those of the PRO.

For more than a hundred years – until the 1960s – these were, with a few exceptions on isolated occasions, the only publications the PRO produced: texts and calendars, lists and indexes, and successive guides. All these are finding-aids to the records, but they are not for the faint-hearted, nor for the searcher who is pressed for time. In their general character, and in their language and organisation, they reflected and reflect the notion of the records user as a literary researcher, either from an academic background or from the then larger world of leisured antiquaries. By the 1960s, however, several important changes had occurred among the clientele of the PRO and the services they required. First, the development of higher education meant that increasing numbers of intelligent novices – the graduate students with dissertations to do – were (literally) queueing at the gates and requiring more attention than could be afforded to them. Second, the increasing volume of modern departmental records, and the increased access to them after 1958, both swelled the numbers of researchers in new subject areas and burdened the staff with obligations to provide wisdom over an impossibly wide range of records, topics, and periods. Third, and perhaps the most conspicuous, was the steady surge of interest in genealogy, which brought to the PRO many people who had not previously thought of themselves as researchers and who had (in many cases) no familiarity with research procedures or research institutions of any kind, let alone the daunting fastness of the Public Record Office.

These problems had to be faced, and panaceas (though not, perhaps, cures) were developed pragmatically. In terms of publications, two new types were introduced. One was the handbooks, which started as supplementary finding-aids of similar types to the old Lists and Indexes, but on a smaller scale, but which have come to include other, more elaborate works: guides to the records of particular departments (such as the Colonial Office, the Cabinet Office, the Foreign Office), guides to the records of particular procedures (such as the general eyre, and the census), guides to particular types of research (such as family history). These handbooks have proved extremely useful and (with a few exceptions) they have been deservedly popular.

The other new publication in response to new pressures was the leaflet. Beginning in the mid 1960s with a provisional leaflet on records of births, marriages, and deaths, a series of free leaflets on popular subjects of research has now grown to more than a hundred titles, from the Jacobite risings to medieval genealogy, from maps and plans to the Royal Irish Constabulary. These leaflets give brief guidance (three or four pages, on average) on the likeliest sources for a particular line of enquiry, and they help the searcher to find a narrowly defined area of information without requiring a general acquaintance with the administrative structures behind the creation of the records.[7]

A third response to changing problems, which does not obviously count as a publication but which is, at the very least, the direct successor to one, is the *Current guide*. Early in this century it was decided that the *Guide* could no longer take the form of an alphabetical encyclopaedia; in the early 1970s it was decided that it could no longer take conventional book form at all. The 1963–8 published guide had its third volume to cope with the revisions required since the publication of its first two volumes, and it became increasingly obvious that the rate of accessions of records would continue to make any printed guide obsolete – and grotesquely obsolete – long before it was published. Today the oft-quoted figure of one shelf mile of records accessioned every year may be sufficiently convincing; put another way, in publications terms, there are between eight and ten thousand new pages of lists a year, each requiring consequential amendments to the guide. A pioneering use of computers by means of an agency proved serviceable,[8] though increasingly cumbersome as technology advanced around it, and the system has been transferred in-house. We now have a *Current guide* whose administrative histories are in most cases adequate departmental handbooks in their own right, while the class descriptions can be updated directly on computer as required. The publication of this guide is not wholly satisfactory; the class descriptions and their index are available on microfiche for a few pounds, but the administrative histories, running to several four-inch binders, are not yet available save as sheet-by-sheet photocopies,

[7] Current lists of leaflets available are on display, or available on request, in the Search Departments at Kew and Chancery Lane.

[8] M. Roper, 'Modern departmental records and the Record Office', *Journal of the Society of Archivists*, 4(5) (1972), 400–12 explains the genesis of the *Current guide*.

although plans for a microfiche publication by Her Majesty's Stationery Office have been announced.

One other innovative publication in recent years has been the popular publication which is designed to appeal to the non-specialist, however scholarly its underlying research may be. A series of museum pamphlets made a useful start, in the 1970s; more recently, glossy picture books, like Stephen Constantine's selection of 1930s posters, *Buy and build*, and N. A. M. Rodger's authoritative synopsis of *The Armada*, have shown that the PRO has the material with which to provide attractive, informative, and profitable publications at a modest price.

The PRO can look back on a rich and varied tradition of publication, and all these types of works are represented in the publishing plans for the next few years; but it is important to review forces and factors which may or must make for changes in the future. Not all changes are desirable, and not all will prove necessary, but it would be perilous to ignore their potentialities.

The first factor is one of resources. When the royal commission on the public records was gathering evidence in 1912, nineteen assistant keepers were preparing calendars or transcripts for publication. Today that figure is nil. Apart from one executive officer working on the calendar of Patent Rolls for Elizabeth I, no records publications, in the narrow sense, are in preparation by the permanent staff. Admittedly more than twenty volumes are in some stage of preparation at the hands of outside editors – mostly, of academics who do the work for love and honoraria – but the days when assistant keepers' time could be spared for such luxurious work have finally departed. Increasingly, the same is likely to be true of the handbooks; apart from one or two in the later stages of drafting, no more can be projected because of the difficulties in giving assistant keepers enough time, either in hours per week or in length of posting to a particular department, to see a substantial scholarly work through to completion. Many pressures, from the steadily increasing volume of readers and the steadily increasing volume of records, have not been met by commensurate increases in the complement of professional staff, and the effect upon the 'literary' work of the PRO has been decisive.

The problem of limited resources leads ineluctably to the problem of priorities, and in this context the dwindling of the PRO's traditional publishing programme may seem justifiable. If the massed ranks of texts and calendars redound to the PRO's credit, the massive amounts of unsorted or poorly arranged records wipe that credit from the slate. The deputy keeper who devoted so much official time to Rymer's *Foedera* was well aware of the shameful state of the 'ancient miscellanea of the Exchequer', while even now the unsorted miscellanea of the Court of King's Bench and the Court of Common Pleas, going back to the middle ages, occupy an estimated nine hundred sacks – an uncharted archive comparable in scale to the entire holdings of the British Library's Department of Manuscripts. In the face of such chronic neglect, it is arguable that expensive archival scholarship should be bestowed upon making the unavailable available rather than upon editing one more roll.

Priorities may change, however, for more positive reasons, of which technological advance is one, and a very forceful one. When Rymer was editing *Foedera*, and when Brewer and Gairdner were editing the *Letters and papers . . . Henry VIII*, the printed transcript was the only means whereby the contents of original documents could be made available to the remote scholar. Even in Gairdner's day, however, at the turn of the century, Maitland was using photographs in lieu of manuscript originals,[9] in order to keep working while convalescing in the Canaries; the PRO's first piece of reprographic equipment was inherited from a Canadian project after the First World War; large quantities of records were microfilmed for the Library of Congress upon the cautious assumption that Britain would be overrun in the Second World War.[10] Today, when the PRO sells millions of reprographic images of documents each year, the business of getting documents to students, as a substitute for getting students to documents, can be managed more efficiently, more cheaply, and less subjectively by the camera than by the editor.

This does not mean that there can never be any future place for texts and calendars; merely that the scarcity of editorial resources, and the availability of facsimile reprography, inevitably change the approach to the problems which were tackled a century ago. There is, too, a new problem, or at least an old problem with a new urgency: the economics of publication. A century ago, the PRO merely despatched its completed copy to HMSO and awaited the arrival of proofs. Today, financial factors have to be taken more seriously; production costs are very heavy, while the public-sector library market for specialist works is contracting. The combined effects are an expensive printing, a low print-run, and an extortionate cover price. So far, no PRO text or calendar has cost more than one hundred pounds, but the time may come. Consequently, the PRO has to look at ways of producing its mightier publications at prices less discouraging to the institutional librarian and less nearly prohibitive to the individual researcher.

Two expedients for reducing production costs are under active consideration. One is the production of future volumes with the apparatus (introductions, keys, tables, indexes) typeset as at present, but with the main texts microfiched and placed in wallets bound within the back covers of the books. Since many users of calendars turn to the indexes, fail to find what they want, and proceed no further, the proportion of users inconvenienced would be small, and, indeed, fewer and fewer people regard microform as a serious inconvenience at all. If, as provisional costings suggest, this process reduces cover prices by seventy or eighty per cent, the economic argument will be difficult to resist.

Another expedient which the PRO must explore is publication on computer disk. Much work already is typed on word processors, and more will be in future as computer investment increases. There is no intrinsic reason why editorial work should not be produced, in time, in an industry-standard format and sold on floppy disks. This would have the advantage of cheapness; it would also have, from the

9 *The Letters of Frederic William Maitland*, ed. C. H. S. Fifoot (Selden Society Supplementary Series, 1, 1965), e.g. nos 315, 316, 361, 363.

10 *British Manuscripts Project. A checklist of the microfilms prepared in England and Wales for the American Council of Learned Societies*, ed. L. K. Born (Washington, D.C., 1955), introduction.

purchaser's point of view, the very distinct advantage of making the material available to be searched, manipulated, and rearranged to individual requirements.

This appraisal of PRO publication, with its ambitions and its constraints, must include consideration of the PRO's publisher. With the exception of leaflets and other materials produced in-house, all publications have been published by HMSO, for a long time by right and more recently by practice. Not everyone thinks this a good idea. The Publications Committee of the Advisory Council on Public Records expressed some disquiet in 1979:

> . . . the major publishing problem of the Public Record Office concerns its traditional reliance on Her Majesty's Stationery Office as its publisher. The Committee stand aghast at the consequences: H.M.S.O. appears to embody some of the least desirable characteristics one might fear to find in a publisher.[11]

The report went on with a familiar catalogue of grievances: slow production, poor marketing, high cover prices. To be fair to the Committee, it must be said that the PRO's relationship with its publisher was then at its nadir; to be fair to HMSO, a good deal has changed in the intervening years. The use of new technology, such as laser printing, is being explored as a means of cutting costs, while the display of publications and the persuasive publicity leaflets at the anniversary conference itself showed the degree of commitment to attractive presentation and varied interest. Yet it is easy to overlook HMSO's most important characteristic: that it publishes all the PRO's publications. It has become very clear that other commerical publishers, while potentially or (in one or two cases) actively interested in taking over some of the PRO's titles (such as the Modern Records Department handbooks, or the genealogical guides), would not take over the whole range, and it is equally clear what would happen to the valuable but more specialised works if the glossy and popular items were hived off. While HMSO may not trade any single title as a loss leader, at least the balance of the PRO list, with some distinctly profit-making items among the slower-selling reference works, allows goodwill and good public relations to offset any difficulties or lack of enthusiasm for the less commercially attractive works.

For this reason – and it would apply equally to any publisher, or to the PRO itself, if publishing the full list – it is desirable to have a balanced programme of publications, serving the economic historian as well as the genealogist, the casual visitor to the museum as well as the assiduous record agent. Reservations have been expressed, within the PRO and outside, about the use of PRO resources to provide lighter and commemorative and frankly glossy publications when more fundamental work, in publications and elsewhere, remains to be done; but the economics of publication and the aims of the PRO alike argue for the broader approach, not only as a means of keeping the weightier publications in being, but as a means of reaching the widest possible public. The PRO's constituency has diversified dra-

[11] 'The twenty-first report of the Advisory Council on Public Records', in *The Twenty-first Annual Report of the Keeper of Public Records . . . 1979* (HC 801, 1980), 31–2.

matically in the last twenty or thirty years, and the PRO would be open to criticism if its publications list did not reflect this.

This retrospect and prospect is intended to show that the PRO is not complacent about the content or the means of its publishing, nor determined upon change for change's sake. Rather, its developing policy is one of continuous appraisal of all the problems and all the demands, protecting its high standards in an age of change and remaining optimistic in an age of constraint.

10. The Public Record Office, the Historian, and Information Technology

Edward Higgs Assistant Keeper of Public Records

In the comparatively limited space available here it will not be possible to give a comprehensive survey of the ways in which information technology (IT) has affected, or is likely to affect, historical research or archives. All that one can hope to do is to make a few general points about the manner in which the use of computers by historians has 'impacted' upon the Public Record Office (PRO), and about the uses of IT within the Office itself. Other archival institutions will have had different experiences in both those fields, according to the types of records that they hold, their specialised clientele, and the different relationship they have with the providers of IT services.

The last point in particular needs to be amplified. Many archives which have had experience of using IT are small parts of much larger institutions, such as local councils, county library services, universities, and so on. They characteristically have a day-to-day working relationship with the large and complex computer departments of the institutions of which they are a part. The PRO on the other hand is large enough, and independent enough, to have its own small IT Unit. That has had the advantage of allowing the PRO to find its own IT solutions to its own problems, rather than relying on hand-me-downs from other departments. But it also means that the staff of the IT Unit is spread very thinly over the many specialised functions of the Office. In such circumstances the generation of a 'critical mass' of computer consciousness within the Office can be a difficult task.

Before reviewing the development of IT within the PRO, however, it would be useful to turn to the role of computers in historical research and to consider it from the point of view of the archivist. The use of computers in history is intimately bound up with the use of mathematics to elucidate aggregate patterns in human society. Before one can use statistics in that manner it is necessary to perceive society as a mass of individual, autonomous units, rather than in terms of the personal ties formed by feudal bondage or aristocratic patronage. It should be no suprise to discover, therefore, that the origins of the use of statistics to measure society lie in the period of the Industrial and French Revolutions which created the modern democratic state. The attempt to mathematicize social relationships can be found in Malthus, the early statistical movement in England, the Victorian medical statisticians, and in the statistical theories of the nineteenth-century eugenicists.[1]

In a similar manner, historical research has moved away from the doings of kings and queens, towards the study of mass society. This is seen clearly in the development of economic and social history. Such research has always been implicitly quantitative, abounding in references to 'most', 'few', 'many', 'considerable numbers', and, of course, 'the popular'. But it has only been in the last twenty-five years that that quantification has been made explicit under the influence of American quantitative history, itself dependent upon the development of the computer and statistical packages, such as SPSS (Statistical Package for the Social Sciences), which were designed to facilitate the analysis of social science data.

Computers and quantification have in recent years been used in many fields of historical research in this country. Statistical models have been created to allow an input-output anlysis of the economy during industrialisation, or to simulate changes in the standard of living. Statistical techniques have been used to facilitate the analysis of large populations from comparatively small samples. This has been especially common in studies based on nineteenth-century census records. Perhaps the most striking example of the use of computers in historical research has been the reconstruction by the Cambridge Group for the History of Population and Social Structure of the pattern of vital events and population growth from the sixteenth century to 1871, based on an analysis of the ecclesiastical registers of baptisms, marriages, and burials.[2]

In almost all those cases computers have allowed historians to analyse large data sets. That in turn has led to demands for the PRO to preserve individual case files, or, to use current archival terminology, particular instance papers (PIPs). With the use of computers historians can now reconstruct the aggregate characteristics of populations from files which give standard information on particular individuals. Before those methods of aggregate analysis were commonly used such record series were seldom selected *in toto* for preservation since the individual files were of comparatively slight importance on their own account. With the use of sampling theories historians do not need the entire population of individual case files but only a representative sample. That in turn creates a new demand on the Office which has in the past either kept entire series, such as the census records, or selections of 'administrative epitomes' to show the development of administrative practices.[3]

It is unnecessary to repeat here the substance of Kelvin Smith's paper on current PRO policies on sampling and selection. The use of PIPs and sampling strategies

1 M. J. Cullen, *The statistical movement in early Victorian Britain* (Hassocks, 1975); John M. Eyler, *Victorian social medicine: the ideas and methods of William Farr* (London, 1979); Donald A. Mackenzie, *Statistics in Britain, 1865–1930* (Edinburgh, 1981).

2 See, for example, Donald N. McCloskey, *Econometric History* (London, 1987); Michael Anderson, *Family structure in nineteenth-century Lancashire* (London, 1971); E. A. Wrigley and R. S. Schofield, *The population history of England 1541–1871* (London, 1981).

3 Edward Higgs, '"Particular instance papers": the historical and archival dimensions', *Social History*, X, 1 (1985), pp. 89–94.

plainly raises all sorts of questions about the integrity of file series prior to sampling, which comes down in the end to the control exercised over files in departments. There is no point in sampling from case papers if one is not certain that the entire population of original files has survived. There are also problems over the storage of PIPs both during the process of sampling and in subsequent years. By their very nature samples of case papers relating to individuals have to be closed for many years on the grounds of personal sensitivity. But whilst they are lying dormant their storage still has to be paid for. This has important implications for archival funding and accommodation. Also, how can the demand of historians for statistical samples of case papers be squared with the needs of the genealogist for entire record series?

There is, however, another issue which needs to be addressed, and that is the meaning of the information contained in the sources which historians quantify. The current generation of computers lack a sense of irony. If you ask a computer to do something stupid, it will do so with the greatest of pleasure, and to excess. This is what is meant by the old computer adage 'Garbage in-garbage out', shortened to GIGO. The use of computers and quantification does not absolve the historian from assessing the quality of the data he or she is handling.

Computer analyses of records can reveal unexpected patterns in the data. The computer analysis of Domesday Book by Snooks and MacDonald has revealed some unexpected structures in the document which threaten to overthrow the conventional wisdom regarding William's great survey which originated with Round in the nineteenth century.[4] On the other hand, recent attempts to show the geographical distri bution of wealth during the Industrial Revolution from the records of direct taxation have been undertaken in apparent ignorance of the nature of these records. The fact that the historians have accepted this research without demur, seems to indicate the power of the mystique of quantification, and a decline in standards of archival scholarship.[5]

If the definitions or administrative conventions used to structure records or data change, then any simplistic attempt to construct statistical series from them is fraught with dangers. One need only think of the current controversy over unemployment statistics to see the havoc which such changes can play with attempts to illustrate social trends.

An example from the field of census analysis might make this point clearer. The census household is one of the more problematic entities found in the nineteenth-century returns. Tillott and Anderson, working on the enumerators' books of 1851 and 1861, have argued that the householder was defined as an occupier who rented space in a house. There was, therefore, considerable confusion over the status of boarders and lodgers. Single lodgers and lodger families are shown as forming separate households in the returns by the conventional marks used for this purpose

4 John McDonald and G. D. Snooks, *Domesday economy. A new approach to Anglo-Norman history* (Oxford, 1986).

5 For a discussion of the problems in using this source see Michael Jubb, 'Income, class and the taxman: a note on the distribution of wealth in nineteenth-century Britain', *Historical Research*, LX (1987), pp. 118–24.

but are still recorded as 'lodger' in the relationship to head column. In the absence of the sociological definition of the household as a group of people eating together such confusion was, Tillot argues, inevitable. Tillott and Anderson have chosen to ignore the conventional marks for households, and have defined the household as all those persons grouped under a person designated as a head in the relationship to head column.[6]

Although this may facilitate comparability across the same census, the convention does not, unfortunately, allow comparison between all censuses. This is because the definitions given to the enumerators after 1851 were quite specific, and changed over time. Contrary to Tillott's belief, enumerators were told in 1861 that lodgers boarding together separately from the rest of the people in a house should form a separate household, even though they should still be regarded as lodgers in relation to the principal occupier of the house. The separate lodger households found in the returns could quite correctly constitute definite social entities, although there was plainly still grounds for confusion. The Cambridge Group may well be justified, therefore, in excluding all boarders, lodgers and visitors from their analysis of household structure.[7]

Tillott was misled by regarding the enumerators' books as the sole source of instruction on this matter. But much fuller rules for defining the household survive at the PRO in the instruction books given to enumerators. These show a gradual progression after 1881 towards constituting the lodger or lodger group boarding separately as distinct households with household heads. This may lead, other things being equal, to an illusionary decrease over time in average household size, as the proportion of solitaries in society increases.[8]

Neither the Tillott/Anderson conventions, nor those used by the Cambridge Group, can fully deal with this problem because the people included in the household in the former case, and those excluded from it in the latter, changed over time. The solitary lodger in 1861 included in the head's household by Tillott and Anderson, and excluded from consideration by the Cambridge Group, would have been constituted as a solitary head in the returns by 1901, although his or her social position might not have changed. The Cambridge conventions give complete comparability across time for a comparatively brief period of twenty years in the mid-nineteenth century when the census definition of the household was stable. They

6 P. M. Tillott, 'Sources of inaccuracy in the 1851 and 1861 censuses', in *Nineteenth-century society*, ed. E. A. Wrigley (London, 1972), pp. 90–105; Michael Anderson, 'Standard tabulation procedures for the census enumerators' books 1851–1891', in *Nineteenth-century society*, ed. Wrigley, pp. 134–45.

7 This appears to be the convention implicit in Peter Laslett, 'Introduction: the history of the family', in *The household and family in past time* eds Peter Laslett and Richard Wall (London, 1974) pp. 1–73; and in John Knodel, 'An exercise on household composition for use in courses in historical demography', *Local Population Studies*, XXIII (1979), pp. 10–23.

8 For a more detailed discussion of such problems see Edward Higgs, 'Structuring the past: the occupational, social and household classification of census data', *Computing and History Today*, IV (1988), pp. 24–30.

do have the advantage, however, of concentrating analysis on 'clean' data. The Tillott/Anderson conventions, on the other hand, do neither.

It is not only in the historical community that IT is creating new opportunities, and new problems. Archives, as institutions dedicated to the storage, handling and dissemination of large amounts of information, are increasingly affected by modern computer technology. The PRO was in the fields of computerised data-handling, sorting, and stock control at a very early date. Indeed in some ways it has paid the price for attempting to innovate at an early stage in the Information Technology Revolution. Many of the problems which the Office met in the late 1960s and early 1970s in terms of programming, limited processing-capacity, and the lack of flexibility in computer systems, are no longer constraints today.

In the first phases of the planning of the PRO's Kew repository it was recognised that there was a need for an efficient requisitioning system that would transmit a reader's request for a document from the public reading rooms to the appropriate storage area in the repository; record the issue of the document; monitor its subsequent correct replacement; maintain a permanent record of the transaction; and produce statistical information required for management purposes. This was the basic specification for what became the PRO's PROMPT requisitioning system. The system, which was originally installed at Kew in 1977 and later extended to Chancery Lane, has increased the capacity of the repository to produce records to an ever-expanding readership, and has provided readers with much fuller information about the availability of those records.[9]

The system has worked well but has its limitations. When readers order records they are expected to be able to distinguish between group, class, and piece references. Since the staff of the PRO themselves disagree on the meaning, or even the existence, of such entities, it is not surprising that readers are often baffled by those terms. In the final analysis the problem is one of computer capacity. The computer can only hold information on record classes, that is, series of files or papers: it does not validate the reference of each piece, the individual orderable items which are produced to readers. The original minicomputer which ran the system was purchased before the precipitous decline in the relative cost of computer processing capacity. Indeed, as a 16 bit machine with 32K of core memory, its capacity can be compared unfavourably with that of many modern desk-top micros. The computer has, of course, been enhanced but the inherent limitations of the system remain.

At much the same time that the design of PROMPT was under way, the Office was also facing up to the limitations of the printed *Guide to the contents of the Public Record Office*, which explained the arrangement of the Office's holdings to readers. The latest version of the printed *Guide*, covering transfers up to 1960, had been published in two volumes in the early 60s, and a supplementary volume, taking the coverage up to 1966, was issued in 1968. But the constant accessioning of records

[9] Michael Roper, 'PROMPT: the computerised requisitioning system of the United Kingdom Public Record Office at Kew', *International Journal of Archives*, I, 2 (1980), pp. 20–9; Mary Wilkinson, 'Enhancements to the PROMPT computerised requisitioning system at the Public Record Office, Kew', *ADPA*, IV (1982–83), pp. 49–51.

meant that the printed *Guide* was always out of date, and the production of further supplements would only lead to confusion. The arrangement of the printed *Guide*, based on grouping the records of discrete departments in distinct chapters, was also very inflexible. With rapid changes in modern departmental responsibilities and structures, such an arrangement rapidly became artificial.

In any modern repository there are likely to be three main approaches to the use of archives: *via* a knowledge of administrative history; *via* archival classification and arrangement; and *via* a particular subject. Any new *Guide* had to take those differing types of search strategy into account.

A computerised system which would allow constant updating of its database, and produce guides in different formats from the same data, appeared to offer a solution to those problems. The Office subsequently developed the concept of the *Current guide*. This was in four parts: a set of administrative histories of all departments linking their functions to the records they produced; a set of descriptions of each record class in the PRO, arranged alpha-numerically by class code; and two indexes to Parts I and II. Part II and its index were computerised through an adaption of the INSPEC system developed by the Institute of Electrical Engineers for the production of abstract-journals and indexes. The PRO's version of that system came to be known as PROSPEC.[10]

The inputting of PROSPEC data was, however, a very cumbersome process. Each PROSPEC record, containing all the elements needed to produce the *Guide* and its associated catalogues and indexes, had to be entered in manuscript on specially prepared data sheets. These were then punched onto tape and sent to the Institute of Electrical Engineers for input into their computer system. Quality control, updating, corrections, and trouble-shooting were all laborious administrative exercises because of the Office's lack of direct control over the PROSPEC database. The PROSPEC system was intended to produce other finding aids in addition to the *Guide*, such as location lists, site lists, and microfilm and search room catalogues. The final system was not, however, used to support all these facilities.

The limitations of the PROSPEC system have been partly overcome by bringing it in-house, and running it on PRO hardware. That has allowed greater flexibility and easier data input. But the Office is looking at a much larger project which might possibly lead to the *Current guide*, data on other supplementary finding aids, the requisitioning system, and information necessary for the transfer and processing of records, being combined in a single, comprehensive, Records Information System (RIS). This would allow data currently kept in numerous discrete systems to be combined, thus enhancing its value, and cut down on the duplication of data inputting throughout the various departments of the PRO.

Before the Office makes any decisions on what, if anything, should be included in RIS, a lengthy process of consultation and planning has to be undertaken by the

10 Michael Roper, 'Modern departmental records and the record office', *Journal of the Society of Archivists*, IV, 5 (1972), pp. 408–9; P. Simmons, L. Bell and M. Roper, *ibid.*, IV, 5 (1972), pp. 423–7; C. D. Chalmers and J. B. Post, 'A flexible system for the cumulative general index', *ibid.*, VI, 8 (1981), pp. 482–92.

IT Unit. The staff of this section are currently mapping the existing systems within the Office, to identify overlaps and duplications of effort. Members of other departments, who will end up as users of any RIS system, are being fully involved in the process. This will lead eventually to the presentation of a series of options to senior management for possible implementation.

This paper has been concerned so far with the Office's use of computers at the macro-level for gaining intellectual and physical control over the public records as a whole. But the Office has also been active in using computerised indexing programmes to produce finding aids to individual classes of records. In the 1960s the PRO was experimenting with the Newcastle File Handling System, developed at Newcastle University, for indexing Memoranda Rolls and other records. The Office also looked at other computer systems such as KWIC (Key Word in Context), KWOC (Key Word out of Context), and PRECIS (Preserved Context Indexing System).

These experiments showed that indexes could be produced via computers but at considerable cost, and the use of computers to index particular documents or lists was suspended. A number of serious problems had been revealed: the limitations of computer systems in indexing complex and heterogenous documents or list descriptions; mechanical and human constraints in producing indexes as part of the process of providing lists, catalogues, or calendars; limitations on using computer indexing systems developed for library or bibliographic purposes for the varied levels of finding aid needed in a large archive; difficulties in training staff in the use of such systems; and finally problems of resource allocation involved in any commitment to large-scale indexing projects.[11] Many of these early indexing experiments also involved using computers owned and run by other institutions in other parts of the country, which greatly increased the complexities of the process.

The resource implications of such projects need to be stressed. In the absence of really accurate optical character readers, computers can only sort data which has already been keyed into them. That is an extremely tedious and time-consuming business, and is perhaps the major constraint on using the indexing capacity of computers to their full potential. In many archives and libraries today records are being laboriously keyed into computer databases, and one wonders if this is a proper use of scarce resources. Conservation microfilming is surely a cheaper method of protecting records, and their proper arrangement and listing is a more urgent priority.

Some of those problems have been overcome by the recent revolution in desktop micros, and the purchase of database management packages designed for commerce and business. Such user-friendly systems are now being utilised throughout the Office to produce and analyse databases of information on finding aids, documents, legislation, objects of special interest, library books, and so on. They are easy to use, extremely flexible and comparatively cheap.

The purchase of such equipment has, however, been very much on an ad hoc

[11] Duncan Chalmers, 'Computer indexing in the Public Record Office', *ibid.*, VI, 7 (1981), pp. 399–413.

basis, and the Office now has the inevitable problems of incompatibility between systems and machines. This is especially acute at the interface between database management and word-processing. Because of the rigid distinction between word-processing on word-processors, and database management on microcomputers, the creation of lists in piece-number order, and the sorting of them to create indexes, have been quite separate processes. Data has been input twice by different staff, using incompatible hardware and software.

The scale and complexity of some of the projects being run on existing micros are also stretching the capacity of those machines to their limits. That has caused numerous problems for the management of computer projects because of the delays associated with data processing and backup.

Many of those difficulties will hopefully be overcome in the near future. With the appointment of a microcomputers support officer in the IT Unit, and the establishment of a Microcomputers Users Group, the Office is moving towards an integrated microcomputer strategy. With the increasing introduction of integrated packages such as Smart, which combine database management, spreadsheets, word-processing and the like, problems of software incompatibility can be overcome. At the same time, the use of newer, and more powerful, micros, and their possible integration into networked systems, hold out the possiblity of overcoming hardware incompatibility and limitations of capacity. All this could lead to a revolution in the listing and indexing of records.

The PRO is also exploring the possibility of setting up a machine-readable data archive using optical-disk technology. This involves testing the suitability of optical disk as an archival medium; exploring the implications of public access to computer records, particularly with regard to the conversion of computer tape formats; and establishing standards for the documentation of computerised records transferred to the PRO. The tests carried out so far seem to indicate that optical disk does offer a technically suitable solution to the problems of archival storage. But the relative cost of setting up such an archive is still high. There are also some doubts about the physical suitability of such disks for long-term storage and use. The interim reports on the project speak darkly about the horrors of 'downward plastic creep', and 'plastic spin flow'.

It is, of course, unwise to attempt to forecast the future course of the IT Revolution in the office and archival environments. If the present author were capable of doing so he would not be employed as a assistant keeper of the public records. But there are some straws in the wind. As the BBC Domesday project has shown, optical disks can be used to store images of documents as well as computerised data, and might eventually replace microfilm or fiche as a means of archival storage. It could even be possible one day for readers to access such data from outside the Office on national, or even international, computer networks. The idea of the twenty-first century historian sitting in his or her study in Australia calling up files from Kew is perhaps fanciful, but perhaps no more ridiculous than Sir Hilary Jenkinson might have found the idea of RIS.

The main constraint on such means of access might not be technological but intellectual; knowing what to access rather than how to access it. For the academic the solution might be in having the *Current guide* on-line but less experienced researchers would require guiding through a search strategy. There is, however, considerable interest currently being shown in the creation of such 'expert computer systems' which will guide people via series of questions and answers to the particular pieces of information they require. Nor is remote access to such systems a flight of fantasy. There are several commercially produced videotext systems for micros which currently support such facilities via Prestel-type links.

The Information Technology Revolution will plainly affect historians and archivists profoundly. Groups so intimately concerned with the storage and communication of information could hardly fail to feel its impact. But inevitably IT throws up as many problems and challenges as it provides solutions and opportunities. Nor should it be allowed to undermine the traditional standards of archival and historical scholarship. As yet the computer is merely a powerful extension of the human mind: it cannot replace it.

11. THE NATIONAL REGISTER OF ARCHIVES AND OTHER NATIONWIDE FINDING AIDS

Brian S. Smith Secretary of the Royal Commission on Historical Manuscripts

It is perhaps a little strange, but is really very appropriate, that in this series of celebratory lectures to mark the 150th anniversary of the Public Records Act 1838 and the centenary of the British Record Society one should be specifically devoted to those historical records which lie outside the terms of the Public Records Acts. It brings to my mind that aside in a presidential address by a past Deputy Keeper of Public Records in which, compared with the bulk of the public records, he likened the contents of the British Museum's department of manuscripts to the boot of an Austin Seven. I thought at the time, which from the terminology you will place before 1958, that the Grand Old Man had failed to take account of both the quality of the British Museum's collections and the existence of quantities of non-official records elsewhere. However, presidents speak *ex cathedra* and we all dutifully kept silent. Since then more scientific measurements, like the latest survey by the Royal Commission on Historical Manuscripts in 1984, have shown that of 750 kilometres of records held in publicly funded repositories in the United Kingdom only one-fifth is in the PRO.[1] But whilst it is my function to divert your attention briefly to the means of discovering the existence and whereabouts of the other four-fifths of the records of the nation – and of the additional unmeasured quantities remaining in private hands – it also gives me this welcome opportunity to pay tribute to the Public Record Office for fostering and harbouring both the Historical Manuscripts Commission and the National Register of Archives in those earlier, simpler days between the Public Records Acts of 1838 and 1958, when the Master of the Rolls as the titular keeper of the public records was also the singular office holder under the Crown in England and Wales to whom all matters relating to historical records could be referred.

Thus it happened that when the attention of historians turned from the government's archives to the nation's wealth of non-official records, and the Rolls Series was launched in 1857 to publish at public expense the literary sources for the history of the middle ages, a task it accomplished by the end of the century in some

1 B.S. Smith, 'Record repositories in 1984', *Journal of the Society of Archivists*, VIII, 1 (April 1986), 1–16.

250 volumes, it was the Master of the Rolls who was made responsible for the venture.[2] It was to the Master of the Rolls also that the Prime Minister, Lord Palmerston, naturally turned for advice on receiving in 1858 a memorial for the appointment of a commission to survey historical papers in private hands, employing either independent inspectors or keepers from the British Museum. The Master of the Rolls, Lord Romilly, advised against the proposal. Almost immediately, however, in 1860, he submitted a similar plan, its chief distinction being to keep executive control in the hands of the Deputy Keeper of Public Records, an arrangement which persisted until 1959.[3]

The appointment of the Royal Commission on Historical Manuscripts in 1869, under Lord Romilly's chairmanship, to make enquiry into the location of privately owned historical manuscripts throughout the United Kingdom of public interest for the nation's history, law, science or literature, to make abstracts or catalogues of them and to present reports, was the first attempt to carry out a national survey of historical records. The result was quite remarkable. In its first nine reports between 1870 and 1884 the Commission reported on 424 collections, two-thirds owned by individuals, one-third by institutions. They included most of those of outstanding national importance, forming an impressive roll-call of the aristocracy, Rutland, Salisbury, Manchester, St Germans, Lothian, Ormonde, Bath, Devonshire, Northumberland, Bute and many other noble and long-established landed families, ancient corporations and burghs, cathedrals and colleges.[4] Then having surveyed all the major collections made open to them the Commissioners began in 1883 with the Cecil papers at Hatfield House their more detailed examination of the most important papers they had discovered, published in the great Reports and Calendars series, of which 236 volumes have appeared.[5]

In taking this change of direction they were well aware that they had left unfinished their original object of carrying out a comprehensive survey of all the nation's surviving historical records. With the much reduced resources allowed them after 1914, they later considered how they might renew this task with voluntary assistance.[6] Abortive attempts in the 1920s and 1930s exposed the impracticality of this method, whereas by contrast their secretary, R.L. Atkinson, successfully conducted a more limited enquiry in 1941 to record the changes in composition and ownership of the HMC reported collections which was published in 1946.[7]

2 P. Levine, *The amateur and the professional: antiquarians, historians and archaeologists in Victorian England, 1838–1886* (Cambridge 1986), pp. 115–119; E.L.C. Mullins, *Texts and calendars* (Royal Historical Society, London 1958), pp. 42–60.

3 *Manuscripts and men:. . . The Royal Commission on Historical Manuscripts 1869–1969* (London 1969), pp. 1–11.

4 Mullins, pp. 61–90.

5 Historical Manuscripts Commission, *Calendar of the manuscripts of the Most Hon. the Marquis of Salisbury preserved at Hatfield House*, 24 vols. (London 1883–1976).

6 *Nineteenth report of the Royal Commission on Historical Manuscripts* (London 1926), pp. 8–9; *Twentieth report. . .* (1928), p. 4; *Twenty-first report . . .* (1938), pp. 11–12.

7 *Twenty-second report. . .* (1946), pp. 12–13, 15–103.

These ventures represented one strand in the formation of the National Register of Archives. Another was provided by the British Records Association to which, as members here will know, the British Record Society had given birth in 1932.[8] With the prompting of the small company of local archivists and manuscript librarians who then existed and fired by the fertile, some might say over-fertile, imagination of Hilary Jenkinson, then principal assistant keeper in the PRO, the Association presented in 1943 an ambitious programme of legislative proposals for the post-war custody and regulation of archives.[9] Amongst these, and even in that period of state controls the only one to find favour with the government, was the creation of a National Register of Archives. Treasury approval was given for its initial two and a half years' funding and under a special directorate shared by the PRO and the Historical Manuscripts Commission the first registrar, Lt-Colonel G.E.G. Malet, was appointed in 1945. At the same time separate funding from the Scottish vote was provided for a register to be administered by the Scottish Record Office in Edinburgh.

The history of the National Register of Archives has yet to be written, and though entertaining it would take too long to recite here.[10] An early emphasis was placed on recording the many local collections of archives not reported by the Commission and for this purpose Malet set about forming a network of county committees of volunteers and advocating the establishment of county record offices, several of which like those in Berkshire, Cornwall, Leicestershire, Wiltshire and Worcestershire directly owe their origin to his pressure and advice. He overcame the many obstacles placed in his way so that by the time of his death in 1952 he had created 37 such committees and there were about 35 county record offices in existence. These in due course absorbed the activities of local NRA committees, allowing them to wither away. Meanwhile in London, where Malet and his assistant were housed in the PRO, like the part-time secretary of the Historical Manuscripts Commission, the Register was advancing so well under the energy of its own momentum, that the directorate ceased to meet in 1952 and support thenceforth rested with the Commission's self-effacing secretary. This arrangement was regularised in 1959 when under its revised royal warrant the Commission was formally required to maintain the Register.

Other changes were more or less coincidental. In 1957 Roger Ellis, principal assistant keeper in the PRO, was appointed the Commission's first full-time secretary on Atkinson's death, and in 1959 the Commission moved with the NRA out of the PRO into its present offices nearby in Quality Court. These three events, which

[8] *The British Records Association 1932–1947, being a report from the joint secretaries on their retirement* (1948).

[9] The Master of the Rolls Archives Committee, *Proposals for the control of English archives* (1946).

[10] The progress of the National Register of Archives is charted in the twenty-second to twenty-sixth *Reports of the Royal Commission on Historical Manuscripts*, (1946–1987), the *Bulletins of the National Register of Archives* (1948–1967), and the annual *Secretary's report to the Commissioners* (1969–1987). All are published for the Commission by Her Majesty's Stationery Office.

combined to remove the Commission from the shadow of the PRO, allowed its new secretary to develop the potential of both the Commission and the Register. Slowly the Register was integrated with the Commission's longer established sources of information and working practices, a process not completed until the early 1970s.

By then about 15,000 reports, as all the lists and catalogues are collectively known, had been registered. The great majority, reflecting the origins of the Register, related to archives in local record offices or to papers in private hands examined by the local volunteers, to which were added the reports compiled by the Commission's own staff continuing their work of inspection and listing, but now feeding the results into the Register. However, at that stage, though nationwide, the Register was not national in the sense that the nationally important collections of the national libraries and other repositories were poorly represented. A deliberate effort to correct this imbalance then began, expanded determinedly by Godfrey Davis, appointed the Commission's secretary in 1972 from the British Museum's department of manuscripts, in order to strengthen the Register's holdings of reports from the national libraries, record offices and museums in London, Edinburgh, Aberystwyth and Belfast, from the universities and other specialist institutions and from the most fruitful sources overseas in North America and Australasia. The results may be gauged from the origin of reports added to the Register. In 1987–88 these came from 84 local record offices, 60 national, specialist and university institutions, and 70 private owners and other sources.[11] The extent of the net may be further judged if it is recalled that there are 234 publicly funded record repositories in the United Kingdom which collect and care for archives other than those of their own administration and provide facilities for their study, whilst the NRA contains reports from 900 record offices, libraries and museums and 5,000 private owners, individual and institutional, who are willing to make their records accessible to scholars. At the start of this conference the Register contained 31,117 reports, and this total is being enlarged or amended at the rate of about 2,000 a year. It is this rate of addition and amendment which renders any attempt to publish or microfilm the Register of dubious academic value and poses the biggest challenge in keeping the Register and its indexes up to date. Its essence is its immediacy.

Coming from so many sources and embracing lists compiled from the seventeenth century onwards, made in all manner of ways and variety of detail, it is the Register's first task to record these reports accurately, extract the essential information from them consistently at a common level, and index them to the highest scholarly standards to exercise intellectual control over them. The material covers every sort of historical record, with notable strengths in the reports on personal papers, family, estate and business records, and the archives of major institutions. There are separate series, arranged topographically, of parish, nonconformist, schools, and local authority records, and of small miscellaneous reports. It cannot be stressed too much that the usefulness of the Register to scholars depends ultimately upon the quality and quantity of the reports reaching it from archivists and librarians. It is their testimonial. In general, rather than attempt to isolate its strengths,

[11] Royal Commission on Historical Manuscripts, *Annual review 1987–1988*.

it would be easier to note its omissions. These fall into three categories: minor groups of papers held in the expected places; recent accessions not yet properly catalogued, which can include material acquired twenty years ago and in fact available for research; and papers of modern origin which have not yet fully emerged although privileged scholars may have been allowed access to them. In practice, to some extent these deficiencies are made up by incorporating into the Register brief details trawled from printed guides, annual reports and similar sources.

Entry to this storehouse of historical information is by the central indexes to the Register and to the contents of the reports, which are compiled by the Commission's staff. Malet's complex card indexes and the prodigious memory of his assistant and successor, Miss W.D. Coates, gave way in the 1960s to a short title index and location index to the Register, and to personal, topographical and subject indexes to the reports. But again the systems broke down with the sheer weight of the material.

The topographical index was abandoned in 1964 and the subject index some ten years later. The subject index was then radically reformed, leaving behind it ghosts in those local record offices which had adopted the earlier scheme, and in the late 1970s a separate index of business records known as the companies index was hived off. The personal index was also overhauled. It was always in the most demand, for the majority of enquiries to the Register are for the papers of identifiable people of historical interest. These words are chosen with care. The Commission has limited resources and all its indexes are necessarily selective. Indeed were they otherwise, scholars would be plunged into a thicket of useless entries and in dealing with material at a national level the indexes cannot aim at the same detail as those of a single repository. The personal index refers to people whose names can be found in the standard reference books and to substantial groups of their papers, not for instance to isolated letters written by them. It is not designed for genealogical searches which are better served by the worldwide indexes compiled by the Mormons. Yet even within these limitations the personal index now contains over 107,000 entries relating to nearly 32,000 people of historical significance. It was computerised in 1970, some ten years ahead of computerised indexing in record offices, and as part of the Commission's current computerisation programme for the whole National Register of Archives and its indexes it has been converted to a new on-line system. The Register and all the other indexes are part of the same programme. In July 1987 new entries began to be made on-line, and the daunting task of backloading 225,000 existing titles and entries going back to 1945 and totalling a million elements, all requiring editing and verifying, has largely been carried out; only the subject index, with its peculiar complexities, remains to be finished over the next two or three years. The benefits in terms of consistency, speed and versatility of control and use of the Register are already evident, and as soon as the conversion has been completed and satisfactorily tested these search facilities will become available to the public.

Although a few percipient scholars were quick to appreciate in 1945 that the Register provided them with a powerful new tool for their research it was not until 1965, after leaving the cramped quarters which were all that could be spared in the crowded PRO building in Chancery Lane, that the Register was provided with a search room. Although enlarged in 1984 it is not really big enough for the 31,000 reports which are on open access, the 2,000 and more readers each year, of whom in 1987–88 44 per cent were postgraduate scholars and 36 per cent people using the Register for professional purposes, and the computer terminals which will shortly be introduced. On the other hand, contrary to most reading rooms, the success of the Register might best be measured by an absence of readers, for this would indicate that its information was being effectively disseminated elsewhere.

For its search room is only one, and perhaps the least original, way in which the Register's accumulated and centralised information is disseminated. Since 1954 it has supplied duplicate copies of reports to donor repositories for their own circulation and has itself distributed copies of the more important to nine copyright and national libraries for consultation. More important, as a means of broadcasting information on the topics in which the Register is richest and which are most in demand by historians, the Commission in 1973 launched a new series of Guides to Sources for British History based upon the National Register of Archives. Six volumes have been published since 1982, two more are approaching the press, and others are on the stocks.[12] These volumes are slim frigates packed with concentrated information compared with the dreadnoughts of the Reports and Calendars. Being well received by scholars and publised at a cost of only £4 to £8 they are a triumph for the Register and HMSO.

But this is only one way in which the Register can claim to be still at the front of the field. It was the first of its kind, a unique British achievement which has attracted imitators in other national archives, beginning with Holland in 1965 and more recently the Scandinavian countries, South Africa, New Zealand, Australia, and Pakistan, and also commercial copyists. However, it remains the most comprehensive, academically strongly based, and up-to-date National Register of Archives in the world, which (such being the way of things) draws perhaps more appreciative comments from scholars overseas who lack such a register at home than from academics and archivists in this country to whom it has become familiar.

This is not to claim that it is incapable of improvement. The preparation of every volume in the Guides series has exposed gaps in the Register's coverage which have had to be filled by painstaking research. It is not enough for the Register to boast, like the undergraduate verse about Jowett, 'What I don't know isn't knowledge'. It must seek out what it should know. For the Register is not just a passive recipient of reports, but actively looks for a large proportion of its holdings, perhaps 20 per cent each year. For example, in preparing the current volume on the sources for British business and industry 1760–1914 the editors last year more than doubled

12 *Papers of British cabinet ministers 1782–1900* (1982); *The manuscript papers of British scientists 1600–1940* (1982); *Guide to the location of collections described in the Reports and Calendars series 1870–1980* (1982); *Private papers of British diplomats 1782–1900* (1985); *Private papers of British colonial governors 1782–1900* (1986); *Papers of British churchmen 1780–1940* (1987). All are published for the Commission by H.M.S.O. *Papers of British politicians 1782–1900; Sources for the history of British business and industry 1760–1914: part 1 textiles and leather*.

the number of entries in the Register relating to the textile industries from 1,100 to 2,400 and still have 60 repositories and 24 manufacturers to approach, in the course of which they will, like other archivists and historians, be examining the contents of dirty store rooms, discovering hidden caches of records forgotten by their owners, and listing unsorted papers.

Moreover, with its limited resources and the quantity of the material to be covered the Commission has always recognised that the Register cannot enter into that detail which some scholars would wish. It has, therefore, always welcomed the work of others in specialised fields, freely supporting their initial efforts by providing material from the Register and gratefully receiving into it the results of their more detailed investigations. There is, after all, no shortage of work to be done.

In the 1940s, for instance, it stood aside from recording ecclesiastical archives because these were the subject of the survey given limited publication in 1951 at the expense of the Pilgrim Trust.[13] It has long had a special and mutually supportive relationship with the Business Archives Council in its surveys of banking and insurance records and of the oldest surviving limited liability companies. It took on itself and published in 1982 a survey of the papers of British scientists begun by a joint committee with the Royal Society, and one way or another it has participated in similar nationwide surveys of the papers of economists, of feminists, of missionary societies, of shipbuilding, and others. Such surveys, resulting in published nationwide finding aids range from those of particular kinds of documents, like medieval cartularies, bishops' registers and hearth tax returns, to wider topics like the contents of medieval libraries, English legal manuscripts, and the papers of twentieth-century politicians. There are also many such finding aids concerned with records relating to other parts of the world to be found in this country. Their grand total is surprisingly large, and it would extend this brief overview inordinately to refer now to even a fraction of the 180 or so. A bibliography of them is in hand for publication next year which will serve as a guide to them all, some being of special interest to genealogists.[14] This bibliography will also include the thirty surveys currently in progress, some of which lie outside the terms of the Commission's present warrant, such as literary manuscripts (Reading University) and the records of national health service hospitals (Wellcome Institute with the PRO).

Two features of contemporary surveys deserve comment. First, they sometimes seem to be motivated less by individual scholars perceiving a need in their own discipline than by universities seeking research projects to satisfy the government's criteria for general university funding. Second, instead of having the finite aim of publication some surveys have the infinite aim of creating a computerised database. There are dangers in these approaches which have not been fully addressed. The two surveys just named have arranged for the publication and eventual continuation of their work by the British Library and PRO respectively. But will other universities, whose enthusiasms in archival matters have in the past tended not to

13 Pilgrim Trust, *Survey of ecclesiastical archives* [1951].

14 *Surveys of historical manuscripts in the United Kingdom: a select bibliography*. In preparation at the Commission.

outlast special grants or the departure of the director of such projects, be willing to accept the permanent drain on their own resources of maintaining the database? And how can their databases be integrated, like the publications which preceded them, into the National Register of Archives to save scholars from embarking upon inefficient rounds of unnecessary enquiries?

These disturbing questions, as yet unanswered, may serve as the introduction to more certain concluding forecasts of other developments in comprehensive nationwide finding aids to historical records. The NRA was suited to British circumstances in the 1940s and 1950s. If we were starting out now it would be done differently. The purpose of its computerisation programme of 1987–92 is to make that new start so that the Register is ready to advance into the twenty-first century. One can foresee not only the computerised retrieval of information in the Commission's own search room in the near future, but thereafter from other points in the kingdom. Just as the Register's indexes have for years been used in some of the national libraries as the most useful key to their own and related collections elsewhere, so it may be expected that local record offices, and their readers, will use them in the same way. Whilst for the reasons already given it would be unrealistic to expect the Register to obtain 100 per cent coverage of the nation's historical records, it would seem not unreasonable to increase this from the present 70 per cent or so to 85 per cent. And why should not the public records, or at least initially those in repositories outside the PRO, be included in this target? Furthermore, other specialist surveys will multiply as tools for historians and ways will be found of harmonising these with the National Register of Archives.

I hope that this brief review will assure both the PRO and British Record Society that the National Register which they, both directly and vicariously, promoted and fostered has fulfilled their expectations and is well set to celebrate its own half-century in 1995.

12. THE INDEX LIBRARY: A CENTENARY HISTORY, 1988[1]

Peter Spufford General Editor, *The Index Library*

It is hard to find an exact date to celebrate the centenary. Work on the first volume of its *Index Library* began in the autumn of 1887. The first monthly instalment was dated January 1888, the first volume was completed in November 1888, but the British Record Society was not formed to manage its publication until November 1889.

The Public Records – Phillimore and Selby's Original Scheme

It was in the autumn of 1887 that the British Record Society really began. The prime mover was a young solicitor, the thirty-four year old William Phillimore (b.1853, d.1913). He was a distant relative of the more famous members of an eminent legal family. Phillimore was addicted to publishing, beginning his extraordinarily lengthy list of publications with a work on church bells in his native Nottinghamshire, which appeared before he went up to Oxford as an undergraduate. In 1887 he had just published the first edition of his *How to write the History of a Family*, which was to prove the standard genealogical textbook for the next generation. The *Index Library* was launched by him from outside the Public Record Office. However, he had the active co-operation of Walford Selby (b.1845, d.1889) from within the Public Record Office, where he had been working for over twenty years, and was by then the superintendant of the search room. In 1889 Phillimore acknowledged how much 'most valuable advice' Walford Selby had given him when 'engaged in planning the index library'. They not only lamented the lack of printed indexes to the British public records, but also set about doing something to provide them. The volumes of the Record Commissioners had come to an end some fifty years earlier, and the only official publications then being printed in England were the vast series of *Calendars of State Papers*, and the much smaller series of *Calendars of Treasury Papers* and *of Documents Relating to Ireland* and the class lists sporadically printed as appendixes to the Deputy Keeper's Reports. However, no indexes to the

[1] An earlier version of this paper was published in the *Genealogists' Magazine*, xxii (1988), pp. 322–6 and 362–7, and distributed to those attending the *Records of the Nation* conference.

public records were being produced at all. The major historical publishing enterprises of the day, the Rolls Series, the Camden Society, the Hakluyt Society, the Harleian Society and the Pipe Roll Society, were all concerned with producing a limited number of select documents in full.[2] Selby himself was the Director and Treasurer of the Pipe Roll Society, which he had founded only four years earlier, for the publication in full of 'all public records prior to 1200', and was in the process of editing *The Red Book of the Exchequer* for the Rolls Series. As well as editing documents Selby had recently published guides to Lancashire, Cheshire and Norfolk records to be found in the Public Record Office, was engaged in calendaring the MSS at Hatfield, and was editor of *The Genealogist*.[3] Selby and Phillimore felt that something different was needed as well, but they did not intend to start yet another society. Instead, with the financial backing of Charles Clark, the legal publisher, they embarked upon a private scheme for the publication of a 'series of indexes to the principal English Records', which they grandly entitled *The Index Library*, of which Phillimore was to be editor.

The Index Library, 1888

Phillimore and Selby began by issuing monthly instalments of several indexes at once, to interest the maximum number of people. The first, dated January 1888, consisted of the first sixteen pages of a calendar of Chancery Proceedings under Charles I, sixteen pages of an index to late sixteenth and early seventeenth century Bills of Privy Signet, and sixteen pages of an index of names to the Royalist Composition Papers of the Commonwealth period. These were all transcriptions of manuscript indexes already in the Public Record Office and easily accessible to Selby, who was responsible for their selection. Phillimore did not at first see any point in their producing fresh indexes of their own. In December 1887 he wrote:

> The aim of the Editor is not so much to compile new Indexes and Calendars to the Records as to render available old ones now in manuscript, which have stood the test of long use.

He was soon compelled to write of one of their sources:

> These indexes, unfortunately, have been done very badly, and the only thing which can be said in their favour is, that a bad index is, perhaps, better than none at all. They were evidently compiled by persons unable to read the handwriting of the Stuart period, and unacquainted with even the elements of indexing.

They found the work more complex than anticipated as they began to check the existing indexes and correct their inadequacies. For example, some of the old

2 For something of the flavour of historical enterprises in the 1880s see below pp. 171–2.
3 For Walford Selby, see Frederick Boase, *Modern English Biography*, iii (1901, reprinted 1965).

indexes were only divided up by the first letter of the names and arranged within each letter chronologically, rather than strictly alphabetically. Soon they were involved in the much slower task of compiling rather than copying indexes. Nevertheless they persisted for two years in issuing forty-eight pages of index every month to anybody who was prepared to buy. They sold their monthly parts at two shillings each or a guinea a year for twelve instalments. In 1889 Selby contracted typhoid and died at the age of forty-five, leaving Phillimore to carry on alone. Selby's death raised speculation about whether the scheme would continue, and this brought other troubles in its train. In January 1893 Phillimore was to write:

> Financially it did not prove a success owing, apparently, to a fear that the serial might not continue long enough to complete the works being issued in it, and the publisher suggested that the subscribers to the *Index Library* should be invited to form a society.

The British Record Society, 1889

The publisher's suggestion became a reality on 28 November 1889. The British Record Society was brought into being to put the project on a more secure basis. Phillimore later wrote:

> The wisdom of this step was soon shown by a marked accession of new subscribers, which was clearly due to the increased stability given to the *Index Library* by the formation of the Society.

He became the first Secretary and remained General Editor of its publications,[4] which now came out in larger, quarterly, instalments. The Society's publications continued to come out in quarterly instalments until 1920. They then came out in half-yearly sections, still unbound. It has only been since 1947 that the Society has produced its volumes ready-bound.

The need for a private scheme, or even a society, to publish indexes to the records in the Public Record Office was removed almost as soon as the Society had been formed. Henry Maxwell Lyte, the new Deputy Keeper, who had been appointed in 1886, brought about a change in official policy in 1890, which not only resulted in the official series of calendars being extended in the first instance to the Patent and Close Rolls (1891 and 1892) and later to other classes of record, but also in the production of an official series of Lists and Indexes in 1892.[5] Selby and Phillimore's initiative had helped stimulate official action that, with public resources at its disposal, could be infinitely more effective than anything done in the private sphere. As the scale of official indexing was extended, so the need for the Society's original activities diminished. The Society produced six volumes of in-

4 For a list of the officers of the Society during the first century of its existence see the first appendix to this chapter, below pp. 133–5.

5 See above pp. 20 and 93–4.

dexes to Chancery Proceedings before this series was made redundant by the inclusion of indexes to chancery proceedings among the official List and Index series from 1896 onwards. The Society produced twelve volumes of indexes to *Inquisitions post mortem*, but this series also became redundant after the introduction of two official series of calendars of *Inquisitions post mortem* in 1898 and 1904.

The Lists and Indexes published from the Public Record Office naturally ceased during both World Wars. However, when such publication was not revived after the Second World War, pressure built up among historians for continuing publication by private enterprise. This eventually brought about the formation of the List and Index Society in 1965, which is now once again printing copies of existing indexes in the Public Record Office. This had nothing to do with the British Record Society, which had by 1965 moved into other fields, but there was a remarkable similarity between the aims of the founders of the List and Index Society and those of Selby and Phillimore's original *Index Library* scheme eighty years before.

The Index Society, 1877–90

In May 1890 the young British Record Society took in the older Index Society, which had been founded at the end of 1877 by Henry Wheatley, the bibliographer and topographer of London. Wheatley had been the first secretary of the Early English Text Society and has been described as the 'father of modern indexing'. The present Society of Indexers' award for the best index of the year is a medal named after him. The Index Society was founded to produce 'Indexes of Standard Works, Subject Indexes of Science, Literature and Art, and a General Reference Index'.[6] Publication began in 1878, but by 1890 the Index Society was in financial difficulties. At its final meeting Dr Wheatley, as its director, proposed the merging of his society in the British Record Society on condition that the latter should discharge the printers' bill for the second and third volumes of the *Index of the biographical and obituary notices in the Gentleman's Magazine 1731–1780*, which the Index Society was unable to meet. In return the British Record Society received an influx of new members and a number of new council members, like Wheatley himself and Sir Leslie Stephen, the editor of the *Dictionary of National Biography*. In addition it took over the remaining stock of the extraordinarily wide variety of indexes published by the Index Society. The eighteen volumes, which followed Wheatley's *What is an index?*, ranged from an index to Trevelyan's *Life and Letters of Lord Macaulay* to an index of *Engravings in the proceedings of the Society of Antiquaries*, and from a bibliography of the literature of *Vegetable Technology* to the *Bibliography and Chronology of Hales Owen*. Apart from the three-volume index to the biographical and obituary notices in the *Gentleman's Magazine*, which broke the Index Society financially, the most ambitious of its productions had been the *Guide to the Literature of Botany* (1881), by Benjamin Daydon Jackson, the Secretary of the

[6] H. B. Wheatley, *How to Form a Library* (1887), p. 213.

Linnaean Society, which was still thought to be worth reprinting in 1964.[7] Dr Wheatley in retrospect very reasonably considered that the aim of the Index Society had probably been too general, and that, had it been confined to history and biography, it might have been more successful.

Local Records

Despite the fact that the Public Record Office had taken over the original functions of the young British Record Society in the 1890s, and made them its own, the Society did not vanish. Instead Phillimore diverted its attention towards material outside the Public Record Office. His interest in provincial records was long-standing. As early as October 1889 he had advocated in *The Times* that something should be done about their preservation, under the supervision of travelling record-inspectors from the Public Record Office. Such travelling record inspectors only came into existence as a result of the 1958 Public Records Act.[8] 'In every county town', he wrote, 'there should be provided a suitable building under the direction of the county council to be styled "The County Record Office" ', and even prepared bills to promote their foundation. The only 'local' record office in existence at that time was that for London at Guildhall. It took over a quarter of a century for Phillimore's ideal to begin to materialise. The first English county record office was started in a small way by Dr G. H. Fowler in Bedfordshire in 1915, shortly after Phillimore's death.

When the Society's printer went bankrupt in 1892, in order to avoid disastrous financial consequences in future it was transformed into a limited company. Phillimore took the opportunity of this incorporation of greatly enlarging the declared aims of the Society from its merely indexing function by adding a clause permitting it 'to take any measures necessary or desirable for the protection or preservation and custody of any records or documents in the nature of records'.

Although Phillimore resigned as General Editor and Secretary in 1893, he remained a member of the Council until his death in 1913, and he continued to edit some of the volumes until 1907, including the special volume in 1897 for Queen Victoria's Diamond Jubilee. This was the complete text of the Coram Rege roll for the Trinity Term, 1297, and is the only volume of the *Index Library* to date which is neither an index nor a calendar. In 1896 he mooted the idea of a Scottish section for the Society which began publishing indexes to Scottish testaments in the following year. In 1898 a totally independent Scottish Record Society came into existence to take over the Scottish Record Series already being published by the British Record Society.[9] He tried the same technique a third time in 1909 when he

7 For a list of the Index Society publications see the second Appendix to this chapter, below pp. 136–7.

8 See below pp. 139–48.

9 The first three volumes of the Scottish Record Society's publications are in fact volumes 16 and 20 of the *Index Library*.

began an Irish Record Series, once again initially as a private venture. He started, of course, with testamentary records, but failed to get his projected Irish Record Society off the ground. In 1897 he founded the Thoroton Society as an historical society to serve his native Nottinghamshire. He attempted, but failed, to found record societies for Gloucestershire, Bristol, and Derbyshire, but in May 1904 he successfully launched the Canterbury and York Society for the publication of medieval episcopal registers, and edited its first volume, the register of Hugh of Wells, bishop of Lincoln, 1209–35.[10] His private enterprise, as Phillimore and Co. Ltd from 1897, in publishing extracts of marriages from parish registers also proved a great success, and he had edited over two hundred volumes before he died at the relatively early age of fifty nine. His continued interest in local records had borne remarkable fruit.[11]

This interest in local records and in local record societies was maintained by Phillimore's successors in running the British Record Society. Of the first fifty volumes of the *Index Library* no fewer than thirteen had been issued by the British Record Society in conjunction with nine different county societies, and many of these, like the initial Scottish Record Society volumes, were the first, or among the first, of the county societies' publications. The wave of interest in record publication that Phillimore tapped had not only brought about the foundation of the Huguenot Society and the Selden Society at a national level at almost the same time as the British Record Society, but also, within a very few years, county record publishing societies in Lancashire and Cheshire, Staffordshire, Yorkshire, Somerset and Worcestershire, in addition to the older Surtees Society which had been publishing 'Northumbrian' records for over fifty years. Most, but not all of these societies were primarily concerned not with producing indexes or calendars, but still, as Sir Frank Stenton was to write of Canon Foster when he launched the Lincoln Record Society in 1911, with 'providing complete texts of important records, presented in the language of their composition, and illustrated by a full apparatus of notes and references'. Phillimore, by contrast, was interested in making the large bulk of less individually significant records more accessible.

All this was, however, record indexing or publication, not record preservation. In the 1920s this was to be remedied by Miss Joan Wake, already the dominant figure in the Northamptonshire Record Society, and Miss Ethel Stokes, who had edited several of the British Record Society's volumes. In 1928, under their initiative the Society began to take the work of record preservation seriously. This had become urgently necessary because, since the Law of Property Acts of 1922 and 1924, and the Land Registration Act of 1925, the preservation of manorial records was no longer a legal necessity and many such documents were in danger of destruction. The Public Record Office had set up a Manorial Documents Committee in 1925, and the Manorial Society had been engaged in listing collections of manorial

10 Dorothy M. Owen and R. L. Storey, 'The Canterbury and York Society', *Archives*, xii (1976), 170–5.

11 See *Who was Who, 1897–1916* for brief biographical details, as supplied by Phillimore himself.

documents since 1906.[12] A few more county record offices had already been founded, and the Master of the Rolls had designated these and a number of other repositories as proper places for the custody of manorial records.

However, Miss Wake and Miss Stokes felt that not enough was being done to see that such records reached the right places. In 1928 the British Record Society began to give advice on where such documents should be deposited. In 1929 the Manorial Society was merged in the British Record Society, and the enlarged Society hired premises for sorting documents and sending them to record offices. In the first full year, 1930, no less than 30,000 documents were sorted and sent to repositories in twenty-eight counties. This work expanded in successive years.

In 1930, 1931 and 1932 the British Record Society held a series of three annual 'Congresses of Record and Allied Societies' concerned with the work of preservation of historical records. As a consequence of the last of these, the British Records Association was formed, to take over the records preservation activities of the British Record Society, which handed over to it, at the beginning of January 1933, the premises it had rented for sorting documents. Dr Wake was to inspire the new Association for a quarter of a century. The lists of manor court rolls in private hands that the Manorial Society began to keep, and which the British Record Society briefly maintained, combined with the lists of the Manorial Documents Committee of the Public Record Office, became the Manorial Register of the Historical Manuscripts Commission and eventually evolved into the National Register of Archives.[13]

Thus the British Record Society in its infancy had, by its very existence, spurred the Public Record Office into the publication of great series of calendars, lists and indexes, and nearly half a century later had been instrumental in setting up an organisation for the sorting and distribution of records for preservation. Although the Society had seen its prime function taken over once again, it was not wound up in the 1930s any more than it had been in the 1890s.

Probate Records

From the 1930s onwards the Society has concentrated almost exclusively on publishing indexes to wills, administrations and probate inventories. Wills and inventories are, in some ways, the most intimate records that individuals leave behind them, and are neglected at their peril by any historians who are at all concerned with people. The Society had already been doing some work in this field from its inception. Phillimore's first choice for a publication outside the Public Record Office fell on the index to wills proved in the court of the Archdeacon of Northampton, between 1510 and 1652. Although it was not the first index to be started,

12 This list was partially published by the Manorial Society, which also published reprints of sixteenth and seventeenth century works on holding manorial courts. For a list of the Manorial Society publications see the third Appendix to this chapter, below p. 137.

13 Oliver D. Harris, 'The drudgery of stamping – a physical history of the Record Preservation Section', *Archives*, xix (1989), 3–17 and see above pp. 111–18.

it was the first for which a complete set of parts was issued. Phillimore's initiative in printing this index to Northamptonshire and Rutland wills was to point the way in which the Society was to develop, because the probate registries, unlike the Public Record Office, were then in no position to publish their own indexes.

Up to 1915, when publication slackened because of the First World War, the Society had produced no less than forty-nine complete volumes, of which just over half were indexes to wills and administrations. Almost all the remainder were indexes to records in the Public Record Office. Between the two World Wars the pace was much slower than it had been before. Only sixteen further volumes were then completed, but the proportion of volumes devoted to probate material was even higher.

Ever since the Society decided to create fresh indexes as well as print existing ones, there has always been an extremely long period of time between the starting of a new index and its final publication.[14] The current indexes of probate material begin with the writing of index slips to each separate document in the order in which it is to be found in the record office. These slips are checked back for accuracy and cross-checked against related documents; original wills against registered wills, for example, or probate inventories against both wills and administrations. Only then can the slips be re-arranged in alphabetical order of testators. When this is done queries arise over possible misreadings of names as well as about how to arrange and cross-reference grossly mis-spelled names so that they can be found by users of the volume. At last the slips can be typed, and, after checking the text and seeing that it conforms to a standard set of abbreviations and conventions, it can be sent to the printer. However, with this sort of work, there is still a long way to eventual publication. Not only are index volumes troublesome for the printer to set and for the proof-reader to correct, but once they have been set and corrected, a fresh group of indexers start work on producing extensive supplementary indexes of occupations and places, including ships as well as hamlets. The 'Place Indexes' in particular demand an extraordinary topographical flair for correct identification.[15]

New printing technology is being used experimentally with volumes at present in the press and it is hoped that these will enable the supplementary indexes to be produced more quickly. However, any indexes produced by machine will still need extensive editing by hand. Without these supplementary indexes the volumes would only be of direct use to biographers and genealogists and of much less value to

[14] In 1935 J. H. Morrison reckoned that the compilation and publication of the volumes of the *Index Library* took eight years or so, *Prerogative Court of Canterbury Wills, Sentences and Probate Acts 1661–1670*, preface. Since Morrison knew that he was about to die when he compiled this index, he published it himself since he could not wait for the British Record Society to publish it.

[15] The labour of producing such supplementary indexes has sometimes daunted editors of individual volumes and the Society has not always been as rigorous as it is now in demanding them. The earliest supplementary index of places was provided by Challenor Smith to his first Prerogative Court of Canterbury will volume in 1893, and the earliest supplementary index of occupations by Ethel Stokes, also to a Prerogative Court of Canterbury will volume, in 1912. However, as late as 1950 the Society allowed a volume to go out with neither a place index nor an occupation index.

social and economic historians, whether local or national. Until the recent surge of interest in family history, local historians probably formed the larger part of the users of the volumes and may indeed still do so. Only when the supplementary indexes have been completed, and the further queries raised in making them resolved, can the volume go to press. There is thus a time-lag of many years between starting on a new project and eventual publication.

Dr Marc Fitch

Marc Fitch originally joined the Council of the British Record Society in 1949 as Honorary Treasurer and remained in this office for ten years. However, it rapidly became clear that he was to be one of the dominating figures in the history of the Society and much more than a mere receiver of subscriptions and balancer of books. In 1956 he became Chairman of the Council in succession to Sir Anthony Wagner, and remained as Chairman until 1967. He was the obvious choice of successor when Harold Ridge, the General Editor, died in 1957. In a Society devoted to publishing the General Editor is the key officer around whom the other officers, Chairman, Secretary and Treasurer, revolve. Marc Fitch characteristically proposed instead that the General Editorship be divided amongst an Editorial Committee, of which he was to form only a part, although, as it transpired, the leading part. Although not called General Editor he actually occupied this position for many years. It was not until 1987 that a new General Editor was appointed.

When Marc Fitch began editing the Society's volumes in 1957 the work of the Society was suffering from the effects of the war and the hard post-war years. But for him, it might well have ceased in the next few years. When he took charge, the Society's printers only had a single index in their hands, that to the wills proved in the Prerogative Court of Canterbury between 1686 and 1693. His first task was to compile the supplementary indexes himself and to see the book through the press. It came out in 1958 as volume 77 of the *Index Library*. Ready-written slips were in hand for only one following index volume, that to the wills proved in the same court, between 1694 and 1700. This appeared in 1960. The publication of even these volumes was only possible because of the generosity of the Pilgrim Trust, from whom Marc Fitch had, as Honorary Treasurer, obtained a handsome grant in 1953. Otherwise there was no work in progress, apart from a project that he had himself introduced to the Society in 1954, long before he became responsible for editing. This was for a complete index to all the wills of the whole complex of probate jurisdictions that covered Essex and part of east Hertfordshire from 1400 to 1858.

In the following year Frederick Emmison, then County Archivist of Essex, joined the Council and slip-writing began. It was natural that when Marc Fitch took over the editorial responsibilities in 1957 that he should choose Emmison as one of his colleagues on the Editorial Committee, along with Guy Strutt and later Russell Muirhead. The Society was very fortunate that Marc Fitch was able to recruit so eminent a topographer as Russell Muirhead to compile many of the 'Indexes of Places'. Marc Fitch recruited Guy Strutt not only for his general advice, but also to compile indexes, those to 'Trades and Occupations'. When Dr Emmison retired from the editorial committee he was replaced by the Sussex archivist, Francis Steer. Dr Fitch later added Jeremy Gibson, a publisher, to the committee and Roy Stephens, a printer. The then Secretary of the Society, Peter Spufford, became a member of the editorial committee in 1975. He gradually came to co-ordinate its activities, and was eventually given the revived title of General Editor for this work.

The three volumes which arose from this Essex project, entitled *Wills at Chelmsford*, appeared in 1958, 1960 and 1969, all under Emmison's personal editorship, and set a new standard of accuracy and usability for this sort of index work. Essex was thus the first county for which an index was published of all the wills before 1858. This has given local historians of that county an inestimable advantage in their work. No county yet has a complete index to all the probate records created before 1858. Cornwall has a complete index to all its wills and administrations, but not to its other probate records. Bedfordshire and Cambridgeshire are likely to be the first counties to have complete indexes to all their probate material.

However, the Essex testamentary project was only the fore-runner of a wide range of work initiated by Marc Fitch. He conceived an overall plan of building on past index work by concentrating for a period of years exclusively on testamentary material, with the intention of producing indexes to all the probate records throughout England before the year 1700.

The Prerogative Court of Canterbury

A great deal had already been done on the most extensive and important series of probate material in the country, that of the Prerogative Court of Canterbury (frequently abbreviated as P.C.C.). This is, of course, the most generally useful of any group of British testamentary records, because the P.C.C. was the supreme probate authority up to 1858. In practice it exercised its jurisdiction whenever called upon to do so by executors or administrators and when a dead man had property in two or more dioceses in the province of Canterbury, which, very approximately, covered all England south of the river Trent and the whole of Wales. In the seventeenth century more than three out of four Englishmen and all Welshmen lived in this area. Executors in the colonies, particularly those in North America, and even in Ireland and occasionally Scotland, also brought business to this court. Therefore most people of any prominence were likely to have their wills proved in the Prerogative Court of Canterbury. Furthermore, between 1653 and 1660, there was a central civil jurisdiction, the Court for Probate, for the proving of wills and granting of letters of administration for the whole country. This was set up in place of the ecclesiastical courts, whose work had ground to a standstill from 1643 onwards during the Civil War and the subsequent abolition of bishops.[16] The records of this

16 Thomas M. Blagg and Josephine Skeate Moir (eds), *Index of Wills proved in the Prerogative Court of Canterbury*, vii, 1653–6 (British Record Society, Index library, liv, 1925), preface; and Christopher Kitching, 'Probate during the Civil War and Interregnum', *Journal of the Society of Archivists*, v (1976), pp. 283–93 and 346–56.

civil court are to be found with those of the Prerogative Court of Canterbury, which was re-established, with the rest of the old system of church courts, after the restoration of the monarchy in 1660.

The two unpublished volumes which Marc Fitch took over from his predecessor completed, when issued, an index (in seventeen volumes) to the wills proved in this court from their beginning in 1383 to 1700. Work on this index had been begun by the Society as long ago as 1893. It was an enormous undertaking and the volumes in this long series have been correspondingly bulky. The largest runs to nearly 900 pages, with between fifty and sixty wills listed on every page.

The letters of administration granted by the probate courts in cases of intestacy form a supplementary series to the wills, although they are of much less historical value. When Marc Fitch took over, eight volumes of index to these administrations had been published, from the earliest surviving ones of 1559, up to 1595, for the critical Commonwealth years 1649–60, and for 1620–30. He decided that, as a first priority, the gaps in this series should be filled, and, as a lower priority, that it should be continued to 1700. Three volumes of index to these administrations, covering the gaps of 1596–1619 and 1631–8, were compiled from scratch under his supervision and came out over his name in 1964, 1967 and 1986. He has since organised the writing of slips for the administrations granted in the P.C.C. during the remainder of the century. These are currently (1988) being edited into a series of volumes by Mr Gervase Hood.

The third principal group of testamentary records of the P.C.C. is formed by the probate inventories that list the moveable goods of those who had died. They were made when executors and administrators applied for probate of wills and administration of property. Social and economic historians had been clamouring for access to these inventories for some years, but they remained inaccessible until arranged and indexed. They were transferred in 1964 from the Principal Probate Registry in Somerset House to the Public Record Office, ahead of the other records of the P.C.C. The British Record Society does not need to index these inventories, since indexes are being compiled in the course of their arrangement, itself a lengthy process. The first of the resulting indexes have already been published by the List and Index Society, and it is to be hoped that it will issue further volumes as they become available.

The fourth group of probate records, of executors' and administrators' accounts, is not very numerous in the P.C.C., and such accounts as there are will be indexed with the accounts from other courts in a single volume covering the whole country.

London Wills

Apart from the wills proved in the P.C.C., the largest group of wills in the country are naturally those relating to London, since one-tenth of the population of England and Wales already lived there by 1700. Most of these are divided into two major divisions, those proved in the Court of the Commissary of the Bishop of London, and those proved in the Court of the Archdeacon of London. The records of both these courts are now in Guildhall Library, London. If any progress was to be made towards achieving his aim of producing a complete index to all the probate records throughout England before 1700, Marc Fitch saw that it was most necessary to start on the London records as rapidly as possible. As well as being strategically right, this also fitted in with his own long-held interests in the history of London. One of his first actions in 1957 was therefore to approach the City of London for help. As a result the Corporation made a generous grant towards the cost of compiling the index. It is a measure of the slowness of publishing in this field that, although slip-writing began in 1960, the first of the four 'volumes' of the index to the Commissary Court wills proved between 1374 and 1700 did not appear until 1969. The second volume appeared in 1974, the third volume in 1985, and the three parts of the fourth volume are at present (1988) in the press. The first two volumes of the Commissary Court of London wills index were published jointly by the Society and the Historical Manuscripts Commission. Meanwhile an index for the period 1363 to 1700, to the other major group of London wills, those proved in the Archdeaconry Court, appeared in two volumes in 1979 and 1985. The Society's London indexers, under Marc Fitch's supervision, have also completed the slip writing of the probate records of the Consistory Court of the Bishop of London, now in the Greater London Record Office, where the costs of their work were partially met by another generous grant, from the Greater London Council. They will appear in the final volume of Marc Fitch's London probate index for the British Record Society with an index to the probate records of the Archdeaconry of Middlesex and the minor London probate courts.

Provincial Wills

A general quickening of tempo in the editorial work quickly became apparent under Dr Fitch's guidance. Not only did he carry forward the P.C.C. index at a faster pace and attack the great mass of London material for the first time, but he also approached archivists in many parts of England to see if they were prepared to emulate Frederick Emmison's example of active co-operation with the Society by producing will indexes on the Essex pattern.

Ten of the Society's most recent publications have been such provincial probate indexes. Four of them have come from Suffolk, two each for the records of the archdeaconry courts of Suffolk (1444–1700, now at the Ipswich Record Office), and of Sudbury (1354–1700, now at the Bury Record Office). Two have come from Oxfordshire, for the records of the Bishop and Archdeacon of Oxford (1516–1732 now at the Oxfordshire Record Office), and one each from Berkshire, Cambridgeshire, Cornwall and Northamptonshire. Volumes approaching publication include further indexes to provincial probate records. At the time of the conference a second set of microfiche, a further index to Lincoln Wills, two volumes of index to Bedfordshire Probate Records were in the press. Coming up rapidly behind these volumes were three more volumes of index to the Cambridgeshire and Isle of Ely probate records, two volumes of index to the probate records at Hertford, and two of index to Surrey probate records. And behind these come three more volumes for which slips are already fully written, and yet more for which slips have partially been written, from Herefordshire, Surrey, Lincoln, Hampshire and Kent, and a third set of microfiche.

I wrote earlier of the problem of the time between the initiation of an index project and the publication of volumes. The long delay has worked in both directions. Volumes have gone on appearing when no new work was being undertaken, and no volumes have been printed when a great deal of work was being done. Volumes, most improbably, continued to appear during the Second World War and during the extremely difficult period after it, although little or no new work could be started. On the other hand, in the 1960s, during a period when Marc Fitch was stirring the Society to great activity, relatively few completed volumes were published. It was not until 1969 that the results of all this work began to become accessible. In Marc Fitch's first twelve years, up to 1969, only six volumes were produced, a slightly slower rate than between the two World Wars, but in the following eighteen years a further fifteen index volumes, a supplementary volume, and a set of microfiche came out, a faster rate than at any time since 1915. In his last two years as General Editor three volumes came out. The real measure of his achievement is that, whereas when he started one volume was in the press and one in preparation, at the moment of handing over to a new General Editor in 1987 shortly before his eightieth birthday, a second set of microfiche was being made and the text of six volumes was being set at one time, four further volumes were virtually ready to go to press, and no less than twelve more volumes were in various stages of preparation, making a total of twenty-three volumes in all, as against two when he began. At no time in the history of the Society has so much work been going on at once. At this point in time it is impossible to assess the impact not only of the twenty three volumes already produced by the society under Marc Fitch's direction, but also of the twenty three, and no doubt more, volumes to be produced because of his work. By the time all these volumes have come out the Society's indexing work will have covered wills, inventories and administrations in the old counties of Bedford, Berkshire, Cambridge, Cornwall, Cumberland, Derby, Devon, Dorset, the Isle of Ely, Gloucester, Hampshire, Hereford, Hertford, Kent, Leicester, Lincoln, London and Middlesex, Northampton, Nottingham, Oxford, Rutland, Shropshire, Somerset, Stafford, East and West Suffolk, Surrey, East and West Sussex, Warwick, Westmoreland, and Worcester.[17]

Neither volumes published in the past, nor those contemplated for the immediate future, apart from those for Cumbria, cover wills proved in the ecclesiastical province of York, largely because of the admirable series of will indexes published in the north of England by such local societies as the Lancashire and Cheshire Record Society and the Yorkshire Archaeological Society. It is now possible to believe that Marc Fitch's aim of producing printed indexes to all wills, inventories and adminis-

[17] For a list of the British Record Society's publications see the appendix to chapter 16, below pp. 181–6.

trations before 1700, whether in the province of Canterbury, or that of York, will be achieved within a reasonable time. A fair indication of the ground already covered and of the ground yet to be traversed is provided by Anthony J. Camp's authoritative, *Wills and their Whereabouts* (4th edition, London, 1974), or by J. S. W. Gibson's more popular brief and up to date *Simplified Guide to Probate Jurisdictions: Where to Look for Wills* (3rd edition, Solihull, 1985). Besides indicating the present custody of the original probate records, these books list the printed indexes to wills, inventories and administrations in the British Isles, whether published by the British Record Society or by any other record society.[18]

It is not clear if, in the long run, the Society will pursue indexes to eighteenth and early nineteenth century probate material, or turn to the production of indexes to documents other than wills, inventories, administrations and probate accounts. Some of the provincial probate indexes that are being created at the moment stop in 1700, whilst others run to 1858, so the 1700 finishing line is already blurred. Furthermore, the Society of Genealogists, under the direction of A. J. Camp, is at present producing an index to P.C.C. wills from the period between 1750 and 1800. However historians of later centuries, apart from family historians, do not seem to have the same interest in probate material as their early modern counterparts. During Marc Fitch's direction of the publishing work only one non-probate index has appeared, that to *Cases in the Court of Arches, 1600–1913*, but there is no reason why the fourth and later stages of the Society's existence should not pursue different lines of activity. Ought the Society to continue indexing other documents of the sixteenth and seventeenth centuries, which is where the whole thrust of its full century of publication has been. If so what? The whole of a hearth tax, if one had survived complete, could be published is only fifty volumes! That would perhaps be a marvellous opportunity for cooperation between a national society and local societies. Perhaps that in itself is the clue to what the Society ought to do. Is its role to do what the Historical Manuscripts Commission did in its Joint Publication Series inaugurated by Dr Roger Ellis in 1959. The highly successful series of co-operative volumes which appeared as a consequence from 1962 onwards came to an end in 1980. Col. Malet had actually suggested that the Society might do this in 1949, although it was the Historical Manuscripts Commission that took up the proposal in the event. But is that what the *Index Library* should do next? Or perhaps it could go back to its very beginning, to Chancery, and index Chancery Exhibits – that most extraordinarily rich of all historians' lucky dips? Before looking at other fields the Society has also to consider whether it has a duty to see that existing probate indexes are kept in print or brought back into print. Many British Record Society volumes are available in Kraus reprints and Chadwyck-Healey microfiche – but ought non-British Record Society volumes of Prerogative Court of Canterbury

[18] The Table, on pp. 178–9 below, summarises the current state of play and emphasises that it is no idle dream to hope for all probate records before 1700 to be indexed in the not too distant future.

indexes be reprinted, in particular those by Morrison and the Matthews for the mid-seventeenth century, of which the British Record Society has had the copyright?[19]

Whereas the first stage was concerned with the indexing of public records and provoked the publication of official indexes to these records, and the second stage was concerned with the preservation of local records and stimulated the formation of the British Records Association, the third stage, associated with Marc Fitch, has assuredly been concerned with the indexing of probate records. The fourth stage has yet to be defined. This definition of the future means that the Society is now at an exciting moment in its development.

12. APPENDIX I

Officers of the British Record Society 1889–1989

It is ironical that a society dedicated to the preservation of records should have preserved its own records so badly that it is no longer possible to establish a complete list of its own officers. The following list is as complete as its records allow.

Presidents

The Earl Beauchamp, first President, elected 1890, d.1891
The Marquess of Bute, 1891, d.1900
Lord Hawkesbury, 1900, became Earl of Liverpool 1905, d.1907
Lord Aldenham, elected 1907, d.1907
Sir Alfred Scott Scott-Gatty, Garter Principal King of Arms, 1907, d.1918
Sir Henry Farnham Burke, Garter Principal King of Arms, 1919, d.1930 (also Chairman of Council)
Lord Hanworth, Master of the Rolls, 1931, Viscount Hanworth 1936, d.1936
Sir Wilfred Greene, Master of the Rolls, 1937–49, Lord Greene 1941, d.1952
Sir Francis Evershed, Master of the Rolls, 1949–62, Lord Evershed 1956, d.1966
Lord Denning, Master of the Rolls, 1962–82, Vice-President since 1982
Sir John Donaldson, Master of the Rolls, since 1982, Lord Donaldson of Lymington 1988

19 Most clearly worth reprinting, although perhaps after rearrangement, is the matter relating to the period from 1630 to 1652 in J. and G. F. Matthew's *Year Books of Probate* for 1630 to 1655, in eight volumes (1903–27); and in J. H. Morrison, *Prerogative Court of Canterbury Wills, Sentences and Probate Acts 1661–1670* (1935); and perhaps also in his *Prerogative Court of Canterbury: Letters of Administration 1620–30* (1935).

Hon. General Editors

William P. W. Phillimore 1887–1893
Leland L. Duncan and G. S. Fry from 1893 jointly
Sidney Madge by 1902
E. A. Fry until 1908
R. H. E. Hill 1908–10
T. M. Blagg 1910–1936
J. F. Ainsworth 1936–1940
C. Harold Ridge 1940–1948 and 1950–1957
J. C. H. le B. Croke 1948–1950
Dr Marc Fitch and an editorial committee 1957–1987
Members of the Editorial Committee 1957–87
Guy Strutt 1957–87; Frederick G. Emmison 1957–69; L. Russell Muirhead 1967–76; Francis Steer 1969–75; Jeremy S. W. Gibson 1975–87; Peter Spufford 1975–87; Roy Stephens 1978–87
Dr Peter Spufford 1987–

Chairmen of Council

Charles Elton, Q.C., M.P., 1889–90
G. E. Cokayne, Norroy King of Arms, 1891–1905
C. H. Athill, Clarenceux King of Arms, 1906–22
Sir Henry Farnham Burke, Garter Principal King of Arms, by 1925–1930
The Revd T. C. Dale by 1934–1937
A. T. Butler, Windsor Herald, 1937–46
A. R. Wagner, Richmond Herald, 1947–56
Marc F. B. Fitch 1956–67
George Squibb Q.C., Norfolk Herald Extraordinary, 1967–86
Dr Peter Spufford 1986–

Honorary Secretaries

William P. W. Phillimore 1889–93
E. A. Fry (Assistant Secretary 1892–3) 1893–1900 and 1902–8
Sidney Madge 1900–2
R. H. E. Hill 1909–14
G. S. Fry 1915–18
Bower Marsh 1918–22
R. M. Glencross 1922–3
A. J. Guimarens 1923–9
(Ethel Stokes, Hon. Secretary, Organizing Committee, 1928–32)
Clarence G. Paget 1929–?46
H. S. Pocock ?1946–1952
Col. H. K. Percy-Smith 1952–60

Dr Peter Spufford 1960–79
(Dr David Palliser, Acting Hon. Secretary 1969–70)
Patric Dickinson, Rouge Dragon Pursuivant 1979–

Honorary Treasurers

Charles Athill, Richmond Herald, 1889–92
Edwin Holthouse, from 1892
G. S. Fry 1897–1919
Arthur Campling 1919–21
H. G. Harrison from 1921
C. G. Paget by 1929–49
Marc F. B. Fitch 1949–59
Richard E. M. Fitch 1959–65
David Bedford Groom 1965–70
Malcolm Kitch 1971–7
Carolyn Busfield 1977–

Centenary Year President, Vice Presidents and Council 1988–9

President: The Master of the Rolls, The Rt Hon. The Lord Donaldson of Lymington, P.C.

Vice Presidents: G.E.Aylmer, M.A., D.Phil., F.B.A., President of the Royal Historical Society; The Rt Hon. The Lord Denning, P.C., formerly President when Master of the Rolls; F.G.Emmison, M.B.E., D.U., F.S.A., F.R.Hist.S.; Marc Fitch, C.B.E., D.Litt., Hon.F.B.A., F.S.A., F.R.Hist.S., formerly Chairman, General Editor and Treasurer; G.H.Martin, C.B.E., M.A., D.Phil., F.S.A., F.R.Hist.S., Keeper of Public Records; G.D.Squibb, L.V.O., Q.C., B.C.L., M.A., F.S.A., F.R.Hist.S., Norfolk Herald Extraordinary, formerly Chairman; Professor F.M.L.Thompson, M.A., D.Phil., F.B.A., F.R.Hist.S., Director of the Institute of Historical Research; Sir Anthony Wagner, K.C.B., K.C.V.O., M.A., D.Litt., F.S.A., F.R.Hist.S., Clarenceux King of Arms, formerly Chairman.

Ordinary Members of the Council: Miss D.M.Barratt, B.A., D.Phil., F.R.Hist.S.; Philip H.Blake; A.J.Camp, B.A.; Miss Stella Colwell, B.A.; Mrs.J.M.Cox, B.A.; Miss Rosemary Dunhill, M.A.; J.S.W.Gibson, F.S.A., F.R.Hist.S.; The Revd. D.Bedford Groom, F.C.A., F.R.S.A.; John Post, M.A., D.Phil.; William Serjeant, B.A., F.R.Hist.S.; Roy Stephens; The Hon. Guy R. Strutt, M.A.; Peter Walne, M.A., F.S.A., F.R.Hist.S.; C.R.Webb, M.A., John Whyman, B.Sc., Ph.D.; Thomas Woodard, L.V.O.

12. APPENDIX II

Publications of the Index Society 1878-90

Rules for obtaining uniformity in the indexes of books. 1878

1. Henry B. Wheatley, *What is an Index?* 1878, 2nd ed., 1879
2. Mabel G. W. Peacock, *Index of the Names of the Royalists whose estates were confiscated during the Commonwealth*, 1879
3. G. Laurence Gomme, *Index of Municipal Offices*, 1879
4. *Report of the First Annual Meeting of the Index Society*, 1879
   with four appendixes:
   (i) A.H.Huth, 'Index to Books, etc., on Marriage between near kin'
   (ii) W.de Gray Birch, 'Index of the Styles and Titles of English Sovereigns'
   (iii) E.Solly, 'Index of Portraits in the *European Magazine*, *London Magazine* and *Times*'
   (iv) 'Index of Obituary Notices for 1878'
5. Edward Solly, F.R.S., *Index of Hereditary Titles of Honour*, 1880, reprinted 1968
6. Perceval Clark, *Index to Trevelyan's Life and Letters of Lord Macaulay*, 1881
7. *Report of the Second Annual Meeting of the Index Society*, 1880
   with three appendixes:
   (i) Robert Bowes and James Douglas, 'Indexes of Portraits in the "British Gallery of Portraits", Jerdan's, Knight's, and Lodge's "Portrait Galleries" '
   (ii) 'Index of Abridgements of Patents'
   (iii) 'Index of Obituary Notices for 1879'
8. Benjamin Daydon Jackson, F.L.S., *Guide to the Literature of Botany*, 1881, reprinted 1964
9. *Index of Obituary Notices for 1880*, 1882
10. Walter Rye, *An Index to Norfolk Topography*, 1881
11. Benjamin Daydon Jackson, F.L.S., *Vegetable Technology: A contribution towards a Bibliography of Economic Botany*, 1882
12. *Index of Obituary Notices for 1881*, 1883
13. Edward Peacock, *Index to English-speaking Students at Leyden*, 1883
14. *Index of Obituary Notices for 1882*, 1884
15. *Index of Biographical and Obituary Notices in the Gentleman's Magazine, 1731–80*

    Part I, A–Gi, ed. R. Henry Farrar, 1886
    Part II, Gi–Mi, ed. Henry B. Wheatley, 1889
    Part III, Mi–Z, ed. E.A.Fry, 1891 (British Record Society)

Occasional Indexes

1. *Engravings in the Proceedings of the Society of Antiquaries*, 1885
2. Henry Ling Roth, *Bibliography and Chronology of Hales Owen*, 1887

12. APPENDIX III

Publications of the Manorial Society 1906–29

1. Alfred L. Hardy (ed.), *List of Manor Court Rolls in Private Hands, Part I*, 1907, 2nd ed. 1913
2. *List of Manor Court Rolls in Private Hands, Part II*, 1908
3. Nathaniel J. Hone (ed.), *A Mannor and Court Baron (Harleian MS 6714)*, 1909
4. *List of Manor Court Rolls in Private Hands, Part III*, 1910
5. Herbert W. Knocker, *The Special Land Tenure Bill of 1911; A Critical Analysis*, 1911
6. William Barlee, *A Concordance of all Written Lawes concerning Lords of Mannors, their Free Tenantes, and Copieholders. 1578*, 1911
7. Herbert W. Knocker, *Kentish Manorial Incidents*, 1912
8. (Jonas Adames), *The Order of keeping a Court Leet and Court Baron*, facsimile of 1650 edition, 1914
9. *The Method of holding a Court Baron with view of Frank Pledge*
10. Charles Calthrope, *The Relation betweene the Lord of a Mannor and the Coppy-Holder His Tenant*, reprint of 1635 edition, 1917
11. E. Margaret Thompson, *A Descriptive Catalogue of Manorial Rolls belonging to Sir H.F.Burke, Part I*, 1922
12. E. Margaret Thompson, *A Descriptive Catalogue of Manorial Rolls belonging to Sir H.F.Burke, Part II*, 1923
13. Herbert W. Knocker, *Manors and the New Acts. The Freehold Tenement*, 1926
14. Herbert W. Knocker, *Manors and the New Acts. The Freehold Tenement. Extinguishment of Incidents*, 1926
15. Herbert W. Knocker, *The Ancient 'Greenways' of Suffolk*, 1928
16. T. F. Hobson, *A Catalogue of Manorial Documents preserved in the Muniment Room of New College, Oxford*, 1929

13. LIAISON: PUBLIC RECORDS HELD IN OTHER RECORD OFFICES

Alexandra Nicol Principal Assistant Keeper of Public Records

It is a great pleasure to be at this conference today and to have the opportunity of addressing you. When I was asked to give this talk I was the Liaison Officer in the Public Record Office with the responsibility for public records held outside the Public Record Office. I have since changed my job and no longer have that responsibility, so I hope you will forgive me if you feel that I am speaking under false pretences.

I shall devote the first part of my talk to discussing records which are held outside the Public Record Office, before moving on to the role of the Liaison Officer. In the Public Records Act 1958 section 4 allows for public records worthy of permanent preservation to be deposited in what is known as a Place of Deposit. Records not considered worthy of permanent preservation in the Public Record Office may be presented to other repositories under section 3(6) of the Public Records Act if they have not yet been transferred to the Public Record Office, and under section 6 if they have been transferred to the Public Record Office and a decision is then taken that they are not really worthy of permanent preservation there. I shall start with those records considered worthy of permanent preservation, i.e. those held under section 4 of the Act.

The reason for the inclusion of this section in the Act arose because of the records of Quarter Sessions, of Magistrates Courts, and of Coroners Courts which are specifically mentioned in section 4(2) of the Act. The Act was based on the recommendations of the Grigg Committee which reported in 1954. Records of the Courts of Law were, however, outside its terms of reference.[1] It was decided, however, that in the Act legal records must be included.

With some legal records there was no difficulty. There was no problem with the records of the Supreme Court of Judicature. These were covered by the Public Record Office Act 1838 and were regularly transferred into the custody of the Master of the Rolls in the Public Record Office.[2] The position of the records of Quarter Sessions and Petty Sessions was, however, more difficult. A memorandum prepared by the Lord Chancellor's Department in 1956 states that 'It appears to

1 Committee on departmental records *Report*, HMSO 1954, Cmd 9163.
2 PRO 54/36 p. 15.

have been generally accepted that the PRO Acts 1838 to 1898 applied to these records' (i.e. the records of Quarter Sessions) 'as destruction schedules have been operated since the 1890s. Records have in no cases been transferred to the PRO but have in numerous instances (without objection by the Master of the Rolls) been deposited in muniment rooms maintained by local authorities.'[3]

A similar situation applied to the records of Petty Sessions. The same memorandum states that 'The application of the PRO Acts appears to have been accepted, as destruction has been carried out under a schedule (provisions of which are repeated in respect of the Metropolitan Magistrates Courts in one of the current schedules of the Home Office). No transfers to the PRO have been made of records of these courts; but steps have been taken in a few counties within recent years, with the approval of the Master of the Rolls, to secure their deposit on loan in the County Council's Muniment Room.'[4]

The view that each of these were public records is based on an opinion expressed in 1877 by Sir George Jessel, then Master of the Rolls. Sir George, giving evidence before the Select Committee on the Public Record Office in 1877 said: 'As I understand the 20th section of the Public Record Act, though the Clerks of the Peace do not seem to know that, the Master of the Rolls has a technical jurisdiction over those records now, because they belong to the Queen. They are all Her Majesty's records, but they are not within the terms of the sections which empower a warrant to be issued, which would bring them into the Public Record Office; but I have no desire to bring more documents into the Public Record Office than are there already.'[5]

The position with regard to Coroners was clearer. Although they kept in their own custody all records except murder cases etc., where the inquisition must be sent to the court of trial or to the director of prosecutions they were seen as traditional officers of the crown and their records were, therefore, subject to the Public Record Office Acts and a schedule was made in 1921 for their records.[6]

It seems that it was not the status of the records but their possible removal from local keeping to the PRO that was the main worry. In one draft of the 1877 Public Record Office Bill there was a clause which related to the transfer of some records of the sessions of the peace from the county to the PRO. This prompted the Clerks of the Peace for Surrey and for Middlesex to appear to give evidence before the Select Committee discussing the Bill, arguing in favour of the records being retained locally, as a result of which the clause was withdrawn.[7]

Similarly the third report of the Royal Commission on Public Records in 1919, discussing local records in particular, for the records of Quarter Sessions and Petty

[3] Ibid. p. 20.
[4] Ibid. p. 22.
[5] PRO 1/137.
[6] PRO 54/36 p. 23.
[7] PRO 1/137.

Sessions recommended their transfer not to the Public Record Office but to a local repository in the locality to which the documents relate.[8]

Nevertheless there was obviously a lack of clarity about the status of these records which it was decided in the middle 1950s must be faced. Although it has been generally accepted that the records of the Courts of Quarter Sessions and Magistrates were public records the draft instructions to Parliamentary Counsel, written later than the Lord Chancellor's Department memoranda, whilst they included Coroners records within the definition of public records, did exclude records of Quarter Sessions and Petty Sessions.[9]

The problem was tackled in 1957. In April a meeting was held with representatives of the Lord Chancellor's Office, the Home Office, and the Ministry of Housing and Local Government with members of the Public Record Office. They had before them a memorandum by the Lord Chancellor's Office. This paper suggested that the Bill should declare the records of Quarter Sessions and Petty Sessions to be public records and it should state what authority was responsible for custody of those records prior to their transfer to a local repository for permanent preservation. The paper also stated that it seemed appropriate that Coroners' records should go to local archives centres as their final destination.[10]

As a result of this the Bill as introduced in the House of Lords on 28 November 1957 included the clause 'if it appears to the Lord Chancellor that a place outside the Public Record Office affords suitable facilities for the safekeeping and preservation of records and their inspection by the public, he may, after consultation with the authority who will be responsible for records deposited in that place, appoint it as a Place of Deposit as respects any class of public records selected for permanent preservation under this Act.'[11] In introducing the Bill the Lord Chancellor did not consider this clause controversial, he referred to it only briefly: 'certain classes of records which have a strong local interest are best preserved locally, and this clause will enable such records to be placed, after consultation with the local interest, in local repositories.'[12]

The clause was welcomed in the House of Commons by Mr Edward du Cann who commented that the clause 'provides for the local storage of records, and that is a very good thing'.[13] However, before the Act was passed there was one important amendment to section 4(1). The Bill provided for a place to be appointed as a Place of Deposit 'after consultation with the authority who will be responsible for the records'. Mr Chuter Ede, the member of Parliament for South Shields and President of the County Councils Association commented on this and on the fact that 'there is no requirement that the authority in whom the building is vested shall consent to it being used. If, after consultation, the Lord Chancellor says "it is a good place and

8 Report of the Royal Commission on Public Records, vol. 3 (part 1) HMSO 1919, Cmd 367, p. 35.
9 PRO 54/36 p. 5.
10 PRO 54/37 pp. 22–4.
11 House of Lords: Bill as Introduced, 28 November 1957.
12 Hansard, House of Lords, Monday 16 December 1957 col. 1152.
13 Hansard, House of Commons, 26 March 1958, cols 518–19.

whether you like it or not, that's where they are going to be", it might be the cause of some difficulty.'[14] As a result of that a government amendment was introduced and instead of a Place of Deposit being so appointed only after consultation with the authority concerned it was changed to 'with the agreement of'.[15]

Following the passing of the Act the clerks of local authorities in England and Wales had their attention drawn to its provisions insofar as they concerned local authorities. They were requested to supply information concerning the records deposited in their repositories or libraries, the accommodation provided, and the facilities for public access. On the basis of the return made to these enquiries over eighty repositories and libraries had been appointed Places of Deposit for public records by the end of 1959. The bulk of the records were those Quarter Sessions, Petty Sessions, Coroners Courts and Courts of Probate for their pre-1858 records.[16]

In his first report the Keeper of Public Records commented on the visits which he and the Deputy Keeper had made to several of the counties of England and Wales to discuss the arrangements made for the safekeeping and inspection of the public records in the county record offices. He observed that they had been much encouraged by the interest and concern shown by the clerks in this matter and the zeal of their archivists.[17]

Since then various other classes of public records have been identified as suitable for deposit under section 4(1) of the Act. NHS records had always been held locally and their position has been regularised with the appointment of many record offices as Places of Deposit for NHS records. The bulk of these records causes some particular difficulties. The administrative records cause less of a problem than clinical records. Anyone who has visited a records store in a hospital will appreciate what we are up against. There is a particular difficulty at the moment with the number of psychiatric hospitals that are closing down. When I took over as Liaison Officer in 1982 I baulked at the prospect of having to cope with NHS records. As I had previously worked in the Medieval Department I thought that one way of getting to grips with it was to have a card index; every hospital in England and Wales would have a card on which details of their records would be entered. However, before I embarked on this I visited the Contemporary Medical Archives Centre at the Wellcome Institute for the History of Medicine as I knew that they had done surveys on the whereabouts of hospital records. As a result the PRO and the Wellcome Institute for the History of Medicine in association with the King's Fund Centre undertook a survey of hospital records held in record offices and in some hospitals and has at the same time gathered together a wealth of other relevant information. This has been fed onto a computer with a specially written program at the Wellcome Institute. One of the advantages of this (and there are many advantages) is that we now know what clinical records are being held, for

14 Ibid. col. 537.

15 Parliamentary Debates, House of Commons, Standing Committee E, Official Report, Public Records Bill (*Lords*) Wednesday 21 May 1958, cols 79–80.

16 First Report of the Keeper of Public Records (for 1959) paras 52–3.

17 Ibid. para. 56.

what kind of hospitals, covering what dates, and in which part of the country. This means that if an archivist is confronted by a hospital closing down it will be easier to take a decision on what clinical records should be saved as it will be known what else survives. This Hospital Records Project is proving extremely successful and I should like to pay tribute to the work of local archivists in undertaking a great deal of work filling in complicated and detailed forms. The response from them was quite fantastic – when the researcher to the project finished work in April she reckoned we had had a 99 per cent return. The project is now being transferred to the PRO where it will be regularly updated. It is not yet available for searching as some forms have still to be fed into the computor but we hope it will be soon.

In addition to hospital records there are other classes of records deposited under s.4(1). There are the pre-vesting date records of colliery undertakings, which are the records of Colliery Companies before the Coal Industry Nationalisation Act of 1946. The PRO now takes in the National Coal Board records. The records of collieries since 1946 are very mundane as things such as policy decisions are no longer taken at that level. There are Territorial and Auxiliary Forces associations records. The eighty-six forces were dissolved on 1 April 1968 and replaced by fourteen new Territorial Auxiliary and Volunteer Reserve associations. Certain of their records, such as signed minutes of associated meetings and correspondence files were transferred to Places of Deposit. So also are HM Customs and Excise Shipping Registers of outports. These are not a record of the movement of ships but registers which constitute a document of title to property and therefore provide full details of dimensions, ownership, and history and ultimate fate of each ship registered in each port in chronological order of registration. Records of Area Rating Assessment Committees are also held locally. These committees were established in 1925 to revise and approve draft valuation lists. These minute books record meetings to examine, approve, and assign valuation lists, and to hear and determine objections from individuals against assessments. The Lord Chancellor mentioned on Monday his responsibility for appointing Justices of the Peace. The Advisory Committees on Justices of the Peace, who advise the Lord Chancellor on who should be appointed as JPs, have recently been in the news as the present Lord Chancellor has decided that their names should no longer be secret, as they had been, but that they should be made known. The records of these advisory committees are also held locally. There is no regular pattern of record keeping amongst these committees and some of their papers, especially as they are remaining in the localities to which they relate, are personally sensitive. Consequently there is a blanket of 75 year closure. However, archivists responsible for them are allowed to authorise access to them at their discretion.

Another important group of public records held under section 4(1) are county court records. It had originally been decided that they should come to the Public Record Office, but recently this decision was reversed, with the agreement of the Advisory Council on Public Records.

I have discussed so far public records held on the whole in local authority record offices. There is also a group of repositories known as specialised repositories. These hold the records of the organisation of which they are part and sometimes other related records. Thus the national museums and galleries whose records are public records have been appointed as Places of Deposit for their own records. Some hospitals hold their own records, as do some military establishments. So does the Post Office. Another specialised repository is the Royal Greenwich Observatory. You may have read that this is being transferred to Cambridge. Arrangements are in hand for the proper housing of the records when this happens.

I said at the beginning that there were held in local record offices not only records considered worthy of permanent preservation but also that presentations had been made of records not considered worthy of permanent preservation in the PRO, but which were of considerable local interest and which local record offices might wish to accept. The exact words of section 3(6) of the Act are 'public records which, following the arrangements made in pursuance of this section, have been rejected as not required for permanent preservation shall be destroyed or, subject, in the case of records for which some person other than the Lord Chancellor is responsible, to the approval of the Lord Chancellor, disposed of in any other way'. This power had first been granted in the Act of 1877. This empowered the Master of the Rolls to dispose of documents of insufficient value to be preserved in the PRO otherwise than by destruction. In accordance with the rules made in 1890 for the administration of the Act such documents might be transferred to the authorities of any library in Great Britain or Ireland and by an Order in Council of 1908 certain colonial office documents could be transferred to the colonial governments which were interested in their contents. The Royal Commission on Public Records in its first report drew attention to this facility and, writing in 1912, commented that only eight transfers had taken place. It was critical of this. If I may quote them: ' It is perhaps to be regretted that no steps should have been taken to ascertain whether such transfers could not have been made in many other cases with advantage to local students. It will be evident from instances given in an appendix to this report [the appendix lists the eight instances of transfers taking place] that the principle of such transfers is fully established. Your commissioners venture to believe that presentations of duplicate records would be gladly accepted by public institutions in every part of the United Kingdom if an appropriate selection were made.'[18]

Henry Maxwell Lyte was Deputy Keeper of Public Records at that time. He was far from happy with those parts of their report. In his own report for 1912 he states 'At the present time it might be premature to offer any comment on the evidence, or even on expressions of the commissioners' views. As, however, their report within the future will be regarded as an authoritative statement of the conditions prevailing in 1912, similar to the reports of 1800 and 1837, which they have frequently consulted in the course of the investigations, it seems desirable to give publicity to the following memoranda calling attention to certain matters of fact as to which they as a body, or a minority of them, have, it is submitted, fallen into error, of course unwittingly.' Maxwell Lyte in his comments on the report was quite outspoken. The commission had included a paragraph about the port books:

[18] First Report of the Royal Commission on Public Records, vol. 1 (part 1) HMSO 1912, p. 19, and appendices pp. 44–5.

Maxwell Lyte says 'the commissioners claim to have made "a discovery" with regard to these documents. They appear to attach considerable importance to the subject, as, in addition to taking oral evidence about it, they mention it several times in their main report and they have printed various reports, letters and memoranda about it, occupying more than six pages in an appendix. Whatever their "discovery" may have been, some of their statements of fact and some of their inferences therefrom are manifestly incorrect.' A little further on he starts a paragraph 'to this it is necessary to give a flat contradiction'.[19]

However, to their criticisms of the few transfers made to public institutions he makes no response. Despite the strictures of the commissioners the PRO does not seem to have altered its policy towards presentation of records. Before the 1958 Act the great majority of records transferred from the Public Record Office were returned to the Department which had originally transferred them to the PRO. On other occasions records were transferred to local repositories, because they had been found not to be public records. For example in 1933 a vestry book for Holbeck in Leeds was transferred to the Town Clerk of Leeds; in 1934 a church warden's account book for Monmouth from 1673 to 1746 was transferred to the representative body of the church in Wales. In 1936 the Prince Regent's papers relating to the trial of Caroline, Princess of Wales, were transferred to the Royal Archives at Windsor again on the grounds that they were not public records. The largest transfer of records before the 1958 Act to another repository was to the Scottish Record Office following the passing of the Public Records (Scotland) Act in 1937. These, however, were records considered worthy of permanent preservation and were transferred under section 4 of that Act.

Since 1959 there has been a steady trickle of records presented to local record offices under sections 3(6) and 6 of the Public Records Act 1958. Some of the presentations have been of large collections of documents, such as the census of distribution maps which were a collection of maps produced for the census of distribution taken in 1971 by the Business Statistics Office at Newport. The maps are large-scale maps of town centres in various parts of England and Wales showing the location of business premises with names and trades of occupiers. Two copies of each map were produced; one was selected for permanent preservation at the PRO and the other was offered under sections 3(6) to local record offices. Another example of a large group of documents being offered were the Charity Commission accounts. Other presentations have been made to particularly relevant authorities. In 1962 surplus aerial photographs relating to Iraq were presented to the Iraqi government. In 1971 gramophone records not required for permanent preservation were presented to the British Institute of Recorded Sound. The majority of the presentations are made to local record offices. If the authority responsible does not want the records that are offered in this way then the records are destroyed.

Few presentations are made under section 6, the great majority being under section 3(6). We rely on the Departmental Record Officers and the Inspecting Officers to identify material for presentation. If in the course of their work review-

[19] 74th Report of the Deputy Keeper of the Public Records (for 1913) pp. 14–15.

ing records for permanent preservation at the PRO they come across something of local interest they alert the Liaison Officer who makes all the arrangements. Records which have been presented cease to be subject to the Public Records Acts. However, the PRO does not lose total control of them. An assurance is required that no disposal of the records to a third party would be made without the concurrence of the Lord Chancellor, and they may be destroyed only with the agreement of the Keeper of Public Records. On the whole presentations are widely welcomed by the recipients. Where disposal schedules exist for records held locally as they do, for example, for Quarter and Petty Sessions records, local archivists often express the view that destruction is recommended for too much material which they think should be preserved. The PRO can take account of this feeling by the use of presentations.

I hope that has given you some idea of the kind of public records held outside the Public Record Office. I shall now turn to the last part of my talk, which is the role of the Liaison Officer. Section 4(1) of the Public Records Act 1958 says that 'if it appears to the Lord Chancellor that a place outside the Public Record Office affords suitable facilities for the safekeeping and preservation of records and their inspection by the public he may, with the agreement of the authority who will be responsible for the records deposited in that place, appoint it as a Place of Deposit as respects any class of public records selected for permanent preservation under this Act'. It is the responsibility of the Liaison Officer to see that these suitable facilities are provided. The Royal Commission on Historical Manuscripts also has an interest in seeing that records are stored properly and made available to the public and the Liaison Officer has always worked closely with colleagues there.

What exactly are 'suitable facilities'? When it comes to 'suitable facilities for the safekeeping and preservation of records' we have a British Standard, *Recommendations for the preservation and exhibition of archival documents* (BS 5454). This goes into detail on a lot of matters, but the four main requirements are the need for security, for good environmental control, and for adequate precautions against fire and flood. The repository should be a solid structure with a heavy door, strong locks and preferably no windows. There should be an intruder alarm. There must be no possibility of unauthorised entry. The main danger is from vandalism. Thefts are more likely from the Search Room. If a vandal thinks that such a secure building must hold valuables and manages to get in, anger at what is found can lead to wanton damage. Secure buildings need not be unattractive. In one converted building the windows were blocked up but the glass on the outside was painted with reflective paint so that the fact that they were blocked up was not apparent.

On environmental controls the British Standard is unequivocal. 'Unsatisfactory environmental conditions have damaged documents more extensively than any other single factor.' It is recommended that the temperature be between 13°C and 18°C with a relative humidity of 55 to 65 per cent. Great stress is laid on the need for both temperature and relative humidity to be constant; sudden fluctuations in either are especially bad for documents. Air movement is also critical. There is a considerable amount of debate at the moment as to whether air-conditioning is the best means of providing proper environmental control. It is expensive, and as we at the PRO know only too well, it can go wrong. On the other hand it can provide a proper stable environment and it has the added advantage of washing the air. Some recent archival buildings are concentrating on a solid structure rather than on air-conditioning. This has proved successful in Germany.[20]

One result of recent tragic fires is that it is now easier to persuade councils of the importance of proper fire precautions. All surfaces surrounding the repository area should have a four hour fire resistance. In one purpose-built repository on more than one floor an architect misinterpreted the meaning of four hours. He provided doors with only two hours' fire resistance. His argument was that if a fire started inside one room it would take two hours to move outside and then another two hours to enter the room upstairs. However, we had to point out that we were protecting the inside of the repository area from any fire that would start outside, and that in this case two and two did not make four. Other precautions against fire include, of course, smoke detectors, fire compartments, and, preferably, an automatic extinguishing system, although not a water-based one. Hand-held extinguishers should also be provided.

Precautions also need to be taken against water getting into the repository. The site is important here: a repository should not be sited where there is any danger of flooding. Any supply of water within the building which houses the repository should be well away from it, and with no possibility of its penetrating the repository area. Flat roofs must be avoided; they are notorious for leaking.

The records are thus kept safely. Suitable facilities must also be provided for their inspection by the public. This means not only that there must be a Search Room but also that lists must be provided. Security in the Search Room is a major consideration, and there must be proper invigilation. A short time ago there was a series of thefts from record offices by a user which has led to new safety precautions being introduced. The popularity of record offices continues to grow and they have become busier and busier. This can make invigilation difficult, but it is essential that there are sufficient numbers of staff manning a Search Room to provide for the security of the documents.

One of the most rewarding aspects of my time as Liaison Officer was to see what practical steps many councils were taking in order to cope with the increased use of their record offices. A considerable number of new record offices, whether purpose built or converted, have been opened or work is going ahead on them. Others are still at the planning stage. One noticeable trend has been the opening of branch offices. This caters for local pride, and when a branch office opens an influx of deposits usually follows. This expansion of record offices has been greatly helped by their users. Perhaps foremost amongst these are genealogists. In the past the relationship between archivist and genealogists has not always, perhaps, been as harmonious as it could have been. The British Records Association a short time ago had as a theme for its Conference the relationship between the two. If there were indeed differences between the two I think that these no longer exist. Genealogists are recognised as important friends (with a large or a small F) of record offices. The

[20] British Standards Institution, *Recommendations for the storage and exhibition of archival documents* (BS 5454) 1977.

Society of Archivists has recently organised courses on marketing. On these courses the importance of targeting has been stressed. Archivists attending these courses have acknowledged the critical importance to them to their users. There may be one or two exceptions, but the vast majority of archivists now recognise that they need those who use their services.

CONTRASTING CONSUMERS

14. A GENEALOGIST'S VIEW OF THE PUBLIC RECORDS – IDEALS AND REALITY

Stella Colwell

My first encounter with the Public Record Office was in the sticky heat of July 1965, when, like countless other genealogists before and after me, I came to examine the Census Returns. Then, it was a matter of securing a seat in the Long Room in Chancery Lane (and in those days you needed to be early or you had to queue), and of trying to find your way through the maze of references to the 1841, 1851, or 1861 Census. I note with interest in the recent HMSO publication, *The Nation's Memory*, a string of similar customers photographed outside the premises eagerly waiting their turn. Nor was it a simple matter to locate addresses, for there was no street index available except for parts of London and a few selected cities. Until you had the box of Returns before you you had no idea whether what you wanted was even there, or was lurking in some other box. A one-and-a-half hour wait for material was the norm. If a mistake was made, a wrong reference for example, then the waiting time was doubled for it to be rectified. The hot sticky heat evolved into the cold sweat of panic and disillusionment – searching the Census in those days was not for the faint-hearted.

Through time I came to enjoy scanning the pages of those volumes, quickly finding the appropriate Enumeration District, folio, and page numbers, and expanding the territory covered to the enumeration districts on either side of where my subject's family lived and learning who and what his neighbours were. Then, horror of horrors, the Census Returns were removed and replaced by microfilm copies when the 1871 Census became available and the whole lot was transported to the Land Registry Building in Portugal Street, together with the Non-Parochial registers. Being naturally cautious, I regularly sent my assistant to use the new-fangled equipment before I had the courage to try it out for myself. The adage that the best way to preserve records was by keeping them from the public was coming true! The room was kitted out with high, unyielding tables, on which were set strange boxes with cards containing detailed instructions and diagrams on how to operate them. Working in close contact with other researchers, gazing into a box and winding a handle, I felt much as early textile-factory workers must have done, as around me genealogists and others struggled to master the system, shiftily glancing at their neighbours to see how the reels should be mounted, and valiantly trying to decipher the cards. The Census overnight became remote, clinical, and curiously inaccessible. No longer could you flit from page to page, turn them backwards and forwards for more information, and thus the personal and intimate involvement with history was lost, at least to me.

Now, acquiring the correct Census microfilm is much more straightforward, provided you have a seat. Ten minutes and the microfilm should be ready for collection. In the Rolls Room in Chancery Lane you can even help yourself to the microfilmed 1841 and 1851 Census, arranged like a row of toys in boxes on the open shelves. Perhaps that is a foretaste of things to come, for the Non-Parochial registers for England and Wales are similarly microfilmed, as are the huge and unwieldy registers of PCC wills. Gone are the days of the Literary Department in the basement of Somerset House, when poor red-faced Mr Cheape staggered backwards and forwards all day long bringing the cumbersome and treacherous metal-clasped volumes of wills from the strong room, and when you were allowed merely to take the briefest of abstracts of the information they held.

And yet, for me, this is technology going mad – the screen is vertical, the reels sometimes so worn away that the handle will not wind them on, the filming rendering some pages so bright as to be illegible, and where the blue pencil of the Superintendent Registrar or Registrar General's Office has been at work, names and ages are almost obliterated, for the camera is unable to discern the nuances of pen and pencil superimposed on each other. Our eyes were brought up to see, to read the horizontal, and have now to be manipulated to match this new technique. I find it difficult to read an upright image, especially on a small screen, glance down, take notes and resume my place in reading all at the same time. With the variety of magnifications you can find yourself winding the frame up and down, and sometimes sideways, without your aid, in your attempts to scrutinise a frame. How many lines of a will, for instance, have my eyes skipped over in recognising repetitive legal jargon, wrongly thinking I had refound my place? A marker line on the screen would help to overcome this problem. My poor eyes are confused and contorted with their constant darting about. Two hours at a microfilm reader and I am exhausted, and if by some error the 'bright light' has been switched on, my eyes are dazzled and temporary nausea ensues. The concentration involved in reading material at such close range and in so confined a space is far greater, I maintain, than in poring over the pages of a book, where eyes can and do frequently look up and away into the distance. If I, with good eyesight, encounter problems, what about people wearing spectacles? As I see it the only people to gain from this exercise are the opticians. Regular breaks are recommended by the manufacturers of the machines – perhaps a notice to this effect would help readers. Then, there are inevitably the reels which somehow contrive to turn themselves inside-out. To a total non-technician this can lead to lots of interesting adventures trying to sort out the problem before seeking help.

The microfilm readers packed closely together on tables not wide enough apart for seats to be comfortably placed, inadequate ventilation, blinds to cut out the sun, and lack of plant life to break the monotony of the surroundings, create a tension all of their own, heightened when the person next to you is noisy, untidy, mobile, and sweaty. There is a photocopying service, but the film may not be suitable for this process and by definition you have to find what you want before it can be photocopied. What else is there to help? There are now some personal name indexes for a limited number of places, but more importantly, since 1979 Jeremy Gibson has been steadily and relentlessly collecting and publishing information on provincial holdings and finding aids to simplify the genealogist's task. The first of these, of local dispositions of the Census Return microfilms, ran to 2,000 copies. It is not surprising that it is now in its fifth edition, as more and more family historians want to know the whereabouts and accessibility of source material and local repositories purchase copies of records held elsewhere. A visit to the County Record Office is therefore now a very real alternative to the PRO, provided that it is geographically closer than London. But in its wake has come increasing demand and shrinking supply of seating facilities and staff. There can never, it seems, be enough room set aside for the voracious record users. What *is* the answer? Perhaps the loan and sale of microfilms of the most popular genealogical sources for private use or study in other centres may be a possibility. With increased leisure-time, earlier retirement, and the growth of school and university projects involving the use of original archives, the problem will not go away.

What do genealogical researchers seek? What *they* want to know is what to look for, where it is, how it will be useful to them, whether it will be indexed or in print, and how best to set about their task. It seems to me that the first three pose no problem for the properly-prepared researcher, but that the last two have been neglected. The sheer volume and scale of many of the genealogical sources in the PRO makes the indexing and publishing of them at present quite uneconomic or time-effective, but technology is advancing at such a pace that I am hopeful that in my lifetime it will be done. The last lies with teachers of genealogy – the setting of a clear standard of research technique and display of results with a more critical analysis of findings among the records. As yet there is no effective guideline, and something perhaps ought to be done now as more and more people tread the path to the PRO and other repositories in pursuit of their own and others' antecedents.

The genealogist's ideal is the centralisation of resources at a convenient place, with flexible opening hours to take cognizance of a 9 – 5 working day, with clear and simple guides to what is there, tacit instructions on how to locate individual categories of document, personal and place-name indexes, finding aids like well-indexed printed calendars or transcripts, subject indexes and publications to explain in more detail the background to, the period covered by, and the actual genealogical content of sources within these groups. We also need guidance on the language, terminology, palaeography, and dating schemes employed in creating them. Of the PRO the genealogist wants all his sources readily to hand, if not all in one building, at least in buildings within a close vicinity to each other, with the records of births, marriages, and deaths, and perhaps probates since 1858 gathered in. Is that too much to hope for, at least at some future time? At the moment the fact that the General Register Office is the only place where you can consult the centralised indexes to life's three main events means fighting the crush for space and a £5 fee for the privilege of a certificate. Since 1984 the indexes have been microfiched: what about microfiches of the lot being made available at the PRO? If records and indexes are made available to the public they should surely be made *available*.

Let us take a closer look at those ideals. Firstly the siting of the PRO – from a genealogist's point of view Chancery Lane is almost ideal, with the nexus of bus and underground networks close by, with banks and food supplies a few minutes' walk away. But the increasing volume of governmental deposits has rendered the sole use of this building impossible, for there is now no room to expand, unless the records are withdrawn elsewhere for storage and all we see are microform copies. Secondly there is the nature of the building – a veritable beehive of interconnecting corridors and cells, yet only four Search Rooms of uneven size and shape, and records kept maybe an hour's journey away from where the searcher sits. Compare it with Kew and its single level storage, its wide gangways, jolly trolleys and chutes to hurtle the crates of boxes and bundles down to their destinations. On a day when the computer terminals have broken down you realise what a difference that system has made to the waiting period for documents. A genealogist using certain categories of legal records may find himself at Kew looking at the Annual Criminal Registers for traces of a miscreant ancestor, and on learning that he appeared before an Assize Court be faced with a trip back to Chancery Lane, some three-quarters of an hour away; and if the discovery is made in the early afternoon, probably it comes too late to do any more searching. A phone call to one of the Search Rooms at Chancery Lane, having located the relevant reference in the duplicate class lists at Kew, may well put in hand the collection and production of the record before the reader arrives back in central London. Then he may find the name of the gaol in which his antecedent languished, and so another journey to Kew is called for.

Before the Kew repository was opened in 1977 readers were given a questionnaire seeking their opinions on an extension of the opening hours to include one or two evenings each week, in addition to the existing Saturday morning service in Chancery Lane. To a professional genealogist wanting to pursue his own historical interests and to the working amateur the Saturday facility was a real boon. Hearts sank when nothing came of the project and the Saturday morning opening ceased. Yet the British Library can offer three nights a week and is open on Saturdays to its readers.

My next point, that there should be clear and simple guides to the contents of the PRO, is in my experience well met in a rudimentary way by the subject indexes to the two volumes of the *Guide to the contents of the PRO*, published in 1963. Like their predecessors edited by Giuseppi in 1923, those are sadly out of print and therefore cannot be referred to at home unless second-hand copies can be purchased. To make up for this mystifying lacuna a growing welter of free leaflets has mushroomed. There are now over one hundred titles and the production line is still at work setting out the background to, content of, and class references of certain groups of record many of which are essential to the genealogist. Yet there is not one on the different handwriting styles and abbreviations employed by the government departments, with an alphabet to help decipher the documents. Instead we have to turn to general Latin glossaries not specifically addressed to the public records. Look at the list of titles, find the leaflet number you want, and either help yourself at Kew, or request it from the Enquiries Room in Chancery Lane. Some leaflets seem to fly away between my visits as they constantly seem to be out of stock. This cannot be of much comfort to a reader with only a limited amount of time to carry out his investigations.

How much time is saved by spending a few minutes reading these leaflets, learning what records would best suit your needs, and to which classes they belong. Indeed, certain groups have been the subject of lengthier studies, such as the probate material, Royal Naval and Army records. The fact that Cox and Padfield's book, *Tracing Your Ancestors in the PRO*, has gone to four printings with a revision to come, shows that the genealogist's thirst for information on the public records remains unquenched. Parties of family historians from evening classes and local societies now stream through the two repositories learning how to find their way round, lectures are regularly given to the public by the staff, and now we have a Family History Desk at Kew to cater for the newcomer's and lost searcher's needs. But how do you locate the class lists, how do you use them, and how do you know whether your required document has been indexed, transcribed, calendared or printed, and where those aids can be found? I remember being able to refer to a drawerful of cards in the Round Room in Chancery Lane which revealed this information at a glance. They were arranged alphabetically by class letters and then chronologically by class number. A recent visit referred me to a non-existent shelf in the fireplace. Constant updating of these cards would prove of immense value to searchers.

I have found in every Record Office I have used different opening hours, different classification systems, different means of reference, different microform systems – those systems are supposed to make the searcher's task easier, yet in some cases I have had to explain the system to the search room staff. Surely there could be some consistency among them all?

My further ideal is for personal and place-name indexes to all the public records. I know in my heart that as things stand this is fantasy. But who could have predicted in the 1950s what a huge difference the International Genealogical Index of parish registers and other vital records listings would have made to the genealogist? It has been compiled and regularly updated from microfilms of original material, indexed and fed into computers. Enterprising genealogists like Charles Bernau, Gerald Fothergill, and George Sherwood and the Genealogical Co-operative of the first decades of the century did not have computers, yet they compiled a myriad of indexes to the public records, for example to the deponents in the Courts of Chancery and the Exchequer. Later on there appeared the typescript indexes of apprentices on whom a levy was imposed, covering the years 1710 until 1774, and of course the PCC wills indexed to 1700, and then from 1750 until 1800, saving much valuable time as well as the wear and tear on the originals, and allowing people to consult them outside the PRO.

Photocopying and borrowing of microfilm copies has made transcription, and word-processing has made the typing-up, very much simpler for the family historian. The indexing could be expanded to take in sources like the Attestation and Discharge Papers of Army personnel with a certain amount of teamwork. Friends of the PRO might care to have an 'Adopt an Index' scheme, whereby funds could be raised for specific indexing projects. However, index compilers need to be trained, need time as well as expertise. I personally have long appreciated the value of the published transcripts and calendars of the early Chancery records such as the Patent, Fine, and Close Rolls. Their excellent general indexes have made the medieval period accessible to the non-Latinate scholar and to the searcher with a limited amount of time. They can be viewed in libraries outside London, so saving time at the PRO. Mostly the records have been translated, but full translations are not always available. The Patent Rolls have not been calendared after 1575, nor the Close Rolls after 1509, yet on the dorse of the latter are hundreds of enrolments of deeds of bargain and sale which by a statute of 1536 had to be recorded in one of the Courts at Westminster or locally with the Clerk of the Peace. The original deeds will in many cases have disappeared, and so this wonderful source of land transactions is all that survives. The Inquisitions Post Mortem, in printed calendar form, grind to a halt in the late fourteenth century, temporarily revive in the reign of Henry VII, and they too would merit a completed series.

Yet the genealogist is tracing his ancestry *back* – many of the above calendars relate to a period when many people had no legal or landed status and did not bear hereditary surnames, so whilst being of historic interest they are usually of little practical value to the family historian unless he wants to know the distribution and occurrence of his surname in place and time. There seems also to be a lack of printed material in the PRO for the Stuart and Georgian periods, an era of growing prosperity and litigation. I still cannot solve the mysteries posed by the confusing array of calendars to the Chancery Proceedings, and the Court of the Exchequer is virtually unknown ground to me, whilst for the Tudor and Stuart dynasties the class lists of Lay Subsidy and Hearth Tax assessments present problems of dating schemes. The Feet of Fines are divided into Regnal Years and Exchequer Terms, albeit by county, but few have been published, let alone indexed. When perhaps over half of freehold land was held in fee tail at this time, can we afford to ignore this source, and the Common Recoveries, similarly arranged? What I should like to see is a thorough survey of these sources, with a detailed explanation of their evolution and history, their content for the genealogist, and an account of how they can be used, with a programme for their calendaring or indexing set in train. There is not one yet, but it would be so worthwhile.

All this may seem unappreciative of the tremendous changes which have taken place since Charles Bernau and his companions set to work. The main emphasis of the readership is now genealogical, and the weeders take note of their requirements from the records when sorting what is to be saved and what destroyed, a policy not followed a few decades ago. Publication of material ought now perhaps to concentrate on this market. The leaflets, the handbooks, and, yes, the dreaded microforms, have all contributed to the greater accessibility of our recorded heritage, together with the photocopying and other reproduction processes. To have ideals is to avoid complacency with what we have. It is the will and determination which need to be harnessed.

Finally, by holding more conferences such as this, perhaps mounted jointly with other academic institutions, we as readers are given a chance to air our views and perhaps help in making many of the above ideals a reality.

15. Records for the Primary School

Joan Blyth

In 1980 I talked to a meeting of the British Records Association at the University of Liverpool on *The Use of Archives in Schools* (for pupils aged five to eighteen). My brief this afternoon is less extensive and therefore can be treated in greater depth. I am now concerned with children aged five to eleven in primary, first and middle schools and their teachers, the majority of whom are not historians.

You cannot be unaware of the Government's desire to provide national guidelines for History as a foundation subject in primary as well as secondary schools. The use of records telling of important events and personalities in British history may become an interesting way of introducing children to national history. A national curriculum does not suggest methods of teaching, only broad topic areas. At present, most primary schools include historical strands in their topic approach, teaching history together with geography and other components of the curriculum. Therefore a topic such as Domesday Book or the Spanish Armada, recently prominent themes well documented in the Public Record Office, could involve children in the use of documents and therefore of record offices. Most primary class teachers have a great advantage over their secondary colleagues, in that they teach one class all the time and can undertake topic work for two or three whole afternoons a week. Therefore, a top class of juniors, aged ten to eleven, can undertake in-depth study of a small area of the past and can produce work of a high standard – a good preparation for GCSE work.

My talk will be divided into four parts:

1. What parts of the past are typically studied in primary schools?
2. Which types of records are suitable?
3. How may those records be used?
4. A look at some examples of such records housed in the Public Record Office and their use with different age-groups.

1. *What parts of the past?*

Topics chosen by primary teachers are usually the outcome of spontaneous decisions leading to visits outside school and to practical activity by children. Five very popular topics are:

(a) *Local history of the near environment* often includes, for example, a visit to a local building or museum. In the nine to eleven age-range, this can involve reading original documents short in length, without transcriptions after about 1700, and with transcriptions between about 1500 and 1700, depending on the calligraphy. Medieval records involving Latin or Anglo-Saxon are not suitable except for glancing.

(b) *Family history and reconstitution* is popular with children as well as adults, though care has to be taken not to probe too deeply into sensitive family situations. The years 1900 to 1988 can be successfully studied through oral history, interviewing older people who often bring records such as letters and diaries into school. Parents often become very interested in this work. Study of one's own family can lead to study of a quite different family in the past.

(c) *Drama and role-play* have become a favourite means whereby children experience the feelings of people in the past. In many cases teachers, drama groups (such as the Young National Trust Theatre), lecturers in institutions of higher education and the advisory staffs of Local Education Authorities have studied original documents and developed work with children based on those documents. For example, lecturers at La Sainte Union College in Southampton, co-operating with an Adviser in Hampshire, worked on the 1566 Court Leet records for Southampton and involved each child, in three classes, playing the role of a person living in a particular street in the city at the time, with a 'real' name and occupation.

(d) As a topic, *The Normans*, including the Conquest and Domesday, lends itself to some use of documents, notably the Bayeux Tapestry (a largely non-verbal record) and the Domesday Book itself, from which teachers can select the relevant extract (in translation) for their own district. The Victoria County History is a particularly useful reference for teachers, and can be found in most large public libraries; Elizabeth Hallam's *The Domesday Project Book* is an excellent guide for work of this kind.

(e) *Victorian and Edwardian Schools* has become a hackneyed topic in some schools, but much good work can be done on log books, inspectors' reports and absence books. This topic is popular as it can involve children in role-playing in class with slates, canes, blackboards, strict discipline and rote-learning, also wearing appropriate apparel.

2. *Which types of records?*

In the context of this paper I mean written records on parchment or paper, such as letters, diaries, posters and advertisements, old books, parish registers, census returns, probate inventories, school log-books, other legal documents, manuscripts (where these include illuminated capitals, there can be additional interest), maps and photographs; even film. Teachers and pupils find them in record offices, libraries, museums, newspaper offices, cupboards in co-operative commercial and other concerns. Sometimes they have been worked up by Local Education Authorities and record offices in published form [e.g. *A Tudor House: Speke Hall and the Norris Family 1500–1700* (1970) and *Some Kent Children 1594–1875* (1972)]. Other more personal records are to be found in the attics and bottom drawers of homes. Teachers should take care not to get so immersed personally in records that children do not 'see the wood for the trees' and fail to understand the broader aspects of what they are studying.

3. *How may these records be used?*

This depends upon the preparation of teachers, the ability and age of the class, and the availability of numbers of documents for classes of between twenty and thirty children. Several Local Education Authorities, for example Liverpool, provide in-service courses for teachers in palaeography, in which they are helped to select suitable documents, read them, and work out appropriate activities for their classes. A service would be rendered to schools if transparencies could be lent or bought for whole-class viewing or group viewing. Knowledge of documents and access to them affects use in the whole five to eleven age-range.

At the infant stage (five to seven), documents in the form of pictures are the most useful. In any case, children just learning to read glean much information from picture reading. Thus illuminated capitals, advertisements, posters, and clear small maps such as the 1611 Speed map of Southampton are invaluable. Young children are always very careful to look after genuine records of the past.

Children of seven to nine are usually able to read clear handwriting in late eighteenth, nineteenth, and twentieth century documents, if they are not too long, the context is explained, and transcriptions are provided.

The most rewarding ages for work of this kind are from nine to eleven, when more able children, already at a stage of mastery in the basic skills, are needing the challenge of new work. Collaborating in pairs or trios, those with patience and determination view a document as they might view a crossword or jigsaw puzzle, while they have less feeling of examination urgency than older pupils. Archive Teaching Units have been found very useful at this stage; the best of these are divided into, say, six topics suitable for six groups. (See Marilyn Palmer's article in the *Journal of the Society of Archivists*). This age-group can cope with clear sixteenth- and seventeenth-century hands with the safety net of transcriptions.

4. *Examples from the Public Record Office*

(a) *For five- to seven-year olds*

The *Fifteenth Century Plan of Chertsey Abbey* comes from a source, perhaps a cartulary, showing a plan of the abbey buildings: most teachers would need to seek a translation of the medieval Latin. As far as I can decipher (with the help of Simon Harrison of Chester Record Office) the top building is the abbot's lodging (villa = house); the one at the bottom is the monastery church; above the monastery is a barn (horreum); to the right are two mills (molendina), one being a water-mill and wheel; the river has a tributary or minor channel (calamus) used as a conduit, and there are woods in each field. After doing some work on this monastery, children could work out what the different buildings were used for, and could then make their own plans, labelling the buildings from English words provided on the blackboard or worksheet.

The *Portrait of Charles II* comes from the Plea Roll of 1673. The capital P surrounds a portrait of the king, as being the first letter of 'Placita coram domino rege' (pleas before the lord king). In this case, both 'placita' and 'domino' are conventionally abbreviated: this would be explained. The portraits are said to become more lifelike as the years pass, but the 1643 and 1660 capitals resemble Charles I and Charles II respectively more closely than in this case. Material of this sort could figure in a study of Royalty starting in the present and developing into the past, including a comparison of modern photographs of the Royal Family with this kind of representation of Stuart monarchs. Children should know that most of his subjects never saw Charles II or knew what he looked like!

Nineteenth-Century Advertisements could well illustrate Victorian life. Using *A Sheffield Dog Show* in 1885, teachers could get children to notice the different types of dogs wearing Victorian costume, and using Victorian furniture. Such questions as 'Do you have a dog and go to dog shows?' should be asked. In the case of *Menotti, a wire cyclist*, children should be asked to compare him with a modern tight-rope walker in a circus. They should notice the town of 1899 in the background, the contact with Europe through a foreigner, and the difference between the advertisement and real life (Menotti could not possibly be balancing on so many wires at the same time!). A *Safety Skirtholder* of 1898 shows two lady cyclists, one using the skirtholder and the other without. Teachers should get children to notice the costume and the bicycle without a bar. What was the danger with no skirtholder? The picture also presents a problem as there is no skirtholder actually to be seen on the safe bicycle or anywhere else! The 1907 advertisement for *Chlorinol Soda Bleaching* is more controversial, as it shows two coloured boys wanting to use the bleach to make them into 'white niggers'. It could be used as part of a topic on Edwardian children and their attitudes towards multi-cultural issues, compared with attitudes today.

(b) *For seven- to nine-year olds*

These children are capable of more than picture reading, but find untidy and/or very early handwriting difficult. John Speed maps and plans from city and county record offices are very manageable.

Second World War Posters give plenty of scope for amusement and activity. For example *Fuel Saving* shows parents and brother chastising the sister for putting too much coal on the fire. A gender lesson could be taught here, as the girl is being blamed for doing all the heavy work! But it does show the strength of patriotism in the 1939–45 war years. It could lead to children making their own humorous posters for today, such as ridiculing people who are late for meals or have the television on too loud and long. *Use Shanks' Pony* was intended to persuade people to walk, and to leave public transport for war purposes. Children can make their own posters against litter in the streets or dogs fouling pavements, or encouraging children to help old people who are neighbours.

A *Seventeenth-Century Mince-Pie Recipe* and its transcription form the basis for a topic on food. 'Six mince pies of an indifferent bignesse' could actually be made and baked at school or at home, using the recipe. This would involve discussion of methods of cooking without electricity or gas or fire ovens.

William Shakespeare's Signature at the end of his will in 1616 could be used in a topic on Tudor life or on Elizabethan and Jacobean drama. Discussion could start from whether this is his genuine signature, as many people signed with a mark, and could bring in the legal importance of a signature today.

(c) *For nine- to eleven-year olds*

As already indicated, this is the best age to use records, as these children can read many documents without help and have more time than in the secondary school.

John Shakespeare's name is mentioned as not attending church because he was in debt (1592). This was William's father. 'It is said that these last nine come not to church for fear of process for debt'. John was one of the nine, and this refers to his position as a recusant, fined for not attending church. It could be used along with the 1616 signature of William in a topic on Tudor life. Recusancy could be explained partially at this age, through such a document.

First World War Diaries were written by officers about the activities of their units and were sent regularly to their commanding officers. They were usually handwritten and some are clear and brief. Captain Cochrane sent one of his in late, in 1916, because of 'strenuous duty in the trenches'. In the same batch of records a typed document recommended the V.C. for Private Miles in 1918 'for conspicuous gallantry and splendid initiative'. Children can transcribe the documents in pairs and then each write their own imaginative account by the soldier concerned. This could be done with the help of the many suitable books and pictures available on the First World War.

From this paper it is clear that archivists can be of great assistance to primary teachers. They can seek out pictorial, short, and legible documents on topics likely to interest children, and can show these documents to teachers. They can provide or lend packs of fifteen copies of one document and information about it. They can issue or lend slides and information about these, as the Public Record Office has done in the case of the slides discussed here. They can respond to teachers' requests for help. They can go into primary schools, or welcome classes of children into record offices for a specific exhibition relevant to the topic being taught, for example William Shakespeare or the Second World War. They can conduct palaeography courses for teachers. Record offices such as those in Essex, Lancashire, and Kent have provided these liaisons with teachers for many years through having a teacher-archivist on their staff. Archivists do well to remember that children aged ten and eleven are about to become secondary pupils and perhaps future historians and archivists, and are capable of reading and understanding documents effectively, with a modicum of help.

Bibliography

Books and Pamphlets

Blyth, J.E., *History in Primary Schools*, Open University Press, 1988 (chapters 3 and 4)
DES, *Archives and Education*, Education Pamplet 54, HMSO, 1968
Dunning, R., *Local Sources for the Young Historian*, Muller, 1973
Emmison, F.G., *How to Read Local Archives, 1550–1700*, Historical Association, H 82, 1967
Hallam, E., *The Domesday Project Book*, Hodder & Stoughton, 1986
Noble, P., *Understanding History*, Help Your Child series, W.H. Smith, 1986
Macdonald, C.K., *Using Evidence*, Blackwell, 1986
Palmer, M. and Batho, G., *The Source Method in History Teaching*, Historical Association, TH 48, 1981
Steel, D. and Taylor, L., *Family History in Schools*, Phillimore, 1973
Stephens, W.B., *Teaching Local History*, Manchester University Press, 1977
Thompson, K.M., *The Use of Archives in Education; A Bibliography*, Society of Archivists, 1982
West, J., *History Here and Now*, Teacher Publishing Company, 1966
Wood, R., *Children 1772–1890*, History at Source, Evans, 1968

Pamphlets published by the Public Record Office

Cocoa and Corsets by Michael Jubb, 1984 (Victorian and Edwardian posters)
Domesday 1086–1986, 1986 (pack)
Mary, Queen of Scots, by Jennifer Baker, Museum pamphlet no. 12, 1981

Royal Portraits from the Plea Rolls: Henry VIII to Charles II by J.D. Miller and Margaret Post, 1974
Shakespeare in the Public Records by David Thomas and Jane Cox
The Armada, in the Public Records by N.A.M. Rodger, 1988
This is Your War by Marion Yass, 1983

Articles

Fines, J., 'Archives in Schools' in *History*, vol. LIII, no. 179, October 1968
Palmer, M., 'Archive Packs for Schools: Some Practical Suggestions' in *Journal of the Society of Archivists*, vol. 6, no. 3, April 1979
Woodhouse, J. and Wilson, V., 'History through Drama: an Enactive Approach to Learning' in *Education 3–13*, vol. 15, no. 3, October 1987

Articles in *Teaching History*

Blyth, J.E., 'Archives and Source Material in the Junior School', no. 1, May 1969
Glendinning, H. and Timmins, G., 'Population History with Juniors', no. 36, June 1983
Mason, I., 'The Records Road Show on Documents in Essex Classrooms', no. 31, October 1981
Rogers, G., 'The Use of Primary Evidence in the Junior School Classroom', no. 38, February 1984
Ross, A., '"Faction and History": Solving some Problems in Primary Children's Understanding of the Past (Kelly's Street Directory)', no. 34, October 1982
Wheeler, S., 'Young Children, Documents and the Locality', no. 3, May 1970

THE PROBATE RECORDS OF THE NATION: NEW APPROACHES TO WILLS, INVENTORIES AND ACCOUNTS

16. 'A PRINTED CATALOGUE OF THE NAMES OF TESTATORS'

Peter Spufford Chairman, The British Record Society

> Of the early wills we do not possess even a printed catalogue of the names of Testators, much more any work which should communicate to the public the choicer portions of the information, topographical, historical, biographical, literary, which is lurking, unseen by every eye, in the dispersed, the dark and dusty depositories of the testamentary evidence of England. I am persuaded, by experience in such enquiries, that there is no department of antiquarian research, topography, public or literary history, lives of our eminent men in every department, manners, language, which would not be essentially benefited by a publication of matter, which to an experienced eye would appear of importance, in Wills of the Plantagenet, Tudor and Stuart reigns, while a better acquaintance with these evidences would be the creation of a new world in our gentilitial Antiquities.

My quotation comes from the Revd Joseph Hunter's preface to the second volume of his work on South Yorkshire published in 1831.[1] Joseph Hunter was one of the most productive and accurate antiquaries of the early nineteenth century.[2] In 1831 he was still a Unitarian minister in Bath, but in 1833 he became a sub-commissioner of the public records and, in 1838, on the foundation of the Public Record Office, he became one of Sir Francis Palgrave's four new assistant keepers of whom he and Sir Henry Cole were the ablest. At almost exactly the same time he was helping to found the Camden Society. His rolling prose will serve both as the brief for these probate essays, and also for much of the work of the British Record Society over the last hundred years.

Joseph Hunter, was not, however, the first to see the advantage of publishing 'matter of importance' from wills. In 1780, three years before Hunter was born, John Nichols, the great Leicester antiquary and publisher of the *Gentleman's Magazine*, had already printed a *Collection of all the wills now known to be extant of the Kings and Queens of England and every branch of the blood royal*. To the best of my knowledge he

1 Joseph Hunter, *South Yorkshire. The History and Topography of the Deanery of Doncaster*, ii (London, 1831).

2 Charles Drury, 'Joseph Hunter, F.S.A.', *Transactions of the Hunter Archaeological Society*, i (Sheffield, 1918), 12–17, and David Crook, 'The Reverend Joseph Hunter and the Public Records', *Transactions of the Hunter Archaeological Society*, xii (Sheffield, 1983), 1–15.

was the first to do so, which should make the him the patron saint not only of the Leicester School of Local Historians, but also of all those who work in 'the dispersed, the dark and dusty depositories of the testamentary evidence of England'. In 1826, the year that John Nichols died, Sir Nicholas Harris Nicolas published *Testamenta Vetusta, being illustrations from Wills, of manners, customs &c as well as of the descents and possessions of many distinguished families*. Even before he left Bath, Joseph Hunter was in correspondence with Nicholas Harris Nicolas, whilst John Nichols' son, J. B. Nichols, and his grandson, J. G. Nichols, were later in close contact with Joseph Hunter and were co-founders with Hunter of the Camden Society.

In part, at least, Joseph Hunter's clarion call for publication was heard almost at once. Three years later, in December 1834, the council of the infant Surtees Society, then a few months old:

> RESOLVED – that four hundred copies of a Selection from unpublished WILLS AND INVENTORIES of all Classes of Persons from the Eleventh Century downwards, illustrating the History, Manners, Language, Statistics, &c., of their respective Periods to be made and transcribed under the superintendance of the Secretary, be printed by the Society.

It came out the next year as the Society's second volume. James Raine the secretary was conscious that he was for the first time printing wills of people of all classes, including husbandmen, fishermen, blacksmiths and parish priests as well as knights and earls. He wrote

> Neither [Sir Nicholas Harris Nicholas] nor Mr. Surtees, nor any other country historian, has even attempted to make the Wills and Inventories of the Middle and lower ranks contribute their share of information to the general stock of historical and social knowledge.

This was responding very strongly indeed to Joseph Hunter's call, and James Raine was equally aware that he was drawing attention for the first time to the enormous value of probate inventories by printing a fascinating selection of them. The Surtees Society has since published no fewer than fourteen further volumes of selections of wills and inventories from northern England.[3] An attempt to emulate this in southern England in 1848 ran into difficulties, because of the obstructive attitude of the officers of the Prerogative Court of Canterbury who, fearing a diminution of their fees thwarted the attempt. It was not until 1863, after secularisation, that the Camden Society was able to produce the proposed volume of wills of eminent persons.[4] The tradition of publishing selections of wills and inventories or abstracts

[3] Six volumes of *Testamenta Eboracensia*, four volumes of *Wills and Inventories from the Registry at Durham*, two volumes of *Wills and Administrations from the Knaresborough Court Rolls*, two volumes of *North Country Wills . . . at Somerset House*, and a single volume of *Wills and Inventories from the Registy of the Archdeaconry of Richmond.* Details of all these are given in A. Hamilton Thompson, *The Surtees Society 1834–1934* (Surtees Society, Durham, 1939).

[4] Charles Johnson, 'The Camden Society', *Transactions of the Royal Historical Society*, 4th ser., xxii (1940), reprinted in R. A. Humphreys, *The Royal Historical Society 1868–1968*

from them is very much alive today. Series of volumes of abstracts of wills from Essex and Suffolk are currently in progress, for example.[5]

However, Joseph Hunter also pointed out 'of the early wills we do not possess even a printed catalogue of the names of Testators'. This call took a little longer to elicit any response. It was not until after the abolition of the ancient ecclesiastical probate jurisdictions in 1858 that anything was done. From the beginning, the new Principal Probate Registry produced printed annual indexes to new grants of probate for consultation both in the Principal Registry and in the forty district registries. It also tried to produce indexes to the ecclesiastical probate records that had been taken over by these civil registries. Sixteen volumes of indexes to wills and administrations of the Prerogative Court of Canterbury were printed, but these only reached back to 1853, whilst only a single index was produced to the testamentary records of any other court, and that was a very tiny one – the court of the Dean and Chapter of Westminster. At the same time Oxford University had an index published to the university wills.[6] In 1864 the scheme of official printed indexes to old material was abandoned. This was not to be wondered at, in view of the scale of the operation involved.

The magnitude of surviving probate records is still a little daunting. Even now it is not yet clear how many probate records do survive. In 1958 and 1961 Dr Emmison produced an index of all the wills then at Chelmsford from the beginning (1400) up to 1720. There were some 41,500 of them, nearly all proved since 1520. The slightly dubious early statistician, Gregory King, deriving his information from Charles Davenant's work on the last Hearth Tax,[7] estimated 35 to 40,000 households in Essex in 1688. In other words there was approximately one will from every Essex household over two centuries. I cannot as yet tell how typical or atypical was the survival of wills in Essex. Historians begin to know that Essex was not always typical. However, if in this regard it was typical, then Gregory King's estimate of 1⅓ million households for the whole kingdom would suggest that we might expect something of the order of 1⅓ million wills of the sixteenth and seventeenth centuries to survive in provincial record offices. On top of this are the wills proved in the Prerogative Court of Canterbury. These have been indexed to 1700, largely

(Royal Historical Society, 1969), pp. 59–60, gives details of the attempt. The volume that eventually resulted was John Gough Nichols and John Bruce (eds), *Wills from Doctors' Commons. A selection from the wills of eminent persons proved in the Prerogative Court of Canterbury, 1495–1695* (Camden Society, Old series, lxxxiii, 1863). In the meanwhile the Society had managed to produce Samuel Tymms (ed.), *Wills and inventories from the registers of the commissary of Bury St. Edmunds's and the archdeacon of Sudbury* (Camden Society, Old Series, xlix, 1850). For the administration of the Prerogative Court of Canterbury in its last years see G. D. Squibb, *Doctors' Commons: a history of the College of Advocates and Doctors of Law* (Oxford, 1977).

5 See below pp. 172–3 nn. 19 and 20.

6 John Griffiths, *An Index to Wills proved in the Court of the Chancellor of the University of Oxford and to such of the records . . . of that Court as relate to matters testamentary* (Oxford, 1862).

7 G. S. Holmes, 'Gregory King and the Social Structure of pre-industrial England', *Transactions of the Royal Historical Society*, 5th ser., xxvii (1977), 41–68.

by the British Record Society, and there are around 280,000 of them. There are also those proved in the Prerogative Court of York. Fifteen volumes of indexes to them, produced by the Yorkshire Archaeological Society in their Record Series, have reached 1688, and suggest that around 150,000 wills from before 1700 survive in the records of the Prerogative Court of York. Would it be too wild to guess that 1¾ million wills altogether have survived from the sixteenth and seventeenth centuries?[8] Most of these wills are represented by two documents, a file copy and a registered copy. If the experience of the Prerogative Courts of Canterbury and York is anything to go by, there was one administration for every two wills, but this too may be atypical.[9] Nevertheless, I would guess that evidence for ¾ million or more grants of administration still exist, making 2½ million wills and administrations in all, with many hundreds of thousands of inventories,[10] and much smaller numbers of guardianship documents and probate accounts. Probably under 30,000 of the latter survive. Nevertheless I think we are talking of something in the order of four to five million documents from before 1700, but I could be wrong by as much as a million documents either way!

It is no wonder that the new probate registries gave up producing 'a printed catalogue of the names of testators'. There were, of course, the calendars maintained

8 Since the conference Mr Motoyasu Takahashi has attempted to produce some exact statistics for wills in early modern England. This has never been done before and his very interesting results appear as chapter 17, 'The number of Wills Proved in the Sixteenth and Seventeenth Centuries', below pp. 187–215. His detailed work suggests that my guess at the numbers of wills surviving from the sixteenth and seventeenth centuries may be rather on the low side. If Mr Takahashi's figures are at all representative they would imply that Essex had fewer will-makers than elsewhere and was atypical in this respect also. See also the paper of Anthony J. Camp, 'The Genealogist's Use of Probate Records', below pp. 287–98, a paper of very wide interest in which, amongst other things, he also discusses the numbers of people making wills, and suggests how the proportion declined during industrialisation.

9 In the Prerogative Court of Canterbury between 1558 and 1660 approximately 178,000 wills were proved and 85,000 letters of administration were granted, according to J. S. W. Gibson, *Wills and Where to Find Them*, (Phillimore for British Record Society, Chichester, 1974), p. 2. whilst in the Prerogative Court of York between 1514 and 1680 approximately 103,000 wills were proved and 51,000 letters of administration were granted. Evidence from the Consistory Courts of Lincoln and Chichester suggests that the proportion of wills to administrations in provincial courts was roughly the same. Around 21,000 wills survive at Lincoln from 1601–52, whilst around 10,500 letters of administration were granted there from 1601–59. Just under 20,000 wills survive at Chichester from 1555–1800, whilst just over 10,000 letters of administration were granted there at the same period. *Index Library*, vols xli, lii, xlix and lxiv. For details of these volumes see Appendix below, pp. 183–4.

10 Mark Overton, 'English Probate Inventories and the Measurement of Agricultural Change' in Ad van der Woude and Anton Schuurman (eds), *Probate Inventories* (A. A. G. Bijdragen, xxiii, Landbouwhogeschool Wageningen, 1980), p. 208 counted 27,440 inventories from Norfolk and Suffolk, excluding those in the Prerogative Court of Canterbury. John S. Moore, 'Probate Inventories: Problems and Prospects', in Philip Riden (ed.), *Probate Records and the Local Community* (Gloucester, 1985), pp. 16–17, guesses at a total of 'well over one million' English and Welsh probate inventories, including some 70,000 Prerogative Court of Canterbury inventories and rather more York ones.

for current reference in the sixteenth and seventeenth centuries themselves, when the wills were newly proved, but, as William Phillimore, founder of the British Record Society, discovered to his cost, many of these were appallingly bad. However, some individual men in individual registries produced fresh manuscript lists of the probate documents in their care.

When in 1881 Frederick Furnivall, the Shakesperian scholar and founder of the Early English Text Society, wanted to print the fifty earliest wills in English from the late fourteenth and early fifteenth centuries, for the Early English Text Society he was guided to these by Challoner Smith, the superintendant of the department for literary enquiry at the Principal Probate Registry, who had 'long since' been making a list, as Furnivall explained, 'in the faith that I, or some grubber of like kind, would turn up and ask where he should go to work'.[11] The British Record Society printed Challoner Smith's 'list' in two volumes in 1893 and 1895. Furnivall had worked his way in vain through twenty-eight boxes of Prerogative Court of Canterbury inventories in the hope of finding these of 'Shakespeare and his fellows' and expressed the wish that Challoner Smith would 'compile and print a Catalog of the Inventories'. It was nearly a hundred years later, in the 1970s, that the List and Index Society was able to print the first volume of the Public Record Office's new 'Catalog of the Inventories'.[12]

Furnival's optimism in the 1880s, hoping for instant catalogues of inventories, was matched by his contemporaries. When Walford Selby and James Greenstreet founded the Pipe Roll Society in 1883 they anticipated that within a very few years they would have put into print every scrap of documentary evidence for English history dating from before 1200. The launching of our *Index Library* in 1887-8 also by Walford Selby, this time with William Phillimore, was intended to produce indexes to all 'the principal English Records' in a relatively short space of time.[13] Another all-embracing plan of the 1880s was G. E. C(ockayne)'s *Complete Peerage*, the first volume of which came out in 1887. 'All' and 'Complete' seemed possible. It was riding the same wave of optimism that enabled the new Deputy Keeper of Public Records, Henry Maxwell Lyte, who was appointed in 1886, to embark on major building works for the Public Record Office and at the same time, to launch out on various grandiose publishing enterprises. These included the List and Index series in 1892 which made the original intention of the *Index Library* redundant almost as soon as it was started. The Selden Society and the Huguenot Society were launched as record publishing societies at a national level at almost the same time as the British Record Society, and within a very few years, county record publishing societies came into existence in Lancashire and Cheshire, Staffordshire, Yorkshire, Somerset and Worcestershire.[14] The *English Historical Review* was launched in 1886, and the Royal Historical Society, released from the rapacious hands of Charles

[11] Frederick J. Furnivall, *The Fifty Earliest English Wills in the Court of Probate, London. 1387–1439* (Early English Text Society, lxxviii, 1882, reprinted 1964), p. ix.

[12] See below p. 174, n. 25.

[13] For Walford Selby see Frederick Boase, *Modern English Biography*, iii (1901, reprinted 1965).

[14] R. H. C. Davis, 'Record Societies in England', *History*, lx (1975), 239–46.

Rogers in 1881, took off in the 1880s. New Fellows elected between 1884 and 1886 included Acton, Maitland, Creighton, Lecky, Seeley and Cunningham.[15] The School of Modern History at Oxford and the Historical Tripos at Cambridge, both creations of the 1870s, were beginning to have an effect in the 1880s. Henry Maxwell Lyte had himself been one of the first to read History at Oxford. The Royal Historical Society ran a conference on historical teaching in schools in 1887. History was the coming subject and record publishing and indexing were all the rage. Henry Wheatley and his new Index Society were promoting indexing almost as a universal panacea for ignorance.

Since the abandonment of official indexing in 1864, the publication of indexes to wills has been very largely in the hands of voluntary societies. Joseph Hunter's plea for a 'printed catalogue of the names of testators' found a more vigorous response from voluntary societies in the north, perhaps not surprisingly since the plea was made in a work on Yorkshire. The first society to produce an *index* to wills was the Record Society of Lancashire and Cheshire in 1879. They had produced no fewer than five volumes of index to the wills at Chester by 1888, when the Yorkshire Archaeological Association produced its first volume of will indexes. These two northern societies have produced more will indexes than any other society except the British Record Society. The first will index in the society's *Index Library* also appeared in monthly parts in the course of 1888. Over the hundred years that have since elapsed, no fewer than seventy two of the British Record Society's publications have been concerned with probate records and the provision of indexes to them.[16]

When I spoke to the British Records Association's Annual Conference, in December 1985, I tried to point up the competition for scarce resources between the publication of indexes and that of abstracts or selections. In this paper I want to emphasise the complementary rather than the competitive aspect of the two activities. Jules de Launay had then just produced abstracts of all the wills for Cranbrook in Kent from before the Civil War,[17] Messrs Brinkworth and Gibson had done the same for Banbury a few years earlier,[18] and Dr Frederick Emmison had already launched into his series of Essex will abstracts from the reign of Elizabeth. By now five volumes of Essex will abstracts are out and seven volumes are yet to come.[19] Since then a series of seventeenth century Suffolk will abstracts edited by Nesta Evans, Marion Allan and Richard Allnut, has also reached publication point.

15 R. A. Humphreys, *The Royal Historical Society 1868–1968* (Royal Historical Society, 1969) and A. Kadish, 'Scholarly exclusiveness and the foundation of the *English Historical Review*', *Historical Research*, lxi, 1988, pp.183–98

16 The Appendix to this chapter, pp. 181–6 below, gives details of these and other British Record Society publications. This shows that in the Society's second half century its publications have been almost exclusively concerned with probate records.

17 Jules de Launay (ed.), *Abstracts of Cranbrook Wills proved in the Diocesan Courts of Canterbury . . . 1396–1640* (Kent Record Collections, Canterbury, 1984).

18 E. R. C. Brinkworth and J. S. W. Gibson, (eds), *Banbury wills and inventories* Part 1 1591–1620 and Part 2 1621–50 (Banbury Historical Society, 1976).

19 F. G. Emmison,*Essex Wills (England)* i, 1558–65 (National Genealogical Society, Special Publication li, Washington D.C., 1982); ii, 1565–71 and iii, 1571–7 (New England

The fourth volume has just appeared,[20] as has another volume of Kent abstracts.[21] The period covered by the East Anglian abstracts, from Essex and Suffolk, has been specifically chosen to pick up stray references to the earliest migrants to New England and their immediate ancestors. This is not only of value to American genealogists, but is important to historians who are interested in the social framework from which migrants came and how it relates to that which they established in their new settlements.

However, the scale of the two sorts of publication, index and abstract, must be very different. The three volumes published by the British Record Society since I then spoke have indexed some 22,000 wills, some 11,000 wills and 19,000 administrations respectively. The Cranbrook volume covered 659 wills, the Archdeaconry of Sudbury volume 894 wills, and the Essex volumes approach a thousand wills each. It is patent that it would never be possible to abstract all the wills in England before 1700. Nevertheless, wills and inventories do make compulsive reading. It is very appealing for local historians to have all the wills of a community now fully in print, as in Cranbrook or Banbury, or those that relate to the parents of the first wave of migrants from East Anglia to the New World. The great advantage is the abundance of extra information given, particularly personal names. The 659 Cranbrook abstracts mention over 6000 personal names. These are often of people with the same surname as the testator, but not always. The eight Hordens mentioned in the 1504 will of Joan Hindle, a Cranbrook widow, would never have been apparent in a simple index entry to Hindle. A tenfold increase in the number of names available by abstraction rather than indexing seems fairly general.[22] The latest Suffolk volume abstracts 894 wills and mentions over 8000 personal names. The volumes of Elizabethan Essex will abstracts each contain up to 1000 wills and mention around ten thousand personal names. Abstracting is obviously desirable not only for genealogists, but also for social historians enquiring into provision for widows, for daughters, and for younger sons, or for historians seeking hints at religious opinions in will dedicatory clauses. However it is totally impracticable on any large scale for lack of manpower and public money. With something in the order of four million probate documents surviving from before 1700 I continue to feel strongly that where there is competition for scarce resources, indexing must still take priority over abstracting as the most useful means of opening up probate documents to family historians as well as to more general historians. In those cases

Historic Genealogical Society, Boston, Mass., 1983 and 1986); iv and v, Archdeaconry Courts, 1577–84 and 1583–92 (Essex Record Office, Chelmsford, 1988 and 1989).

20 Marion Allen, Richard Allnutt and Nesta Evans (eds), *The Wills of the Archdeaconry of Suffolk*, 3 vols, 1629–36 and 1637–40. (New England Historic Genealogical Society, 1986) and 1620–4 (Suffolk Record Society, xxxi, 1989); and Nesta Evans (ed.), *The Wills of the Archdeaconry of Sudbury 1630–35*. (Suffolk Record Society, xxix, 1987).

21 H. C. F. Lansberry (ed.), *Sevenoaks Wills and Inventories in the Reign of Charles II* (Kent Archaeological Society, Kent Records series, Maidstone, 1988)

22 This was still so in the mid-eighteenth century, see Anthony J. Camp, 'The Genealogist's Use of Probate Records', below pp. 289–90.

where full indexes have been published first, in Essex or Suffolk, or at Banbury, for example, abstracts admirably complement and amplify the indexes.[23]

I also feel the same about probate inventories. Probate inventories have also been printed in full, by James Raine the elder in the nineteenth century, and more recently by Frederick Emmison, Francis Steer, Michael Havinden, David Vaisey and others.[24] We now know what to expect of them. In general I do not foresee the value of any further volumes of full transcriptions of inventories from particular localities. On the other hand volumes of full transcriptions of inventories of specific economic or social groups, such as potters or shopkeepers, culled from a wide area, would still be very useful to early modern historians. Otherwise indexes to guide historians, whether economic or social historians, family historians, or even Shakespeare scholars, are surely enough.[25]

23 F. G. Emmison, *Wills at Chelmsford (Essex and East Hertfordshire)*, i, 1400–1619 (British Record Society, Index Library, lxxviii, 1958); M. E. Grimwade, W. R. and R. K. Serjeant, *Index of the Probate Records of the Court of the Archdeacon of Suffolk 1444–1700*, 2 vols (British Record Society, Index Library, xc and xci, 1979 and 1980); M. E. Grimwade, W. R. and R. K. Serjeant, *Index of the Probate Records of the Court of the Archdeacon of Sudbury 1354–1700*, 2 vols (British Record Society, Index Library, xcv and xcvi, 1984); and J. S. W. Gibson, *Index to Wills proved in the Peculiar Court of Banbury* (1959).

24 F. G. Emmison, *Jacobean household inventories, 1606–20* (Bedfordshire Historical Record Society, xx, 1938); F. W. Steer, *Farm and cottage inventories of mid-Essex, 1635–1749* (Essex Record Office Publications, viii, 1950); M. A. Havinden, *Household and farm inventories in Oxfordshire, 1550–90* (Oxford Record Society, xliv, 1965); D. G. Vaisey, *Probate inventories of Lichfield and district, 1568–1680* (Collections for a history of Staffordshire, 4th ser., v, 1969); E. R. C. Brinkworth and J. S. W. Gibson, *Banbury wills and inventories, 1591–1650* (Banbury Historical Society, 1976); J. M. Bestall and D. V. Fowkes, *Chesterfield Wills and Inventories, 1521–1603* (Derbyshire Record Society, i, 1977); J. S. Moore, *The goods and chattels of our forefathers: Frampton Cotterell and district probate inventories, 1539–1804* (1977) and *Clifton and Westbury probate inventories, 1609–1761* (1981); C. B. Phillips and I. H. Smith, *Stockport Probate Records 1578–1619* (Record Society of Lancashire and Cheshire, 1985) and others, for Nottinghamshire (1963), Devon (1966), Worcestershire (1967) and Yorkshire (1972), listed in Mark Overton, *A Bibliography of British Probate Inventories* (Department of Geography, University of Newcastle upon Tyne, 1983).

25 The lead has been given by the List and Index Society, which has been publishing the Public Record Office's lists of inventories: lxxxv P.C.C. *Inventories. Series II (PROB 3)*, part 1, 1702, 1718–82; lxxxvi, P.C.C. *Inventories. Series II (PROB 3)*, part 2, 1734–82, with index to both parts; cxlix, P.C.C. *Paper Inventories (PROB 5) 1661–c.1725* (1978); cciv, P.C.C. *Filed Exhibits with Inventories (PROB 32) 1662–1720* (1984); and ccxxi, P.C.C. *Parchment Inventories Post 1660 (PROB 4/1–6416)* (1988). These volumes list by far the larger part of the available inventories from the Prerogative Court of Canterbury. A few further inventories are to be found listed in clxxiv, P.C.C. *Cause Papers, later series (PROB 37) 1783–1858*. Published lists or indexes are still lacking for PROB 2, Inventories 1417–1660, a relatively small group of 825 documents for which a typescript list and index does exist, the remainder of PROB 4, and PROB 31, Exhibits Main Series 1722–1833, for which a Card Index exists. For details of all these classes see Jane Cox, *Wills, Inventories and Death Duties. The Records of the Prerogative Court of Canterbury and the Estate Duty Office. A Provisional Guide* (Public Record Office, 1988), pp. 25–6. A very few provincial indexes to inventories have also been produced, for example the new index of over 7000 Bristol inventories, E. and S. George, *Guide to the Probate Inventories of the Bristol Deanery*

What have not yet been printed in full are the accounts of administrators and executors, apart from a few scattered examples.[26] I would therefore suggest that we need many more of these in print in full, so that we can realise their value, particularly as a corrective to some of the illusions presented by inventories.[27] Even so, a couple of volumes from different places, possibly Kent and Lincolnshire, should be enough. After that indexes will again be adequate. In view of the fewness of those that have survived, an index to them all should only fill two volumes.

Joseph Hunter's anticipation that there would be 'no department of antiquarian research, topography, public or literary history' that would not benefit from probate material has been amply borne out in recent years.

Five years ago Dr Overton was able to compile a bibliography of probate inventories listing nearly five hundred references to works that published inventories or made use of them for the history of agriculture, industry, retailing, vernacular architecture, material culture or literacy.[28] The importance of inventories for historians and the use already made of them, is indicated by the fact that he could even then find so many works related to them, excluding those that have made use of wills, but not inventories. In that bibliography the name of Professor William Hoskins stands out with sixteen entries. This is not surprising since Dr Joan Thirsk has pointed out that it was William Hoskins 'The Leicestershire farmer in the sixteenth century' that pioneered the use of probate inventories for the study of early modern agriculture as long ago as 1945.[29] Oddly, only four of Dr Thirsk's numerous works appear in the list. This is the more surprising as inventories provided the underpinning for the two early modern volumes of the *Agricultural History of England and Wales* which Dr Thirsk edited. They thus made possible the whole of her influential regional approach to early modern England.[30] However, Dr Havinden's classic study of the introduction of new crops is there,[31] and so are Barry Trinder and Jeff Cox's study of mining, agriculture and shopkeepers on the Shropshire coalfields,[32] and David Hey's work on metalworking, agriculture and trade in

of the Diocese of Bristol 1542–1804 (Bristol Record Society and Bristol and Gloucestershire Archaeological Society, 1988). However, most recent general indexes to probate records naturally include inventories.

26 For example in Brinkworth and Gibson, *Banbury Wills*, nos 256, 265, 283, 289; in Phillips and Smith, *Stockport Probate Records* pp. 93–4 and 96–9; or in Margaret Spufford, *The great reclothing of rural England: petty chapmen and their wares in the seventeenth century* (1984), pp.154–5 and 231–5.

27 See Margaret Spufford, 'The unreliability of probate inventories' in John Chartres and David Hey (eds), *English rural society, 1500–1800. Essays in honour of Joan Thirsk* (Cambridge, 1990).

28 Mark Overton, *A Bibliography of British Probate Inventories* (Department of Geography, University of Newcastle upon Tyne, 1983).

29 *Transactions of the Leicestershire Archaeological Society*, xii (1945), 33–95.

30 Recently summed up in Joan Thirsk, *Agricultural Regions and Agrarian History in England, 1500–1750* (1987).

31 M. A. Havinden, 'Agricultural progress in open-field Oxfordshire', *Agricultural History Review*, ix (1961), 73–83.

32 B. Trinder and J. Cox, *Yeomen and Colliers in Telford . . . 1660–1750* (1980).

South Yorkshire.[33] There was nothing yet of the Norwich Survey's work on housing and lifestyle. In that bibliography only two of the earliest works of Dr Lorna Weatherill were included. As the historian of the early modern pottery industry she has written a great many more since. In this volume she writes about her current major work on changes in consumer behaviour in early modern England, and demonstrates the vital importance of probate inventories for this undertaking.[34] Professor Cole's work on inventories as a means of reassessing wealth is yet to come, as is Mrs Garrard's on change in domestic interiors, systematising our impression of such interiors derived from Francis Steer's collection of inventories.[35] The latter may well be as revealing in its sphere as Dr Havinden's was on the introduction of new crops.

Because of its limitation to inventories, Overton's bibliography underestimated the work of historians who have heavily used wills for their work in social history, as pioneered by my wife with her work on rural society.[36] Only four of her books and articles appear in Overton's list as a consequence – More had already appeared by then, and yet more have come out since, like her work on chapmen.[37]

In words bringing Joseph Hunter up to date she wrote in 1974:

> Wills are the only personal record any individual villager ever left behind him. They are therefore the only source from which his private life can ever be reconstructed. Wills are largely unused by local historians, compared with the almost too well-known probate inventories which should accompany them. They tend to be thought of as the province of the genealogist. However, they provide a mass of information which is not obtainable elsewhere. Quite apart from giving almost the only slender information which exists on the personal religious beliefs of the ordinary man behind the plough, a dying man in his will makes provision for his widow, gives dowries to his daughters, and provides for his sons. In the process, he usually states whether his land is copyhold, freehold or leasehold, and therefore gives much more comprehensive information than, say, a court roll entry, to which a will often acts as a corrective.[38]

Because of the exclusion of wills there was nothing in Overton's bibliography of

33 David G. Hey, *The rural metalworkers of the Sheffield region. A study of rural industry before the Industrial Revolution* (University of Leicester, Department of English Local History, Occasional Papers, 2nd ser., v, 1972).

34 See Lorna Weatherill, 'Probate inventories and Consumer Behaviour in England, 1660–1740', below pp. 251–66 and Lorna Weatherill, *Consumer behaviour and material culture in Britain 1660–1760* (1988).

35 A foretaste of this work is provided by Rachel P. Garrard, 'English probate inventories and their use in studying the significance of the domestic interior, 1570–1700', in van der Woude and Schuurman (eds), *Probate Inventories* (1980), pp. 55–81.

36 Margaret Spufford, *Contrasting Communities* (Cambridge, 1974).

37 Margaret Spufford, *The great reclothing of rural England: petty chapmen and their wares in the seventeenth century* (1984).

38 Spufford, *Contrasting Communities*, p. 56.

Keith Wrightson's work on rural Essex, which had then already appeared, and more recently he has been using probate material in his work on the Durham coalfield.[39]

Because of its limitation to inventories there is also nothing in the Overton bibliography of the argument among historians of popular religion of the weight to be placed on the dedicatory clauses in wills. When Dr Overton's bibliography came out, Professor Dickens and my wife, among others, had already used dedicatory clauses extensively, but there is more work to come from a new generation of younger scholars, like Professor Carlsen and Drs Plumb and Marsh, working on the reformation period, from the Lollards to the Family of Love.[40] Only one item by Professor David Cressy appeared in Overton's bibliography, but he has since used wills extensively to build up seventeenth century kinship networks, from those spreading across the Atlantic from old England to new England.[41]

The last stage in the probate process, the accounting, has so far been the least used. Five years ago, Dr Clare Gittings was the first to use them for her work on funerals.[42] More recently, my wife has used them for her study of petty chapmen. In a later chapter[43] Amy Louise Erickson explains why they are the probate source that is going to be exploited by historians in the next few years as vigorously as inventories have been in the half century since Dr Emmison revived our interest by printing some in 1938, and Professor Hoskins took them up for his work on Leicestershire farming at the end of the Second World War.[44]

But to return to my main theme – how much has been done to produce Joseph Hunter's 'printed catalogue of the names of Testators'. At the British Record Society, during Dr Marc Fitch's editorship of the *Index Library*, we have been attempting to do just that for all periods up to 1700, and, where opportunity presents itself we have not hesitated to go on to the eighteenth and even the nineteenth centuries, with the reservation that we might conserve precious resources by using microfiche for the nineteenth century. During its first half century, the British Record Society did a great many different things, from the indexing of the Public Records to the conservation of local records, as well as the publication of indexes to probate material. However, in its second half century it has concentrated almost

39 Keith Wrightson and David Levine, *Poverty and Piety in an English Village, Terling 1525–1700* (New York, 1979), and Keith Wrightson, *Whickham: The making of an industrial society* (Oxford, forthcoming).

40 I had hoped that my wife would write something for this volume about this new work in progress. Instead she had an idea and suggested to Christopher Marsh that it would be fruitful to search for disputed will cases to assemble a picture, built up from incidental details, of how wills were made. The very interesting results, which overset some received opinions, appear as Christopher W. Marsh, 'In the Name of God? Will-Making and Faith in Early Modern England', below pp. 215–50.

41 David Cressy, *Coming over: migration and communication between England and New England in the seventeenth century* (Cambridge, 1987).

42 Clare Gittings, *Death, Burial and the Individual in Early Modern England* (1984).

43 'An Introduction to Probate Accounts', below pp. 273–86.

44 F. G. Emmison (ed.), 'Jacobean household inventories, 1606–20', *Bedfordshire Historical Record Society*, xx (1938).

TABLE: Probate Records without published Indexes, before 1700 (1988)

PROVINCE OF CANTERBURY

Diocese	*Court*	*Years*	*Current state*
Provincial	P.C.C.	1661–1700	Admons index being edited
	Deaneries of Shoreham and Croydon	1614–1700	Ts index
Canterbury	Consty of Canterbury	1577–1639 1650–1700	slip writing interrupted
	Archdy of Canterbury	1577–1639 1659–1700	slip writing interrupted
Chichester	Archdy of Lewes (2 pecs)	1600–1700	index in ts?
Ely	Consty of Ely (1 pec)	1449–1700	editing in progress
	Kings College, Cambridge	1449–1700	
Hereford	Consty of Hereford (3 pecs)	1500–1700	) Index complete. new
	Dean of Hereford	1660–1700	) document numbers being added before publication
Lichfield	Consty of Lichfield (23 pecs)	1652–1700	
Lincoln	Consty of Lincoln	1660–1700	Wills being set, admons being indexed
	Archdy of Bedford (2 pecs)	1484–1700	Index being set
	Archdy of Buckingham	1483–1700	Modern card index
	Archdy of Huntingdon	1660–1700	
	Archdy of Huntingdon – Hitchin Division	1557–1700	Index being edited
London	Consty of London	1507–1700	Index ready to edit
	Commy of London – London div	1626–1700	In course of publication
	Archdy of Middlesex – Middlesex Division	1608–1700	Index ready to edit
	Archdy of St Albans	1415–1700	Index being edited
	Dean and Chapter of St Pauls	1535–1700	Index ready to edit
	Pec of St Kath by Tower	1545–1700	Index ready to edit
Norwich	Archdy of Norwich	1469–1700	
	Archdy of Norfolk	1603–1700	In course of indexing (Norfolk & Norwich Genealogical Society)
Oxford	Peculiars in Berks, Bucks & Oxon. Some formerly in Sarum, some in Lincoln.		MS index
Peterborough	Consty of Peterborough	1541–1700	
	Archdy of Northampton	1652–1700	Indexing in progress (Northants Rec. Office)
Rochester	Consty of Rochester	1437–1700	) modern card
	Archdy of Rochester	1561–1700	) index

Diocese	Court	Years	Current state
Sarum	Consty of Sarum (25 pecs)	1526–1700	) In course of
	Archdy of Sarum	1528–1700	) indexing (Wilts.
	Archdy of Wilts	1557–1700	) Record Office)
Winchester	Consty & Archdy of Winchester (48 pecs)	1398–1700	In course of indexing
	Archdy of Surrey	1480–1649	Index being edited
		1649–1700	Slip writing started
	Commy of Surrey	1662–1700	Slip writing started
Worcester	Consty of Worcester (11 pecs)	1652–1700	Ts index (part Mormon)
	Ct of Stratford upon Avon	1559–1700	Ts Index
Miscellaneous			
	Ct of Dean of Windsor	1662–1700	
	Ct of Eton College	1457–1666	

The Welsh Dioceses have been intentionally omitted. The National Library of Wales is supposed to be indexing and publishing them.

PROVINCE OF YORK

Diocese	Court	Years	Current state
Provincial	P.C.Y. (c.30 pecs)	1688–1700	Mormon Index (Ts)
Carlisle	Consty of Carlisle (2 pecs)	1564–1700	Indexing in progress
Durham	Consty of Durham	1540–1700	) Mormon index (Ts)
	Pec of Allerton	1666–1700	)
York	Exch. & Chancy of York	1658–1700	
	Archdy of Richmond – Eastern Deaneries (4 pecs)	1474–1700	
	Archdy of Richmond – Eastern Deaneries non-Lancs Wills	1457–1700	
	7 Nottingham pecs (including Southwell)	1520–1700	

exclusively on this field, particularly in the past thirty years under the general editorship of Dr Marc Fitch. Despite its title, the Society has concentrated heavily on the publishing of indexes to *English*, rather than British, records. The Scottish Record Society, which took off from us in 1898, long ago completed the publication of indexes to Scottish testaments. Furthermore we have in practice not only concentrated on England, but on the province of Canterbury. The publishing efforts of our Society have been complemented in the north by the vigour with which the Lancashire and Cheshire Record Society and the Yorkshire Archaeological Society have prosecuted the publication of indexes to their probate material, and in Wales by the efforts of the National Library of Wales to publish indexes to Welsh probate material.[45]

A survey of the field as a whole is provided by the Table on pp. 178–9, which reveals which English probate courts do not yet have indexes to their pre-1700 probate records published either by the British Record Society, the Lancashire and Cheshire Record Society, the Yorkshire Archaeological Society or, indeed, anyone else. We need to ask now what needs to be done to ensure that, when the present flood of volumes have been produced, there are yet more ready to print. The preparation of fresh indexes to early modern probate records is a singularly time consuming business, especially when secondary indexes of places and occupations are also compiled. The British Record Society has commonly found that it takes eight or nine years, and frequently even longer, from the beginning of slip writing to the printed page. Consequently it is necessary to plan ten years ahead. A first glance suggests that in order to tackle the largest concentrations of population first, work at Canterbury ought to be encouraged vigorously, and questions ought to be asked about the Consistory Courts of Lichfield and Durham. However, other options may prove simpler. Indexes currently being prepared, that are still unknown to me, may be finished and offered for publication long before those that I know about. The British Record Society is, of course, not alone in this work. Other societies, like the Norfolk and Norwich Genealogical Society are also publishing probate indexes. The List and Index Society is intermittently producing lists of Prerogative Court of Canterbury probate documents as they are prepared in the Public Record Office. Seven such volumes have come out during the past decade.[46]

As well as looking at the records of particular courts it is essential to pay attention to the needs of the users of such volumes, the successors to those people that Joseph Hunter had in mind. To this end, the British Record Society is considering an index devoted to all the probate accounts throughout the country – a small, but particularly valuable group of documents that has the potential of giving historians many new insights into the seventeenth century.[47]

We must also consider whether any of the sixteenth and seventeenth century works on probate, from Swinburne in the sixteenth to Burn in the eighteenth ought to be reprinted,[48] perhaps by the British Record Society, as an 'extra volume'? There

45 So far the only published index volume is Nia Henson, *Index to the probate records of the Bangor Consistory Court*, i, pre-1700 (National Library of Wales, Probate Indexes, i, Aberystwyth, 1980)

46 See above p. 174 n. 25 for lists of inventories. In addition the List and Index Society has also published clxi P.C.C. *Cause Papers, early series (PROB 28) 1642–1722* For the whole range of Prerogative Court of Canterbury probate records see Cox, *Wills, Inventories*, pp. 46–58, where she lists all the different classes of Prerogative Court probate material now in the Public Record Office.

47 For a fuller consideration of these accounts amd their potential see Amy Louise Erickson's paper, below pp. 273–86.

48 Henry Swinburne, A *brief Treatise of testaments and last wills* (First edition, 1590) was the earliest such work. Swinburne himself augmented it considerably c.1611. He died in 1624, but a third, further augmented edition came out in 1635, and a fourth in 1677, with reprints in between, for example in 1640. A number of less successful works came out at

is also a need for a volume of examples to show what use has been, and can be, made by different sorts of historians using probate documents, together with a glossary and formulary to assist in understanding them. Is this another 'extra volume' for the British Record Society? Ought the British Record Society to lend its patronage, or not, to works using probate material to explore particular historical problems, like the evolution of shop-keeping in early modern England?

But all that is fantasy. At the moment, as Joseph Hunter told us in 1831, we still 'do not possess even a printed catalogue of the names of Testators'.

16. APPENDIX

Complete List of Volumes of the Index Library issued to subscribers 1888–1988

1. NORTHAMPTONSHIRE & RUTLAND WILLS 1510–1652, pp. xvi + 210
2. CHANCERY PROCEEDINGS: Bills and Answers temp. Charles I, Part I (A–D), pp. vi + 265 (See *Guide to the Contents of the Public Record Office*, I, p. 34 also for vols, 5, 6 and 14 below)
3. ROYALIST COMPOSITION PAPERS. Index Nominum. Series I and II (A–F), pp. viii + 84
4. SIGNET BILLS 1584–1624. A key to the Patent Rolls, with lexicographical Index, pp. xvi + 236
5. CHANCERY PROCEEDINGS: Bills and Answers, temp. Charles I, Part II (E–L), pp. iv + 264
6. CHANCERY PROCEEDINGS: Bills and Answers, temp. Charles I, Part III (M–R), pp. iv + 190
7. LICHFIELD WILLS & ADMINISTRATIONS 1510–1652, pp. xii + 687 (Issued jointly with the Shropshire Archaeological Society and the William Salt Archaeological Society. This volume relates to Staffordshire, Shropshire, Derbyshire, Warwickshire and small parts of six other counties)

the end of the seventeenth century and in the early eighteenth century. Dr Dorothy Owen in her Sandars lectures in 1988 (Cambridge, forthcoming) referred to Clark's *Praxis*, which circulated in manuscript before being printed in 1666, to John Godolphin's *Repertorium Canonicum* of 1678, Consett's *Practice of the Spiritual Courts* of 1681, and a work by Horton which appeared in 1738. The new standard work was created by Richard Burn, *Ecclesiastical Law*, (First edition, 1763). New editions appeared in 1767 in four volumes, of which the last was concerned with probate law, and in 1775 and on into the nineteenth century. Perhaps even books, or parts of books, on godly dying like Thomas Becon, *The Sicke Mans Salve* (c.1558–9), as quoted by Christopher Marsh, below pp. 269–11, ought also to be reprinted at the same time.

8. BERKSHIRE WILLS & ADMINISTRATIONS 1508–1652, pp. viii + 199 (Issued with the Oxford Historical Society)
9. GLOUCESTERSHIRE INQUISITIONS POST MORTEM, Vol. I 1–11 Charles I, pp. x + 233
10. PREROGATIVE COURT OF CANTERBURY WILLS, Vol. I 1383–1558 (A–J), pp. xxxvi + 308
11. PREROGATIVE COURT OF CANTERBURY WILLS, Vol. II 1383–1558 (K–Z), pp. vii + 392
12. GLOUCESTERSHIRE WILLS, Vol. I 1451–1650, pp. xvi + 316
13. GLOUCESTERSHIRE INQUISITIONS POST MORTEM, Vol. II 12–20 Charles I, pp. xii + 190
14 CHANCERY PROCEEDINGS: Bills and Answers, temp. Charles I, Part IV (S–Z), pp. viii + 240 (about 50,000 references)
15. LONDON INQUISITIONS POST MORTEM, Vol. 1 1485–1561, pp. viii + 259 (Issued jointly with the London and Middlesex Archaeological Society)
16. COMMISSARIOT OF EDINBURGH. Testaments 1514–1600, pp. iv + 304. Scottish Section
17. BRISTOL CONSISTORY WILLS 1572–1792, with wills in the Great Orphan Books 1379–1674, pp. x + 136
18. PREROGATIVE COURT OF CANTERBURY WILLS, Vol. III 1558–1583, pp. xxvii + 433
19. CORAM REGE ROLL Trinity Term 25 Edward I (1297), pp. xxvii + 315 (not an index but a transcript)
20. COMMISSARIOT OF INVERNESS: Testaments 1630–1800 and COMMISSARIOT OF HAMILTON AND CAMPSIE: Testaments 1564–1800, pp. 32 + 85. Scottish Section
21. GLOUCESTERSHIRE INQUISITIONS POST MORTEM, Vol. III Miscellaneous Charles I, pp. viii + 175
22. DORSET WILLS AND ADMINISTRATIONS 1568–1799, pp. x + 268
23. WILTSHIRE INQUISITIONS POST MORTEM, Vol. I Charles I, pp. viii + 501 (Issued jointly with the Wiltshire Archaeological and Natural History Society)
24. SUSSEX WILLS AT LEWES 1541–1652, pp. xix + 529
25. PREROGATIVE COURT OF CANTERBURY WILLS, Vol. IV 1584–1604, pp. xxiv + 568
26. LONDON INQUISITIONS POST MORTEM, Vol. II 1561–1577, pp. x + 223 (With London and Middlesex Archaeological Society)
27. LEICESTER WILLS 1495–1649, pp. xii + 314 (With Leicestershire Archaeological Society)
28. WILLS AND ADMINISTRATIONS AT LINCOLN, Vol. I. Wills 1320–1660, pp. xvi + 349 (Mainly Lincolnshire and small numbers from eight other counties)
29. CHANCERY PROCEEDINGS, Reynardson's Division, 1649–1714, Vol. I (A–K), pp. xxiii + 259
30. GLOUCESTERSHIRE INQUISITIONS POST MORTEM, Vol. IV 1236–1300, pp. xvi + 241
31. WORCESTER WILLS, Vol. I 1451–1600, pp. viii + 535 (With Worcestershire Historical Society. Covers Worcestershire and half Warwickshire)

32. CHANCERY PROCEEDINGS, Reynardson's Division 1649–1714, Vol. II (L–Z), pp. vi + 238
33. FACULTY OFFICE MARRIAGE LICENCES 1632–1714, pp. iv + 427
34. GLOUCESTERSHIRE WILLS, Vol. II 1600–1800, pp. viii + 448
35. WILLS AND ADMINISTRATIONS EXETER PRINCIPAL REGISTRY 1559–1799 (Devon and Cornwall), WILLS AND ADMINISTRATIONS ARCHDEACONRY OF EXETER (Devon) 1540–1799, pp. xxiv + 878 (Two calendars in one volume)
36. LONDON INQUISITIONS POST MORTEM, Vol. III 1577–1603, pp. ix + xxxiii + 348 (With London and Middlesex Archaeologicl Society)
37. WILTSHIRE INQUISITIONS POST MORTEM, Vol. II Henry III to Edward II, pp. xv + 505 (With Wiltshire Archaeological & Natural History Society)
38. LEICESTERSHIRE MARRIAGE LICENCES 1570–1729, pp. vii + 542
39. WORCESTER WILLS, Vol. II 1601–1652 (With Worcestershire Historical Society. Covers Worcestershire and half Warwickshire)
40. GLOUCESTERSHIRE INQUISITIONS POST MORTEM, Vol. V 1302–1358, pp. ix + 375
41. WILLS & ADMINISTRATIONS AT LINCOLN, Vol. II Wills 1601–1652, pp. viii + 234
42. HUNTINGDONSHIRE WILLS 1479–1652, pp. xii + 222
43. PREROGATIVE COURT OF CANTERBURY WILLS, Vol. V 1605–19, pp. vii + 611
44. PREROGATIVE COURT OF CANTERBURY WILLS, Vol. VI 1620–29, pp. viii + 395
45. TAUNTON ARCHDEACONRY WILLS 1537–1799, pp. vi + 437
46. EXETER CONSISTORY WILLS AND ADMINISTRATIONS 1532–1800 (Devon and Cornwall), pp. vi + 324 (With Devonshire Association)
47. GLOUCESTERSHIRE INQUISITIONS POST MORTEM, Vol. VI 1359–1413, pp. x + 266
48. WILTSHIRE INQUISITIONS POST MORTEM, Vol. III Edward III, pp. vi + 461 (With Wiltshire Archaeological and Natural History Society)
49. CHICHESTER CONSISTORY WILLS 1482–1800, pp. viii + 415
50. WILLS AND ADMINISTRATIONS AT CANTERBURY 1396–1558 and 1640–50, pp. viii + 603 (With Kent Archaeological Society Record Series)
51. WILLS AND ADMINISTRATIONS AT LEICESTER 1660–1750, pp. viii + 391
52. WILLS AND ADMINISTRATIONS AT LINCOLN, Vol. III Administrations 1540–1659, pp. xxii + 410 (With Lincoln Record Society)
53. DORSET WILLS AND ADMINISTRATIONS, Vol. II, pp. viii + 184, TAUNTON ADMINISTRATIONS, pp. viii + 130 (Together)
54. PREROGATIVE COURT OF CANTERBURY WILLS, Vol. VII 1653–1656, pp. xx + 786
55. ACT BOOKS OF THE ARCHBISHOPS OF CANTERBURY 1663–1859, Part I (A–K), pp. iv + 587
56. CORNWALL ARCHDEACONRY WILLS AND ADMINISTRATIONS, Vol. I 1569–1699, pp. vi + 373
57. WILLS AND ADMINISTRATIONS AT LINCOLN, Vol. IV Archdeaconry of Stow etd, p. xvi + 501
58. NOTTINGHAMSHIRE MARRIAGE LICENCES, Vol. I Archdeacon's Court 1577–1700; Peculiar of Southwell 1588–1754, pp. xvi + 696

59. CORNWALL ARCHDEACONRY WILLS AND ADMINISTRATIONS, Vol. II 1700–1799, pp. vi + 243
60. NOTTINGHAMSHIRE MARRIAGE LICENCES, Vol. II Archdeacon's Court 1701–1753; Peculiar of Southwell 1755–1853, pp. xii + 751
61. PREROGATIVE COURT OF CANTERBURY WILLS, Vol. III 1657–1660, pp. xvi + 891
62. LONDON MARRIAGE LICENCES, Vol. I 1597–1648, pp. vii + 436
63. ACT BOOKS OF THE ARCHBISHOPS OF CANTERBURY 1663–1859, Part II (L–Z), pp. 612
64. CHICHESTER CONSISTORY ADMINISTRATIONS 1555–1800 (and two Peculiars), pp. xii + 269
65. WILLS AND ADMINISTRATIONS AT CANTERBURY 1558–1577 (and administrations 1539–45), pp. viii + 149
66. LONDON MARRIAGE LICENCES, Vol. II 1660–1700, pp. vi + 214
67. PREROGATIVE COURT OF CANTERBURY WILLS, Vol. IX 1671–1675, pp. xii + 292
68. PREROGATIVE COURT OF CANTERBURY ADMINISTRATIONS, Vol. I 1649–1654, pp. xiv + 503
69. WILLS IN THE CONSISTORY COURT OF NORWICH, Vol. I 1370–1550, pp. xiv + 423 (With Norfolk Record Society)
70. NORTHAMPTONSHIRE ADMINISTRATIONS 1677–1710, pp. vii + 255
71. PREROGATIVE COURT OF CANTERBURY WILLS, Vol. X 1676–1685, pp. x + 481
72. PREROGATIVE COURT OF CANTERBURY ADMINISTRATIONS, Vol. II 1655–1660, Part I (A–F), pp. viii + 153
73. WILLS IN THE CONSISTORY COURT OF NORWICH, Vol. II 1550–1603, pp. vi + 188 (With Norfolk Record Society)
74. PREROGATIVE COURT OF CANTERBURY ADMINISTRATIONS, Vol. II 1655–1660, Part II (G–Q), pp. vi + 175
75. PREROGATIVE COURT OF CANTERBURY ADMINISTRATIONS, Vol. II 1655–1660, Part III (R–Z), pp.128
76. PREROGATIVE COURT OF CANTERBURY ADMINISTRATIONS, Vol. III 1581–1595, p.173
77. PREROGATIVE COURT OF CANTERBURY WILLS, Vol. XI 1686–1693, pp. vi + 407
78. WILLS AT CHELMSFORD, Vol. I 1400–1619, pp. viii + 509
79. WILLS AT CHELMSFORD, Vol. II 1620–1720, pp. viii
80. PREROGATIVE COURT OF CANTERBURY WILLS, Vol. XII 1694–1700, pp. viii + 556
81. PREROGATIVE COURT OF CANTEBURY ADMINISTRATIONS, Vol. IV 1596–1608, pp. ix + 187
82. COMMISSARY COURT OF LONDON WILLS, Vol. I 1374–1488, pp. xv + 239 (Joint volume with Historical Manuscripts Commission)
83. PREROGATIVE COURT OF CANTERBURY ADMINISTRATIONS, Vol. V 1609–1619, pp. viii + 192
84. WILLS AT CHELMSFORD, Vol. III 1721–1858, pp. viii + 405
85 CASES IN THE COURT OF ARCHES 1660–1913, pp. viii + 624

86. TESTAMENTARY RECORDS IN THE COMMISSARY COURT OF LONDON, Vol. II 1489–1570, pp. xvi + 340 (Joint volume with Historical Manuscripts Commission)
87. BERKSHIRE PROBATE RECORDS 1653–1710, pp. x + 174
88. ARCHDEACONRY OF ELY PROBATE RECORDS 1513–1857, pp. xii + 228
89. ARCHDEACONRY COURT OF LONDON PROBATE RECORDS, Vol. I 1363–1649, pp. xx + 476 (ISBN 0–901505–05–6)
90. ARCHDEACONRY COURT OF SUFFOLK PROBATE RECORDS AT IPSWICH 1444–1700, Vol. I (A–K), pp. viii + 319 (ISBN 0–901505–06–4)
91. ARCHDEACONRY COURT OF SUFFOLK PROBATE RECORDS AT IPSWICH 1444–1700, Vol. II (L–Z), pp. vi + 321–617 (ISBN 0–901505–07–2)
92. NORTHAMPTONSHIRE ADMINISTRATIONS, from 1710, pp. x + 158 (ISBN 0–901505–08–0)
93. PROBATE RECORDS OF BISHOP AND ARCHDEACON OF OXFORD 1516–1732, Vol. I (A–K), pp. xiii + 337 (ISBN 0–901505–09–9)
94. PROBATE RECORDS OF BISHOP AND ARCHDEACON OF OXFORD 1516–1732, Vol. II (L–Z), pp. x + 338–651 (ISBN 0–901505–15–13)
95. PROBATE RECORDS OF THE COURT OF THE ARCHDEACON OF SUDBURY 1354–1700, Vol. I (A–K), pp. viii + 330 (ISBN 0–901505–13–7)
96. PROBATE RECORDS OF THE COURT OF THE ARCHDEACON OF SUDBURY 1354–1700, Vol. II (L–Z), pp. vi + 331–667 (ISBN 0–901505–14–5)
97. TESTAMENTARY RECORDS IN THE COMMISSARY COURT OF LONDON, Vol. III 1571–1625, ed. Marc Fitch, pp. xiv + 527 (ISBN 0–901505–11–0)
98. TESTAMENTARY RECORDS IN THE ARCHDEACONRY COURT OF LONDON, Vol. II 1661–1700, ed. Marc Fitch with TESTAMENTARY RECORDS OF THE DEANERY OF ARCHES 1620–1845, ed. Janet Foster, pp. xxiv + 284 (ISBN 0–901505–17–X)
100. PREROGATIVE COURT OF CANTERBURY ADMINISTRATIONS, Vol. VI 1631–1648, ed. Marc Fitch, pp. xii + 572 (ISBN 0–901505–18–8)

Forthcoming:

Lincoln V. Consistory Court Wills (1660–1700)
Bedfordshire Probate Records (1480–1858), 2 volumes
Commissary Court of London Probate Records IV (1626–1700), 3 parts
Consistory Court of Ely Probate Records (1449–1858), 3 volumes
Probate Records at Hertford, 2 volumes
Prerogative Court of Canterbury Administrations VII (1661–1700), 3 parts
Archdeaconry Court of Surrey Probate Records (1480–1649), 2 volumes
Consistory Courts of Dean and Bishop of Hereford Probate Records (c.1480/90–1700)
Lincoln VI. Consistory Court Administrations (1660–1700)
Winchester Wills (1305–1700)
Surrey Archdeaconry and Commissary Courts (1660–1751)
Archdeaconry and Consistory Courts of Canterbury (1577–1639)
Probate Accounts

MICROFICHE SERIES (Supplementary Series)

MS 1 CORNISH PROBATE RECORDS AT CORNWALL RECORD OFFICE 1800–1857, ed. Brenda L. Hull, pp. iv + 380, on four fiche (ISBN 0–901505–10–2)

MS 2 HEREFORD PROBATES ADMINISTRATIONS AND WILLS 1407–1581, ed. M. A. Faraday and E. J. L. Cole, pp. xxxii + 628 on seven fiche (ISBN 0–901505–24–2)

EXTRA VOLUMES

EV 1 J. S. W. Gibson, *Wills and Where to Find Them*, Phillimore for the British Record Society, 1974

Subjects covered by volumes

ENGLISH NATIONAL RECORDS: Archbishop of Canterbury Act Books vols. 55, 63; Chancery Proceedings 2, 5, 6, 14, 29, 32; Coram Rege Roll 19; Court of Arches 85, 98; Faculty Office Marriage Licences 33; Prerogative Court of Canterbury Wills and Administrations 10, 11, 18, 25, 43, 44, 54, 61, 67, 68, 71, 72, 74, 75, 76, 77, 80, 81, 83, 100 and forthcoming; Royalist Composition Papers 3; Signet Bills 4.

ENGLISH LOCAL RECORDS

(General): Probate Accounts forthcoming;

(by old Counties): Bedfordshire forthcoming; Berkshire 8, 87; Bristol 17; Cambridgeshire 88 and forthcoming Cornwall 35, 46, 56, 59 and MS1; Derbyshire 7, Devon 35, 46; Dorset 22, 53; Isle of Ely 88 and forthcoming; Essex 78, 79, 84; Gloucestershire 9, 12, 13, 17 (Bristol), 21, 30, 34, 40, 47; Hampshire forthcoming; Herefordshire MS 2 and forthcoming; Hertfordshire forthcoming; Huntingdonshire 42; Kent 50, 65 and forthcoming; Leicestershire 27, 38, 51; Lincolnshire 28, 41, 52, 57 and forthcoming; London and Middlesex 15, 26, 36, 62, 66, 82, 86, 89, 97, 98 and forthcoming; Norfolk 69, 73; Northamptonshire 1, 70, 92; Nottinghamshire 58, 60; Oxfordshire 93, 94; Rutland 1; Shropshire 7; Somerset 45, 53; Staffordshire 7; Suffolk 90, 91, 95, 96; Surrey forthcoming; Sussex 24, 49, 64; Warwickshire 7, 31, 39; Wiltshire 23, 37, 48; Worcester 31, 39.

SCOTTISH RECORDS: 16, 20

Fuller details of the Society's publications are to be found in E. L. C. Mullins, *Texts and Calendars. An Analytical Guide to Serial Publications*, I (to 1956) & II (1957–82) (Royal Historical Society, 1958 and 1983) and of the probate records themselves in A.J. Camp, *Wills and their Whereabouts* (4th edition, London, 1974), and J. S. W. Gibson *Simplified Guide to Probate Jurisdictions: Where to Look for Wills* (3rd edition, Solihull, 1985).

17. THE NUMBER OF WILLS PROVED IN THE SIXTEENTH AND SEVENTEENTH CENTURIES. GRAPHS, WITH TABLES AND COMMENTARY[1]

Motoyasu Takahashi Churchill College, Cambridge

Although the existence of wills as historical evidence has been famliar since the eighteenth century, their systematic use is not so old. Less than twenty years ago Dr Margaret Spufford was one of the pioneers in the systematic use of wills for early modern English social history.[2]

Among the problems that have constantly perplexed systematic users of probate material is the question of what proportion of the population, at any one time, made wills or had their goods formally administered after death. Beyond this lies the question of whether this proportion changed over time, and, if so, for what reasons. Did the numbers making wills increase within the same social groups? or did the will-making habit spread to other groups? Within these larger problems lie the less significant question of whether the proportion making use of the Prerogative Courts changed.

In order to provide some indication of the answers to these problems the number of wills proved annually in the Prerogative Court of Canterbury, the Consistory Courts of Ely and Worcester and the Archdeaconry Court of Leicester have been tabulated and graphed for the period from 1480 to 1629.[3] No doubt due to the tremendous labour involved, no such graph has ever been drawn before. It speaks for itself.

The graph and tables have been drawn up from the volumes of indexes published, and about to be published, by the British Record Society in their *Index Library*.[4]

1 The tables and graphs are presented here as I drew them up, but I am much indebted to Dr Peter Spufford for improving the English of my accompanying text when editing it for publication, and to the supervisor of my research in Cambridge, Dr Margaret Spufford, for much helpful advice, and for suggesting this particular line of enquiry to me. I would also like to thank Mr Christopher Marsh for his assistance at an early stage in this piece of work.

2 For example in *Contrasting Communities: English villagers in the sixteenth and seventeenth centuries*, Cambridge 1974.

3 See Graph I, p. 190 and Table I: Wills proved in four courts 1480–1629, pp. 193–6.

4 For the Prerogative Court: *Index of Wills proved in the Prerogative Court of Canterbury*, i & ii, 1383–1558, ed. J. Challenor C. Smith (1893 & 1895); iii, 1558–1583, compiled S. A. Smith, ed. Leland Duncan (1898); iv, 1584–1604, compiled S. A. Smith, ed. Edward

All wills, whether registered or original, have been counted, but administrations and unattached inventories have been excluded. Where bundles or registers cover more than one year, and the indexes do not give any indication of the date of individual wills, the number of wills involved has been arbitrarily divided equally between the years with which the bundle or register concerned is labelled.[5]

The Prerogative Court of the Archbishop of Canterbury was the superior probate court for the whole of England and Wales. In theory this only meant that testators dying with property in more than one probate jurisdiction in southern England had to have their wills proved in this court. The Prerogative Court of York had a similar jurisdiction in northern England, whilst executors dealing with property in both the provinces of Canterbury and York had to go to the Canterbury court. In practice large numbers of executors in southern England went to the Prerogative Court even though they did not need to do so, and it thus came to be the normal probate court for many of the more important people in the country.

The provincial jurisdictions were chosen because of the convenience of the indexes to their probate records. However they also represent different geographical areas of the country, East Anglia, and the West and East Midlands respectively The jurisdiction of the Consistory Court of Ely covered most of the ancient county of Cambridgeshire and the old Isle of Ely, with the exception of the town and university of Cambridge and of the deaneries of Bourne, Shingay and Fordham. The jurisdiction of the Consistory Court of Worcester covered most of the ancient county of Worcestershire, with the exception of some twenty parishes in the diocese of Hereford, but it also included over seventy parishes in Warwickshire, forming the south-western third of that county. The jurisdiction of the Archdeaconry Court of Leicester was almost exactly coterminous with the ancient county of Leicestershire.

General Trends

Any discussion of the general trends in the quantities of wills to survive, is complicated by both the particularly large numbers of wills surviving from years of epidemics, and by the strong impression that in the early years only a very small

Alexander Fry (1901); v, 1605–1619, ed. Ethel Stokes (1912); vi, 1620–1629, ed. Ethel Stokes (1912), *Index Library*, vols 10, 11, 18, 25, 43 and 44.

For Ely: *Index of the probate records of the Consistory Court of Ely, 1449–1858*, 3 vols, compiled C. A. & D. Thurley, ed. E. Leedham-Green (in the press). I am indebted to Dr Rosemary Rodd of the Literary and Linguistic Computing Centre of Cambridge University for access to this unpublished material. For this court I used the date of making the will if given, and the date of registration if the date of making is not given, rather than the date of probate.

For Worcester: *Calendar of Wills and Administrations in the Consistory Court of the Bishop of Worcester*, i, 1451–1600 and ii, 1601–1652, ed. E. A. Fry (1904 and 1910), *Index Library* vols 31 and 39.

For Leicester: *Calendars of wills and administrations . . . in the Archdeaconry Court of Leicester*, i, 1495–1649, ed. Henry Hartopp (1902), *Index Library* vol. 27.

5 This affects the totals for Worcester for 1538, 1539, 1542, 1543 and 1544, and for Leicester for 1611, 1612, 1613, 1614, 1615, 1628 and 1629.

proportion of the wills made and proved are available to us. The number of wills surviving from Worcester from the second half of the fifteenth century and the first quarter of the sixteenth was very limited. The earliest will to survive from the Consistory Court of Worcester dates from 1439, but a regular annual sequence of wills from that court is not available until 1527. Comparison with figures of wills referred to in the court books in the neighbouring diocese of Hereford,[6] suggests that the surviving Worcester wills for this period were not representative of the numbers that were likely to have been proved. Although the number of fifteenth century wills surviving at Ely was much more substantial than at Worcester, it was still not up to the level of those proved at Hereford. The earliest wills from the Consistory Court of Ely date from 1450, but the great fluctuation in numbers from year to year suggest that regular keeping of wills only began in 1479, although they may not survive fully until 1537.[7] The earliest will from the Archdeaconry Court of Leicester dates from 1495, but the regular sequence there only began in 1515.

The surviving wills proved in the Prerogative Court of Canterbury began in 1383, but they have not been graphed until 1480 when wills from the Consistory Court of Ely begin to survive in reasonable numbers. For the late fourteenth century never as many as twenty wills proved in the Prerogative Court have survived from any one year. However for the first quarter of the fifteenth century there were nearly always over thirty surviving wills proved each year and frequently over fifty.[8] The numbers increased markedly from the late 1480s as they also did for the Ely court. Whether it is only that a greater number have survived from this period or that will making increased around this date must be a matter for speculation. By the end of the century there were regularly over two hundred wills a year, that have survived, proved in the Prerogative Court, and in Ely normally over fifty. After a burst of activity in the first years of the sixteenth century the surviving wills from the Prerogative Court returned to the level of the 1490s, some two hundred a year, until the 1530s. Wills proved in the Archdeaconry Court of Leicester only really survived from 1515 onwards. In the following decade the numbers increased both there and at Ely, even discounting the plague year of 1521.

Worcester wills effectively started from 1527. The 1530s show mild increases in numbers at Leicester and sharp rises in the Prerogative Court and at Ely and Worcester. At the latter the surviving wills from the plague year of 1538 even exceeded the Prerogative Court numbers as they did again in the next plague wave in 1546. In the 1540s all the provincial courts proved greater numbers of wills than

6 See below pp. 198–200.

7 From the decade up to 1536 an average of 51 wills per year have survived, and from the decade after 1537 an average of 148 wills per year have survived, The 1540s may therefore mark the commencement of full record keeping rather than an abrupt increase in will making. For Ely wills survivng from before 1479 see Table II, p. 196. For the change from the 1520s to the 1540s see Table I, p. 194 and Graph III, p. 191.

8 See Table III, pp. 197–8: Prerogative Court of Canterbury wills to 1479.

GRAPH I. Wills proved in four courts 1480–1629 – Annual Totals

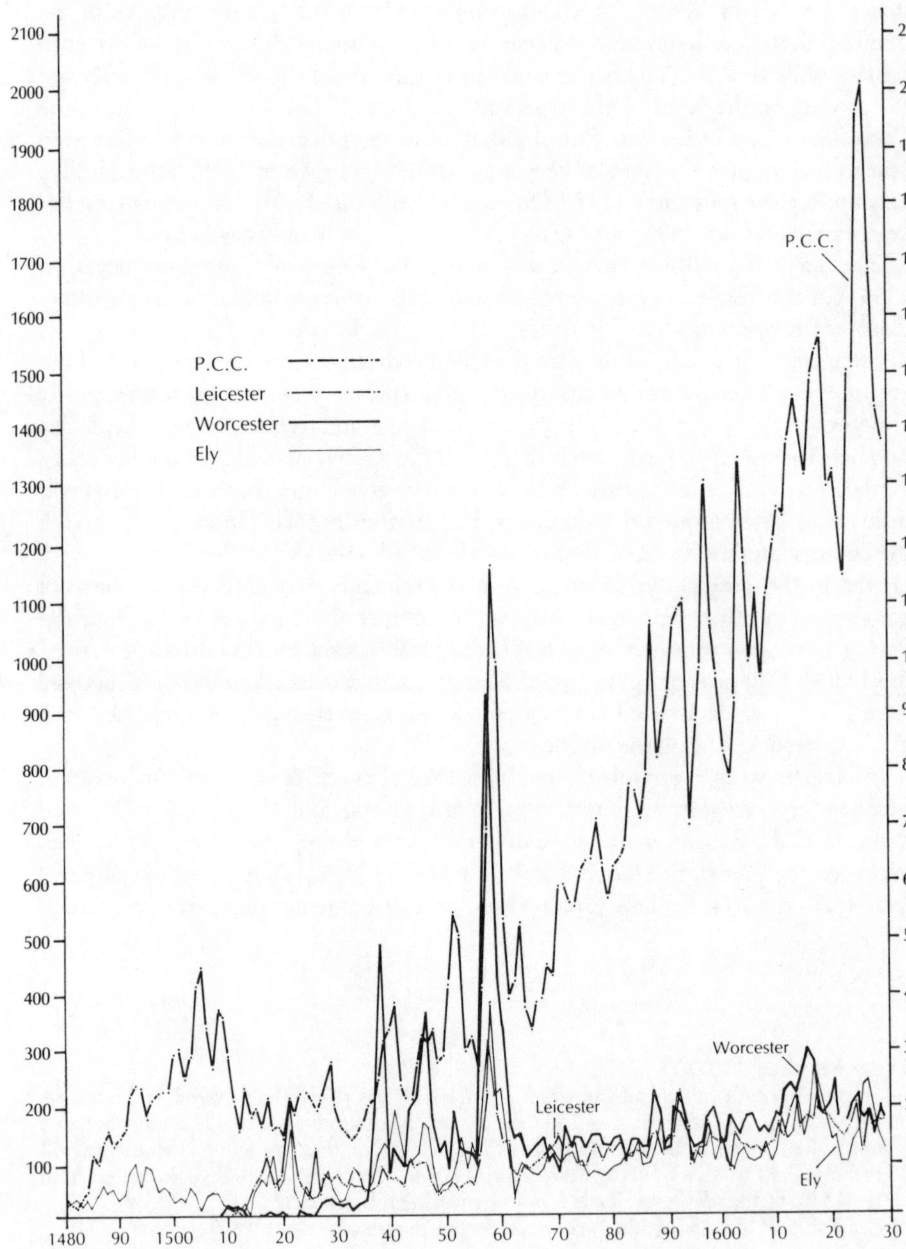

GRAPH II. Wills proved in the Prerogative Court 1480–1630 – Annual Totals

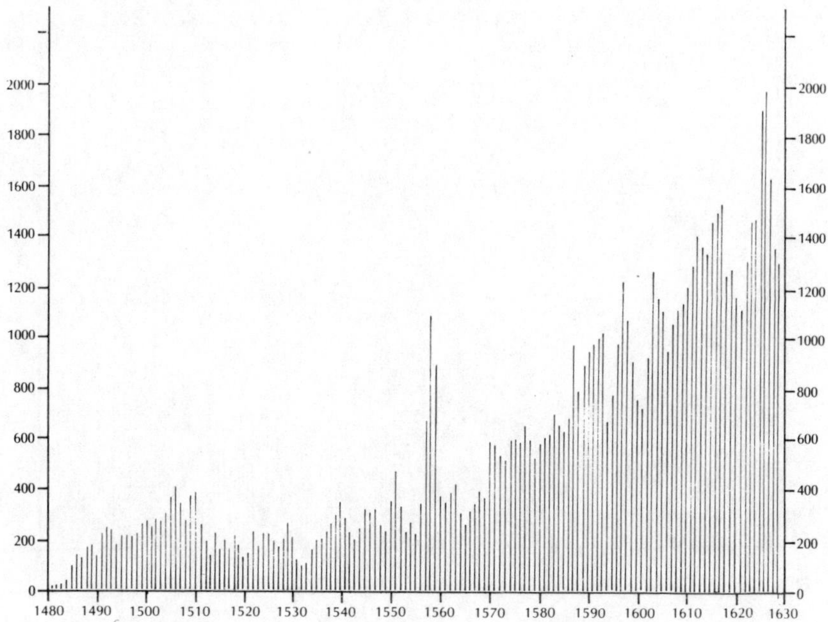

GRAPH III. Wills proved in the Ely Consistory Court 1480–1630 – Annual Totals

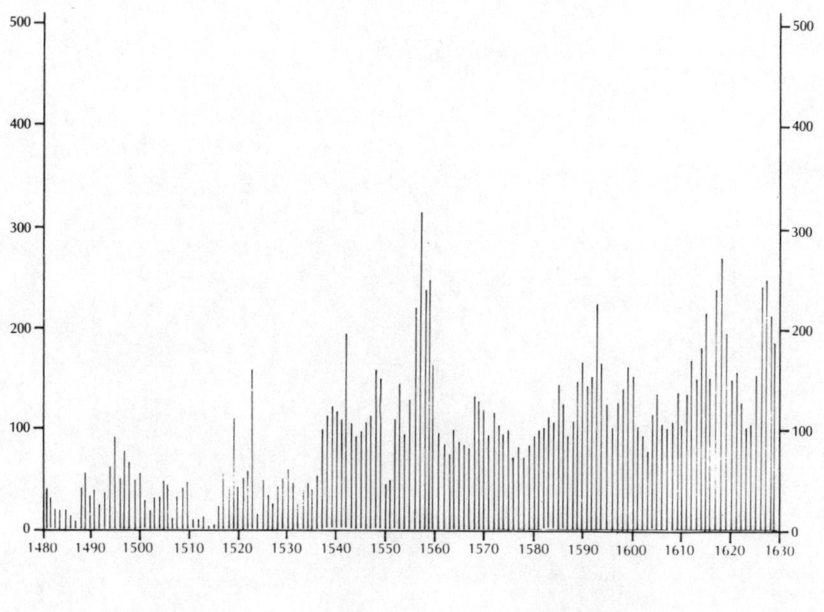

GRAPH IV. Wills proved in the Worcester Consistory Court 1480–1630 – Annual Totals

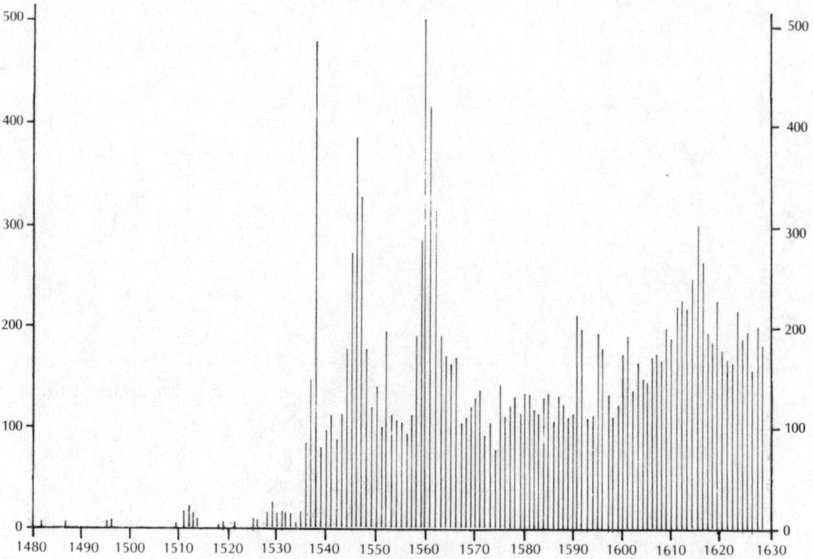

GRAPH V. Wills proved in the Leicester Archdeaconry Court 1480–1630 – Annual Totals

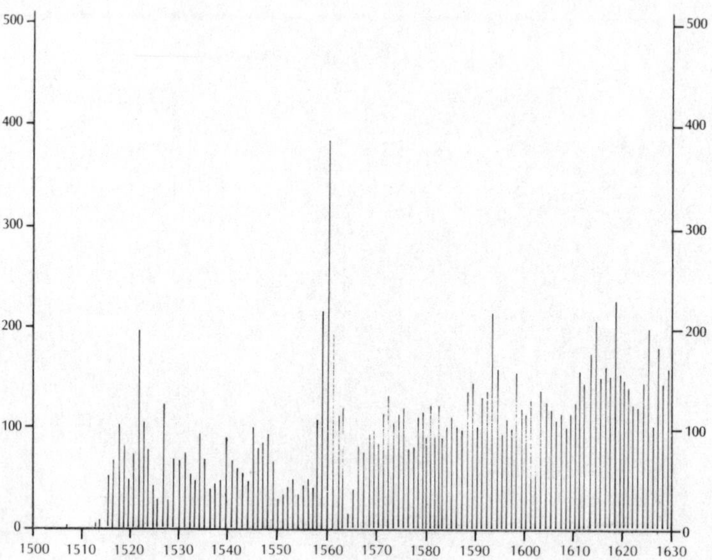

TABLE I. Wills proved in four courts 1480–1629[9]

Year	P.C.C.	*Ely*	*Worcester*	*Leicester*
1480	27	35	2	
1481	24	23	–	
1482	21	27	–	
1483	43	20	1	
1484	54	29	1	
1485	116	13	2	
1486	100	33	–	
1487	141	56	–	
1488	166	41	–	
1489	134	43	–	
1490	149	28	–	
1491	160	39	–	
1492	223	73	–	
1493	244	97	1	
1494	239	51	2	
1495	179	86	3	1
1496	216	85	–	–
1497	225	47	–	–
1498	228	51	–	–
1499	228	42	–	–
1500	295	24	–	2
1501	303	31	–	–
1502	250	25	–	–
1503	290	50	–	1
1504	415	44	–	–
1505	448	9	–	–
1506	340	35	–	1
1507	264	41	–	1
1508	375	42	–	4
1509	364	19	6	–
1510	288	13	18	1
1511	205	8	14	4

9 Where bundles or registers cover more than one year, and the indexes do not give any indication of the date of individual wills, the number of wills involved has been arbitrarily divided equally between the years with which the bundle or register concerned is labelled. In this way the 108 undated wills in the Worcester 1538–9 bundle have been attributed 54 to 1538 and 54 to 1539, the 95 undated Worcester wills in the 1542–3 bundle attributed 48 to 1542 and 47 to 1543 (although more are likely to have been 1542), the 6 undated Worcester wills in the 1543–4 bundle attributed 3 to 1543 and 3 to 1544. The 115 undated wills from Leicester 1611–15 have been attributed 23 to each of the five years. The 403 Leicester wills labelled 1628–9, and the 163 Leicester wills labelled 1628, 1630, 1631, have been combined and attributed 163 to each of the four years 1628–31.

Year	P.C.C.	*Ely*	*Worcester*	*Leicester*
1512	157	12	13	8
1513	237	21	11	1
1514	177	7	–	6
1515	198	46	–	53
1516	164	66	1	70
1517	216	53	3	107
1518	158	108	5	91
1519	163	44	1	49
1520	149	66	3	72
1521	231	155	1	200
1522	185	46	–	112
1523	225	17	8	65
1524	227	52	5	47
1525	215	33	1	31
1526	193	37	1	122
1527	217	62	22	35
1528	282	73	25	72
1529	206	48	26	62
1530	169	23	18	69
1531	152	31	16	55
1532	146	56	19	51
1533	158	54	7	84
1534	169	54	17	72
1535	200	45	22	38
1536	215	65	70	39
1537	247	108	183	51
1538	317	131	479	88
1539	337	122	73	67
1540	382	190	119	65
1541	239	127	101	61
1542	214	89	83	50
1543	214	98	182	102
1544	276	113	212	88
1545	327	167	293	90
1546	315	158	360	94
1547	337	83	168	55
1548	276	43	113	34
1549	288	55	132	40
1550	417	67	80	44
1551	546	95	188	57
1552	400	138	118	40
1553	292	86	111	53
1554	323	130	108	57
1555	281	104	77	51
1556	409	203	174	105

Year	*P.C.C.*	*Ely*	*Worcester*	*Leicester*
1557	697	312	275	219
1558	1160	221	935	374
1559	987	226	429	178
1560	531	159	323	128
1561	386	81	164	129
1562	421	71	136	17
1563	524	94	141	65
1564	373	81	101	87
1665	332	74	110	80
1566	383	73	128	93
1567	390	83	140	101
1568	451	123	97	90
1569	432	112	112	119
1570	589	90	77	140
1571	591	108	158	113
1572	562	111	125	121
1573	552	92	136	130
1574	613	94	137	85
1575	636	64	121	85
1576	639	74	139	106
1577	707	71	138	120
1578	634	68	127	93
1579	566	77	124	117
1580	622	83	135	105
1581	640	90	141	129
1582	659	106	99	96
1583	768	103	134	102
1584	756	133	133	114
1585	705	84	121	107
1586	787	93	120	99
1587	1061	116	220	139
1588	815	162	189	145
1589	889	126	117	102
1590	934	139	117	135
1591	1052	213	193	135
1592	1079	196	181	219
1593	1098	148	158	151
1594	698	90	119	87
1595	880	115	122	108
1596	973	119	132	99
1597	1308	148	170	163
1598	1062	93	189	132
1599	963	138	120	125
1600	822	93	127	129
1601	770	76	172	71

Year	P.C.C.	*Ely*	*Worcester*	*Leicester*
1602	920	103	147	140
1603	1345	117	143	133
1604	1165	99	172	127
1605	978	95	175	112
1606	1108	99	144	117
1607	956	127	156	107
1608	1105	89	142	119
1609	1200	113	184	128
1610	1259	168	173	162
1611	1241	132	208	142
1612	1376	147	234	181
1613	1454	204	213	208
1614	1399	136	253	152
1615	1318	176	295	169
1616	1491	266	266	162
1617	1539	227	185	219
1618	1567	178	175	168
1619	1296	133	195	162
1620	1329	139	233	156
1621	1234	94	168	138
1622	1133	95	166	135
1623	1500	132	189	152
1624	1505	149	213	199
1625	1961	230	165	109
1626	2013	239	180	179
1627	1679	184	140	154
1628	1435	148	194	163
1629	1376	114	165	163

TABLE II. Ely Wills to 1479

Year		*Year*	
1450	8	1465	16
1451	0	1466	9
1452	12	1467	24
1453	21	1468	13
1454	35	1469	14
1455	46	1470	12
1456	33	1471	13
1457	57	1472	5
1458	64	1473	17
1459	39	1474	18
1460	1	1475	3
1461	2	1476	2
1462	2	1477	10
1463	–	1478	9
1464	13	1479	40

TABLE III. Prerogative Court Wills to 1479

Year		Year	
1381	–	1424	22
1382	–	1425	34
1383	2	1426	46
1384	6	1427	26
1385	1	1428	37
1386	2	1429	24
1387	3	1430	34
1388	2	1431	26
1389	2	1432	37
1390	4	1433	26
1391	17	1434	8
1392	18	1435	18
1393	12	1436	34
1394	5	1437	14
1395	7	1438	15
1396	1	1439	30
1397	–	1440	14
1398	–	1441	1
1399	–	1442	27
1400	16	1443	27
1401	40	1444	23
1402	46	1445	20
1403	52	1446	8
1404	45	1447	26
1405	48	1448	35
1406	42	1449	32
1407	51	1450	34
1408	44	1451	17
1409	34	1452	21
1410	38	1453	–
1411	29	1454	50
1412	32	1455	60
1413	46	1456	38
1414	31	1457	84
1415	61	1458	63
1416	54	1459	43
1417	55	1460	32
1418	58	1461	36
1419	61	1462	–
1420	64	1463	37
1421	37	1464	90
1422	32	1465	84
1423	32	1466	64

Year		*Year*	
1467	84	1474	105
1468	59	1475	57
1469	52	1476	63
1470	59	1477	38
1471	74	1478	35
1472	49	1479	38
1473	70		

in the 1530s and this general gradually rising trend continued decade by decade until the second decade of the sixteenth century.[10]

After the influenza epidemic of 1557–9 the fortunes of the Prerogative Court and the provincial courts diverged markedly. Whilst the number of wills proved in the latter only increased in line with the growing population, the numbers proved in the Prerogative Court increased quite startlingly. By the second decade of the seventeenth century over thirteen hundred wills a year were normally proved in the Prerogative Court, compared with only two hundred a year in the early decades of the previous century. This more than sixfold increase in the use of the Prerogative Court contrasts with probably less than a doubling in the numbers of wills in the provincial courts. This is very difficult to calculate because of the problem of survival in the first decades of the sixteenth century. Moreover whereas the numbers of wills proved in the provincial courts probably only continued to keep pace with the number of burials,[11] those passing through the Prerogative Court continued to increase much more rapidly. In the 1620s over fifteen hundred wills a year were normally proved in the Prerogative Court of Canterbury. Between 1661 and 1685 they averaged over nineteen hundred a year, between 1686 and 1693 over two thousand two hundred a year, and in the later 1690s around three thousand a year.

Survival of Wills from the Fifteenth and early Sixteenth Centuries

We have supposed that the unevenness of each of the provincial series of wills in its early years represents a situation in which it was not yet normal to preserve or copy every will that was presented to the court for probate. The problem is highlighted by the immense number of entries in the court books of the bishop of Hereford for the fifteenth century, each representing a will presented for probate which has not been preserved.[12]

10 See below pp. 204–6.

11 Only the Ely wills have been counted up to 1700 and there is an intriguing correspondence between the trends in the Ely will figures and in the annual burial totals for England. There is equally a relatively close match with the burial totals for the fen-edge village of Willingham within the diocese itself. Spufford, *Contrasting Communities*, Graph 1. Nine year moving averages of Willingham population 1560–1740.

12 M. A. Faraday and E. J. L. Cole (eds), *Calendar of Probate and Administration Acts 1407–1541 and Abstracts of Wills 1541–1581 in the Court Books of the Bishop of Hereford*, (British

The diocese of Hereford covered the county of Hereford and parts of six adjacent counties. Herefordshire is the immediate neighbour of Worcestershire to the west and yet the numbers of wills of which we are being made aware are utterly different.[13]

TABLE IV. Annual Totals of Probate Acts from the Diocese of Hereford 1442–1541

Year	Acts	Year	Acts
1442–3*	216	1491–2*	125
1445–6	412	1494–5	250
1447–8	188	1499–1500	325
1453–4	321	1500–1*	223
1455–6*	173	1501–2	317
1456–7*	184	1502–3	409
1458–9	242	1507–8*	193
1459–60	165	1508–9	434
1467–8	62	1514–15	300
1468–9	215	1517–18	239
1471–2*	213	1522–3	258
1472–3	201	1523–4	244
1473–4*	122	1525–6	272
1475–6*	214	1527–8	399
1479–80*	564	1529–30	351
1480–1	232	1530–1	313
1481–2	228	1534–5	202
1486–7	390	1535–6	227
1487–8	317	1537–8	387
1488–9	240	1538–9	180
1489–90	193	1539–40*	227
1490–1	168	1540–1	273

* incomplete, some deaneries missing in this calendar.

Record Society, 1990). I am indebted to Dr Peter Spufford for access to this unpublished material. Mr Faraday has already published a discussion of this material as M. A. Faraday, 'Mortality in the Diocese of Hereford 1442–1541', *Transactions of the Woolhope Naturalists Field Club*, xlii (1977), pp.163–74.

13 No amount of social differentiation could adequately explain such a difference. The survival of gavelkind in parts of Herefordshire, the poverty of many of its inhabitants, the lack of secondary employment there, and the growing emphasis on large scale sheep farming and corn growing may have made minor differences to the numbers of wills made, but cannot account for the totally disparate numbers with which we are concerned. For the economic and social situation in rural Herefordshire see J. Thirsk (ed.), *The Agrarian History of England and Wales*, iv 1540–1640 (Cambridge, 1967), p.109 and J. Thirsk, 'Industries in the countryside', in F. J. Fisher (ed.), *Essays in the Economic and Social History of Tudor and Stuart England* (Cambridge, 1961), pp. 70–88.

In the introduction Mr Michael Faraday explains that in the period 1407–8 to 1540–1 they had calendared no fewer than 12,000 probates. Over the whole period of time some two hundred wills were proved annually. Compared with other figures the Hereford figures are enormous.

For the isolated year 1407–8 there were 82 wills proved in the Hereford Court, coming from only two of the thirteen deaneries in the diocese. This should be compared with 51 surviving wills from the Prerogative Court for 1407 and 44 for 1408. The Hereford probate acts are almost continuous from 1442–3. There are peaks in 1445–6, 1479–80, 1502–3 and 1508–9. In the first of these peaks, 1445–6, over 400 wills were proved in Hereford. At the same time less than fifty survive from the Prerogative Court. By the late 1460s and early 1470s the number of Hereford probates had stabilized at around 200, at the same time the number of Prerogative Court wills had also stabilized, but at around eighty. Despite such initial disparity of numbers the Hereford numbers and the Prerogative Court numbers generally exhibit rises and falls at about the same dates from the 1440s to the 1530s. Although the same phases of change affected both, the Prerogative Court survivals do catch up in number with those which passed through the Hereford court. By the 1490s both are in the two to three hundred range.[14]

Mr Faraday has analysed his probates by Deanery, and it is quite extraordinary to realise that in a single sparsely inhabited deanery in Herefordshire on the marches of Wales, more wills were proved than have survived from the same period from the whole diocese of Ely in eastern England.[15]

In the light of this evidence from Herefordshire we have to push back the period when will making became common at least as far as the middle of the fifteenth century. Earlier commentators who believed that they saw the beginning of widespread will making in the late fifteenth and early sixteenth century need to be corrected.[16] What began then was not the widespread making of wills, but the widespread survival of the wills made.

Epidemics and other Crises of Mortality

Dr Paul Slack has already used probate records to investigate the impact of plague in Tudor England in his recent book on plague and the social responses of the English

[14] For the annual totals of probate acts calendared in the diocese of Hereford, 1442–1541, see Table IV p. 199.

[15] Faraday, *Hereford*, Introduction, p. xiv.

[16] For example Dr Barbara Hanawalt, using Bedfordshire evidence, believed that will making only became common in the late fifteenth century, *The Ties That Bound: Peasant Families in Medieval England* (Oxford, 1986), p.14; and Dr Cecily Howell and Mr S. Coppel, using Leicestershire and Grantham evidence respectively, believed that will making only became common in the sixteenth century, Cecily Howell, *Land, Family and Inheritance in Transition: Kibworth Harcourt 1280–1700* (Cambridge, 1983), pp. 62 and 70; and S. Coppel, 'Wills and the Community: A case study of Tudor Grantham', in Philip Riden (ed.), *Probate Records and the Local Community* (Gloucester, 1985), pp. 77–8.

people to it in the sixteenth and seventeenth centuries.[17] For his probate evidence he also used volumes of the *Index Library* to help establish the chronology of epidemics between 1485 and 1560. As well as the Consistory Court of Worcester and the Archdeaconry of Leicester, he used the volumes of indices of London Commissary Court wills, of Wills at Chelmsford, of Berkshire Probate Records, of Archdeaconry of Lewes wills, and of wills from the dioceses of Lichfield and Exeter.[18] He did not use the Prerogative Court indexes, and the Ely index had not been compiled when he was undertaking his research. He did not tabulate the numbers of wills involved, nor did he graph his results, apart from the London Commissary Court before 1565, so that for probate evidence of epidemics the work presented here complements and expands that already published by Dr Slack.

In addition to probate material, Dr Slack also used the extensive parish register material collected by the Cambridge Group for the History of Population and Social Structure,[19] and a range of urban sources from fourteen selected towns. Although he expressed reservations about the weakness of his sources, including both wills and parish registers, as indicators of the frequency and severity of mortality crises, Dr Slack concluded that there were at least 17 periods of crisis mortality between 1500 and 1670, once every decade on average.[20] He also pointed out that his evidence was heavily weighted towards towns, and that rural experience did not always correlate with urban. Probate evidence comprehends the differing experience of towns and countryside alike.

Dr Slack found that the Commissary Court of London wills greatly increased in numbers between 1497 and 1500, and concluded that this was evidence of plague in the city, which fitted neatly with the strong literary evidence for plague in various parts of the country between 1498 and 1504. However our new evidence helps confirm Dr Slack's suspicion that it was confined to the city, despite the literary evidence. The Prerogative Court figures rise in 1500 and 1501, but not markedly beyond the general rising trend, whilst the number of wills preserved from Ely actually falls.

Dr Slack found evidence of an epidemic, possibly plague, in London and Essex in 1504. The considerable rise in the Prerogative Court wills in that year and 1505 suggests that on this occasion the epidemic was much more widespread, but Ely was not affected.

The sweating sickness and plague of 1517–18 which Dr Slack noticed in London, Essex and Leicestershire is also evident in Ely in 1518, but is barely reflected in the Prerogative Court wills.

In his consideration of probate records Dr.Slack found much evidence of disease outside London through the 1520s, in Berkshire in 1521 and 1529, in Leicestershire in 1521 and 1526, and in the diocese of Lichfield in 1524, 1527 and 1530. He also

17 Paul Slack, *The impact of plague in Tudor and Stuart England* (London, 1985).

18 Slack, *Plague*, p. 57, Table 3.1: Years of high mortality 1485–1560, p.147, graph of wills from London Commissary Court 1478–1565, and p. 358 n. 8.

19 Summarised in Table A10.2 of E. A. Wrigley and R. S. Schofield, *The Population History of England 1541–1871. A reconstruction* (London, 1981), p. 653.

20 Slack, *Plague*, pp. 54–9.

misconstrued the beginning of regular preservation of wills at Worcester in 1527 as an epidemic-related increase in numbers. It is very easy to confuse the aberrations of record survival with external events at this period. Indeed much of the evidence for the 1520s may represent irregular increases in preservation of wills rather than increased mortality. However the new evidence from Ely supports the notion that there was an epidemic in 1521, but not later in the 1520s. On the other hand the new evidence from the Prerogative Court might point to an epidemic in 1528, but not earlier in the decade. Dr Slack's consideration of non-probate evidence suggested to him that there were urban epidemics in Norwich in 1520, in London and York in 1521 and in Worcester in 1528.[21]

Literary evidence indicates that bubonic plague returned to England from Germany and the Low Countries in 1535, and the urban evidence shows just such a return of bubonic plague in the middle and late 1530s, in Bristol in 1535, in Shrewsbury in 1536–7, in Reading, Exeter and Hull in 1537, and in York in 1538–41. Dr Slack discerned probate evidence of plague in the Diocese of Worcester in 1538, and in London, Essex and Berkshire in 1540. Our new evidence from Ely and the Prerogative Court is confirmatory. Both courts show greater numbers of wills from 1538–40, particularly from 1540. This, particularly the Prerogative Court evidence, suggests that plague was widespread in these years and not merely limited to a few towns.

Plague continued through the 1540s. Dr Slack's urban evidence particularly emphasises the middle years of the decade, London in 1543, Reading in 1543–4, Bristol, Norwich, Worcester and Newcastle in 1544–5, and Salisbury, Exeter and Lincoln in 1546. His probate evidence confirms this from Berkshire, East Sussex and the diocese of Worcester for 1545 and for the diocese of Exeter for 1546. Our new evidence from the Prerogative Court and from Ely also produces a fresh peak in numbers for these years, again indicating that plague was yet more widespread.

The fact that the numbers of wills available to us so closely reflects the waves of plague suggests both that the onset of the disease was sufficiently slow for those who were to die of it to have the opportunity of making their wills, and that friends or acquaintances were prepared to risk the contagion to come in to act as scribes at the bedsides of the dying.[22] It was not until Burghley's plague orders of 1578 that continental notions of quarantine were introduced into England, and that harsh and strict rules for the isolation of infected households began to be enforced.[23] Dr Slack discusses at length how far the public was prepared to accept these rules, and cites examples of testators being reduced to making their final wishes known orally when the rules were enforced, even on one occasion to strangers through a window when the house was boarded up.[24]

21 Slack, *Plague*, p. 61, Table 3.3 and p. 358 n.14.

22 See below, Christopher W. Marsh, 'In the Name of God? Will-Making and Faith in Early Modern England', pp. 226–30, for a discussion of the time taken to make wills.

23 Slack, *Plague*, pp. 207–26.

24 Slack, *Plague*, pp. 284–310, particularly pp. 287–8 and 413 n.17.

The great influenza epidemic of 1557–9 exerted a terribly baneful influence upon almost all areas of England. Its effects seem to have been worse than any of the visitations of plague in the sixteenth and seventeenth centuries. The Ely and Prerogative Court evidence amply bear this out. The number of wills proved at Ely in 1557 was never reached again before I stopped counting in 1700. Although the number of wills proved in the Prerogative Court was regularly exceeded from 1608 onwards with the great general rise in the number of wills passing through that court, as well as in the crises of 1597 and 1603, never again did those proved in any single year so greatly exceed the general number being proved at the time.

In 1563 Dr Slack observed a 24 per cent increase in the number of wills passing through the London Commissary court, and Prof. Wrigley and Dr Schofield noted crisis mortality from April to October, with particularly large numbers of deaths in June and July. Our new Prerogative Court of Canterbury figures indicate an increase in will numbers in this year, but not as marked as in London. Our figures from the provincial courts show no significant increase at all.

After the peak years from the 1540s to the 1560s crisis mortality did not recur for a whole generation.

The harvest failures of 1586 and 1587 produced the first of the late Elizabethan subsistence crises. Famine and famine related disease lifted the number of deaths entered in parish registers in 1587 and 1588 more than 25 per cent above the normal level for the period. Our new material from probate records also suggests that deaths greatly increased in these years. The number of wills increased significantly in all three provincial courts that were examined, but more markedly at Worcester than at Ely and Leicester. However at all three the number of wills in these two years was greater than at any time since the influenza epidemic of three decades earlier. In the Prerogative Court too the number of wills increased markedly in 1587.

Plague spread through England from Devon between 1591 and 1593, ravaging London in 1592. The Worcester, Ely and Leicester wills increased as a consequence in 1591, and those in the Prerogative Court during all three years.

Harvest failures produced another subsistence crisis in 1597 and 1598, and Dr Slack found evidence of crisis mortality in eleven of his fourteen towns. Although the Ely, Worcester and Leicester wills increased in number by about a fifth over the preceding years, this was not so marked as in the plague of 1591. However in the Prerogative Court the number of wills proved passed 1300, around 40 per cent more than in the preceding years. This was more marked an increase than in 1591–3. Is it not extraordinary that famine-based diseases should produce such mortality even amongst those substantial enough to have their wills proved in the Prerogative Court? That surely deserves further investigation.

Plague recurred very violently in London in 1603, and the number of Prerogative Court wills increased to over 1300 again, presumably reflecting this high metropolitan mortality. Our probate evidence suggests that it may not have spread extensively to the provinces. There were only mild increases in the wills proved at Leicester in 1602–3, and at Worcester in 1604–5, and no increase at all at Ely at this time.

Moreover Dr Slack only found urban evidence of plague in three towns outside London.

Our probate evidence would suggest that the next crisis of mortality took place around 1616–17. There were peaks in the numbers of wills proved in the Prerogative Court in 1616–18, and in all three of our provincial courts – in Worcester in 1614–16, and in Ely in 1616–17. This perhaps provides another minor corrective to Dr Slack's comprehensive survey of epidemics. It does not fit with any of the periods of crisis mortality picked out by him. However, Prof. Wrigley and Dr Schofield did pick out January 1616 as one of their 'national crisis' months, with a monthly death rate 50–99 per cent above normal. This, combined with the will evidence, might suggest that 1616 ought to be added to Dr Slack's seventeen selected crises.[25]

The harvest failures of 1623–5 produced the third and last of the English subsistence crises of this period, magnified by a major plague in 1625. Deaths recorded in parish registers leapt to more than 40 per cent above the normal level for the period. Those producing our probate records did the same. In 1625 and 1626 wills in the Prerogative Court increased by around a third, to some two thousand each year; in the Worcester and Leicester courts by much the same proportion; but in Ely by an even larger percentage.

There is a close correlation between probate evidence and parish register evidence for the chronology of crisis mortality, from the inception of parochial registration onwards. This close correlation suggests that, even if we no longer have all the wills that were made and proved, those which survive do so in proportion to those which were made.[26] This argument cannot, for lack of parish registers, be pressed further back than 1541 and we believe that, outside the Prerogative Court, the survival of fifteenth century wills was wholely capricious.[27]

Population Growth

Having established that the surviving wills correlate well with the mortality crises of the sixteenth and seventeenth centuries, we can look at the underlying trends and ask whether or not the growth in the numbers of surviving wills, and by implication the numbers of wills made, correlates with what we now know about the numbers of deaths.

A detailed comparison of our graph with the overall graphs provided by Prof. Wrigley and Dr Schofield generally coincides.[28]

25 Slack, *Plague*, p. 339.

26 Amy Louise Erickson's work on probate accounts suggests that even in the late seventeenth century considerable numbers of wills were made and proved which survive neither as originals, nor as registered or office copies. She hopes to throw further light on this in future research.

27 See above p. 189.

28 Wrigley and Schofield, *Population History*, figure 2.3, pp. 58–9, pullout 1, and figure 7.1, p. 207. The latter graph also appeared in R. M. Smith, 'Population and its geography in

Unfortunately they have no firm evidence before 1538 because of the lack of parish registers.[29]

The graphs, both of burials and of wills in the 1540s and 1550s are dominated by recurrent crises. As already seen the latter follow the former closely.

Deaths show a fall, followed by a steep rise in the decade of the 1540s. The Prerogative Court and Worcester wills show almost the same trends, whilst the Ely and Leicester wills exhibit the same pattern but more modestly.

The 1550s contrast with the 1540s, deaths rose at the beginning of the 1550s, fall by the middle 1550s and rise steeply by the end of the 1550s. The same trends are shown by the Prerogative Court and Worcester wills.

The underlying trend of deaths after the crisis year of 1563 was downwards, a natural compensatory movement after a major mortality crisis. The numbers of wills from Worcester remains little changed, but in Ely and Leicester, and even more in the Prerogative Court the numbers of wills rose, against the trend in deaths. In other words this was a period when the proportion of will makers was rising. In the 1580s deaths remained low until the crisis of 1587, but in our provincial courts, except Worcester, the numbers of wills went on creeping upwards, before rising sharply in 1587. The same trend was even more marked in the Prerogative Court. The generation between the plague of 1563 and the susbsistence crisis of 1587 was marked by an increasing proportion of will makers amongst those who died.

The next decade was dominated by mortality crises, but it was followed by another compensatory fall in the number of deaths in the first decade of the seventeenth century. Apart from the London plague of 1603 and the winter epidemic of 1616, there was no major crisis until 1623. The long term trend in the number of deaths was however rising gradually, along with the overall population. All three provincial courts, and, more markedly, the Prerogative Court have rising number of wills at this time. However, once again will makers in a period between crises can be seen to be an increasing proportion of those who died.

Comparing numbers at the beginning and end of the period should determine whether the rising proportion of will makers among those who died in the periods between crises, had any long term effect when combined with what happened in the crisis periods themselves.[30]

In the first quinquennium for which Prof. Wrigley and Dr Schofield calculated deaths, 1540–4, they estimnated that 425,000 people died in England. For the last quinquennium for which we have counted wills, 1625–9, they estimated that 647,000 people died.[31] This is an increase of 52 per cent. Unfortunately both

England 1500–1730', in R. A. Dodgshon and R. A. Butlin (eds), *An Historical Geography of England Wales* (1978), p. 205, fig. 8.2.

29 For the period before 1538 see below p. 206.

30 I would like to thank Dr Peter Spufford for this idea.

31 Wrigley and Schofield, *Population History*, p. 495. See also below, pp. 212–13, for a more detailed comparison of the 1560s and 1620s. The number of deaths is the proper standard for comparison, not the overall population. The first date for which Prof. Wrigley and Dr Schofield calculated the total population was 1541, when they estimated a total population of 2,774,000 for England. For 1631, the next 'census' date after we stopped counting

periods were subject to epidemic mortality. In the same quinquennia in the three provincial courts, 1680 people made wills that have survived in 1540–4, and 2527 people in 1625–9.[32] This is an increase of 50 per cent. In other words the number of will makers whose wills have survived from these three provincial courts increased almost exactly in proportion to the number of deaths in the country as a whole. However in the Prerogative Court, 1325 people made wills that have survived in 1540–4, and 8464 people in 1625–9. This is an increase of 538 per cent, and it is quite clear that a vastly increased proportion of executors proved wills in the Prerogative Court in 1625–9 than in 1540–4.

For the period before 1540, although we do not have parish registers to give us a clear picture of the population, some indications can be gleaned from other sources. The muster books of 1522 and the subsidy returns of 1524 and 1525 have been used by Julian Cornwall to suggest that the population of England was then some 2,300,000, and already increasing rapidly towards the 2,700,000 estimated by Prof. Wrigley and Dr Schofield for 1540.[33] Prof. Wrigley and Dr Schofield have themselves postulated notional figures for deaths for the years before 1540 to fit in with such estimates of population growth. They guess that, in the five years after the 1521 plague, around 67,000 people were dying annually.[34] The numbers of wills surviving from this period include just over two hundred from the Prerogative Court.[35] If the numbers from the Prerogative Court are not unusable because of the problem of survival at this period, they would suggest that in the 1520s and 1530s the number of will makers whose wills passed through the Prerogative Court increased by 27 per cent, almost exactly in line with the number of deaths postulated by Prof. Wrigley and Dr Schofield.

The Prerogative Court and the Provincial Courts

Our overall impression is that the numbers of wills proved in the sixteenth and early seventeenth centuries in the Prerogative Court and our three provincial courts followed divergent patterns. The number of wills proved in the Prerogative Court followed the number of burials from at least the 1520s through the crisis years up to 1563, but then expanded much faster than the number of burials. The number of wills proved in our three provincial courts together continued to follow the number of burials as far as we have traced them, although the three courts exhibited rather different characteristics.[36]

wills, they estimated the total population at 4,893,000. (*Population History*, pp. 208–9.) This is an increase of 76%, compared with the increase of only 52% in deaths.

32 In 1540–4: 697 at Worcester, 617 at Ely, 366 at Leicester; in 1625–9: 844 at Worcester, 915 at Ely, 768 at Leicester.

33 Julian Cornwall, 'English Population in the Early Sixteenth Century', *Economic History Review*, 2nd ser., xxiii (1970), 32–44.

34 Wrigley and Schofield, *Population History*, p. 736.

35 See Table I, pp. 193–6. The total for 1522–6 is 1045 from the Prerogative Court.

36 The will makers increased by only 21% at Worcester, by 48% at Ely and by 110% at

It is clear therefore that not only was there a much greater use of the Prerogative Court by executors from 1563 onwards, but that the total number of wills made increased, for the switch to the Prerogative Court by executors did not bring about any diminution in the number of wills proved in the provincial courts. The numbers were kept up by wills made by people whose predecessors would not have made wills at an earlier date.

It is difficult to estimate the overall impact of the sixfold increase in wills proved in the Prerogative Court, for we do not yet know how many wills were proved in the whole range of provincial probate courts. The three courts we have examined are only a small proportion of the whole range. There were no less than fifty major probate jurisdictions in the sixteenth and seventeenth century province of Canterbury of which the largest was the huge Commissary Court of the Bishop of London, and in addition hundreds of minor courts down to those of minute peculiars covering single tiny villages. It is not even clear if the experience of our courts was typical. If it was typical, we would estimate that in the 1620s approximately seven times as many wills were proved in the provincial courts of the province of Canterbury than in the Prerogative Court.[37]

In the first half of Elizabeth's reign a similar calculation would suggest that only one fourteenth part of the wills of the province of Canterbury passed through the Prerogative Court.[38]

It is not easy to pick out the social status of the executors who came to use the Prerogative Court whose predecessors would not have done so. The occupational index to the *Index of Wills proved in the Prerogative Court of Canterbury* for the period 1605–19 reveals that in these fifteen years the wills of over eight hundred husband-

Leicester. It is not yet possible to know whether the experience of any of these courts was typical. The Ely figure most closely conforms to the overall increase in burials throughout England.

37 Between 1620 and 1629 an average of 70 wills a year from Worcestershire, Leicestershire, and Cambridgeshire with the Isle of Ely were proved in the Prerogative Court, whilst 480 wills a year were proved in the Leicester Archdeaconry Court and the Worcester and Ely Consistory Courts together. This can be only a very approximate correspondence as it ignores the proportion of Worcester Consistory Court wills which came from Warwickshire, and the proportion of Cambridgeshire and Isle of Ely wills proved in the Ely Archdeaconry Court. These ommissions probably more or less cancel each other out. In the 1620s the total number of wills proved in the Prerogative Court annually averaged 1,517. On this basis one might conclude that something of the order of ten thousand wills were being proved annually in the provincial courts of the province of Canterbury at this time.

38 Calculated on a similar basis to the 1620s, but for the period 1558 to 1583, covered by the *Index to the Prerogative Court of Canterbury*, iii. This period includes the beginning of the vast expansion of the use of the Prerogative Court by executors. In this quarter century the total number of wills proved in the Prerogative Court annually averaged 583, but this is an average of very different figures for the beginning and end of the period. In the 1560s, after the epidemics were over, there were normally fewer than four hundred wills proved each year, but by the 1580s there were normally over seven hundred wills proved each year. If an average of such different figures is of any use at all it might suggest that in the first half of Elizabeth I's reign something of the order of six to eight thousand wills a year were being proved in the provincial probate courts of the province of Canterbury.

men and even those of fifty two 'labourers' and 'day labourers' were taken to the Prerogative Court. Common sense would suggest that the wills of husbandmen and labourers were much less frequently taken to the Prerogative Court at the beginning of Elizabeth's reign, but unfortunately the volume of index for 1558–83 was not provided with a supplementary index of trades and conditions. It is therefore not possible to say how many fewer wills of husbandmen and labourers were taken to the Prerogative Court at that period. It is also probable that the number of yeomen's wills taken to the Prerogative Court also increased considerably in the second half of the sixteenth century and the early years of the seventeenth, but this cannot be measured either. Considerable numbers of yeomen's wills were of course already being taken to the Prerogative Court at the beginning of Elizabeth's reign, as well as those of the gentry, the nobility, the higher clergy and leading townsmen. Social and local historians need to know that from Elizabeth's reign onwards it is worth looking in the Prerogative Court for the wills of quite ordinary people that they might not previously have expected to find there.

Although London was beginning to grow very rapidly indeed at this time, the bulk of the additional wills came from provincial, rural, England. This shift to the Prerogative Court correlates with a growth in centralisation in many fields and is yet one more indicator of the increase in the importance of the 'nation' as opposed to the region at this time.

The new computerized index to the Ely wills allows us to measure the downward social spread of will making in one part of provincial England at least. Prof. Hoskins was one of the first to look at the spread of will making. He cited the will of a rich labourer in Leicestershire as early as 1560–1,[39] and pointed out that such cases were exceptional but not rare. He found a few examples in every year covered by the Leicestershire probate inventories. He nevertheless suspected that the habit of making wills did not spread widely among ordinary people until the 1670s. He placed this in the context of the great improvement of living standards involved in the widespread rebuilding of smaller houses in the late seventeenth century, which followed his 'great rebuilding' of larger houses in rural England earlier in the century.[40]

It is now possible to see whether Prof. Hoskins was correct in his guesswork. Wills proved in the Ely Consistory Court do not give status or condition in the fifteenth century apart from those of priests and women. In the first half of the sixteenth century a small number of others do so, although it was not yet common, and the large majority have no indication of status. The largest group of those whose status was given were the husbandmen. The numbers of these gradually increased, but averaged just over three a year over the whole half century. The earliest wills of people specified as labourers were proved in 1518, and by the 1540s wills of men picked out as labourers were proved in most years. Can we take it for

39 With personal estate of £32 18s 8d, William G. Hoskins, *The Midland Peasant*, p.174.

40 Hoskins, *Midland Peasant*, pp. 200 and 301, and for another aspect of this improvement of living standards see Margaret Spufford, *The Great Reclothing of Rural England: Petty Chapmen and their Wares in the Seventeenth Century* (London, 1984).

granted that most of the will makers who did not specify their occupation were in fact yeomen? although no-one bothered to call himself a yeoman when making his will until 1530. In the second half of the sixteenth century it became much more common to specify a status when making a will, and from the 1580s over half of the testators whose wills were proved in the Ely Consistory Court did so.[41] In the 1580s and 1590s, of 2,495 wills proved as many as 1,416 gave some indication. Of those which did, the largest group, apart from the 283 women, was still the husbandmen. There were 430 of them. There were also 232 labourers. There were still only 201 who called themselves yeomen and a mere score of gentry. Of those who declared themselves, 38 per cent called themselves husbandmen and 20 per cent called themselves labourers.[42]

In the 1620s and 1630s 3,146 wills were proved in the Ely Consistory Court. By now well over two thirds of the testators gave themselves a status. Again, apart from the 446 women, the largest groups were the 510 husbandmen and the 391 labourers. Yeomen now much more commonly declared themselves. 368 did so. Of those who declared themselves, 29 per cent called themselves husbandmen and 22 per cent called themselves labourers.[43] If it is borne in mind that self-estimation by will makers was frequently higher than the estimation put on them afterwards in probate inventories by their neighbours when appraising their goods, it is evident that many of those who called themselves yeomen were regarded by their neighbours as husbandmen, and that many of those who called themselves husbandmen were regarded by their neighbours as labourers. In other words from the second half of Elizabeth's reign up to the outbreak of the Civil War at least a quarter and possibly well over a half, of the wills passing through the Consistory Court of Ely were made by labourers and husbandmen. Prof. Hoskins had guessed wrong. It was not at the end of the seventeenth century that the habit of making wills spread among ordinary people, but at the end of the sixteenth century. It may even have been earlier, but the proportion giving themselves a status was then too small to make any safe generalisations. This is much more useful as evidence than the small numbers from individual places. Terling in Essex has been intensively studied by Drs Wrightson and Levine. It was a moderately sized settlement, with 122 households assessed for the hearth tax, and had 192 wills proved in the local probate court. Yet even in a place of this size, the numbers were such that in the sixteenth century husbandmen and craftsmen left only isolated wills. It was not until a century later that it was common for Terling husbandmen and craftsmen to make wills, and for labourers to begin to do so there. Over the whole period from 1550 to 1699 only seven labourers and cottagers did so. On the basis of these small numbers, Drs Wrightson and Levine had to conclude that, even at the end of the seventeenth century, it was a

41 See Table V, Percentage of Ely wills giving status or occupation, 1540–1639, and Graph VI p. 210; and Table VI, p. 211, Numbers of different declared status in Ely wills, 1560–1639, and Graph VII, p. 211, Numbers of different declared status in Ely wills, 1580–1639.

42 17% of the whole body of will makers called themselves husbandmen and 9% called themselves labourers.

43 16% of the whole body of will makers called themselves husbandmen and 12% called themselves labourers.

'highly unusual step for persons of their social position to make formal wills distributing their small stocks of goods'.[44] The new material from the diocese of Ely suggests that, seen on a larger stage than the single village, it was by no means unusual for persons of this social position to make formal wills at the end of the sixteenth century, let alone the end of the seventeenth.

TABLE V. Percentage of Ely wills giving status or occupation, 1540–1639

Decade	Total No. of Wills	Declaring Status	Not declaring Status
1540–9	1123	17%	83%
1550–9	1582	25%	75%
1560–9	951	35%	65%
1570–9	849	39%	61%
1580–9	1096	54%	46%
1590–9	1399	59%	41%
1600–9	1011	63%	37%
1610–19	1767	65%	35%
1620–9	1524	69%	31%
1630–9	1622	71%	29%

GRAPH VI. Percentage of Ely wills not giving status 1530–1629

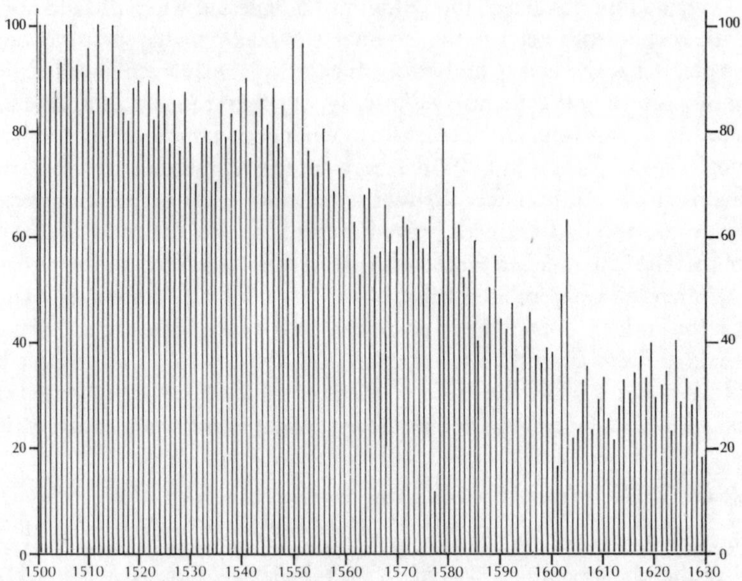

[44] Keith Wrightson and David Levine, *Poverty and Piety in an English Village. Terling, 1525–1700* (New York, 1979), pp. 34, 92–3, 96–7.

TABLE VI. Numbers of different declared status in Ely wills, 1560–1639

Decade	*Women*	*Men*					*Status*	*No Status*
		Gent.	*Yeo.*	*Husb.*	*Lab.*	*Misc.*	*Declared*	*Declared*
1560–9	70	4	45	107	32	79	337	614
1570–9	75	5	31	115	57	49	332	517
1580–9	122	9	77	208	88	84	588	508
1590–9	161	12	124	222	163	146	828	571
1600–9	132	9	115	144	131	108	639	372
1610–19	252	19	181	234	263	202	1151	616
1620–9	197	14	174	256	226	177	1044	480
1630–9	249	14	194	254	186	253	1150	472

The heading 'Lab(ourer)' also includes servants and poor, e.g. almsman.

GRAPH VII. Numbers of different status declared in Ely wills, 1580–1639

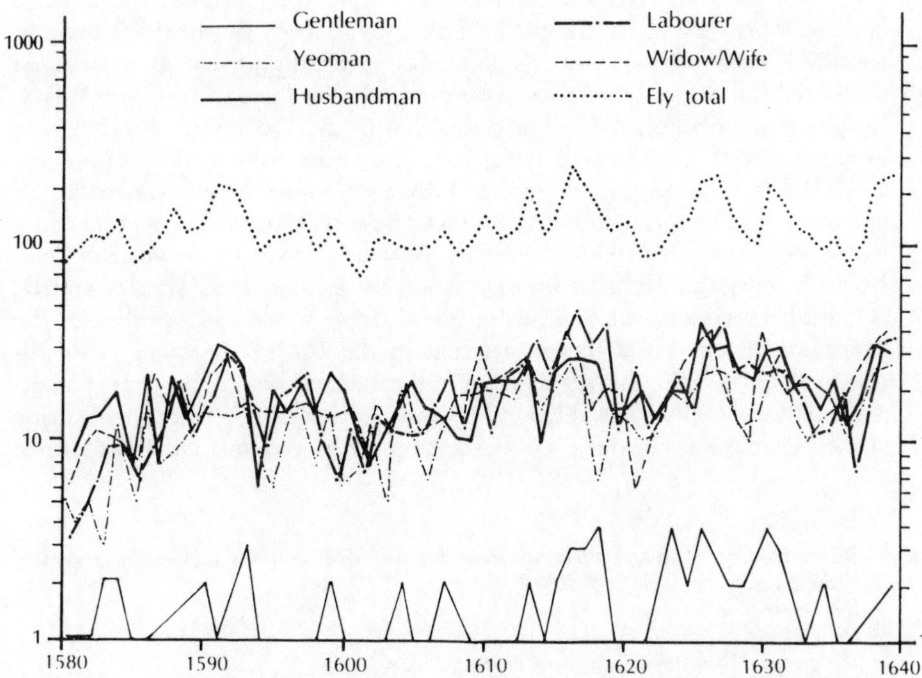

Conclusion

What then has this laborious counting, tabulating and graphing revealed? As well as producing supporting evidence on the crises of mortality in the sixteenth and seventeenth centuries, particularly on the extent of the influenza epidemic of 1557–9, the tables and graphs have revealed a number of interesting facts.

The Hereford evidence now makes it clear that we have to push the period when will making became common back at least to the middle years of the fifteenth century, if not earlier. Previous commentators who believed that they saw the beginning of widespread will making at the very end of the fifteenth century or in the early sixteenth century need to be corrected. What began then was not the widespread making of wills, but the widespread survival of wills. We do not believe that the majority of wills from the courts we have examined survive until the 1530s. It was a change in record keeping that took place in the first half of the sixteenth century, not a change in the habits of the dying. Can the widespread making of wills, now pushed back into the fifteenth century, be associated with the great increase in literacy, now also pushed back into the fifteenth century?

For the period from the 1540s, we do have an adequate proportion of the wills that were made available to us. The close correlation between probate and burial evidence suggests that even if we no longer have all the wills that were made and proved, those which survive do so in proportion to those made. It is therefore from this period that we can begin to answer some of the questions that have been asked. Professor Vann has posed the critical question: what proportion of the whole population left wills.[45] In the early years of Elizabeth's reign we can tentatively guess that some 6000 wills were proved annually in the provincial courts of the province of Canterbury, and some 400 in the Prerogative Court. By the 1620s we can tentatively guess that some 10,000 wills were proved in the provincial courts, beside the fifteen hundred that we know were proved in the Prerogative Courts.[46] Prof. Wrigley and Dr Schofield have suggested that in the 1560s, after the epidemics were over, some 77,000 were being buried annually, and in the 1620s some 123,000.[47] In other words the percentage that left wills that were proved in the province of Canterbury increased from around 8 per cent to around 9 per cent of the whole population. In addition there were the wills made in the province of York. However, only the adults in the population made wills. Prof. Wrigley and Dr Schofield have estimated that adults over 25 only formed 46 per cent of the population in the 1560s and 49 per cent in the 1620s.[48] Assuming nearly all testators were over 25, this suggests that in the 1560s at least 18 per cent of adults made wills and in the 1620s at least 19 per cent. In view of the uncertainty of many elements in these calculations, it would be proper to propose that virtually the same

45 Richard Vann, 'Wills and the Family in an English Town: Banbury 1550–1807', *Journal of Family History*, iv (1979), pp. 264–5.

46 See above p. 207, footnotes 37 and 38.

47 Wrigley and Schofield, *Population History*, p. 495.

48 Wrigley and Schofield, *Population History*, p. 528.

proportion of adults were making wills in the 1560s and the 1620s.[49] There is also an imbalance of the sexes to be taken into account. The Ely evidence suggests that around 90 per cent of the testators were male, although slightly under half the whole adult population was. This would suggest that in both the 1560s and the 1620s almost exactly a third of the adult men in England left wills that were proved in the ecclesiastical courts of the province of Canterbury. By the 1620s perhaps as many as a twentieth of adult women left wills.

Other historians had already guessed that there was an increasing use of the Prerogative Court in the sixteenth and seventeenth centuries. We have now been able to make clear how much greater this use of the Prerogative Court by executors was from 1563 onwards. This was at the same time that the total number of wills made increased, for the switch to the Prerogative Court by executors did not bring about any diminution in the number of wills proved in the provincial courts. The numbers were kept up by wills made by people whose predecessors would not have made wills at an earlier date. Even those who used the Prerogative Court were not necessarily sufficiently prosperous to have been immune from the effects of famine-based disease.

The material from the Ely court has shown how the habit of declaring the testators' status increased in the course of the sixteenth century, and how from the 1580s there is enough evidence to show how many of the new will makers were husbandmen and even labourers. Any notion that very ordinary people did not make wills until the end of the seventeenth century now needs to be revised backwards by at least a hundred years. It is now clear that by the end of the sixteenth century extremely large numbers of husbandmen and labourers were making wills. The nature of the evidence will not allow us to discover how much earlier they may have been doing so.

We dare to hope that future makers of indexes to probate material, who have the advantage of using computers to arrange their material, will take the opportunity of counting, tabulating and graphing it, so that comparisons can be made with what we have done, and so that our estimates and conclusions can be refined. There are a number of lines of enquiry which we have not been able to touch on which need further examination. How far did the legislation of the first half of the sixteenth century affect the preservation of wills? How far did the growth of London affect the use of the Prerogative Court?[50] How far were the numbers of those applying to the probate courts for letters of administration for the estates of intestates affected by the increase in the numbers of those leaving wills? And finally can the increasing numbers of husbandmen, and particularly labourers, making wills from the end of the sixteenth century be correlated at all with the polarization of rural society that was then beginning to take place in some open-field regions of the country? All these are open questions for future workers in this field.

49 The calculations on p. 207 above suggested that the proportion did increase slightly between the 1540s and the 1620s. If there is enough accuracy in the two sets of calculations, they would suggest that the proportion was increasing between the 1540s and the 1560s.

50 See below A. J. Camp, pp. 290–3.

18. In the Name of God? Will-Making and Faith in Early Modern England

Christopher Marsh Churchill College, Cambridge

Wills remain one of the principal sources for historians of popular religion, although in recent years their status as authentic testaments of individual faith has been called into doubt by several commentators.[1] Few today would agree with W. K. Jordan's description of wills, penned in 1959, as 'completely honest documents' and 'mirrors of mens' souls'. 'Almost every will,' he wrote, 'begins with a carefully considered and eloquently elaborated confession of faith, in which the testator earnestly strives to set out the nature of his beliefs, to confess his own inadequacies, to confirm his confidence in the mercy of God, and to prepare himself for a death which he believes to be imminent.'[2] Such confidence in wills – some might call it wishful thinking – has not been extinguished completely, but a majority of historians would probably feel rather closer to the position of Rosemary O'Day, expressed in 1986: 'Far from revealing the religious beliefs of the average testator, wills and their preambles hide them from the historian's gaze.'[3]

With the advent of Reformation doctrines, greater variety came into the wording of will preambles, though it did not develop uniformly. Late medieval wills,

I should like to express my gratitude to Dr Margaret Spufford with whom I have discussed this paper at length. She originally proposed the subject, and delivered an earlier version of it to the conference on the Records of the Nation in August 1988. There have been certain differences of opinion concerning the interpretation of wills (see below note 38) and this version represents my own work and my own conclusions on the subject.

1 See, for example, Claire Cross, 'Wills as evidence of popular piety in the Reformation period. Leeds and Hull, 1540–1640', in David Loades (ed.), *The End of Strife* (Edinburgh, 1984), pp. 44–51. For a comprehensive review of the recent literature on wills, see Derek Plumb, *John Foxe and the Later Lollards of the Thames Valley*, Cambridge Ph.D. dissertation (July, 1987) pp. 40–50. The most recent paper I have seen on wills is J. D. Alsop's 'Religious Preambles in Early Modern English Wills as Formulae', *Journal of Ecclesiastical History*, Vol. 40, No. 1, (January, 1989). Professor Alsop presents an extremely pessimistic argument concerning the potential of will preambles as historical evidence. The current paper was already completed when Professor Alsop's appeared, and does not, therefore, answer it directly. It will be noted that we discuss some of the same points, with differing emphases.

2 W. K. Jordan, *Philanthropy in England, 1480–1640. A Study of the Changing Pattern of English Social Aspirations* (London, 1959), p.16.

3 Rosemary O'Day, *The Debate on the English Reformation* (London and New York, 1986), p.157.

while displaying a considerable range in the nature of religious bequests, normally opened with a fairly standardised commendatory clause in which the testator bequeathed his soul to God, the Virgin Mary and the saints. Occasionally this was abbreviated, or expanded to include the naming of individual saints, but major differences were rare. Under Edward VI and, particularly, Elizabeth I, the range of expressions used became comparatively wide. It is for this reason that historians have scrutinised will preambles in the search for evidence of individual piety.

From the start, however, there were difficulties. A. G. Dickens, aware that wills were perhaps not all they seemed, cautioned historians against analysing the documents 'in any spirit of statistical pedantry'.[4] Margaret Spufford amplified this warning, and changed the nature of the debate by discussing the actual mechanics of will-making, and by emphasising the importance of considering the broader local context in which any particular will was written.[5] Still the problems remained. Testators whose deep faith is known from independent sources sometimes made wills with short, non-committal, unexpressive preambles, even when they were well enough to sign their names and when their particular brand of faith was in harmony with that established by law. Individual historians have also been frustrated when, after discovering a long, expressive preamble and classifying it as a deeply personal account of beliefs, their attention has been drawn to an identical preamble written a hundred miles away. Were some, or many, testators simply transcribing their preambles from printed formularies?[6]

It has been noted that the wills of particular communities are not necessarily reliable in the way they reflect the ecclesiastical history of those communities.[7] Moreover, it has frequently proved impossible to establish the authorship of individual preambles. Did testators generally compose or select the expressions themselves, or did the scribes they employed simply write down their own set formulae before taking advice on the temporal bequests? We need to know, in short, whether early modern testators viewed their wills as spiritual documents, testaments of faith, or whether the majority – including some people of exceptional piety – were really only concerned with the disposal of worldly posessions. It may be inappropriate to distinguish so clearly between the two attitudes.

The lay people of England themselves were apparently becoming increasingly interested in the idea of making wills as the sixteenth century progressed. Across many dioceses, the numbers of wills proved annually seems to have been rising, though the exact take-off point probably varied. The reasons for this broad increase are unclear and, unfortunately, beyond the scope of this paper. It appears, however, that an examination of attitudes to will-making in the early modern period, particularly the later sixteenth century, may be useful. This paper will discuss the motivations behind making a will, as perceived by godly writers and by the men and

4 A. G. Dickens, *Lollards and Protestants in the Diocese of York, 1509–1558* (Oxford, 1959; reprinted, Hambledon Press, London, 1982), p.171.

5 Margaret Spufford, *Contrasting Communities* (Cambridge, 1974), pp. 333–4.

6 For further discussion of this question, see below pp. 242–8.

7 Margaret Spufford, *op cit.* (1974), p. 335.

women they presumed to instruct on preparing for death. In addition, it will examine the procedures followed in the drafting of wills, with a view to establishing the context in which a testament was set down in writing. Finally, there will be a contribution to the debate surrounding the use of printed formularies.

The Reformation may have changed the nature of religious expression in English wills, but it made little impact on the preoccupation of contemporaries with death and mortality. Literature in what may broadly be called the *ars moriendi* tradition was still written in post-Reformation England, as Helen White and others have shown.[8] Sister Mary O'Connor has suggested that one of the characteristics distinguishing the later books on dying well from those of the older tradition was a new emphasis on will-making and the disposal of worldly possessions.[9] There may, of course, have been important differences in attitude between contemporary godly writers and the will-making laity at large; men like Thomas Becon were presumably more likely than most Elizabethans to set a high importance on the spiritual context of will-making, and on the religious expressions found in most preambles of the period. Nevertheless, the treatises they wrote provide a suitable starting point for this exploration of attitudes to will-making.

Becon's *The Sicke Mans Salve* first appeared in the late 1550s and enjoyed a popularity which necessitated almost thirty reprints to 1632.[10] *The Salve*, though punctuated with aggressive anti-Catholic digressions, owed a considerable debt to works of the older genre. It is written in the form of a conversation between the ailing Epaphroditus and four of his trusted neighbours: Philemon, Eusebius, Theophilus and Christopher. Epaphroditus, aware of his worsening sickness, decides to dispose of his worldly goods, 'that after my departure there be no dissention nor strife for them, among such as I most wishe to be linked together with perpetual amitie and continuall friendship'. He adds 'It shall also I trust, be a great quietnes unto my mind.'[11]

The would-be testator accepts graciously a gentle admonition from Philemon for having delayed the matter so long, and concedes 'that no man is certaine of his life until to morrowe: therefore ought we all to watch,and to provide that we be not founde unreadie when the Lord commeth'. He then turns to 'neighbour Theophilus' and says 'I praie you bring hither pen, inke, & paper, with all expedition, and let my will be written'. While Theophilus runs his errand, Epaphroditus treats his other friends to a self-congratulatory speech on the godly manner in which he has ever viewed his goods: 'I have alwaies made them to serve me, and I never served them, but at al times could be contented to depart from them whensoever the glorie of

8 Helen White, *English Devotional Literature* (Ann Arbor, 1965); Louis B. Wright, *Middle-Class Culture in Elizabethan England* (Huntingdon Library Publ., 1935).
9 Sister Mary Catharine O'Connor, *The Art of Dying Well* (Columbia, 1942), p.194.
10 Thomas Becon, *The Sicke Mans Salve* . . ., (c.1558–9). The STC notes twenty-eight reprints. My references here refer to the 1594 edition.
11 *Ibid*., pp. 89–90.

God, and the commodity of my Neighbour did require.' Suitably impressed, Christopher comments 'Then did you use your goods aright'.[12]

The slowly-dying testator proceeds to dictate the preamble to an exceptionally pious will. His words are worth quoting at length:

> I Epaphroditus, the unprofitable servant of God, weak in bodie, and notwithstanding, strong in mind; doo willingly and with a free heart, render and give again into the hands of the Lord my God, my spirit which he of his fatherly goodnesse gave unto me, when hee fashioned this my body in my mothers wombe, by this meanes making me a living creature, nothing doubting but that this my Lord God for his mercies sake, set forth in the pretious blood of his deerely beloved son, Christ Jesu our alone saviour and redeemer wil receive my soule into his glorie, and place it in the companie of the heavenlie angels and blessed saintes.

Without pausing for breath, the testator goes on to make a similarly long and expressive statement on the future of his body,

> nothing doubting, but that according to the article of our faith, at the great day of the generall resurrection, when wee shall al appeare before the judgement seate of Christ, I shall receive it againe by the mighty power of God, wherwith he is able to subdue all thinges to himselfe, not a corruptible, mortall, weake and vile bodie, as it is now, but an uncorruptible, immortal strong, perfect [body], and in al points like unto the glorious body of my Lord and saviour Christ Jesus'.[13]

Epaphroditus then asks his scribe if these expressions have been accurately recorded. Philemon's reply may sound a little impatient to the modern ear: 'Yea forsooth sir. But what is your mind now concerning your worldly possessions?' It must be assumed that Becon's tongue was some way from his cheek, though the remark does serve to remind us that many genuinely dying Elizabethans probably did not have the time to record their beliefs in such detail.

Epaphroditus continues to dictate, beginning with a personal pronouncement on 'the blessed state of honourable Wedlocke', in which he refers to his wife, 'with whome I coupled my selfe in the feare of God, and refusing all other women'.[14] Not surprisingly, every bequest and statement is underpinned by some religious conviction, eloquently articulated by a testator whose periodic expressions of deepening physical torment ('O Lord how sicke am I?') soon begin to lose their pathos. It is his duty before God to provide for his offspring, and to contribute to numerous pious causes. Epaphroditus forgives all his debtors 'unto the uttermost farthing even as I would God the father should forgive me all my debts for Christ's sake'. He remembers the struggling scholars at Oxford and Cambridge, and directs his overseers to his counting house where, in four bags each labelled 'Money for the poore', they will

[12] *Ibid.*, pp. 90–1.
[13] *Ibid.*, pp. 92–3.
[14] *Ibid.*, p. 93.

find hundreds of pounds for the immediate relief of more commonplace poverty. In addition, the testator leaves money for highway repairs and provides for the delivery of eighty sermons following his departure from this 'vale of myserie'.[15]

Such obvious strength of faith notwithstanding, the will-making forms no more than a short section in a lengthy work. When read in context it does not seem such a fully integral part of the testator's final preparations for death. Certainly, it is the Christian's essential duty to settle his estate, on loan from God, in a manner which demonstrates gratitude and faith, and serves to signal – but not cause – his salvation. This settlement should not, however, have been left until the last sickness set in; there is a clear sense in which the will-making is viewed as a necessary but undesirable distraction, something to be completed in order that the testator can focus on more important matters in the immediate approach to death.

Having made his will, Epaphroditus is free to deliver exhortations to his wife, his children and his servants. There are numerous prayers and a personal confession of faith which far exceeds that seen in the will preamble.[16] The will had been signed and sealed by page 120 (in the 1594 edition); the testator eventually 'gave up the ghost' on page 353. Moreover, the participants in this over-poweringly godly conversation placed no direct emphasis on the dedicatory clause, a significant omission since they were at continual pains to highlight specifically all points of importance. Epaphroditus was an individual of deep faith and therefore felt moved to include in his will a long and pious preamble, but it was rendered almost superfluous by the subsequent oral declarations of belief. An expressive preamble was not, so far as we can tell, a crucial part of his Christian responsibility. The real duty a testator performed in making his will was to dispose of his wealth in a godly fashion.

The same preoccupations emerge from similar works by William Perkins (1595),[17] William Perneby (1599)[18] and Christopher Sutton (1600).[19] All see the rendering of the soul to God as an essential part of the sick man's duty, but none places any emphasis on this being done in a will. For Perneby, the dying man, by making a will, 'dothe . . . procure himself the more quiet in minde, the greater libertie to attend upon God and his pleasure; the best opportunity that may be to frame himselfe to another world.'[20] Perkins was explicit in regarding the will-making as an unwelcome interruption; he decided somewhat reluctantly to discuss it, even 'though the making of wills belong[s] to another place and profession'.[21] Again, the implication is that modern historians, faced with little option, have focussed on will preambles much more intensely than did contemporaries, including those contemporaries who wrote books teaching men and women to die in faith. When William Perkins made his own will in 1602/3 he further reinforced the point; his dedicatory clause ran 'I commend my soul into the hands of God, in Christ

15 *Ibid.*, pp. 93–104.
16 *Ibid.*, pp.155–77, 178–81, 183–92.
17 William Perkins, *A salve for a sicke man* . . . (Cambridge, 1595).
18 William Perneby, *A Direction to Death* . . . (London, 1599).
19 Christopher Sutton, *Disce Mori, Learne to Die* (London, 1600).
20 William Perneby, *op cit.* (1599), p. 237.
21 William Perkins, *op cit.* (1595), p. 84.

hoping assuredly to dye in that faith wch I have professed & preached'.[22] For a full expression of 'that faith', we are to look elsewhere. Amongst these Elizabethan writers, Thomas Becon was in fact unusual in even implying by example that a pious preamble was of any significance.

For authors who stressed the sufficiency of Scripture as a guide in all situations, this lack of emphasis on the desirability of long and expressive will preambles was not, in fact, surprising. Several of them referred to Biblical examples when they instructed people to bequeath their souls to God as death approached. When Stephen was stoned to death, Perkins reminded his readers, he said 'Lord Jesus receive my spirit'. David had been similarly concise. There was little indication that lengthy expression was considered necessary. Protestant theology, with its emphasis on the inner spirit, naturally led writers to set a higher importance on the inward prayers and contemplation required of the sick man, than on the expressions employed in the basically 'outward' act of composing a will. Carefully-considered expression was not, of course, undesirable, but the godly person had performed his duty if he merely followed the examples of David and Stephen. It is a curious fact that if the words of Christ on the cross were to be included in the historian's dedicatory clause classification system, they would be judged 'neutral'. There may then be a fault in our registering surprise that persons of known piety sometimes left neutral will preambles. Becon and Perkins had been dead for many years before one solitary writer made a direct plea for expressive preambles.[23]

Having said this, the disposal of goods – whether through a will or not – was a task with powerful spiritual overtones. The writers all agreed upon the necessity of promoting peace amongst one's friends and relatives. A will, said the worldly-wise Perkins, 'cuttes off much hatred and contention in families and it staies many suits in law'.[24] The man who neglected to settle his estate had failed in his responsibility to God. Perneby pursued the same line and warned that neighbours would say of such a shirker 'It is a great pitie that he did not set all things at a stay. You will not beleeve what ado heere is thereupon in the countrie. No peace among his children, no love betweene his friends, no quiet to any of his neighbours'.[25] The man 'whom God hath indued with grace' was unlikely to leave such turmoil behind him.

The testator, by consensus, had additional related responsibilities. Perkins placed particular emphasis upon an individual's duty before God to provide adequately for his children, and quoted St Paul to reinforce the point.[26] Perneby was especially keen on the notion that, by a godly disposal of goods, the testator was working to the glory of his Maker: 'For a man making his will well and wisely doth thereby provoke others to glorifie God for giving him . . . wisedome so to dispose of the

22 C[ambridge] U[niversity] L[ibrary], Wills proved in the Vice Chancellor's Court, January 1602/3. I am grateful to Dr Ian Archer for bringing the existence of this will to my attention. I thank Dr Peter Spufford for discovering in which court, and when, the will was proved.

23 See below, pp. 221–2.

24 William Perkins, *op cit.* (1595), p. 83.

25 William Perneby, *op cit.*, (1599), p. 237–8.

26 William Perkins, *op cit.* (1595), p. 85.

things of this life, and to imitate him in the like'.[27] Each writer further stressed that the sick man was to restore ill-gotten goods to their rightful owners, and that he had a responsibility to make charitable bequests.

The authors also passed comment on the foolish tendency of people to neglect making wills. Perkins identified as common reasons a desire to conceal wealth and a fear that will-making was somehow tempting to death. Perneby, again following suspiciously hot in Perkin's footsteps, assured the reader that 'though . . . he makes a thousand wills (if it were possible for one man to make so many) yet shall he die never the sooner'.[28] Having scorned such superstitious nonsense, Perneby proceeded to warn, a little inconsistently, that the evil inherent in ill-gotten goods would cleave to them still, bringing nothing but harm to the receiver.[29]

Already, writers like Perneby were sharing space on the bookshelf with legal experts on will-making. Henry Swinburne wrote, in 1590, *A briefe treatise of testaments and last willes* and made no mention of faith.[30] Perneby referred specifically to the work, which he said was 'common in everie Stationers open shop, or in each Civilians private studie'.[31] The seventeenth century saw an equally dry contribution from John Godolphin.[32] In practice too, as several modern commentators have observed, the situation was changing as clergymen steadily lost their traditional role at will-makings, and testamentary causes appeared increasingly in the Court of Chancery, rather than in the church courts.[33]

As the seventeenth century drew to a close, William Assheton, rector of a Kent parish, set his back against what he admitted was a changing fashion, and made one last appeal on behalf of religiously grounded wills. Assheton was clearly a divine on the defensive, and he felt the need to justify his purpose in a way that would have surprised a medieval priest: 'And though it must be granted, That to Discourse of Wills and Testaments is chiefly the lawyer's Province; yet, I hope, it will be thought no unsuitable theme for a Divine . . . For though your lawyer can best direct you to draw your will Legally and in Form; yet a Divine may be allowed to instruct you how to make it Charitably, and I may add Prudently, and consequently to your Comfort.'[34]

Assheton recited some of the motivations described by the Elizabethan writers, and criticised many of the still-common failings. Confusedly, he pleaded with his readers to make their wills 'in the time of health' but persistently described a will-making as the 'last', the 'concluding' act of a person's life. He also sought to

27 William Perneby, *op cit.* (1599), p. 237.
28 *Ibid.*, p. 240. In his opening epistle, Perneby told his readers 'If I have imitated any (as I denie not but that I have) I thinke in so doing, I have rather honoured them than hurt them.'
29 *Ibid.*, p. 251.
30 Henry Swinburne, *A Briefe treatise of testaments and last willes* (London, 1590).
31 William Perneby, *op cit.* (1599), p. 242.
32 John Godolphin, *The Orphan's Legacy: or, A Testamentary Abridgement* (London, 1674).
33 Anthony J. Camp, *Wills and their Whereabouts* (London, 1974), p. xxiv.
34 William Assheton, *A Theological Discourse of Last Wills and Testaments* (London, 1696), pp. 2–3.

imbue England's testators with a sense of their personal place in history, urging them to 'Remember your Will stands upon Record for Publick perusal; and therefore to be idle and extravagant in this last Act of your life, is to be hiss'd off the Stage, and to proclaim your folly to all succeeding ages'.[35]

Assheton differed significantly from his Elizabethan predecessors in his statements concerning the will preamble. He told his readers to 'let your Will be so composed, so framed and worded in the commendatory Part, as to declare your self a Christian'. Too many wills, he lamented, broke off abruptly following a depressingly short dedicatory clause. He insisted that testators should 'give . . . a reason of the hope that is in you', and suggested his own lengthy formula for a preamble.[36]

It seems unlikely that, by the very late seventeenth century, Assheton could have expected much success in having his elaborate clause adopted. Within decades, the whole notion of a religiously worded preamble was under threat and the way was clear for the modern-style, faith-free solicitors' testament, written 'in the time of health' and so lacking in colour that few but the testator's relatives are tempted to study it. Assheton's personal and probably doomed attempt to reverse the process in fact looks like a spirited death-rattle, performed on behalf of the traditional will.

Becon's Epaphroditus was unusual. Very few testators expressed themselves at such length on questions of faith. Even the *ars moriendi* authors, with the exception of Assheton, did not encourage them to change their ways. It is tempting to speculate on the circumstances and motivation of the rare testators who did expound their beliefs at length. The state of an individual's health was an obvious factor, since detailed expression was unlikely from a testator who lacked both time and energy. The depth of an individual's faith must also have been influential, though not as clearly so as one might expect. It may not have been so much the strength of belief that set unusually expressive testators apart, as the fact that they felt *self-consciously* pious as they composed their preambles. Epaphroditus, though only the figment of a godly imagination, was a perfect example. The self-styled 'unprofitable servant of God' was so strikingly aware of his own piety that the description is hard to accept. Fortunately, there were occasionally others who proved similarly expressive.

In December 1571, Thomas Merburie, a student at Christ's College, Cambridge, made a will which he headed 'I believe in God the father, god the sone, and god the holie ghost, three persons, but one eternall and ever lyvyng god, and I do fullie looke to be saved by thys my beleiff'.[37] Merburie drew attention to the uncertainty of life and recalled 'we are admonished in the 24 of matthew contynuallie to watche for that we knowe not what howr our master wyll come'. Owing to this uncertainty, Merburie had decided to make a will 'wherebye god wyllynge yt shalbe evident to

35 *Ibid.*, p. 20.

36 *Ibid.*, pp.18–19.

37 Manuscript volume of wills proved in the Vice Chancellor of Cambridge University's Court, 1558–1602, f. 62.

all that during my lieffe I held the profession & belief of a trew Christian man, and goddes grace so assistynge me wyll firmlie & stedfastlye die in the same'.

There followed an extraordinarily full confession of faith. The testator stated his belief in salvation through Christ's death, passion, resurrection and ascension, 'whitowt all vayne opinion of any mans merites, which I do utterly rejecte, detest & abhore as marvelous Injurious to the bludd of my saviour Jesus'. Merburie, amongst a great many things, also expressed an unshakeable belief in his own election: 'I feele inwardlye in my selfe and in my conscience that before all worldes I am predestinate to eternall liefe'. He asked for a modest burial, shorn of hideous papist trappings, and ended with an affirmation of his belief in the certainty of his own resurrection, 'when I shall heare that joyfull voyce, come ye blessed of my father inherite yee the kyngedome prepared for yow before the begynynge of the world'.

There can be no doubt whatsoever that the faith expressed in this will was Merburie's own.[38] The same was certainly true of the will of John Josselin, a distinguished Anglo-Saxon scholar who died at High Roothing, Essex, in 1603. The will had been written over a year earlier, and included an astonishing preamble:

> I doe first of all thanke god, who havinge compassion on me whom he created & placed in this worlde, hath made me to live the most parte of all my life in the light of the gospell, born aboute the ende of the yere of the lorde 1529 when I was drowned according to that my first bringinge up in most deepe darknes of supersticion and Idolatry, being taught to pray to roode stock & stones only in the latyn tonge aswell publickely as pryvately, whereof I understoode no worde, and this was then the common usage of evry man & wooman in those daies, but praised be god that hath made the gospell so to sprede (except fyve supersticious yeres of Queene Maries reigne), that there is none that hath lyved within his tyme but might have plentifully harde thereof his doctryne of salvation, he has made me (most unworthy) partaker, and by the same his mercy, he hath borne from tyme to tyme most gently with my synnes, for the which notwithstandinge I was worthy to be throwen awey of hym, and I have no other helpe & refuge then his free adoption in the which only my salvation leavth, and with all my soule I imbrace the mercy which he showeth to me by & through Christ makeinge a satisfaction for all my faults with the merite & deathe of his passion that by this meanes for all my synnes & transgressions he is fully satisfied and the memory of them cleane blotted out. As concerning the rest and further that is to be done in my Will/ I will my body to be buried in the Chauncell of highe Rodinge Churche harde by the place & before the place where I was wonte to sitt, with a stone laid over me by the discrecion of myne executor, and I doe persuade my self that I am not longe to reste there, believinge that the tyme draweth nere when I shalbe raised ageyne to meete my saviour the lorde Jesus in the cloudes when his

38 Although Dr Margaret Spufford and I both feel that idiosyncratic preambles *do* reflect directly the personal faith of the testator or scribe, Dr Spufford feels that I have under-emphasised the point in the final writing of the paper. For further discussion, see below, pp. 238–9. I have chosen instead to concentrate on more general contemporary practice and attitudes.

comynge shall not be in humylitie & basenes, as when he toke upon hym the shape of a servant & our nature, and in the same suffered for the synnes of mankinde, but with unspeakable maiestie & glory, to the grete comforte of them that here lyvinge in this myserable world have made hym by faith their only rightiousnes & justificacon, and without hym acknowledge their life to be nothinge but mysery and them selves to be but shame and confusion.[39]

We must be grateful that Merburie and Josselin chose to record the details of their inward belief in such a developed outward manner. Both men appear to have been guided, to some extent at least, by a pronounced polemical instinct. Their attitude towards detailed expression in a will was certainly not shared by all men of faith, and the counter-examples, though much less exciting, are probably more numerous. The will of William Perkins has already been cited.[40] The case of Bishop Cooper of Winchester was similar. His will, written in 1594, opened with an individual-sounding but conventional statement on mortality, but the testator left his soul 'into the handes of my Redeemer', with no further comment.[41] It seems reasonable to assume that the bishop, author of an impressive homily on the 'right use of the Lord's Supper', could have discoursed upon his faith at rather greater length, had he felt that the moment was right.[42]

Equally instructive was the will of Thomas Adam, an innholder from Saffron Walden, dated in December 1572.[43] Adam made his will, 'considring the manyfold myseries, Calamities, maladies & perills of death emynate in my mortall body & howe sodenly in these dayes the mortalitye or lyfe of man is extinct to the ensample that other may learne to be redy . . . When god shall call them'. This is the most conscious attempt so far found on the part of a testator to influence his neighbours for the better. The phrases were not, apparently, used in other wills written in the same area at this time; they would, then, seem to reflect the personal feelings of the innholder or, less probably, of his scribe.

Adam recorded further reasons for making his will: 'And as I am sure to dye so am I unsure & uncertaine when & howe shortlye therfore to the intent I wyll avoyd worldly trobles & vayne affections in the panges & agonye of death the wch at that tyme might perhappes withdrawe my mynde & godlye zeale to depart well and Chrystyanlye And furtermore to establish a direct order in the distribucion of such worldly goodes and riches as God hath lent me for the better quietnesse of my posteritie & succession.'

39 Essex Record Office, D/ABW 21/214. I am extremely grateful to Mrs Elizabeth Sellers for sending me a copy of this preamble, via Dr Spufford. Neither I nor Dr Spufford have ever come across a will which discusses the history of the English Reformation in any comparable way.

40 See above, pp. 219–20.

41 Lincoln Record Society, Vol. 2 (1912), p. 339.

42 Thomas Cooper, A *briefe homily, wherein the most comfortable and right use of the Lord's Supper is very plainly opened and delivered, even to the understanding of the unlearned and ignorant* (London, 1580).

43 Essex Record Office, 336 CR 6.

Despite such expressiveness, the dedicatory clause, when it eventually came, was brief in the extreme. The testator was clearly a man whose faith meant a great deal to him, but he wrote merely 'I bequeath my soul to Almighty God.'

Adam agreed with the godly authors that the will-making was an unwelcome distraction in the approach to death. He made his will in order that he would be able 'to depart well and Chrystyanlye' when the moment arrived. His commendatory clause was neutral by any standards, because he did not regard his will as the appropriate place for a full-blown confession of faith. He may well have made such a confession at another time.

As in the pre-Reformation period, it was the subsequent 'worldly' bequests that really reflected the strength of a testator's faith. In 1586, a yeoman named William Rushbrigg from Emneth in Norfolk made a will which displayed a short and wholly unexceptional dedicatory clause.[44] Rushbrigg demonstrated his piety instead with bequests to his church, his vicar and the poor of his village. If his son died, the will continued, Rushbrigg's entire estate was to be used for the benefit of the poor and the community, despite the implied existence (in the form of a 'cousin') of more distant kin. The testator left money for the erection of an alms house, the construction of a gate at the church stile, the repairing of the church way, the diking of the river and the building of a bridge, 'for people safely to passe'. Additionally, he requested a burial sermon, four further sermons, and made extensive extra gifts to the poor.

If the legatee William Hall was truly the testator's cousin, he may – depending on his temperament and beliefs – have felt a little aggrieved to see such wealth pass out of the family. Hall received bequests that were small in comparison, though they perhaps enabled him to understand better his cousin's motives: 'one pair of spectacles, one service book, and another booke callyd the Sick mans salve'. Rushbrigg was obviously familiar with his Christian duty as described by Becon, and a couple of his phrases remind one of the great writer, yet he ignored completely the implied message that a preamble, like that of Epaphroditus (the not so unprofitable servant of God), should be long and expressive. The Emneth testator was evidently thinking clearly when he made his will – so detailed was it in other respects – but he appears to have seen the full expression of his faith in the preamble as something superfluous and unnecessary. His charitable bequests spoke for themselves.

There appears, then, to have been a common body of motivations uniting godly writers and those testators who expressed themselves, whether by words, deeds, or both. Broadly speaking, a will for the godly man was written because it was the Christian's duty before God to settle his estate, of which he had been but a steward, in such a way as to promote peace, 'stay disputes' and glorify God. In doing so, he hoped also to procure himself a degree of spiritual tranquillity, essential if he were to die 'Chrystyanlye'. There was also an element, sometimes at least, in which the testator saw it as his responsibility to set an example to others, to lead his neighbours into similarly godly practice. Within this framework of spiritual motivations

[44] C[ambridge] U[niversity] L[ibrary], Ely Cons[istory Court] original will, William Russbrigg (1586). I am grateful to Professor Eric Carlson for bringing this will to my attention.

and choices, a pious and eloquently elaborated preamble can perhaps be classified as 'a thing indifferent'.

Most of the evidence discussed so far relates to persons who had taken the message of protestantism to heart, who had been perhaps peculiarly receptive to reformed teachings. For the will-making population at large, conclusions are harder to reach. It was possible, then as now, to decide to make a will on grounds that had little to do with faith; complicated personal affairs, the need, seen in worldly terms, to provide for one's children, a desire to remember close and not necessarily godly friends, a vain urge to influence earthly events after one's death, or a vindictive wish to punish a thankless child. All such concerns could be discussed without reference to God, even in an age when religion in English society was far more pervasive than it is today.

A small but significant minority of wills became the subjects of litigation, most frequently in the ecclesiastical courts. It is to the records of such causes that we must look in an attempt to carry this examination of testamentary motivations out of 'godly' circles and into society as a whole. The following discussion is based upon over forty disputed will cases in the dioceses of Ely, London, Exeter, Durham and Winchester.[45] The sample is a relatively small one, not scientifically constructed, and the observations made here are therefore impressionistic.

Testamentary cause records sometimes yield to the historian a quantity of vivid detail which cannot be guessed at from the wills themselves. They are essential sources for students of death, and frequently reveal striking pictures of deathbed scenes and attitudes. It is often possible to observe the bonds of kinship and neighbourliness in the face of sickness and death. This paper is particularly concerned with what the records reveal of the circumstances of will-making, and the spiritual motivations, if any, that lay behind it.

There are obviously certain questions of reliability to be considered when interpreting these records. Incidents of deception are likely, especially when dealing with men like John Lawson of Darwen (Durham), described by one neighbour as 'but a runner and a slave, that will say as any man will have him for a peic of bread'.[46] Similarly, it can be argued that court records, by definition, describe those cases which fell outside the accepted framework of things. In countering this criticism, it is customary to observe that, even so, such records cast their own perverse light upon the norms of behaviour, the expectations of local societies. Furthermore, in many of the cases, different witnesses presented their own recollections of what were clearly the same events. It does seem possible to establish a core of truth; this is, after all, exactly what the courts were seeking to do.

Evidence relating to the physical circumstances of testators at the time of will-making reveals, not surprisingly, a number of common characteristics. Most were

45 I have used manuscript court records in the dioceses of Ely, London (Essex), Exeter and Winchester. The Durham cases discussed here are taken from James Raine (ed.), *Depositions and other Ecclesiastical Proceedings from the Courts of Durham*, Surtees Society, (1845).

46 *Ibid.*, pp. 265–76.

sick, though by no means all were in the final throes of disease. The 'darts of death' were perceived to be on their way, but impact was not always imminent. The vicar of Sutton (Ely) arrived at the house of William Bateman, 'wheare in a kytecyen . . . he found the sayd testator sitting by the fyr side'.[47] A widow from Little Shelford (Ely) was 'lyinge uppon hir bed in a redd kertle haveing a quilte lyinge uppon hir'.[48] A clerical testator from Swavesey (Ely) was sick 'in his chamber where he used always to lye hanged with paynted clothes wherein was iii beds'.[49] There were many similar examples.

The procedures employed in making wills also display common features. The basic pattern – calling witnesses, making the will, hearing it read, and ratifying it – was followed in numerous cases. When the details are examined further, however, there is found to be a surprisingly wide variety of practices, not all of which will be comforting to historians who count wills among their chief sources.

The Sutton (Ely) testator, William Bateman, went one better than Epaphroditus by deciding to make his will 'in his good health'. The will had in fact been 'conceyved in writing' some time before Bateman chose to finalise it in the presence of witnesses. Still healthy, the testator summoned several villagers to his home, including his scribe – a layman called Daniel Morton – and the local vicar, Simon Nappe. Morton then read the will to the testator, who acknowledged it as his own. The document was not dated at its original writing but at the point when Bateman ratified it for the last time.

Ironically, the testator's commendable foresight was to backfire on the night of his death. It seems that, because of changed circumstances, Bateman had wished to revise his will shortly before his decease. He had, however, been unable to have it set in writing because, as Robert Claybell informed the court, 'one Danyell who should have bene the writer was in Bedd and felt himself not then well and sayd in the morning he would helpe them as earlye as they would'. When Daniel Morton arrived the next day, he may have experienced feelings of guilt at finding the testator no longer 'sitting by the fyr side' but 'dead in a chamber'. Bateman's widow then produced the first will, written by Morton, but another participant in the unfolding drama exclaimed 'whye it skills no matter for that will, For the said William Bateman made another will [by word of mouth] this night and gave his wife all his house goodes lands and Cattells therein'.[50]

The case cautions strongly against assuming, even in the early part of Elizabeth's reign, that a clerical witness was also the scribe. It is also of note that the dating of the written will did not coincide with its composition. In this instance, 'it skils no matter' because the testator lived for two further years, but it is easy to conceive of a will, written months from death, when sickness was not extreme, but then finalised and dated when death loomed larger. The exceptionally pious will of Thomas Merburie, already quoted, is a case in point. The model student wrote or dictated his

47 CUL, E[ly] D[iocesan] R[ecords], D/2/6, f. 22.
48 CUL, EDR, D/2/11, f. 109.
49 CUL, EDR, D/2/7, f. 256.
50 CUL, EDR, D/2/6, ff. 22–7.

will, 'being in health at this present time both of bodie and mynde', but the document was dated just a few days before probate was granted and therefore very close to the time of the testator's death.[51] This may have happened frequently enough to threaten the validity of comparing the date written on a will with that of burial or probate and concluding that most wills were composed very shortly before death.[52] Indeed, on the face of things, Elizabethan testators do appear to have had an uncanny knack of knowing which particular bout of sickness was the final one. The common clause 'revoking all former wills by me made' should also be remembered here. Not all testators left their wills until the final hours.

Standard practice becomes harder to identify as more cases are studied. The right-first-time will-making, though fairly common, was far from universal. The preparation of a will was no easy matter, especially if the testator's affairs were complex, and many scribes must have found it difficult to set the will down in perfect form at the first attempt. Consequently, it appears to have been common for a scribe to carry the first draft away with him, for periods ranging from a few days to several months, in order to make a 'fair copy'. Sometimes, scribes still managed to make crucial mistakes, as in the will of John Salmon of Willingham (Ely).[53] The testator had bequeathed to his wife 'all that she brought' with her at their marriage. The scribe took the original will home with him, and absent-mindedly added the words 'household stuff' to the clause, when he wrote the will neatly. The resultant dispute centred on a heifer ('now grown to a good Cowe') which had been part of the bride's dowry, and which defied classification as 'household stuff'.

In this case, the surviving 'original' is in fact the faulty 'fair copy' which was never read before the testator. It bears the witnesses' names all written in the same hand, that of the incompetent scribe. Such examples have been seen as evidence that the true originals were handed back to the executors and only office copies kept by the court.[54] It is clear, however, that the court never saw the genuine original of John Salmon's will.[55] The scribe added further to the local historian's confusion by omitting his own name from the list of witnesses. He perhaps had good reason for wishing to remain anonymous. Salmon's dedicatory clause was strongly protestant, but the man who may have been responsible for it is known of only through the court dispute. It sounds highly irregular, but the vicar of Meldreth displayed the same frustrating modesty when he wrote Robert Thurgood's will in

51 See above pp. 222–3 and n. 37.

52 See, for example, Margaret Spufford, *op cit.* (1974), pp. 321–2. Also, Derek Plumb, *op cit.* (1987), p. 51. For the most recent statement of this view, see Stephen Coppel, 'Will-making on the Deathbed', in *Local Population Studies*, No. 40, (Spring, 1988), pp. 37–45. I am sure, however, that Mr Coppel is right to state that most testators chose to make wills because they felt that the sickness afflicting them was potentially very serious. (For some eighteenth century evidence see also Anthony Camp's paper below p. 289. Eds.)

53 CUL, Ely Cons original will, John Salmon (1560). For records of the court case, see CUL, EDR, D/2/4, ff. 118–23.

54 See Margaret Spufford, *op cit.* (1974), p. 323.

55 For similar examples, see below, p. 230.

1594.[56] The fact that this omission of the scribe's name occurred in two out of only ten cases where the records of litigation have been compared to the original wills is alarming.

On other occasions, the procedure was not of such dubious reliability. More often, the fair copy was prepared following discussion between scribe and testator. It was then this copy that was read and witnessed. At Lent in 1570, the vicar of Swavesey (Ely) assisted 'Father Stacy' in the final preparations of his will.[57] The document was then read aloud to the testator. The vicar, according to his own evidence, then 'toke it whom [home] wth him to wryte it fayre, & brought it to him aboute Julye following & red it to him in the presence of John Graves.' There were very similar cases in each of the five dioceses under view here.

There were also occasional cases in which the will was written up in its first form by a scribe working at home, unaccompanied by the testator. John Prowse of Brixham (Exeter) decided to summon the vicar, 'for that he . . . felt him self sick and therefore entended to make his will'.[58] The vicar duly arrived, and

> having passed somme talk about the making of the will the sayd vicare then knowing his minde and what he should doe at that tyme went from him And within a day or two or iii after as he remembreth the sayd vicare came agayne to the sayd John Prowse lyeng sick in his bedd and brought the sayd . . . testament reddye written with him.

We cannot tell at which point the preamble was composed, but the implication is scarcely reassuring. In this case, as in a number of others, it was not the making of the will that was witnessed, but a subsequent reading.

Some of the most striking cases are those which demonstrate that the preparation of a will could be a process of evolution through changing times, a fact which is frequently hidden in the once-for-all document with which the courts usually dealt. Sometimes, the situation changed sufficiently that a clean break was made and a wholly new will written. Richard Tickner of Wonersh (Winchester) made a will shortly before his death in 1596.[59] When it had been amended and sealed, the testator 'did teare in peaces another writing wch he . . . termed to be his old will. And he bid his wife to burne the pieces thereof. And he toke his said last will to his wefe & bid her lay it up.'

In other cases, the necessary revisions were not quite severe enough to warrant a fresh start. The last will of a man from nearby Albury (Winchester) was extremely untidy, almost illegible in places, because of extensive amendments made in the late stages.[60] The document was written in three different hands. The Swavesey fair copy to which reference has already been made was just the final stage in a lengthy process.[61] In September 1569, Father Stacy called on Robert Loder 'to beare wytnes

56 CUL, EDR, D/2/9, ff. 40–3.
57 CUL, EDR, D/2/7, ff. 155–8.
58 Devon C[ounty] R[ecord] O[ffice], Chanter 860, ff. 141–44.
59 Hampshire RO, Winchester wills, B68/1–5, (1596).
60 Hampshire RO, Winchester wills, B81/1–8, (1591).
61 CUL, EDR, D/2/7, ff. 155–8.

of his will makinge'. Stacy was sick in bed, attended by his daughter and one Lawrence Milford. Stacy then made his will, which was 'wrytten and drawen' by Milford.[62] The scribe then went on his way, leaving the will with Stacy's wife.

The following Lent, six months on, Stacy again summoned Loder. Present this time was the vicar, 'Syr Curtys', to whom the testator or his wife delivered the will. Stacy then ordered several alterations. An additional witness was called, and Curtis read the will to the testator, who acknowledged it gratefully as 'the last will that ever he wold make'.

At this point, the vicar took the will away to make the fair copy, returning four months later, when he said to the testator 'I have brought your will . . . will you have it redd?' Stacy agreed and, finally, a process which had lasted the best part of a year was concluded; in a document which bore one date and looked for all the world like a straightforward composition. Sadly, there is no trace of the will in the records today, so it is impossible to answer procedural questions about the dating of the document and the fullness of the witness list.

One of the implications of cases like this is that godly advice to people, that they make their wills while in health, could be impractical. Circumstances could change rapidly and radically so that old wills became outdated. A widow from Little Shelford made her will at harvest time in 1575, bequeathing a quantity of corn to certain of her relatives.[63] She then lived longer than had evidently been anticipated and was forced to make amendments hardly less distracting than the original will-making. Harvest had been and gone, and the testator, when asked about the corn bequest, observed testily 'they can not have yt nowe, it is not to be had'. Later still, she made further alterations and, as the vicar recalled with surprise, 'sett hir marcke unto the sayd wyll even blotted, rased, corrected & amended as it was'. The vicar then made a fair copy at home, dating the will at this point. This copy, as in the Willingham case, is the so-called 'original' available for inspection today. It carries no trace of the widow's mark, known to have been placed on the real original. There appears to have been considerable scope for the tightening of probate procedures.

The preparation of a will could, then, be a complicated process, and the testator needed to be in firm control of his or her mental faculties. Cases in which advantage was taken of a deranged or witless testator were in fact rare, though the last week of Thomas Hopper of 'Medomsley' (Durham) was a troubled time indeed.[64] Numerous deponents gave evidence that the testator had been 'raving' during his final days. John Hunter told the court that, a week before the testator died, he 'was neither of good memory nor reason, but all distracte, singinge hey roiffe songs'. Similar tales abounded, as the testator came to sound increasingly like King Lear at a comparable point in his life cycle. One female deponent described the occasion when Thomas had 'cauld for his dagger, and said . . . that if he had his dagger he would sley the fellow that had his goods'. Humphrey Hopper, either the villain of the piece or a

62 For further discussion of Lawrence Milford, see below pp. 234–5.
63 CUL, EDR, D/2/11, ff. 109–12.
64 James Raine, *op cit.* (1845), pp. 265–76.

caring and protective father, had turned all visitors out of the room with the words 'Away, thou troublest him'. Perhaps displaying reason in madness, the testator later told his father 'thou art the black devell of Edeedsbrig' and exclaimed to onlookers 'Tak this man . . . I chardge you in the Quene's name and my Lord of Durham, for he hath stolne all my goodes and caried it to Lyddisdaill'.

This case, though compelling, was highly unusual. The majority of testators were, despite sickness, firmly in control of proceedings. William Bateman was 'in good and perfight mind and memorye for he talked well and ratefyed . . . his testament when the same was read byfour him'.[65] The description was typical. Johane Haryson easily held her own in a quarrel with her grandson over the future of a white curtain.[66] In several cases, witnesses gave shining testimony to the testators' sanity. The scribe in a Devon case said of his testator that he 'did here him talk as wiselye as ever he did heare him talk in his life even almost at his last hour'.[67] Ellen Searle of Kirton (Exeter) had been equally eloquent.[68]

Most of these testators were sick when they made their wills, but they were certainly not putty in the hands of grasping relatives. In a number of instances, it seems likely that they had actually become, through old age and sickness, more short-tempered and confrontational than ever they had been 'in the time of health'. Manipulation was not rife and few testators had lost either the will or the power to control events. Robert Thurgood was mentally, if not physically, agile as his will reached its final form.[69] He altered the document, after careful thought, to remove his wife as executor. He then faced the unenviable task of keeping his decision secret from her, and almost found it beyond him:

> after the said testator had confirmed the said will, he . . . did laye it in the corner of the windowe to drie and Joyce Thurgood his wyef comenge up & takeinge it in her hand & goeinge away with it, he the said testator perceivinge it called her, & desyred her to let hym have it, wch she dyd, & soe he delivered [it] to this deponent.

It appears that the description 'weak in body though sound of mind' had an accuracy which one does not necessarily associate with stereotypical phraseology.

There remained, however, an important role to be played by the friends, neighbours and relatives of the testator. The bonds of kinship and neighbourliness meant different things to different individuals, and for some deponents the motives for advising or speaking with a testator were unashamedly cynical. Urias Spicer of Chesterton (Ely) went out drinking with the testator, Thomas Willowes, and another man; and 'being merrilie disposed said to . . . the testator you and this man are Cosens and he and I are Cosens and why may not you and I . . . be Cosins?' He added, as neighbourly good will gave way to shallow greed, 'I would gladly be your

65 CUL, EDR, D/2/6, f. 22.
66 CUL, EDR, D/2/11, f. 110.
67 Devon RO, Chanter 860, f. 142.
68 Devon RO, Chanter 860, ff. 381–5.
69 CUL, EDR, D/2/9, ff. 40–3.

Cosin for that you are a wealthy fellowe and have no children that I might have some of your goodes'.[70]

Court officials were always anxious to establish whether a deponent had any particular interest in the case. It appears that, cynical worldliness aside, men and women with little to gain were frequently forthcoming with words of advice and comfort. Deponents across the land dropped in on ailing neighbours to make friendly enquiries about the state of body and mind. As Gilbert Atwell passed the gate of Ellen Serle, the Devonshire widow, he met his own brother Nicholas; 'and understanding . . . of the sicknes of the widow Searle, lighted from his horse and went into her house to se howe she did.' He continued, 'after some talke betwene them he this deponent persuaded [advised] her to make her will and to distribute somewhat to the poore . . . and she aunswered she had made her will already and it was in George Trowbridges handes.'[71] Six or more assorted friends and relatives were also present during the exchange. Deathbed gatherings of this sort must have been important social occasions, at which reputations for neighbourliness could be made and lost.

In extreme circumstances, neighbourly duty could be deliberately flouted in order to make a point. John Pottes of Cambridge decided not to visit his former friend, Thomas Willowes, when he fell ill in 1593.[72] Willowes later recovered and confronted Pottes, saying 'that he marveiled that he came not to visite him in the time of his sicknes'. To this Pottes responded 'the cause is for that it is reported by manie and beleeved of some that you have given yor kinsman of horningseye all your goodes except twenty nobles and the lease of the painters house'. The precise reason for Pottes' anger was his feeling that the testator was under-valuing his wife by bequeathing much of his estate to a mere cousin. He further informed Willowes that, if the rumours were true, 'you will goe to the divell for . . . if she had ben yor servant as she is yor wyffe she had ben worthye of xx shillings a yeare and she hathe ben yor wiffe these xx yeares'. Pottes clearly felt that the testator had neglected his duty, and that he, 'the said deponent', was therefore absolved of his own.

Perkins had lamented the fact that many people were far from skilled at talking profitably to their sick neighbours.[73] Later, Assheton alleged that, in too many instances, people were afraid of suggesting to their afflicted friends that a will should be made.[74] Such anxiety to avoid offence was not always evident in the court depositions. William Goodman of Chesterton (Ely), for example, displayed brutal honesty when, on meeting a neighbour in the street, he said 'you have ben sicke you looke not well and you wax old I would wish you . . . to set things at a staye'.[75]

Neighbours at a sick person's bedside could be required to ensure that tempers did not become over-heated. When the Shelford widow clashed with her grandson

70 CUL, EDR, D/2/9, ff. 190–208.
71 Devon RO, Chanter 860, f. 381.
72 CUL, EDR, D/2/9, ff. 190–208.
73 William Perkins, *op cit.* (1595), p. 60.
74 William Assheton, *op cit.* (1696), p.11.
75 CUL, EDR, D/2/9, f. 193.

concerning a white curtain, it was only 'uppon the intrety of the cumpanye then present' that real fury was forestalled.[76] Interestingly, it was the aged widow, rather than her grandson, who was urged to moderate her conduct. Friends and neighbours played an important role in the preparation of a will, and in the broader atmosphere that surrounded it.

Naturally, therefore, testators generally selected their witnesses quite deliberately, basing their choices upon personal friendship and social respect. The testator who was concious of the need to make his will 'as sure as may be' would also have been aware of the need to call 'credible' witnesses. In particular communities, therefore, the same individuals tend to appear repeatedly at local will-makings.

In most depositions, the exact reasons for a particular choice are not articulated, but at the time of will-making, the testators' servants, wives and children were frequently sent out to request the presence of particular individuals. An Essex man was summoned, 'being the nere neighbour & well willer of the testator'.[77] A witness in another case was told by the testator, 'after much familiar and comfortable speeches had betwen them', that 'he had sent for him . . . as his speciall frind that he would have his will made'.[78] Occasionally, witnesses were present for less touching reasons; Roger Hopper happened to walk past a testator's house at the right moment, 'being in the way to se the yought [youth] of Kirkly play at fott ball'.[79] In the majority of cases, however, witnesses – like executors – were chosen quite deliberately.

A reliable scribe could be of crucial significance. The testator needed above all a man who could be trusted to prepare a legally acceptable document. Beyond this basic criterion, factors such as personal friendship, social respect and religious affiliation may have come into play. The testator's choice was further influenced, of course, by the local availability of scribes, and presumably by the amount of money he was prepared to pay in order to employ a good one.

The later sixteenth and seventeenth centuries were part of a very broad period of transition. In medieval villages, the local priest had been the almost inevitable choice as will scribe, through his superior literacy and his extensive experience in what was perceived as a traditional role. By the eighteenth and nineteenth centuries, professional legal experts had come to enjoy a similar dominance. Elizabethan England presents evidence of both these types, and of a third transitional breed of will scribe – the 'capable' local layman, who wrote wills either as neighbourly service, or on a semi-professional basis.

There is very little to indicate that 'public notaries' were widely operative in rural England during the reign of Elizabeth. Will-writing in the towns may have been slightly different. In the corporate town of Wisbech (Ely), just one will from some one hundred and fifty made between 1570 and 1600 was written by a self-

[76] CUL, EDR, D/2/11, ff. 109–12.
[77] Essex RO, D/ACD 1, f. 1.
[78] Essex RO, D/AED 1, f. 48.
[79] James Raine, *op cit.* (1845), p. 79.

proclaimed notary;[80] no similar examples have been found in the wills written in villages like Balsham, Shudy Camps and Horningsea.

The clergy were, nevertheless, already declining in importance as will scribes. It has been argued that, by the middle years of Elizabeth's reign, the number of literate and 'capable' yeomen had increased significantly, so that the pool of potential scribes was wider and deeper than ever before.[81] When Leonard Woolward of Balsham (Ely) made his will in 1578, for example, he could have chosen from a wide range of scribes among his 'friends or acquaintances'. Instead, he eventually asked his barber-surgeon, literate though poor, to perform the task. The fact that they then borrowed writing implements from another neigbour seems to strengthen the case further.[82] Literacy was spreading and a growing number of villagers were skilful enough to draft a will.

Not all the evidence points the same way. Nuncupative wills remained fairly common, indicating that some testators did not share Woolward's perception of a wide selection of possible scribes. William Bateman's last will went unwritten on the night of his death, because the scribe was himself temporarily sick. For some reason, Bateman and his wife failed to find another.[83] Literacy levels were undoubtedly rising, but signing one's name was considerably more straightforward than writing a will upon which much could depend. In 1595, the Wonersh yeoman Richard Ticknor made his will, but 'doubted that it was not set downe sufficiently', 'because it was written but by a young scholler'. Consequently, but unusually, he sent it to a Guildford expert for checking.[84]

This need for security, combined with improving lay literacy, led to the development – in some parts of the country at least – of a body of highly literate individuals who established reputations as will-writers. Such lay specialists could be extremely desirable. Lawrence Milford, scribe of the first draft of Father Stacy's will in Swavesey (Ely), clearly enjoyed a sound local reputation. Milford, a schoolmaster and farmer, was himself resident in nearby Willingham, where he wrote a series of fifty wills between 1570 and 1602.[85] Would-be testators must frequently have waited until Milford could attend them. He did not miraculously appear at sick-beds with the aid of some sixth sense; he was summoned by the testators or their relatives, and successfully cornered the local market.

The Milford monopoly was perhaps an extreme case. Not every community had such a dominant semi-professional lay specialist, chosen primarily for the proven legality of the documents he produced. In villages like Balsham, although watertight wills were equally important, the choice of scribe may have been affected to a greater extent by personal frienship and trust. The task of drafting late Elizabethan

80 CUL, Ely Cons original will, John Robinson (1597).
81 Margaret Spufford, *op cit.* (1974), p. 182.
82 CUL, EDR, D/2/11, ff. 259–61.
83 CUL, EDR, D/2/6, ff. 22–7. See above, p. 227.
84 Hampshire RO, Winchester wills, B68/1–5.
85 Margaret Spufford, *op cit.* (1974), p. 328.

wills seems to have been shared in Balsham by at least half a dozen local yeomen.[86] None of the wills they wrote was called into doubt at the consistory court; the service these literate villagers provided was apparently considered satisfactory.

England's clergymen had not, however, been completely eclipsed from proceedings. Lawrence Milford may have written the first draft of Father Stacy's will, but the final version was in the hand of the minister, Edmund Curtis.[87] In some communities, the vicar continued to write most of the wills. In villages where a range of lay scribes was also available, it can perhaps be argued that a decision to involve the vicar carried with it a significance that had not been there when he was the only literate man in the community. Robert Thurgood of Meldreth (Ely) made a spoken will in 1594, and said 'it should serve untill he could have it written'. It was several days before this was done, despite the fact that the testator's brother and his barber-surgeon were both sufficiently literate to sign the eventual will. Rather than entrust the task to either of these men, Thurgood awaited the arrival of John Gosling, the local vicar. A generous bequest to the poor strengthens the impression that the testator was a particularly religious man. Interestingly, the vicar omitted his own name from the final copy of the will, even though he wrote it 'at home at his owne house'.[88]

The will of William Bateman of Sutton (Ely) was similar, though in this instance the vicar was merely a witness, not the scribe. The testator's elaborate bequests to the poor were set in writing before Simon Nappe, 'clericus', appeared on the scene; without the benefit of court depositions it would have been tempting to see the vicar's hand in such piety. When Mr Nappe arrived at Bateman's house, however, he noticed – without surprise or the anger of one whose office has been usurped – that Daniel Morton was already present, 'haveing the same [will] in his hand for that he was the writer thereof'.[89] The vicar's presence was desired on grounds that had nothing to do with his literacy.

In a couple of cases, there is evidence that the old reliance on the priest as will scribe retained some of its hold. In 1586, Lancelot Morgan of Walsingham (Durham) summoned several of his friends and declared 'Neighbours, here is niether minister nor clerk at home, and I would make my will, and I pray you to beare witness how I dispose my goods'.[90] With no cleric available, it was felt that the will could not be set in writing. John Hind, a Cambridgeshire husbandman, arrived at a testator's house to find the will already completed; he surmised that it was 'wrytten . . . by William Bylducke [vicar of Little Shelford] for that there was no other clercke then & there present'.[91]

The pastoral involvement of local clergymen can occasionally be traced in some detail. The enthusiasm displayed by an individual vicar in the performance of his

86 The parish of Balsham will be discussed at length in my Ph.D. thesis, currently in preparation.
87 CUL, EDR, D/2/7, ff. 155–8.
88 CUL, EDR, D/2/9, ff. 40–3.
89 CUL, EDR, D/2/6, ff. 22–7.
90 James Raine, *op cit.* (1845), pp. 320–1.
91 CUL, EDR, D/2/11, ff. 109–112.

duty could obviously have affected the degree to which testators felt concious of the spiritual importance of a will-making. The vicar of Sandon in Essex proudly told the court that, 'according to his duetye', he had visited a sick member of his flock:

> and after he this deponent had godlye enstructed him and perceived him to be readie to die, he this deponent lykewise perswaded him to sett downe order for the desposinge of his goodes and to make his will and the same testator was verie well content therwithall confessinge that it was his onelye desier.[92]

At Merrington (Durham) the minister was still more precise in performing his Prayer Book responsibilities. William Melmerbye visited the sick man, asked of his welfare, gently encouraged the making of a will and inquired whether a bequest to the poor was intended. The testator, who knew his own mind, replied 'I gyve dayly to the poore, as other neighbours doith, and therefore I will nothing to the poore man box.' He apparently felt that his own duties were increasingly fulfilled through more formal contributions to traditional good causes. A pang of sickness later struck the testator and the will-making was delayed. The priest, fearing that the testator's time was short, said 'Let us goo to the communion, and lett my hoost advyse hym what he wold say or doo afterwarde.' He perhaps felt that, since his own attempts to encourage charity had failed, something a little more persuasive was required. The vicar eventually wrote the will up at home, and returned it to his dogmatic parishioner.[93]

The clergy at Norton and Shotley (both Durham) were similarly active. Robert Blaxton, 'clerk' of Norton delivered his 'goostly counsaill' and administered the communion to a testator, before writing her will.[94] William Strothers, curate of Shotley, also administered the final communion and wrote a testator's will.[95] Although the evidence may be distorted, it seems that northern clergymen – more so than their counterparts in the southern province – were consistently regarded as essential participants at a will-making. The reason may well have lain in the continuing scribal superiority of the clergy in a region where literacy was not advancing so steadily. As these cases reveal, however, there were other grounds upon which the presence of a minister might have been desired.

The influence of the clergy brings us back to the point from which we embarked: the role of religion in motivating lay-people to write their wills, and the importance of dedicatory clauses. There clearly were those occasions when the presence of a dutiful vicar, with his 'ghostly counsel' and pastoral advice, must have ensured that a testator was conscious of the spiritual reasons for writing a will, but how prominent a place did these reasons occupy in the popular mind?

There is little suggestion in any of these cases that, for the majority of testators, the composition of a dedicatory clause was viewed as a matter of any great signifi-

92 Essex RO, D/AED 1, f. 59.
93 James Raine, *op cit.* (1845), pp. 212–15.
94 *Ibid.*, pp. 232–3.
95 *Ibid.*, pp. 265–76.

cance. Unfortunately, none of the testators studied here displayed exceptional puritan zeal as they approached death and will-making. This is in itself significant, but it should be remembered that such individuals did exist, and that details surrounding the making of some of their wills might be found to modify the picture. As we have seen, a handful of testators certainly did put heart and soul into the composition of their preambles. They were, however, unusual.

Deponents were almost invariably required to express an opinion on the testator's sanity at the time of will-making. It is striking that recollections concerning the composition of the preamble were not presented as evidence in any of the cases studied. Deponents spoke of the testators' ability to remember the names of their more obscure aquaintances, or the details of debts, and to express themselves forcefully when faced with difficulties. If the precise wording of preambles was a 'live issue' at the average English will-making, the fact would surely have emerged in evidence of this type.

On the other hand, a great many testators would probably have expressed concern if their scribes had simply omitted the dedicatory clause altogether. Wills which displayed no religious content whatsoever were still extremely rare, and were to remain so for many decades.[96] Such wills were, however, accepted by the probate courts.[97] The religious preamble would surely have had a much shorter life than it did if England's testators had no desire at all for its continuing existence. They may not have agonised unduly over the exact phraseology employed, but they probably desired their wills to be couched in the broadly traditional religious terms. To call the will preamble a matter of form is, on the one hand, to argue that intense concentration by historians on the precise wording of individual wills may be a misguided approach; on the other hand, it is to say that the religious preamble, in whatever form, was one of the few ingredients of a will which could be assumed desirable by virtually all testators. The relationship between fashion, form and individual preference is obviously a complex one, but it seems probable that most testators in Elizabethan England wished their wills to reflect their basic faith, even if they rarely expressed much concern over the precise form of the reflection.

In most cases, the fundamental religious format could be safely assumed by testators, and there need have been no detailed discussion. When the vicar of Merrington (Durham) arrived at William Kirkus' house, he asked 'Will ye make a will?' and 'what will ye give to the poore man box?', but he did not, apparently, ask for direction on the wording of the religious preamble.[98] The testator probably felt that the vicar could be relied upon to reflect the essential nature of his belief.

[96] The wills written in Banbury retained religious expressions at least until the 1730s. See R. T. Vann, 'Wills and the Family in an English Town: Banbury 1550–1800', *Journal of Family History* (Winter, 1979), p. 360.

[97] See, for example, the will of George Wilson, Ely Cons original will, (1628). The significance of such wills is hard to gauge. Wilson sounded disillusioned, referring to the disposal of 'that little wch god hath lent me'. He may have dropped the dedicatory clause deliberately. In most cases, there is no indication of the testator's reasons for departing from the traditional format.

[98] James Raine, *op cit.* (1845), pp. 212–15.

The attitude of the courts is also worth discussing. A great deal of scribal time was spent in transcribing will preambles, word for word, into court registers.[99] The precise religious nature of the documents would then appear to have been of some importance to the authorities. It is normal, at this point in the argument, to refer to the case of William Tracy, the Gloucestershire man who was exhumed, in the 1530s, for writing a radically protestant will preamble. It can then be added, in the words of Dr O'Day, that 'even contemporaries employed the preambles of wills as evidence of men's religious beliefs.'[100] It was, indeed, an important case, but the fact that it seems to be the only one of its kind ever referred to is also revealing. The authorities were not, in general, quite so quick to pounce on such irregularities. Cases where testators made protestant wills under Henry and Mary, or Catholic wills under Elizabeth, and suffered no posthumous punishment, are far more numerous. Ten years into Elizabeth's reign, the Catholic will of Thomas Barnard of Horningsea (Ely) was registered by consistory court officials;[101] fourteen years later, when the executors came of age, it was registered again.[102]

It is hard to explain such cases except by arguing that, in general, the ecclesiastical authorities agreed with the godly writers in seeing wills as primarily concerned with the disposition of worldly estate according to Christian obligations. Only in extraordinary cases was the smooth passage of property considered worth disrupting on the basis of 'heretical' faith as revealed in will preambles.

Testators were similarly reluctant to rock the boat; the risk involved in writing a preamble which expressed prohibited beliefs was smaller than is often assumed, but it was still not a risk worth taking. In the early years of the Reformation there were many more protestant testators than there were protestant wills. This may have reflected a fear of posthumous punishment or an unwillingness to disobey the governors outwardly, but it may also have reflected a perception that the will preamble was not a sufficiently important expression of faith to merit taking even a small risk. This was clearly not true in all cases, as demonstrated by the strikingly radical early protestant wills discussed by A. G. Dickens and others.[103] Derek Plumb has argued convincingly that such wills present indisputable evidence of the existence of deeply committed individuals. Nevertheless, it should not escape notice that nearly half of the Lollard wills he traced opened with 'conservative' preambles. The natural, but misleading, tendency is to concentrate on the 14 per cent of Lollards who left 'radical' wills.[104] Wills were testaments of faith, since individuals were performing a spiritual duty and the way in which they did so reflected their religiosity; but pious actions spoke louder than pious words, and the exact expressions used in a will's preamble were generally of only secondary importance.

From the disputed will cases under discussion here, there is just one which

[99] In the Ely diocese at least, there is little evidence that court scribes abbreviated even lengthy preambles.

[100] Rosemary O'Day, *op cit.* (1986), p.155.

[101] CUL, Ely Cons original will, Thomas Barnard (1568).

[102] CUL, Ely Cons original will, Thomas Barnard (1582).

[103] A. G. Dickens, *op cit.* (1959, reprinted 1982); Derek Plumb, *op cit.* (1987).

[104] Derek Plumb, *op cit.* (1987), p. 60.

reflects on this question directly. The Devonshire widow, Ellen Serle, used no fewer than three scribes in the preparation of her will. The second of these, George Trowbridge, told the court that around 'Candlemas' in 1580 'he this deponent was requested by Elene Searle to write her testament'. He agreed, so the widow 'delivered him a peece of paper which hadd a forme of the beginninge of her testament bearing date the xxix daye of december last past and writen as he nowe remembreth to those words, First I give and bequeath my soule to Almightie god so farre being writen by the handes of one John Hollacomb'. No further details were forthcoming, but it seems that, as Mistress Serle began to feel that a will was in order, she obtained from a man with a local name – whether a friend, a notary or a vicar we cannot tell – a stereotyped will 'forme'. It was then two months before she proceeded to fill in the main body of the document.[105]

An Ely original will, made in the 1590s, implies a similar procedure: the preamble and the main text were written in different hands.[106] There was clearly some demand for will forms, though it is not possible to assess its strength with any confidence. It would be fascinating to know how exactly John Hollacomb operated; at present, it seems most likely that will forms, if desired, were obtained from friends and not from those working more commercially.

There is, however, nothing here to invalidate the original view that an exceptionally expressive and pious preamble does reflect profound and personal faith. Scribes were perfectly well aware for whom they were writing, by whom they were directed. There is no reason found in these cases to suggest that scribes deemed it fitting to impose long and idiosyncratic clauses upon those who had not asked for them. It may well have seemed a waste of time to do so. When John Gosling, vicar of Meldreth, wrote the will of Robert Thurgood, he had not, so far as we can tell, been asked for any particular form of preamble. He wrote, 'First I doe bequeath my soul unto Almighty God'.[107] When the vicar came to make his own will some years later (adding a fluent signature and perhaps writing the document himself) he expanded considerably upon his earlier format:

> First I doe bequeath my soule unto Allmightie god my most mercifull creator & unto Jesus Christ his deare son my onely redemer & unto the holy gost & blessed spirit proceding from them both my sanctifier & sanctifier of all the elect people of God.[108]

Without detailed knowledge of local practice, it is unwise to dwell too long upon the implications of this one example. It seems likely, however, that this scribe, at least, reserved his most thoughtful preamble for those, like himself, who desired (and deserved?) it.

Having said this, will-making appears to have been characterised by a surprising

105 Devon RO, Chanter 860, ff. 366, 381–85. For further discussion of the use of set formulae, see below, pp. 242–8.

106 I am indebted to Professor Eric Carlson for this information.

107 CUL, Ely Cons original will, Robert Thurgood (1594).

108 CUL, Ely Cons original will, John Gosling (1616).

degree of variety, and deviant cases are always a strong possibility. It can no longer be considered appropriate to form any but the most timid judgements from individual wills viewed in isolation; the importance of studying the wills of a community in detail, for evidence of custom, stereotypical formulae and striking individuality, can hardly be emphasised strongly enough.[109]

Not surprisingly, religion played a lesser role in the average will-making than it did for Becon's Epaphroditus. The attitudes expressed or reported in court depositions could, on occasion, be downright ungodly. The case of Thomas Willowes of Cambridge was an object lesson in the trouble that could follow if a man failed to make a will and 'set all things at a stay'.[110] Several deponents reprimanded the sick man for planning to leave a high proportion of his estate to a cousin, at the expense of his own wife, who had 'toiled and moiled' at his side for many years. On one occasion, however, the 'testator' (as he was called, for want of a more precise description) was swift to scotch the rumour: 'my Cozen Willowes of Horningsey shall have a turde he shall have none of my goodes nor thou neither . . . I will live and spend the goodes my selfe'. Epaphroditus would have turned in his 'simple not sumptuous' grave.[111]

Other cases, however, show that several of the motivations commended by Becon, Perkins, Perneby and Sutton did play an important part in the popular consciousness. As John Prowse of Brixham (Exeter) approached death in 1579, he clearly had thoughts of posthumous harmony on his mind.[112] On the day the will was witnessed, he made a touching speech before those present: 'I praye you agree togither and love one an other when I am gonne and let there be no strife among you that menne maye not saye these goods were ill-gotten'. Perneby later made a similar association in print.[113] Prowse was also aware, however, that making a will was not an answer in itself. He therefore made an extra bequest to his daughter, 'because thou maiest be a meane of quietnes betwene the exequitors.' The testator's fears that all would not run smoothly were apparently realised.

The same desire for peace was expressed elsewhere. Alison Chambers of Blackwell (Durham) told her witnesses 'I feele myself not right . . . I pray you all . . . to beare witnes of my will, that their be no comber betwixt my brethren'.[114] She also left a generous 20s to the poor, perhaps implying the same spiritual undertones that influenced the godly authors.

On several occasions, the desire to prevent 'comber' was over-ridden by other concerns, which themselves had the effect of making conflict more likely. The Kerton (Exeter) widow Ellen Serle made her will partly at least to ward off the advances of a grasping relative, whom she felt had already received more than his

109 Acceptance of this argument has been growing in recent years, since it was stated with force by Margaret Spufford, *op cit.* (1974), pp. 333–4.
110 CUL, EDR, D/2/9, ff. 190–208.
111 Thomas Becon, *op cit.* (c.1558–9), p.119.
112 Devon RO, Chanter 860, ff. 141–44.
113 See above, n. 27.
114 James Raine, *op cit.* (1845), p. 328.

fair share.[115] The testator was fully aware that trouble might follow, and she would perhaps have laughed wrily at Perneby's rhetorical question 'for when every one knowes his part and portion, how shal they not accord and agree?'[116] For widow Serle, the interests of her sons ranked above any wish to promote peace.

The spirtual motivations for will-making also ran in opposite directions in the case surrounding Robert Thurgood of Meldreth (Ely).[117] One witness told her questioners that the testator, sick in bed just two days before his death, 'did take this deponent by the hand sayeinge I am a don man, I shall never escape this sicknes I shall never see my children brought up, but I trust the Lord will send them frendes when I am gon, I have made a Newe will, & I knowe there wilbe some stirre aboute it when I ame gon, I shall not heare it, but I hoape it wilbe the better for my children that I have made a newe will & put oute my wyef from beinge myne executor & made Michaell Newlinge myn executor'. He was indeed on dangerous ground; as the case of Thomas Willowes has shown, the perceived neglect of a widow-to-be could unleash a storm of community censure. Robert Thurgood was evidently thinking rationally, though the deponent did add that nobody else had heard the exchange, except for the testator's wife 'whoe was sleepinge in the said chamber'. She may not have been as soundly slumberous as he imagined.

The testator's peace of mind, recommended by Becon as a valuable consequence of will-making, had been almost destroyed in this case. In others, enhanced spiritual tranquility was specifically identified as a reason for making one's will. A Newcastle glover visited his former master in 1568 and, 'according to his dewtie and good will, moved hym, for the quietnes of his mynde, to make his will and dispose his goods, which wold be a greate occasion of such quietnes in his hart, that thereby, by the grace of God, he should recover health the better'.[118] The deponent was mindful of his Christian 'dewtie', but where Perneby saw the peace of mind acquired as necessary for the testator to die properly, this northern glover, aware that even terminal illnes could be stress-related, saw it as a possible route to bodily recovery. Here, in a nutshell, was the difference between will-making as perceived by those of extraordinary piety, and will-making as viewed by less exceptional Christians. Ordinary people may have tended to think more in worldly terms, but many of them knew their duties and operated, expressed themselves, within a commitedly Christian framework.

A testator's friends could also be aware, as William Assheton later was, that an appeal to human vanity – the desire to be remembered – was a useful argument when trying to encourage will-making. Henry Brandlinge, the brother of an ageing Newcastle esquire, first encouraged him to make his will 'for the staye of freindes'. He then advised the testator to make generous bequests to his sisters, 'and so his name shulde florische after hym, as he had lyved worshipfully all his lyfe'. This may have been an idiosyncratic use of the word 'worshipfully', for the brother continued

115 Devon RO, Chanter 860, ff. 381–85.
116 William Perneby, *op cit.* (1599), p. 233.
117 CUL, EDR, D/2/9, ff. 40–3.
118 James Raine, *op cit.* (1845), p. 85.

'They say, in this town, if you had not so many bastardes you would have maid your will er now'.[119] Again, the motivations and anti-motivations could, in practice, be rather more worldly than those influencing Epaphroditus.

There are indications that many of the common failings and misplaced motives criticised by the godly writers did indeed enjoy some popularity. Wills were generally delayed until sickness, although, when seen in practical terms, this was often quite sensible. Some people may even have viewed the making of a will – which carried an unwanted feeling of finality – as more trouble than it was worth. When, in 1569, visitors arrived at the home of William Kirkus of Merrington, this master of the pithy comment told them drily 'Heere is Mr Vicar, which wuld have me make a will with great circumstanc; and many maks a will that he repentith all the daies of his life'.[120] Perhaps the minister had been emphasising the spiritual importance of will-making; if so, his dying parishioner had been unimpressed.

There were also those, as alleged by Perkins, Perneby and Assheton, who deferred the making of their wills because they hoped to live longer, and perhaps felt that a will, once written, gave death the taste of victory. Thomas Wilkinson of Newcastle was, in 1568, 'sore syke and in great danger of deathe, by thestimacion of many discreit men and women that had ben to se as he dyed'. Despite the advice of such people, the sick man would 'in no wyse . . . be moved and persuadyd . . . to make his testament, havinge ever such an hope in his owne amendment'.[121] Similarly, Thomas Willows of Cambridge told an advice-giving neighbour, 'if I mend not within these two or thre daies I will make a will in writenge'. He failed to do so and later became so 'grievouslie tormented with pain' that the will was still unwritten when Willowes died; and all manner of 'strife' broke out.[122]

The criticisms and commendations of the godly writers were, then, both reflected in practice. A significant number of testators clearly did approach will-making with the right reasons in mind; others were equally devoted to the wrong reasons. Not surprisingly, it often appears that even the highest principles were implemented in practice with something of a worldly emphasis. The over-riding function of the will was to dispose of worldly estate for worldly peace, and a detailed and explicit confession of faith was rarely a primary concern. A basic religious framework for a will was assumed and probably desired, but it was through the bequests that testators performed their Christian duty.

As John Hollacomb, the mysterious Devonshire scribe, demonstrated with his 'forme of the beginninge of a testament', there was scope for the distribution of stereotyped skeletal wills for use by the testators of England. One of the debates concerning early modern wills has centred on the use of printed legal formularies in the preparation of English testaments. In 1984, Dr Claire Cross wrote an important

119 *Ibid.*, p.121.
120 *Ibid.*, p. 213.
121 *Ibid.*, p. 85.
122 CUL, EDR, D/2/9, ff. 190–208.

article on the wills written in Leeds and Hull between 1540 and 1640.[123] She quoted the long and seemingly personal preamble of a Leeds chapman, written in 1566, but noted the existence of two almost identical examples in wills of the early seventeenth century, one from each town.

Dr Cross traced the source of these later versions to William West's *Symbolaeographia*, published in 1590.[124] The earlier version, she surmised, must have been taken from a similar legal handbook. West would then have borrowed the formula for his own book. Dr Cross concluded, her faith in wills fading, that 'The wide circulation of these Tudor legal formularies would suggest that lawyers and scriveners were in England excercising considerably more influence upon the composition of wills than has hitherto been recognised'.[125] It was a perfectly reasonable argument; West's book was bulky and expensive, containing draft documents of many types. It was unlikely to have been owned by the less formal lay scribes discussed above.

Other historians had discovered isolated versions of the same formula and concluded that they were looking at evidence of exceptional personal piety.[126] Dr Cross' discoveries appeared seriously to undermine their position. The common assumption underlying this growing pessimism may, however, be open to question. Is it appropriate to reason that a preamble (or any apparently 'personal' statement for that matter) loses much of its value as evidence of individual belief if it occurs in the exact same form somewhere else? The logic seems based upon what may be a distinctly modern view of the relationship between expressiveness and originality. The latter is all-important to many twentieth century western minds, but the same attitude may not be entirely applicable to early modern society. It was certainly important to a small number of testators that their will preambles were full and expressive, but did it necessarily detract from the worth of their pious pronouncements if those pronouncements were not original?

In 1697, Assheton lamented the brevity of many preambles, calling it 'scandal to the Christian Religion'. He urged the use of more detailed (and, we assume, more 'personal') phrases; but Assheton proceeded to recommend a lengthy set formula of his own composition, presumably with the intention that it be employed by others.[127] The value of a will preamble, for Assheton, was to be measured primarily by its expressiveness, not by its originality. Perhaps we should adopt a similar attitude; if will preambles were, as suggested here, generally seen as matters of indifference, then the testator or scribe who used an unusually expressive format, even if it was not 'original', may well have done so because of strong 'personal' religious conviction.

Whatever the merits of this argument, the fact that West's book was a *legal*

123 Claire Cross, *op cit.* (1984).

124 William West, *Symbolaeographia* (London, 1590). The work was reprinted regularly into the seventeenth century.

125 Claire Cross, *op cit.* (1984), p. 48.

126 For example, Margaret Spufford, *op cit.* (1974), pp. 341–2; also, Hartley Thwaite in a letter printed in *Local Population Studies*, 8 (Spring, 1972), pp. 64–7.

127 William Assheton, *op cit.* (1696), pp.18–19.

formulary does certainly appear to diminish the significance of will preambles as testaments of faith. It should be noted, however, that the long format presented by West was just one of four versions available.[128] The preamble differed in each one, implying that public demand may have required a choice, ranging from the very short preamble to the very long. If testators were offered all four alternatives, did not their decision to opt for the longest and most expressive clause say something of their faith?

There remains the problem that several writers have discovered versions of the long clause, later adopted by West, at dates which make the use of his formulary impossible. The preamble was, for example, used by a testator from Milton in Cambridgeshire in January 1569. He wrote

> I Geffrye Homes, the unprofitable servant of God, weake in bodye & yet stronge in mynde do with a free hart, render & geve agayne into the handes of my lord my god, my spirite, which he of his fatherly goodnes gave unto me, by this means making me a living creature . . .'[129]

And so it went on. With minor exceptions, Homes' preamble was identical to that used by Epaphroditus in Becon's *The Sicke Mans Salve*.[130] William West did not, therefore, lift his model preamble from a legal formulary, but from an immensely popular godly work by one of the English Reformation's foremost writers. Testators who used the 'unprofitable servant of God' preamble, before 1590 at least, did so not because they employed professional scribes who owned legal formularies, but because they possessed or had access to a work the exclusive purpose of which was to teach men and women to face death in a godly fashion. A decision to use Epaphroditus' preamble implied that the book had been read and appreciated by one at least of the testator and scribe, and almost certainly reflects unusually strong religious convictions.

Modern computer technology has made it possible to trace all the testators in the Ely diocese (excluding those whose wills were proved in the Prerogative Court of Canterbury) who described themselves as 'unprofitable servants of God'.[131] The results of this excercise provide the final 'angle' from which attitudes to will-making will be examined in this paper. How, exactly, was Epaphroditus' preamble put to use?

The first example was that already quoted, dated on 20 January 1569. The testator (or scribe) used Becon's formula in a very full version, though he did omit certain phrases, abbreviate several expressions and change a number of words. Nothing new was added and the alterations were not significant. It is possible that

[128] William West, *op cit.* (1590), sections 404–405.

[129] CUL, Ely Cons original will, Geffrye Homes (1568).

[130] See above, p. 218.

[131] I am extremely grateful to Dr Elizabeth Ledham-Green for assisting me so generously in this project. My thanks also go to the staff of the Cambridge University Literary and Linguistic Computing Centre.

the testator or his scribe had memorised the preamble and reproduced it without copying directly from *The Salve*. The testator used the clause about matrimony, though when referring to his wife he omitted, perhaps revealingly, the phrase 'refusing all other women'.

The 'unprofitable servant' label was used on a further sixty-seven occasions, with the last example being in the will of a Whittlesey widow named (appropriately?) Faith King in 1693. The enthusiasm Geffrey Homes had demonstrated for the full form was not, however, shared by many of the testators who followed him. Only thirteen of the wills included a reasonably complete version of the preamble, and very few testators indeed retained the clause on 'the blessed state of honourable Wedlocke'.

In many instances the form used by Becon and West was shortened, often drastically. A number of the wills, particularly those later in the run, suggest that the label 'unprofitable servant of God' had assumed an identity of its own.[132] The most revealing cases were those in which the testator shortened the preamble substantially but was still clearly using one or other of the two sources. Fifteen testators fell into this category, and the significance of their behaviour seems likely to lie in the perception, already discussed, that a long and expressive preamble was somewhat excessive and unnecessary. By the same token, it can perhaps be argued that an unusually full use of the preamble implied genuine conviction.

The chronology of the sixty-eight wills is also informative, though in the numerous instances where only the original label was retained, it is possible that neither of the two works was in use. There were only five Elizabethan usages, despite the popularity of *The Salve*. There were probably many more testators, like William Russbrigg of Emneth, who owned or had read the book, but who chose not to employ such an expressive preamble.

West's *Symbaleographia* appeared in 1590, but there was a surprising twenty-five year gap before the formula was used again in the diocese. In 1615, John Thompson of Ely, a gentleman, used a full form of the preamble. He clearly took it from West, whose version differed very slightly from that of Becon. Thompson also bequeathed to a relative 'all my lawebookes, latine bookes, french bookes and storie bookes whersoever they be in England'. His will began a series of testaments using the formulary, from a wide range of parishes, and the wordings by this date are all closer to West's than to Becon's. The sudden increase in the numbers of testators using the preamble from 1615 is not easy to explain. It seems possible that it had been published in a more readily available form, possibly as a broadsheet.[133]

When Edmund Neave, a taylor from Chesterton, made his will in 1618, he retained the 'unprofitable servant' label, but rather than recite the long preamble,

132 The label 'unprofitable servant' is Biblical. See, for example, Matthew 25:30, Luke 17:10. If it had found a place in the godly household vocabulary of the day, I suspect that the credit lay more with Becon than with West. *The Sicke Mans Salve* enjoyed a wide popularity that had nothing to do with its incidental role as an occasional formulary. The same can hardly be said of *Symbolaeographia*.

133 I am grateful to Helen Weinstein for discussing this possibility with me.

he then switched to West's second alternative version. The preamble was still commitedly protestant, though much shorter. Again, there is an implication that the longer form was seen as superfluous.

It is also possible to trace the involvement of individual scribes and to examine the way in which they used the formulary. A number of men adopted a version of the preamble and used it in wills by no means all of which were written in their own villages. Roger Amye acted as scribe in Ickleton, Duxford and Hinxton. Toby Clifford was active in Landbeach and Milton. For sheer numbers of wills written, however, Richard Field was unsurpassed; between 1626 and 1651 he labelled seventeen Ely testators as 'unprofitable servants of God'. He clearly had West's formulary, or a copy of the relevant section, at his disposal, but only in the very first will of the series did he use a relatively full version of the preamble. Thereafter, he perhaps decided that such length of expression was unnecessary.

In one group of wills, the use of the preamble can be traced, in a gradually evolving version, through three generations of scribes from several connected families. In 1618, Roger Amye wrote the will of a Ickleton shepherd and included a very full version of West's formula, omitting only the clause on marriage. Four years later, Amye reappeared in Duxford, a neighbouring village, to write the will of John Willows. He used a shortened, but still quite full, version of the Becon/West preamble, but now added a clause of his own, referring to the goods 'wherwith it hath pleased Almighty God to endue me with all & to make me steward of heare in this world & vale of miserie'. The phrase 'vale of misery' had also issued from Epaphroditus' lips, but it may well have been taken here from the Book of Common Prayer. In 1625, Amye wrote a will in Hinxton, returning to a more complete version of the formula.

This was the end of Roger Amye's visible involvement, but in 1639 a widow named Mary Amye made her will in nearby Great Abington. Her witnesses were Thomas and Henry Amye. In this will, the 'unprofitable servant' label survived, but the Becon/West preamble was replaced by new and completely different expressions. The resultant preamble was still lengthy and commitedly protestant. Interestingly, the clause referring to the stewardship of worldly goods 'here in this life and vale of misery', not supplied by either Becon or West, was retained. It seems likely that one of the the younger Amyes inherited their father's role as a local will scribe, but decided to keep only certain elements of his formula. The 'unprofitable servant' label is the only link with the original Becon preamble but it is clear that, through William West, Roger Amye and one of his sons, the new format had evolved out of the old. Thomas Amye used the new preamble for two more wills, written in Duxford in 1647 and Babraham in 1648.

Even this is not the full picture. The new preamble clearly took on its own identity in the Hinxton area, and was adopted by scribes from the North and Swann families during the 1640s and 50s. Following the Restoration, the preamble underwent yet another transition with the phrase 'vale of misery' dropped and some new expressions added. Still the 'unprofitable servant' designation was retained, together with several phrases from the 'vale of misery' format. A scribe named William Howsden had also taken up the formula and used it in Ickleton and West Wratting.

It was employed for the last time in 1670, when William Swann – one of the earlier scribes – included it in his own will. Possibly, the 'unprofitable servant' was then finally dismissed and the evolution went on.

This fascinating process suggests a far greater fluidity in the way preambles were used than can be detected in the bare fact that some scribes did make use of formularies. In this subset of the 'unprofitable servant' wills, phrases were dropped and added, new expressions were developed, and gradually evolving formulae were passed around – either in manuscript or by memory – amongst neigbours who also served as local scribes. It seems clear that the expressions used must have been the subject of local discussion, though the fact that the apparently 'stock' preamble was such a lengthy form may suggest that we are focussing here on an unusual group of scribes and testators. In a similar series of wills from the parishes of Balsham and Bottisham, written between 1609 and 1619, it is known from other sources that the scribes using another elaborate formula were men of exceptional piety.[134] Perhaps the same was true of the Amye scribe group. Most locally recurrent formulae were considerably shorter.

Without detailed local research, the discussion cannot be carried much further. It is noticeable that the total number of 'unprofitable servant' wills written by each individual scribe was not large.[135] If they wrote no other wills, then the testators they served were a select group (and possibly an 'elect' group). These scribes were probably not in the semi-professional league of the Willingham schoolmaster, Lawrence Milford. It is also possible, however, that each scribe had more than one formula in his repertoire, and offered the testator a choice. Either way, the decision to use a particularly expressive formula at a will-making probably reflects an unusual depth of feeling on the part of one at least of the individuals involved.

Some people were, then, concerned about the precise nature of religious expression in will preambles, and must have discussed the matter. It still seems unlikely, however, that they were typical. It is also improbable that a large number of scribes were using printed formularies. Even if all sixty-eight of the 'unprofitable servant' preambles had simply been transcribed from West, which they certainly were not, they would represent a very small proportion of the total number of wills written in the diocese. Admittedly, there may have been other printed formularies – particularly in the second half of the seventeenth century – but the much more common process seems to have involved locally composed preambles being passed around among acquainted scribes.[136]

A shorter stereotyped formula was used repeatedly in Balsham between 1610 and 1622, by a number of village scribes, but it did not evolve in the manner outlined above. The form was used in the will of John Taylor, a man of known piety. He

134 The leading individuals in this case were members of the Family of Love.

135 None of the thirteen possible scribes from the Amye, Howsden, North and Swann families can have written more than five wills using the label. Most wrote only one or two.

136 For evidence of other seventeenth century will formularies, see Bernard Capp, 'Will Formularies', a note in *Local Population Studies*, 14 (Spring, 1975), p. 49.

apparently did not feel the need to be either unusually expressive or unusually personal. Taylor's bequest to 'the poorest sort of people', however, went beyond what was customary.[137] In the final analysis, most English testators took scant interest in the wording of their will preambles, and the subject was not on the agenda at the average will-making.

Wills are only marginally easier to interpret as a result of this paper. This is not modesty, but rather an acceptance that contemporary attitudes to will-making covered a wide spectrum, encompassing Thomas Merburie of Cambridge University at one extreme and Thomas Willows of Cambridge Town at the other. The vast majority of English testators did not agree with either man. The disputed will cases demonstrate that many testators were fully aware that they were performing a Christian duty. Edward Leach of Milton voiced a widespread feeling in 1644, making his will 'because there should be no controversy after my death for my goods and possessions and for the maintenance of love and peace in the world'.[138] This could be seen today as a purely moral duty, but to the seventeenth century mind such statements carried resonances that were distinctly religious. It is equally clear, however, that the perceived duty did not extend to the inclusion of anything like a full confession of faith in one's will. Thomas Merburie was highly unusual, and his attitude set him apart even from writers like Perkins and Perneby, who were conspicuously silent on the matter.

It is not appropriate to argue, however, that there was no correlation between the beliefs expressed in a preamble and those held by the testator. Full and expressive dedicatory clauses were more likely from unusually religious testators, and such clauses are undoubtedly evidence of personal conviction. The reverse is not true; short preambles certainly did not invariably reflect lack of strong faith. John Bourn of Wisbech, a supposed elder in the Family of Love, bequeathed his soul 'into the hands of god etc' in 1593/4, although he was well enough to put his signature to the document.[139] All Christians were expected to leave their souls to God, but the religious contemplation that went with this act was not often set down for posterity in a document used primarily for the disposal of wealth.

Wills are not a source into which historians can dip for swift and reliable results. When studied with care, however, they can tell us much of lay faith. Local context is all-important if arguments are to be developed fully. Patterns of local giving must not be neglected; even the deeply religious individual was more likely to express his faith through his worldly bequests than through his preamble. The witness lists can also yield invaluable information, enabling the historian to reconstruct local religious networks, albeit imperfectly. Witnesses were, as we have seen, generally chosen deliberately; the 'godly' were naturally more than likely to summon their like-minded friends, as Epaphroditus did in *The Sick Mans Salve*. Becon enabled us to

137 CUL, Ely Cons original will, John Taylor, (written 1616, proved 1624).
138 Margaret Spufford, *op cit.* (1974), p. 343.
139 CUL, Ely Cons original will, John Bourne (1593/4).

observe the final hours of Epaphroditus; the disputed will cases examined here have opened windows, partially at least, through which proceedings at less exceptional will-makings can be viewed. Taken together, the evidence reveals and clarifies many of the problems historians face in interpreting this source. It suggests also that there remains much vital information to be reclaimed from the wills written in early modern England.

19. PROBATE INVENTORIES AND CONSUMER BEHAVIOUR IN ENGLAND 1660–1740

Lorna Weatherill University of Newcastle upon Tyne

Introduction[1]

The study of consumption is not a new activity, for even in the seventeenth and eighteenth centuries there were comments on other peoples' expenditure, condemning it or justifying new habits and new goods; commenting on established patterns in one way or another. For example, these comments in a novel by Defoe, about the different experiences of the lower, middle and upper classes of the early part of the eighteenth century, make us aware that there were both social and economic dimensions to consumption.

> . . . the middle state . . . was the best state in the world, the most suited to human happiness; not exposed to the miseries and hardships, the labour and sufferings of the mechanic part of mankind and not embarrassed with the pride, luxury, ambition and envy of the upper part of mankind.
>
> Daniel Defoe, *Robinson Crusoe*, 1719

Historians have usually looked at consumption from economic or business perspectives. It has long been recognised that increasing demand for a wide range of goods and clothing was as important in industrialisation as production. Yet answers to questions about who consumed what and why they did so have not been firmly established. It is in the search for new evidence and ways of looking at it that probate inventories are of great importance.

In this paper I am going to look at the way that probate inventories can be used to help us understand consumption in the early modern period. Firstly, I take the subject at a high level of generalisation through taking results from a sample of nearly 3000 English probate inventories and trying to answer the question 'Who owned what, where?'

1 The research upon which this paper was based was funded by the Economic and Social Research Council of Great Britain from 1981 to 1985. Results are published in: Lorna Weatherill, 'A Possession of One's Own: Women and Consumer Behaviour in England, 1669–1740', *Journal of British Studies*, 25 (April, 1986): 131–156; 'Consumer Behaviour and social status in England, 1660–1750', *Continuity and Change*, 2 (1986): 191–216. *Consumer Behaviour and Material Culture, 1660–1760*, (London and New York, 1988). This paper was prepared before the publication of this book, and the tables in it are copied from some of those in the book, with the knowledge of its publishers, Routledge.

Secondly, I use some evidence from probate papers to ask 'Why?' This is a more difficult question and the answers have to be looked for in other documents, but the evidence from probate inventories enable social perspectives to be taken into account, and they provide evidence about the expressive roles of material goods.

Ownership patterns of common domestic goods

The first part of this paper contains a series of tables based on a comprehensive collection of probate inventories from eight parts of England. These listings of moveable goods were made by neighbours shortly after a person's death and they were commonly made throughout the seventeenth century and became rare in England after the 1720s. In them are listed, sometimes in considerable detail, the farming, trade and household goods of the deceased person, together with cash and debts due. They do not record debts owed or any real estate, so they do not give a complete account of the person's wealth. They also record other information, notably the date, the parish of residence and occupation or status. Thus each inventory contains some information about factors that may have influenced ownership, with the exception of age at death and details about the size and structure of the household. Scottish testaments contain only partial listings of goods and cannot be sampled in the same ways as those from England.[2]

Many goods are listed in the documents and it simplifies the problem of data collection and analysis to select some of them for particular study. Two criteria were used to select about twenty items for special attention; they had to be reliably and consistently listed in the documents and they had to be representative of other goods or of peoples' domestic behaviour. They range from basic furniture and utensils (tables, pewter and cooking pots) to newly available things like china. Many of them, like knives and forks or utensils for hot drinks, point towards gradual changes in eating and drinking habits. Some, such as books and clocks, show something of a household's cultural interests and point towards contacts with a wider world. The main omission is that textiles were poorly listed, and clothing was not reliably valued. Details about the goods selected are listed in the appendix.

There are a number of variables derived from the inventories themselves and these form a framework for the tables below. That there were variations in all of these confirms that there were a large number of influences over ownership and these are an important starting point in discussing consumer behaviour.

1. *Region*

Differences between different parts of the country are evident from table 1.[3]

[2] See appendix, pp. 266–71, for details about the sample.
[3] See appendix, pp. 271–2, for details of the areas covered.

Note The following tables all show the percentages of probate inventories in which selected goods were recorded. They are copied from Lorna Weatherill, *Consumer Behaviour and Material Culture, 1660–1760* (Routledge, New York and London, 1988)

TABLE 1. Ownership of goods by region

	No. of inventories	*Tables* %	*Cooking pots* %	*Sauce-pans* %	*Pewter* %	*Pewter dishes* %	*Pewter plates* %	*Earthen-ware* %	*Books* %	*Clocks* %	*Pictures* %	*Looking glasses* %	*Table linen* %	*Window curtains* %	*Knives and forks* %	*China* %	*Utensils for hot drinks* %	*Silver* %
London area	367	92	80	43	91	59	53	41	30	29	37	74	67	40	13	12	15	44
North-east England[1]	325	93	76	2	95	77	37	26	10	15	25	44	55	14	3	10	3	34
East Kent	390	97	89	11	95	59	39	58	26	36	16	47	81	19	7	3	6	41
Cambridgeshire	390	96	86	6	93	72	33	32	12	14	9	27	44	9	2	3	2	15
North-west England[2]	390	83	57*	5*	92	17*	11*	75	20	33	9	31	15*	8	2	1	1	13
Hampshire[3]	260	93	73	3	97	50	20	13	24	7	3	19	35	7	2	0[3]	0[3]	27
North-west Midlands	390	87	62	13	94	42	21	17	15	7	4	14	28	3	1	0	1	8
Cumbria[2]	390	75	43*	1*	88	11*	4*	23	17	7	3	6	13*	1	1	2	0	10

TABLE 2. Ownership of goods in town and country

	No. of inven-tories	*Mean value of inventory* £	*Tables* %	*Cooking pots* %	*Sauce-pans* %	*Pewter* %	*Pewter dishes* %	*Pewter plates* %	*Earthen-ware* %	*Books* %	*Clocks* %	*Pictures* %	*Looking glasses* %	*Table linen* %	*Window curtains* %	*Knives and forks* %	*China* %	*Utensils for hot drinks* %	*Silver* %
London	319	153	92	81	46	92	58	54	42	31	29	41	77	66	43	14	13	16	46
Major town	217	97	91	72	11	93	67	46	45	21	18	41	58	55	27	6	8	6	44
Other town	291	135	92	70	10	94	56	37	39	23	20	23	50	55	15	4	7	3	37
Villages & rural	2,075	126	88	69	5	93	43	20	35	17	17	5	21	35	6	2	1	2	16
All	2,902	128	89	70	11	93	48	27	37	19	19	37	33	42	13	4	4	4	23

TABLE 3. Ownership of goods by farmers and tradesmen in town and country

	Occu-pation	No. of inventories	Mean values of inventory	Tables %	Cooking pots %	Sauce-pans %	Pewter %	Pewter dishes %	Pewter plates %	Earthen-ware %	Books %	Clocks %	Pictures %	Looking glasses %	Table linen %	Window curtains %	Knives and forks %	China %	Utensils for hot drinks %	Silver or gold %
London	All trades	199	177	93	80	45	91	61	58	48	31	30	43	78	68	44	16	14	17	42
	Farmers	7	103	100	86	57	100	100	100	43	14	43	43	86	71	43	0	14	14	43
Major town	All trades	125	109	94	70	14	95	72	49	51	22	20	43	63	58	30	7	10	9	46
	Farmers	10	106	80	90	0	100	70	40	30	0	20	30	40	40	10	0	10	0	40
Other town	All trades	144	137	97	74	9	97	62	42	39	19	20	26	53	65	14	3	8	3	40
	Farmers	43	118	93	65	9	95	33	23	37	12	16	5	30	35	7	2	5	0	9
Rural or village	All trades	443	109	93	74	8	96	52	28	46	19	22	9	29	46	9	3	3	3	22
	Farmers	1,224	132	89	66	3	94	38	16	31	14	15	2	17	30	4	1	1	1	10
All	All trades	911	128	92	75	17	95	58	40	46	22	23	24	48	55	21	6	7	7	3
	Farmers	1,284	131	89	66	4	94	47	17	32	14	15	3	18	30	4	1	1	1	10

TABLE 4. Changing ownership of goods in town and country

	Saucepans (%)						*Earthenware (%)*						*Books (%)*					
	1675	*1685*	*1695*	*1705*	*1715*	*1725*	*1675*	*1685*	*1695*	*1705*	*1715*	*1725*	*1675*	*1685*	*1695*	*1705*	*1715*	*1725*
London	11	36	43	57	55	73	14	19	33	52	59	75	18	17	19	41	34	56
Major town	3	3	8	10	13	35	37	26	39	44	54	74	23	23	16	13	23	30
Other town	2	7	5	8	31	37	36	38	35	26	54	74	18	22	24	23	23	42
Rural/village	1	2	5	5	9	12	26	26	34	34	43	51	18	18	16	16	17	13

	Clocks (%)						*Pictures (%)*						*Looking glasses (%)*					
	1675	*1685*	*1695*	*1705*	*1715*	*1725*	*1675*	*1685*	*1695*	*1705*	*1715*	*1725*	*1675*	*1685*	*1695*	*1705*	*1715*	*1725*
London	11	15	19	24	52	51	9	26	21	57	60	60	58	74	79	81	91	80
Major town	7	3	8	28	33	26	30	20	32	49	60	48	50	59	47	67	62	61
Other town	17	16	19	15	31	43	21	24	21	6	43	47	36	45	49	51	69	74
Rural/village	8	8	13	19	29	31	2	3	3	5	9	10	11	16	20	25	30	28

	Window curtains (%)						*China (%)*						*Utensils for hot drinks (%)*					
	1675	*1685*	*1695*	*1705*	*1715*	*1725*	*1675*	*1685*	*1695*	*1705*	*1715*	*1725*	*1675*	*1685*	*1695*	*1705*	*1715*	*1725*
London	23	30	43	39	60	62	0	0	0	7	33	35	0	0	2	7	22	60
Major town	20	20	13	31	33	52	0	0	11	13	13	9	0	0	3	3	12	22
Other town	6	13	17	11	29	26	0	7	8	8	17	11	0	0	2	0	17	16
Rural village	4	5	5	6	7	10	0	1	1	2	2	4	0	0	0	1	3	6

Some of the goods were much more common in some places than others, especially:

china
window curtains
glasses
pictures

In some areas the goods were more frequently recorded than in others. From this it is tempting to argue that consumption was concentrated more in some places than others, but the tables also show a complexity. These patterns warn against taking any one area as 'typical' or 'representative'. The places where new goods were important (apart from London) were north east England, Kent and Cambridgeshire, all to the east of England. Places where domestic goods were more sparce were in the north and west, with a few exceptions, like earthenware and clocks in Lancashire. Hampshire inventories, although sometimes of high value, did not record these small durables so frequently.

There is no one explanation for these patterns. One important factor was ease of supply, and especially ease of trade with London. For example, there was a substantial trade in 'merchant goods' from London to the north east of England, which sent coal in large quantities to London.

2. *Towns*

Table 2 shows comparisons between town and country, table 3 distinguishes urban and rural tradesmen and farmers and table 4 shows changes in town and country.

The urban inventories were drawn into the sample at random and the proportions found (18%) were roughly in keeping with the proportion of people living in all kinds of urban communities at the time.

Towns, and especially London, are often thought of as playing a crucial role in changing consumer behaviour in the pre-industrial era. Evidence from the inventory sample does not entirely fit with this, for the towns were not 'islands' of active consumption surrounded by 'traditional' values in the countryside. On the other hand, goods were often more frequently recorded in urban inventories, although there were distinctions between different types of goods.

There were few differences between 'staple' goods, like pewter; also books and clocks.

New and decorative goods were more common in towns and a few were virtually confined to towns. Pictures and window curtains were scarce in rural areas but quite common in London; looking glasses were twice as likely in towns as in rural areas.

London dominated for some of the indicators of new modes of eating and drinking like utensils for hot drinks.

Table 3 shows that both occupation and locality were important, with the tradesmen in towns more likely to own goods than the tradesmen in the countryside. This raises questions about the everyday experiences that led to ownership. Table 4 suggests that there was some diffusion from town to country. This is clear for utensils for hot drinks, but less so clocks and books.

3. *Change*

The years from 1670–1730 are often presented as economically inactive. Table 5 shows that, as far as increases in ownership of goods at death was concerned, this was not the case, for there are some remarkable instances of rapid growth and change.

I would see this as the gradual permeation of new goods, habits and decorations, rather than any dramatic break with the past. There are three patterns here:

In some cases goods were already well known in the 1670s and there were only slight changes by 1725. These include tables, pewter and books.

Secondly, there were some goods that were used in a few households in 1675, but by 1725 there had been considerable increases in their frequencies. These include pictures, looking glasses, curtains, clocks.

Thirdly, there were a few new goods, such as china and utensils for hot drinks. Here change was rapid and many households recorded these totally new things by the 1720s.

4. *Change by region*

Table 6 shows that change was concentrated more in some areas than others. There are many details here, and these add to the patterns already looked at. For example, notice that utensils for hot drinks appeared in Kent, London and the North East at much the same time. Whilst they were recorded in all areas by 1715, they increased rapidly in London at this time. Earthenware expanded rapidly in some places, but in others there was little change, and even a decline in Lancashire. Notice the differences between the north west and north east in book ownership.

5. *Social status and occupation*

The question that interested me most was – how far was social position and behaviour important in consumer behaviour?[4]

There is no single answer to the relationship between social objectives, behaviour and consumption. Table 7 shows ownership of the goods selected by social status and table 8 shows ownership by some individual trades. This is a start to understanding social constraints on material life. I am not interested here in whether social position *caused* increased consumption. I am interested in *observing* what differences could be seen between the goods owned by people of different status and occupation.

[4] See Weatherill, in *Continuity and Change* referred to in note 1 above.

TABLE 5. Changing ownership of goods

	No. of inventories	*Tables* %	*Cooking pots* %	*Sauce-pans* %	*Pewter* %	*Pewter dishes* %	*Pewter plates* %	*Earthen-ware* %	*Books* %	*Clocks* %	*Pictures* %	*Looking glasses* %	*Table linen* %	*Window curtains* %	*Knives and forks* %	*China* %	*Utensils for hot drinks* %	*Silver or gold* %
1675	520	87	66	2	94	39	9	27	18	9	7	22	43	7	1	0	0	23
1685	520	88	68	6	93	46	18	27	18	9	8	28	45	10	1	1	0	21
1695	497	89	69	8	93	44	21	34	18	14	9	31	41	11	3	2	1	24
1705	520	90	71	11	93	47	34	36	19	20	14	36	41	12	4	4	2	23
1715	455	91	74	17	95	56	42	47	21	33	24	44	44	19	6	8	7	29
1725	390	91	76	23	91	55	45	57	22	34	21	40	37	21	10	9	15	21
All	2,902	89	70	11	93	48	27	37	19	19	13	33	42	13	4	4	4	23

TABLE 6. Regional change in ownership of goods

	books (%)						*earthenware (%)*					
	1675	*1685*	*1695*	*1705*	*1715*	*1725*	*1675*	*1685*	*1695*	*1705*	*1715*	*1725*
London area	18	15	19	38	31	52	15	18	33	46	57	74
North-east England	9	9	12	8	14	–	23	18	22	28	38	–
East Kent	28	25	29	25	23	28	38	49	62	52	62	88
Cambridgeshire	11	12	6	18	14	9	11	14	28	42	43	55
North-west England	17	26	20	18	25	15	82	74	82	69	80	65
Hampshire	29	26	23	18	–	–	14	8	14	15	–	–
North-west Midlands	22	15	15	11	17	9	20	12	15	14	18	20
Cumbria	14	17	15	17	22	15	11	18	18	22	29	38
	pictures (%)						*utensils for hot drinks (%)*					
	1675	*1685*	*1695*	*1705*	*1715*	*1725*	*1675*	*1685*	*1695*	*1705*	*1715*	*1725*
London area	54	69	79	77	89	78	0	0	2	6	22	57
North-east England	26	45	42	48	58	–	0	0	5	2	9	–
East Kent	37	31	48	48	52	68	0	2	0	3	16	15
Cambridgeshire	6	18	18	42	34	45	0	0	0	2	0	12
North-west England	20	28	35	32	38	34	0	0	0	2	2	3
Hampshire	18	15	20	23	–	–	0	0	0	0	–	–
North-west Midlands	11	8	14	14	29	11	0	0	0	0	2	3
Cumbria	3	6	6	8	9	3	0	0	0	0	2	0

TABLE 7. Social position and ownership of goods

Social status	No. of inventories	Mean value: Total inventory £	Mean value: Household goods £	Tables %	Cooking pots %	Saucepans %	Pewter %	Pewter dishes %	Pewter plates %	Earthenware %	Books %	Clocks %	Pictures %	Looking glasses %	Table linen %	Window curtains %	Knives and forks %	China %	Utensils for hot drinks %	Silver %
Gentry	122	320	55	93	84	13	93	55	43	39	39	51	33	62	60	26	11	6	7	61
Trades of high status; clergy; professions	152	193	39	97	75	11	95	54	40	53	45	34	35	62	63	21	7	11	7	51
Trades of intermediate status	344	157	32	93	77	25	94	62	50	49	24	25	29	56	58	29	11	9	10	38
Yeomen; large farmers	952	165	23	91	69	5	95	41	20	33	18	19	4	21	35	5	1	1	1	13
Trades of low status	435	92	19	92	74	12	96	56	31	42	17	18	15	37	50	12	3	3	4	23
Husbandmen; small farmers	332	32	8	83	57	2	89	33	9	28	4	4	0	9	16	2	0	0	1	2
Labourers	28	16	5	79	79	11	89	57	14	43	4	0	4	4	18	4	0	4	0	0
Widows and spinsters	217	82	18	77	66	12	89	47	22	33	18	13	12	36	46	17	4	4	2	37
Tradesmen; trade unknown	56	115	31	98	82	27	88	55	32	50	32	29	32	57	61	38	9	11	13	46
Occupation or status unknown	264	62	17	83	70	16	88	48	31	27	17	14	18	36	40	16	5	5	6	23
Total	2,902	128	23	89	70	11	93	48	27	37	19	19	13	33	42	13	4	4	4	23

Note There are other ways of grouping the occupations given in inventories.

TABLE 8. Ownership of goods by selected occupation

Occupation	No. of inventories	Mean value: Total inventory £	Mean value: Household goods £	Tables %	Cooking pots %	Saucepans %	Pewter %	Pewter dishes %	Pewter plates %	Earthenware %	Books %	Clocks %	Pictures %	Looking glasses %	Table linen %	Window curtains %	Knives and forks %	China %	Utensils for hot drinks %	Silver %
Shoemakers	45	63	17	91	64	8	93	58	33	51	16	8	8	38	47	2	2	4	2	16
Tailors	32	56	16	91	78	16	100	69	41	44	22	16	16	34	44	6	0	0	13	17
Carpenters	32	70	18	90	81	6	97	56	22	38	9	16	3	22	56	13	0	0	0	19
Weavers	48	85	13	88	67	8	96	48	19	44	15	17	2	27	29	4	0	0	2	8
Blacksmiths	49	56	15	82	63	14	90	41	18	35	10	22	8	33	39	12	0	4	0	8
Butchers	37	129	24	97	76	8	97	59	41	32	16	19	19	46	59	11	0	3	3	43
Shopkeepers	87	124	29	98	86	25	95	64	53	48	37	25	34	67	68	40	15	13	11	45
Innkeepers and victuallers	101	151	43	99	81	37	98	72	67	57	19	30	39	70	65	40	21	9	17	46
Mariners	40	85	30	98	70	8	98	68	45	60	18	25	48	70	73	20	3	23	25	60
Merchants	16*	223	46	100	75	6	81	44	38	56	50	38	44	75	56	38	19	25	19	75
Drapers and mercers	21*	303	34	95	81	19	95	43	38	48	43	24	43	67	43	24	5	5	10	43

Note
* Sample too small to be meaningful.

Position of gentry: The gentry did not predominate and, in spite of their superior wealth and social standing, many expressive goods, such as pictures or china, and even earthenware, were less frequently recorded in their inventories than in those of some of the tradesmen. I did not expect this – I think it illustrates the complexity of the term 'gent' and warns us not to jump to conclusions about social processes. It also suggests that ideas about social emulation as a motivation for consumption needs to be re-evaluated and I comment on this at the end of the paper.

Role of farmers: Ownership of household goods amongst yeomen farmers was less than amongst tradesmen, even those of lesser rank. They less often owned newer, decorative things, although they were often well equipped with ordinary goods, like pewter and tables.

Trades people: All trades people had more varied goods than the farmers. The higher status tradesmen tended most often to have decorative and new items. A large number of consumers were to be found amongst these occupational groups.

Lower status people: On the other hand, those of lesser status, such as husbandmen, were not consumers on a large scale. They mark the bottom of the social groups represented by inventories and it is interesting to note that few owned any of the new and decorative goods. From this I conclude that the limit to the markets for household goods lay somewhere between master craftsmen and husbandmen, and did not extend to the lower ranks as some writers have suggested. There were too few labourers in the sample to make valid deductions about their behaviour.

Meanings and material culture

New evidence about ownership patterns, such as that presented here as tables, is not enough, for we also need interpretations of consumer behaviour in the early modern period. This is difficult and uncertain because there are serious shortages of evidence and there are no accepted concepts that the historian can readily use to analyse the material side of peoples' lives. One starting point implicit in the thought processes behind my work is that material goods were indicative of behaviour and attitudes. They had symbolic importance as well as physical attributes and practical uses. Through looking at the problem in this way it is possible to move beyond whether or not something was recorded in a list, to the meaning of ownership in social and other terms. At the same time probate inventories can also be used to give evidence about the contents of whole houses, and thus be revealing of the atmosphere within middle ranking homes. This, in turn, throws light on the use of space and possible meanings of material life.

There are several interrelated approaches to the relationships between material and social life that suggest that physical surroundings had social meanings. These assume that buildings and interiors were constructed to convey non-verbal messages as well as to serve practical purposes. Sometimes symbolism was obvious, such as the wealth and power conveyed by the architecture of large country houses. More often, at a domestic level, the impact of a place or interior was more subtle and its meanings subconsciously achieved. This impact arose partly (as it still does) from the shared expectations and culture of the people using it. Material goods, such as furnishings, made physical and visible statements about accepted values and expected behaviour. They were used to draw lines in social relationships, but at the same time they provided shelter and subsistence.

One useful way of interpreting behaviour and responses to the environment is to take specific account of how people endeavoured to present themselves to others in everyday situations, using ideas derived from studies of the present day.[5] In order to foster particular images, people present themselves to other people in ways that are analogous to actors presenting themselves to an audience. Various techniques are used for fostering particular impressions, such as facial expression, tones of voice, clothing and, of course, physical surroundings. This kind of 'presentation of self' does not apply in all situations and is normally done at an automatic and subconscious level both in the home and elsewhere. In putting forward these views, Goffman distinguished between use of space in different parts of the living area. When people are actively fostering their image their behaviour is different from when people are not showing themselves or are doing essentially private things. Thus there are 'front stages' which are the settings of activities in which people present themselves to others, and can be likened to a theatrical stage. The appearance and ambience of the 'front stage' affects the way that individuals or households can present themselves. Likewise, the 'back stage' is analogous to the backstage of a theatre. This means that we can go some way towards interpreting the social roles of some possessions by observing use of space and assessing the values that were placed on activities.

In early modern houses, as now, space was used in coherent and socially meaningful ways. Inventories show that most households of middle rank had houses with between three and six rooms, although some of the farmhouses were very much larger. In Telford about two thirds of the houses had three to six rooms; in other places houses were larger and a smaller proportion lived in houses of this size.[6] A common arrangement was two or three rooms on a ground floor, with rooms over

[5] I was inspired to think about the subject in this way by Mary Douglas and B. Isherwood, *The World of Goods: Towards an anthropology of Consumption*, Harmondsworth, 1980. I have also used ideas and vocabulary from E. Goffman, *The Presentation of Self in Everyday Life*, (Harmondsworth, 1969; first published in the U.S.A. in 1959); R. A. Gould and M. B. Schiffer edd. *Modern Material Culture: The Archaeology of Us*, (London and New York, 1981). There are also increasing numbers of social anthropological studies that contain ideas about these matters.

[6] Evidence for room use is drawn from inventories although I did not collect details about rooms and house size in the main sample of inventories because such detail was not given often enough to use in a comprehensive way. For example, only 57% of the inventories from Telford give information on rooms. The generalisations are based on the published collections, for a list see Weatherill, *Consumer Behaviour*, p. 243. See especially, Trinder and Cox, *Telford* and Vaisey, *Lichfield Inventories*. For a very useful summary of room use in an advanced urban area, see Penelope Corfield and Ursula Priestley, 'Rooms and room use in Norwich housing, 1580–1730' *Post Medieval Archeaology* 16(1982)93–123.

them. The ground floor rooms were variously called parlour, hall, house-place and kitchen; the rooms over normally called chambers. There were also outhouses for working tools and farming equipment. There were enough rooms for activities to be carried out in separate parts of the house, and this has significance for the use of space within the house.

Some parts of houses were more valued than others. Rooms were certainly used for different purposes but different *values* were attached to different parts of the living space. In both England and Scotland households had a general living room, which in England was variously called the houseplace, house or hall. In the smaller houses this contained furniture and equipment for many household activities, like tables, seating, cooking equipment, storage space, pewter and miscellaneous other goods associated with day time living. In England it was virtually unknown to have a bed in the main living room, although in Scotland enclosed and folding beds were normally to be found in the main living area. In England the main room sometimes had decorative things like pictures, a looking glass, the clock or books.

In Scotland, even amongst the better-off tenants (roughly the equivalent of yeomen) room-use was less specialised and houses were small, even in the mid-eighteenth century. A retrospective description of the farmers' living conditions around 1765 mentions two rooms, the but (or kitchen) and the ben (or parlour). The kitchen was used for a large number of things, much as the English houseplace was, but with some important differences:

> . . . it was the general eating chamber, and one of the principle sleeping-rooms. Besides, it was the place where all the victuals were prepared; where they baked the bread, kirned the milk, washed the clothes and ironed them; . . . it was the general rendezvous of all the *comers* and *gangers* about the family; . . .[7]

The other room, the ben, was used something like an English parlour, with the master's bed and personal possessions, the bible, linen and food storage. In houses such as these the distinction between 'front' and 'back' become blurred, for there were no places devoted to specific activities, although the ben clearly served more private needs for some of the household members, whilst the but was more public. I find the contrast between England and Scotland here of interest, although I am unsure how best to explain it; Scotland was a poorer country and the farmers only came to build larger houses for themselves later in the eighteenth century.

Larger houses had more specialised rooms. The evidence from England is better here and many inventories show that there were service areas, such as a kitchen, a dairy or a buttery, for some of the messier activities. Chambers were common in all houses in England, where they were used for sleeping and all kinds of storage. In Scotland there were houses larger than the 'but and ben' and here too rooms were devoted to sleeping and storage.

That the use of space in houses served social functions can be seen from changes

[7] Robertson, *Rural Recollections*, (Irvin, Scotland, 1829) pp. 73–5; there are extracts in J. G. Fyfe, ed. *Scottish Diaries and Memoirs, 1746–1843* (Stirling, 1942).

in room use. The most interesting change in England in the late seventeenth century was that the parlour, formerly a best bedroom with some seating and storage became a best living room, containing decorative things and new types of furniture. These contrasting parlours of urban tradesmen illustrate the change; the first dates from 1674/5. (John Webster of Doncaster, 14 Jan 1674/5, in Brears, *Yorkshire Inventories*, p.141.)

In the Parlour A fether bedd bedsted and Furniture a Truckle bedd with Furniture a Chest Three Trunckes one Shelfe an old viol & a little range	4 0 0

The second illustrates how the parlour could be used in new ways, in this case as a room for meals, although sometimes they were furnished for other activities too. (Edward Sackley of Rochester, Kent, saylesman, 1st Sept, 1717, in Spufford, *Great Re-clothing*, p. 222.)

In the Parlour 6 cane chaires 2 Elbow chaires One ovell Table 25 picktures great and small One tea Tabble 6 sawcers 6 cupps, two slopp basons one Tea pott One dish one cannister and stand one glass lanthorne 2 bird cages Window curtains and vallence one house Cloath	3 3 6

Yet there was also continuity, for parlours like the first could be found well into the eighteenth century, as this example of 1748 shows. (James Spender of Lilleshall, Shropshire, yeoman, 21st July, 1748 in Trinder and Cox, *Telford*, pp. 246–7.)

In the Parlour			
a Feather Bed, Bedsteads, Bolsters, sheets,			
Blanketts hangings & furniture	1	10	0
a Chest of drawes, one Ovall Table and Eight join'd Chairs	1	2	0
a Clock and Hanging Press	1	19	0

Whether they changed or not, the furniture, fittings and utensils of a house made up the material culture of domestic life. This, in turn, was closely associated with the practical functions and social purposes of households. Relationships between ordinary activities, social mores and material life influenced ownership of household goods. The numerous, time-consuming and arduous activities necessarily undertaken in all households were central to the organisation of space within the house and only the larger houses had space devoted exclusively to things other than cookery, eating, clearing up, sleeping and resting. If ownership patterns and consumer behaviour are to be understood in a social context, it is important to understand patterns of household activities. In this the evidence from probate inventories both sets a context for asking questions and enables us to look into the detail of peoples' possessions. In this respect their importance is hard to exaggerate.

19. APPENDIX
Ways of using probate inventories

Inventories present the researcher with many technical problems both in collecting and analysing them so the purpose of this appendix is to give more detail about the way the sample was taken and some of the decisions taken in selecting the goods.

The sample

Probate inventories are very numerous and they can be sampled and used in a bewildering variety of ways. How it is done in any particular case depends on the questions to be answered, the detail to be examined, and the practical limitations anticipated in data collection. The sample limits, controls and defines the conclusions that can be drawn. In general relatively small, carefully contrived samples are to be preferred, for these give the most flexible results. There are, unfortunately, substantial practical problems in taking a random probability sample of English probate inventories. This is due to the complexity of the mechanisms by which inventories were made and subsequently kept. There was a hierachy of local and church courts with responsibility for probate, so that there are considerable practical difficulties in getting all the inventories for a particular place, even if the indexes are reasonably easy to use, which many are not. If a sample is taken from one of the local diocesan courts alone, it does not cover all the inventories population for, estates could have been subject to probate in consistory, archdeaconry or peculiar courts, or the Prerogative Courts of Canterbury or York. Inventories have mainly found their way into the keeping of county records offices, with the result that the records for some dioceses are split between different county archives. In other cases several counties are to be found in one place, as at Lichfield, where Staffordshire, Derbyshire and parts of Shropshire are held. Each archive has its own method of storage, search facilities and indexes of various kinds. Extracting inventories for selected people or places can be a lengthy undertaking even if it is possible. A truly random sample is therefore complex and time consuming to take, even when the variation in the data is known, which they were not when this study began.

As a result of these practical limitations and because I was not sure of the kinds of problems I would encounter, I opted for a simplified and unsophisticated quasi-probability sample. There is no obvious bias due to the sample technique in the data, but the extent of the error due to the sample cannot validly be calculated. I have taken samples of the same size (65) from each diocese from the middle year of each decade from 1675 to 1725. I have selected which dioceses/counties to examine to give a broad geographical coverage but I did not choose the areas to be examined at random. In the archive itself I have taken the inventories unseen from the boxes in which they were kept, rejecting those which seemed incomplete or which did not give details of the contents of individual rooms. Scottish inventories are less numerous and less detailed, so I have not been able to include them in the sample.

Another possibility would have been to take a random probability sample from a large diocese with good inventories, perhaps Lichfield, which covers much of the midlands. This would have given good results for some questions but it would not have satisfied the requirement that the survey should give expression to change at a national level. Another approach would have been to select parishes at random and look at all inventories from them, but the archive work for this would have been complex.

The most important limitation of the sample is that it does not pretend to be representative of everyone in England, or even of those who might have left an inventory. On the other hand the aim of this study was not to produce national aggregations but to explore the mechanisms behind patterns of behaviour, so, whilst a limitation, it does not render the results meaningless.

The selection of 'key' goods

Inventories contain a great deal of detail about individual items, although sometimes they are annoyingly sparse in their listings. It is tempting to try to examine everything, but the amount of information thus generated is overwhelming, so I have not even tried to collect comprehensive data on all furniture and utensils. Instead I have concentrated on a few goods which seem to have been reasonably fully appraised and which were also representative of patterns of behaviour in a more general way. It is, however, worth pointing to a few problems in making the selection of 'key' goods and it is especially necessary to comment on the extent to which I feel household goods were deliberately, or accidentally, left out of the inventories.

The question of how often goods were present in a household and were subsequently left out of an inventory is obviously a crucial one in interpreting the results of much of the investigation reported in this book. There is no one answer to this problem, simply because we do not have any evidence at all about what was not there, only what was actually listed. A number of points do suggest that care has to be taken and that unexpected patterns may be due to different levels of recording in different places or at different times. Overall, however, the patterns discussed in the paper are not due solely to different levels of recording.

It is evident from the wording of some inventories that minimal detail is being given on some items; 'all the linen', for instance, may or may not have included table linen; 'all the pewter' did not distinguish dishes or plates; 'pewter, brass, iron and treen' does not name vessels such as pots which could well have been present. This would not matter for comparative purposes, if the inventories lacking detail were evenly spread throughout time and space, but this was not so and in some dioceses they were less detailed than in others. In particular, detail was more sparse in the Carlisle, Lancashire and Staffordshire inventories than elsewhere. This problem only influences a few of the goods (notably table linen, saucepans, pots, pewter dishes and plates), although some items were so poorly listed that they were not included in the first place.

The other major reason why things were left out was that some goods may have been too small, or of too little value, to be appraised in detail. Many personal items, such as hair combs, were rarely listed. There may have been some doubt about whether personal effects, including even clothing, should be listed at all, for over 10% of inventories do not record clothes although everyone must have had some items of clothing. More important is the fact that many household utensils were, then as now, part of the clutter of the living area and were sometimes grouped together so that things of low value could be hidden away and overlooked as 'lumber' or just discounted; this was probably the case with the low value but extremely common and useful wooden trenchers and plates, which had to be left out of this study entirely because they were erratically listed. The only other such utensil included here is earthenware, which could have a very low value and was probably overlooked on occasions. On the other hand, the patterns of change in ownership of earthenware are entirely in keeping with what is known about the growth of production of the industry, so that even if it were sometimes overlooked, it was included often enough and consistently enough to give meaningful results. Some of the small items, like china or pictures, were relatively new and unusual and probably caught the eye of the people making the inventory and were less likely to be excluded.

Some things included here were quite large or had a monetary value in themselves, so that they were not so likely to be left out by accident. Silver, for instance, was usually quite valuable, and care was taken in listing it; clocks were sometimes the most valuable single item, valued at more than £1 10s each. In the last resort there is no way we can know for certain if something has been left out, for we are only told about what was put in.

GOODS SELECTED

1. *Furniture*

This research concentrates on utensils and household goods, so furniture was not noted, except for tables. Beds would make a very meaningful study in themselves.

Tables

These were consistently listed and all kinds were noted. Sometimes details are given about sizes, shapes and the woods used, but this was not frequent enough for the data to be cross-tabulated, so no attempt is made here to trace new types.

2. *Cooking equipment*

Inventories often list this in great detail, including all the fire tools, jacks, pots, pans and roasting tools. A few items were selected here to represent different kinds of cookery. Many of the smaller things were not consistently listed in detail. I also noted frying pans, but these were so like pots that I have not included them in the study.

Cooking pots

There is internal evidence in three dioceses (Carlisle, Lancashire and Lichfield) that these were not consistently listed, for they could have been included in entries like 'all the brass' that were common in these areas. They were sometimes singled out, as in 'brass pot and all the other brass and ironware'. I included all kinds of materials, although iron pots were not common. I have also included kettles here, for these were round vessels like pots at this time, rather than vessels with spouts. Some were very large and of high value.

Saucepans

These were rare in the dioceses where metal vessels were not listed separately: elsewhere they seem consistently listed. They were vessels with handles, much as we use, for small amounts of food, such as sauces. They were least useful over the traditional open fire, and more suited to enclosed ranges.

3. *Eating equipment*

Many of the most interesting goods in households were associated with meals and drinking. I would have liked to have had more information on wooden utensils, especially trenchers and bowls, for these were cheap and practical for everyday use. They were often mentioned in accounts and inventories, but are not consistently listed and are not therefore included in the tables.

Pewter

This is consistently listed, usually in some detail. It normally had a relatively high value, at around £2.

Pewter dishes and plates

These were selected for comparison, because the plates were associated with new ways of eating and new table lay-outs. They are not consistently listed, especially in the three diocese already mentioned. I have left them in the tables for interest and to show the differences between them.

Earthenware

This is consistently listed, although it was the kind of low value item that was easy to overlook or include with other things. Here it includes stoneware (becoming more available from the 1680s), white ware and delft ware. It had many different household and dairy functions, but it is normally listed as just 'earthenware' with little detail; some refer to specific vessels like plates or cups; some inventories list it in the buttery or dairy, separately from that in the house itself. But this kind of detail is not given often enough for any of the distinctions to be used in the tables.

Knives and forks

It surprises many people to read that these were not used as we use them until the mid-eighteenth century and later. They seem to have been consistently listed, and listed separately from knives and 'flesh forks' used in cookery. I have included any entries that seemed to be for table use and excluded kitchen equipment.

China

Chinaware was imported in large quantities and was made in England until the 1740s. It was lighter in shape and usually white with blue or coloured decoration. It seems to be well recorded because it was new and decorative. Often the vessels are specified in some detail.

Utensils for hot drinks

These too seem to have been consistently listed, for they were new and obvious. I have included any references to utensils that could have been used for these drinks, such as tea pots, tea kettles, coffee pots, tea cups and tea spoons.

4. *Domestic textiles*

These are the most difficult items to select because there were many different kinds and they were all poorly listed. Some just list 'all the linen', and this could have included table and bed linen, as well as hangings and curtains. Cushions and upholstered furniture would have been interesting as indicators of comfort, but neither are well listed, the former hardly mentioned after 1690, although becoming more common before that. No solution is satisfactory.

Window curtains

These seem to have been consistently listed, possibly because they were appraised *in situ* rather than amongst other things. I did not include references that might have been to bed curtains.

Table linen

This is the least satisfactory of all the selected goods. It includes any references to napkins or table cloths or towels. Some inventories give immense detail, others obviously include table linen with all the linen together, but in these cases I have not included it, for I do not wish to include this kind of assumption in the data.

5. *Other Household goods*

The other goods were included because they were representative of behaviour and because they were consistently listed. Other things of considerable interest were also too infrequently owned for it to be useful to tabulate their ownership, notably musical instruments and ornaments (images).

Looking glasses

All kinds from small to large are included. They were well listed.

Pictures

All pictures and prints are included. They seem well listed. Detail is rare, but where a title is given, they are normally landscapes or portraits.

Books

These too seem consistent. I have not included bibles in the cross tabulations, although these were only recorded in a small proportion of inventories (5%). The titles are almost never given and in some places they are listed with clothing.

Clocks

These seem fully appraised; they were harder to overlook than many things because of their high value. Details are rarely given.

Silver

I have included all silver utensils and oddments, as well as a few references to gold and jewellery. There is a very wide variation, from a few silver spoons to substantial holdings of vessels.

AREAS FROM WHICH THE SAMPLE WAS TAKEN

Diocese of Durham, 1675–1715: Department of Palaeography and Diplomatic, University of Durham. This covers County Durham, Northumberland and Berwick on Tweed. The inventories for the coastal plain are fuller than those from the Pennine areas, so the coverage is biased towards the more economically developed areas. There were too few inventories for 1725 to take a sample.

Diocese of Carlisle, 1675–1725: Cumbria Record Office, Carlisle. This covers the northern part of Cumbria, Carlisle and the Eden valley, but it does not include Whitehaven.

Diocese of London, 1675 and 1695–1725 from the City division of the Consistary Court of the Diocese, which covered the eastern parishes of the city and some places, notably Whitechapel, outside. These are kept in the Guildhall Library, London. The sample for 1685 was taken from the Middlesex division because records of this date were missing in the Guildhall. These are kept in the Greater London Record Office.

Diocese of Winchester, 1675–1705: Hampshire Record Office, Winchester. These cover Hampshire and the Isle of Wight, and the sample is from both archdeaconry and consistory courts. There are too few inventories to sample after 1705.

Diocese of Chester, South Lancashire division, 1675–1725: Lancashire Record Office, Preston. The sample covers Lancashire south of the River Ribble.

Diocese of Canterbury,1675–1725: Kent Record Office, Maidstone. These cover the eastern part of Kent only.

Diocese of Ely, 1675–1725: Cambridge University Library, archive department. The sample is from the county of Cambridgeshire.

Diocese of Lichfield 1675–1725: Lichfield Joint Record Office, Lichfield Public Library. The diocese covers a very large part of the Midlands, including Derbyshire, Staffordshire, Northern Shropshire and parts of Warwickshire and Nottinghamshire. The sample was confined to Staffordshire and North Shropshire.

20 An Introduction to Probate Accounts[1]

Amy Louise Erickson

My purpose in this article is to introduce the possibilities, the conditions of creation, the social provenance, and the survival patterns of a probate document hitherto virtually untapped as an archival source for historians and genealogists alike. This document is the probate account, a creature of late sixteenth to mid-eighteenth-century England. (For ease of reference, I use the term probate account to include both executors' accounts, in cases where the deceased left a will, and administrators' accounts, filed in cases of intestacy,[2] although by far the majority of accounts were filed for intestates.) The executor of a testate or the administrator of an intestate filed an account of the deceased's estate in ecclesiastical court, usually one year after the death. This account listed the inventory value of the estate, with which the executor or administrator (hereafter 'accountant') was charged, and all disbursements out of that estate, including funeral costs, debts, rents, and a variety of other expenses, from back taxes to marital property settlements. For all of these expenses the accountant 'prayeth', 'craveth', or 'demaundeth' allowance from the probate ordinary. The account was the final stage in the process of administering an estate, and served the functions of acquitting the accountant of further responsibility for the debts of the deceased, and of ensuring that the residue of the estate was distributed according to law.

I *Possibilities*

Because of the range of expenses deducted, the probate account has something to offer everyone. For genealogists, the probate account of a man will usually provide his wife's name, their parish of residence, sometimes his occupation or status, and

1 I am grateful to Margaret Spufford for her initial suggestion that I investigate these documents, and for her criticism and encouragement and ideas ever since. Members of staff in the county record offices in Lincoln, Chichester, Northampton, Taunton, Dorchester, and Winchester, and in Cambridge University Library's Manuscripts Department, have all been helpful.

2 In this I follow the practice of the only published full-length study of these documents, Clare Gittings' *Death, burial and the individual in early modern England* (London 1984). They have been used in smaller numbers and recommended for further research by other historians: Barbara Todd, 'Widowhood in a market town: Abingdon 1540–1720' (Oxford

often their children's names and perhaps ages. The probate account of a woman will also give her children, but not usually her husband, since he will almost invariably have predeceased her. The majority of women's probate accounts were filed for widows, and nearly all of the remainder for 'virgins' or 'spinsters'. Married women could not legally own any moveable goods, which obviated the need for probate procedure. Occasionally an account will also mention the deceased's parents or parents-in-law, particularly if the deceased owed them money.

For social historians there is evidence in accounts for burial practices, for the costs of raising children, and for the materials and making of clothing – all for a level of society which is rarely found in records of this period. The only published work which has employed probate accounts on a large scale explored their detail on funerals as social occasions.[3] Payments are recorded for beer and cakes for the celebrants, bread given to the poor, and gifts of gloves or rings for mourning friends, as well as for sermons read and gravestones erected. The deceased's young children required clothing, board, and schooling for both girls and boys. Sometimes these costs are listed in a lump or annual sum; sometimes specifics are mentioned – down to a bodice, a pair of drawers, or pens and ink. Clothing, usually for children but sometimes for adults, was itemised both ready-made, and in terms of yardage, buttons, thread, and tailoring.

For medical historians, accounts detail the cures or 'physic' administered to the dying in their last illness, often involving sack and spices, fees paid to 'chirurgeons' and the occasional apothecary, and payments to those who watched with the dying, along with their expenses in 'fire and candle'. Probate accounts represent a level of society which could ill afford the luxury of caring for its own sick, a level at which it made more sense to pay pauper women a small sum to do the nursing.

For economic historians, accounts provide evidence of the rural debt and credit market before the advent of the county bank in the eighteenth century. Many types of bonds and obligations in common use appear, along with the rates of interest charged and the term of the loans. In addition to credit, there is evidence on wage rates for day labourers and servants, and on the retail costs of a wide range of foodstuffs and household supplies, all of which is otherwise scarce for the early modern period. For historians of consumer activity, it will be of interest that accounts list prices new, whereas inventories list the second-hand resale value of goods.

For those interested in landholding and inheritance, accounts often list back rents owed at the time of death; sometimes the type of land is specified, or the number of landlords a tenant held from. In addition, accounts are the only documents which detail the division of an intestate's residual (after debts) estate among

Ph.D., 1983) p. 217; Margaret Spufford, *The great reclothing of rural England* (1984); B.A. Holderness, 'Widows in pre-industrial society', in *Land, kinship and life-cycle*, ed. R.M. Smith (Cambridge, 1984); and David Vaisey, 'Probate inventories and provincial retailers in the seventeeth century', in *Probate records and the local community*, ed. Philip Riden (Gloucester 1985). Two accounts are included without comment in *Life and death in King's Langley: wills and inventories, 1498–1659*, ed. Lionel M. Munby (King's Langley 1981).

3 Gittings, *Death, burial and the individual.*

the deceased's children, and this information is essential to assessing the impact of primogeniture on the transmission of wealth. Although ecclesiastical courts had legal jurisdiction only over moveable goods, they played a crucial mediating role in the *overall* distribution of property. Accounts show that (at least until 1671[4]) if one child – usually, but not always, the eldest son – was to receive freehold or copyhold land by the operation of inheritance law, then the ecclesiastical court commonly awarded to the non-inheriting children an inordinately large share of the moveable property in compensation. The heir to land, who might be at the parent's death still a minor, was allotted only a token sum in cash from the parent's estate. For historians of the family, as well as economic historians, these pecuniary details of property division illustrate the emotional structure of the relationships between parents, daughters and sons. The relationship between spouses is also refined by the appearance in accounts of marriage settlements safeguarding the wife's right to her personal property, which she otherwise lost to her husband upon marriage, at a social level at which such legal arrangements were not previously thought to have existed.

For legal historians, probate accounts illuminate the operation of the ecclesiastical court in its probate function. Much has been said to cast doubt on the efficacy of the ecclesiastical courts in this period,[5] but these comments draw uncritically on contemporary propaganda to monopolise more business for the common law courts, and on legislation intended to curtail the influence of church courts. And contemporary criticisms were invariably levelled at the courts' enforcement of morality, and not at its 'civil' functions of marriage and probate.[6] Documentary investigations support the widespread acceptance of ecclesiastical marriage jurisdiction.[7] Certainly in the area of probate jurisdiction, the evidence of accounts suggests a detailed court enquiry into each case and a high level of control over actual property division.

4 The distribution of the residual estate was listed at the end of an account *until* the 1671 Act for the Better Settling of Intestates' Estates, which imposed statutory intestate divisions with the (for us) unhappy result that henceforth ecclesiastical probate clerks simply wrote 'Distributed according to the Act' at the bottom of an account.

5 For example, Conrad Russell, *Crisis of parliaments 1509–1660* (Oxford 1971) p. 60, or Lloyd Bonfield, 'Normative rules and property transmission', in *The world we have gained*, ed. Lloyd Bonfield, Richard M. Smith, and Keith Wrightson (Oxford 1986) p. 170. Few historians go so far as Katherine O'Donovan, who asserts that ecclesiastical law was completely overwhelmed by the common law in the fourteenth century. *Sexual divisions in law* (London 1985) p. 33.

6 Donald Veall's comprehensive *Popular movement for law reform 1640–1660* (Oxford 1970) contains not one reference to criticism of ecclesiastical probate or marriage jurisdiction.

7 Ronald Marchant, *The church under the law: justice, administration and discipline in the Diocese of York 1560–1640* (Cambridge 1969) pp. 108–9, 243–5. R.H. Helmholtz, *Marriage litigation in medieval England* (Cambridge 1974) pp. 113–23. Martin Ingram, *Church courts, sex and marriage in England, 1570–1640* (Cambridge 1987) pp. 364–74. Eric Carlson, *Marriage and the English reformation* (forthcoming) Chs 5–6.

II *Conditions of creation*

Probate accounts reveal the complexity of estate administration undertaken by the accountant: travel was usually necessary for court appearances, in company with the required two sureties; debts had to be verified and tracked down; the deceased's goods might have to be transported and sold; crops on the ground had to be harvested; children had to be 'put out' or apprenticed. Despite the fact that both contemporary treatises and secondary works invariably refer to the executor or administrator, the vast majority of accountants were women, properly in the documents themselves referred to as the executrix or the administratrix. This was due to the fact that 90 per cent of all accounts were filed for married men. Most married men who made wills named their wife executrix, and the widow of an intestate man had a legal right to the administration of his estate unless she chose to renounce it. (Some women did renounce their right, particularly in those cases where a husband's debts outran his assets and his estate threatened to end up in the negative.) Probate accounts are even more valuable for the study of women than are wills, where as executrices they appear as passive repositories of their husbands' trust, since in accounts widows actively take care of the business. A widow presented in court both her husband's will and her account of his estate, but whereas he wrote the will or had it written, the account was created at her instigation.

The administration of estates was enforced by apparitors, who reported to ecclesiastical officals their neighbours' offences, including swearing, drunkenness, and sexual trangressions, as well as less exciting lapses like failing to prove a will or take out administration for the estate of an intestate. Apparitors were paid by fines collected from the offending parties, so it behooved them to seek out offences. When a date was set, the deceased's creditors and legatees were called to appear in court at the account's passing by a notice posted in the parish church and by a proclamation from the apparitor.

The accountant had appeared in court previously to exhibit the inventory and take out letters of administration, in the company of two sureties. When it came to filing the account, she was allowed to deduct her administrative costs from the estate, including her sureties' dinner on the day of the court appearance, and travel (horsehire, or ferrying costs in the fens), which varied with the distance the accountant lived from the nearest probate court. It might be necessary to pay a shilling to 'a man for goeing with me to shew me the country', in this case the way from Publoe and Bath in 1709.[8] Journeys might also be required to retrieve and pay debts, as in the case of Elizabeth Lawrence, the widow of a husbandman worth £50 at his death in 1679 in Toynton St Peter, 30 miles from the court at Lincoln. Elizabeth had to pay debts due by her husband to a total of twenty-five men and five women in her own and six other villages and towns up to twenty miles distant;

[8] Anne Horton, £104/22, Somerset Record Office (hereafter SRO) D/D/Ct/H93. All footnotes to accounts read as follows: Name, £Charge/Balance (Date) Parish, Record Office and Reference. If the parish or date is supplied in the text, it will not be repeated in the footnote.

while she probably sent messengers with payment rather than going herself, since the average amount of the debts themselves was only slightly over £1, the relative cost in messengers was high.[9] Elizabeth Steevens *als* Cox, the accountant of her mother's £33 estate in 1639, was granted more than most by the court at Bath when she claimed £8 for 160 days of her husband's travel in his mother-in-law's business.[10] (When a son-in-law assisted with administration, or even filed the account in court on his wife's behalf, as Elizabeth Browne's husband did in 1612 for the £14 estate of her mother Cassander Bushey, all business had still to be conducted in the daughter's name.[11] The same was true in the case of a deceased man's account filed by his remarried relict, if her new husband assisted.[12])

Administrative costs could also be affected by legal changes, like the 1678 Act to bolster the flagging wool trade, which required all bodies to be wrapped in woollen rather than linen for burial. Whether certified by affadavit or, as Elizabeth Daulton did, by giving Goodwife Whitehead a shilling to go to the justice and swear that Elizabeth's husband had been buried in woollen,[13] the proof required a small fee. Failure to comply resulted in a hefty fine, distributed to the poor: in 1685 the accountant of Hester Wood in Lincolnshire paid £2 10s. in penalty for burying Hester in linen.[14]

A sale of the deceased's goods added to the administrative costs. Sales occurred especially when the deceased was female, since her household often had to be liquidated for the maintenance of orphaned children. A sale involved, as, for example, in the case of Sussex widow Mary Thurban's £28 worth of moveables in 1629, payments to a drummer, a cryer, and a man for keeping accounts on the day.[15] If an item sold for less than its ascribed value in the inventory, the difference could be claimed as an allowance in the account, in the same way that if a sheep died after the inventory was taken, its value could be deducted from the account. The cause of death was specified (*i.e.*, 'sheep rot'), to establish that the accountant was not merely slaughtering an animal for meat.

Despite the variety of possible expenses, in general a total of between £2 and £3 was spent on administration,[16] and that included the court's own fees, which amounted to about £1 15s. (the fees for probate of a will and for intestate administration were not very different). In the case of particularly impoverished accountants the court might abate part of its own fees, and this happened particularly in

9 Thomas Lawrence, £50/–3, Lincolnshire Record Office (hereafter LRO) Ad Ac 43/128. The debts were in: Toynton All Saints, adjoining Toynton St Peter; Greetham, 8 miles northwest; Horncastle, 10 miles northwest; East Barkwith, 20 miles northwest; Tothill, 12 miles north; and Tattershall, 12 miles southwest (all distances approximate.)

10 Alice Cox, £33/–14 (1639) Chelwood, SRO D/D/Ct/C16.

11 Cassander Bushey, £14/10 (1612) Mareham in the fen, LRO Ad Ac 11/86.

12 For example, Thomas Pickringe, labourer, £42/36 (1624) Aby, LRO Ad Ac 19/25.

13 Robert Daulton, £29/7 (1680) Carlton le Moorland, LRO Ad Ac 43/101.

14 Hester Wood, £117/68, Messingham, LRO Ad Ac 44/139.

15 Mary Thurban, £28/9, Arundel, West Sussex Record Office (hereafter WSRO) EpI/33/1629.

16 Amy Louise Erickson, 'The property ownership and financial decisions of ordinary women in early modern England' (Cambridge Ph.D., 1990) Table 3.1, p. 88.

Cambridgeshire and Lincolnshire, where more accountants were left in debt than elsewhere.[17] The other standard deduction asked by nearly every accountant was for the deceased's funeral, and this allowance varied with wealth, generally amounting to between £1 and £2, in prosperous Northamptonshire up to £5 or more.[18]

After administrative and funeral costs, the next to be deducted were debts. At the end of the sixteenth century, Henry Swinburne in his *Treatise of testaments* complained about the misuse of debts by accountants:

> many times are debts thrust into the inventary, which are not due by the testator, and so the legataries and children of the deceased are often defrauded, at least of some part of their due, by the unfaithfulnesse of the executor, and the negligence of the ordinary.[19]

But even in Swinburne's own day, debts owing *by* the deceased were very rarely listed in an inventory. And at the passing of an account, the payment of any debt out of the estate amounting to more than £2 had to be substantiated by an aquittance or a cancelled bond. Payments of smaller amounts might be attested to by the accountant's oath.[20] She was to pay debts out of the deceased's estate in specific order: first to the crown; then legal judgments and condemnations; statutes merchant and recognisances; obligations; and simple bills and merchant (shop) books. Debts without specialty (not in writing) the accountant was not legally bound to pay at all,[21] although she often did, especially those which had been confessed by the deceased in his lifetime or on his deathbed.

In addition to debts owed by the deceased in his lifetime, there were expenses in the year following his death to be included. Swinburne's guidelines for accounts directed that 'sumptuous and delicate expences are not to be allowed, but honest and moderate, according to the conditions of the persons'.[22] An accountant might have tried to claim expenses larger than she had actually paid in order to make a profit from the allowances, but considering that the proof of payment required by the court for debts also extended to expenses, the success of dishonest accountants must have been limited. Acquittances sometimes survive pinned to the account, and accounts themselves were closely inspected: deductions deemed inappropriate were crossed out and the addition of sums, though as erratic as one ever finds in this

17 For a discussion of fees, see Henry Swinburne, *Briefe treatise of testaments and last wills* (London 1635; 1st edn 1590), Pt. 6, p. 72, and for a comparison with southern courts, see Marchant, *Church under the law*, pp. 111–12. The amount due might be reduced by as little as 3s. or cut to as much as half the normal fees, but the balance of the account was not always negative in cases of abatement, and there was no standard cutoff point; the court's ordinary charges on accounts with comparable or even lower balances were sometimes *not* abated. Individual circumstances in each case, including the accountant's own wealth, and the number and age of the deceased's children, must have determined the abatement of fees.

18 Erickson, 'Property ownership', Table 3.2, p. 88.

19 *Testaments*, p. 54.

20 *Ibid.*, p. 89.

21 *Ibid.*, p. 78.

22 *Ibid.*, p. 90.

period, was clearly double-checked. In Margaret Parkinson's 1604 account of her husband's estate before the probate ordinary at Ely, marginal notes indicate that some of the accountant's claims were allowed by the court, but others were not. The final balance was crossed out and refigured five times.[23] In 1618 it was alleged against Agnes Crow, of the Isle of Ely, that at least part of the debts she deducted in her account of her husband's estate had in fact already been paid by her husband in his lifetime.[24] Such false expenses would have allowed the accountant to reap a larger residue than appeared in the account balance, but also required extensive cooperation by payees to provide the supporting bonds, shopbooks, and acquittances which were required by the probate court. In 1500 accounts which I have examined, Agnes Crow is one of only two accountants accused of unethical procedures.[25]

Even the amount with which the accountant was charged is sometimes greater than the inventory value of the deceased, either because the accountant reported goods and debts which the inventory appraisers had inadvertently overlooked, or because the amount of money made by the sale of the deceased's goods exceeded that estimated in the inventory. In either case, the correction was reported by the accountant. One example among many is the Sussex widow Alice Hill, whose husband's inventory came to £46 in 1635, but in her account she reported an additional £8 bond and £5 worth of goods which had been overlooked, plus £4 worth of books sold before the inventory was even taken.[26] Some accounts still have attached a list, which can run to several pages, of items disposed of on the day of the sale.[27] In some cases these additional sums significantly augmented the value of the inventory – Maurice Greenfield's accountant, in 1682, for instance, posted church notices of the sales and had them cried, which efforts at publicity brought in an extra £42 to Maurice's estate, nearly half again as much as his inventory was valued[28] – and would have made a significant windfall for the accountant had she covered them up. But she declared them so often that it is difficult to think many accountants either tried or succeeded in falsification.

The efficacy of ecclesiastical probate jurisdiction is further attested by the tenacity of the court in its pursuit of accountants. Occasionally an account was delayed

23 Richard Parkinson, £81/52, Whittlesey, Cambridge University Library (hereafter CUL) EDR A12/1/1604/15.

24 Alexander Crow, £19/2, Elm, CUL EDR A12/1/1618/4.

25 The other was Martha Onn, relict of Lincolnshire husbandman Bartholomew, who was successfully sued in 1632 by Bartholomew's new administrator 'for her rashe administringe of his goods'. This man then charged the litigation costs to Bartholomew's pitifully small £9 estate. LRO Ad Ac 23/76. I can imagine other subversions which would have had more chance of success. For example, upon the disposition of the residual goods an accountant could claim she thought she was with child. The unborn child was awarded a portion and, when no child appeared, the accountant might appropriate that portion herself. But in fact, claims for a child in the womb occur only rarely.

26 Robert Hill, £46/25, Petworth, WSRO EpI/33/1635.

27 For example, Anne Holwell [no totals] (1622) Westonzoyland, SRO D/D/Ct/H31, and Anne Elliott, £55/–24 (1728) Bridgewater, SRO D/D/Ct/E18.

28 Maurice Greenfield, £146/17, Shipley, WSRO EpI/33/1682.

longer than one year after receipt of an estate, in the event that both parents of a minor child were dead and the accountant was personally required to bring up the child, and waited to file the account until the child was of age. These estates were brought to account as many as fifteen years after the death in question, and of course the minor child who subsequently came of age was key to enforcing administration in these cases.[29] The court also had to be persistent in the face of a high turnover of estates. In one West Sussex example, Charitie Figg *als* Vincent *als* Chandler proved the will of her first husband Chandler, a victualler, in October 1605, and that of her second husband Vincent, who died of plague, within two years following. But in John Vincent's inventory had been accidentally included £11 worth of goods belonging to his deceased son, also named John (who was not Charitie's son). When that son's *wife* died, *her* administrator, in October 1607, complained to the court that the £11 of John Vincent the younger's, of which his wife in turn had been rightful administrator, was in the hands of Charity Chandler *als* Vincent. So five months later, now married a third time to Figg, Charity was called to account by the ordinary yet again, for that £11 belonging to her deceased stepson's deceased wife's administrator.[30]

Although we can verify the internal consistency and general veracity of probate accounts, their use as a historical source is complicated by the problem that we do not know under what circumstances an account was originally required by the probate ordinary. Henry Swinburne, in 1590, merely said that the purpose of an account was to avoid 'the utter undoing and spoyling of many fatherlesse, and friendlesse children', but plenty of accounts were filed where no children were involved. He further warned that 'no man can with safe conscience, speake against the rendering of an account',[31] which suggests some men were doing exactly that, although if we review the legislative history it appears that those who spoke against the rendering of accounts did not achieve their aim until a century after Swinburne. Probate courts were first authorised to require an *executor* to account to the ordinary in the thirteenth century.[32] But the next legislative mention does not occur until the 1540 Statute of Uses (31 Hen. VIII c.5), which states that an *administrator* may be called to account, although he cannot be forced to distribute the residual estate.[33] This latter restriction was clearly an anti-ecclesiastical jab, which the ecclesiastical courts in their turn deftly side-stepped by granting the administration of an estate only to that person who would give a bond promising to pay the surplus according to the ecclesiastical rules of division.[34] The 1671 Act for the Better

[29] For example, Alice Hobbs, £21/7 (1619) Othery, SRO D/D/Ct/H64, and Susannah Keen, £142/–67 (1711) Bleadon, SRO D/D/Ct/K9.

[30] Will of William Chaundler, WSRO STC1/15/219b, and accounts of John Vincent, elder, £11/–6, WSRO EpI/33/1608, and Elizabeth Vincent, £67/53, WSRO EpI/33/1607, all in Midhurst.

[31] *Testaments*, pp. 85–6.

[32] Michael M. Sheehan, *The will in medieval England* (Toronto 1963) pp. 217–8.

[33] See George Meriton, *The touchstone of wills, testaments and administrations*, 3rd edn (London 1674) p. 250.

[34] William Nelson, *Lex testamentaria*, 2nd edn (London 1724) p. 19.

Settling of Intestates' Estates (22 & 23 Car. II c.10), mentioned above in connection with the distribution of residual property, laid down that the ecclesiastical ordinary 'shall and may' call an administrator to account, and so allowed for enforcement, but without specifying under what conditions enforcement was to occur.

Because the 1671 Act empowered ecclesiastical courts to compel estate distribution, it has been seen as a strengthening of ecclesiastical jurisdiction.[35] However, the ecclesiastical method of enforcement seems to have been working reasonably well already; if it had been ineffectual, a significant increase in the number of surviving administrators' accounts after 1671 would be expected in light of the newly extended powers granted to ecclesiastical courts by Parliament. *No* such increase occurs in the surviving documents. Furthermore, ecclesiastical enforcement of estate administration was *restricted* by Parliament fourteen years later in the Statute of Distributions (1 Jac. II c.17): henceforth accounting would only be required in cases where there was a specific request, (a) on behalf of a minor, (b) from the next of kin, or (c) from a creditor of the deceased. After *that* Act, in 1685, the number of surviving accounts *drops* markedly; they continue to occur through the eighteenth century, but only where requested, and so are more likely to represent disputed cases.[36] Hence the pattern of document survival argues that Parliament was eroding, not strengthening ecclesiastical jurisdiction with the Act of 1671. On the basis of the only fragment of parliamentary debate on the bill which survives, it appears that the intent was to extend the jurisdiction, and income, of the common law courts.[37] By 1685, those who spoke against the rendering of accounts had gained ascendancy.

Granted that between 1540 and 1685 by no means all estates were brought to account, two reasons in particular which might have caused the ordinary to require an account would suggest a bias in the surviving documents. The first is circumstances of actual or potential conflict over the estate. But aside from a few spectacular instances, like the Cambridgeshire widow Frances Richardson, in possession of her husband's £566, who in 1674 defended four actions at common law and a suit in Chancery in London,[38] evidence of litigation is rare in probate accounts. Of the 140 surviving Northamptonshire accounts, all of which date from the later seventeenth century, only 6 per cent (eight) mention a law suit, either over the whole estate or over payment of specific debts to or from the deceased. Of 95 Cambridgeshire accounts, most from the earlier part of the century, only 12 per cent (eleven) mention litigation. In both places, litigation for recovery of individual debts was far

35 W.S. Holdsworth, *History of English law* III, 7th edn (London 1927) pp. 558–60. This interpretation apparently derives from Nelson, *Lex testamentaria*, p. 18.

36 The decline is sharp in Lincolnshire, Northamptonshire, West Sussex, and Hampshire, but appears more gradual in Kent and Somerset. A complete picture must await the indexing of probate accounts throughout England.

37 This would have been achieved by reviving the medieval writ 'De rationabili parte bonorum', allowing the widows and children of intestate men to sue for their thirds in common law courts. See the debate on two similar earlier bills in Anchitell Grey, *Debates of the House of Commons* I: *1667–1694* (London 1769) pp. 121–2.

38 Robert Richardson, £566/–192 (1674) Chesterton, CUL EDR A12/2/1673/1.

more common than litigation over the management of the estate.[39] The second possible reason that the court might have required the filing of an account is the estate's actual or potential liability to debt. However, only about one quarter of all accounts ended in debt throughout England (with regional variation),[40] so the court would have been extraordinarily inaccurate in its target group if it was calling principally potential debtors to account. Thus while the selectivity of probate accounts' survival is not clear, there is no pattern to suggest its being anything other than random, at least prior to 1685. No obvious bias like suspect management or likelihood of debt appears which might outweigh the wealth of information to be found in this source.

III *Social provenance*

Probate accounts cover a wide range of social strata, including nearly as many husbandmen as yeomen, a considerable number of labourers and a few of the (generally lesser) gentry. Of course many testators and most intestates did *not* identify their social status, but accounts permit the most precise possible assessment of their economic status (always excepting a complete listing of land ownership, which is unobtainable except on a very small scale through painstaking local reconstructions). The initial, or inventory value of the personal estates represented in accounts did not usually exceed £200, which certainly represents a level of society for which detailed information is rarely available. The median initial charge of accounts in Lincolnshire is only £55; in Cambridgeshire it is an even poorer £42. But in West Sussex the median rises to £73, and in Northamptonshire to £131.[41]

In order to approximate any given individual's social status, his wealth can be compared with the wealth of men who were identified by their neighbours as yeomen, husbandmen, and labourers. These strata fall into bands of prosperity, whose upper and lower margins shift according to regional differences in economy.[42] Like countries, however, social groups could be net debtors or net creditors, and that information is vital to their economic status. Probate inventories are an indication of gross wealth only, since inventories rarely list debts owing by the deceased.[43] Accounts are a far more accurate measure of total wealth because they reflect the

39 Whether the discrepancy in litigation levels here is a difference of region or of period might be tested by a study of the frequency of probate suits in ecclesiastical courts, and a direct comparison of accounts with litigation where possible. Both York and Maidstone hold sets of probate accounts already filed *with* ecclesiastical cause papers, which would be a good place to start assessing the types of litigation arising.

40 Erickson, 'Property ownership', Table 3.3, p. 94.

41 These medians are derived from the total number of accounts in Chichester (1227), Northampton (145), and Cambridge, (247, not including University accounts), and from a sample of 379 accounts in Lincoln.

42 For an estimation of these bands, see Erickson, 'Property ownership', pp. 118–20.

43 This despite the 1671 Act for the Better Settling of Intestates' Estates, which required them to do so. C.B. Philips, 'Probate records and the Kendal shoemakers in the seventeenth century', in *Probate records and the local community*, p. 40.

value of the estate after debts paid. Also, where inventories, for procedural reasons rarely mention land, accounts often do so, both for the payment of rents and in the distribution of the residual estate. The difference these expenses made in the final value of the deceased's estate was often significant but always unpredictable, bearing no necessary relation to the size of the estate as recorded in the inventory. In Lincolnshire, the median value of 83 yeomen's inventories in the years between 1599 and 1686 dropped from £110 to a mere £37 after debts were paid. The value of an inventory may possibly reflect the deceased's wealth in his or her lifetime, but it is certainly no indication of the amount of that wealth remaining to sustain the surviving family. In analysing inventories, it has been suggested that the value of the debts the deceased owed (where they are listed) ought to be *added* to the total value of the inventory since debts reflected the credibility of the deceased in the community.[44] While account deductions verify that yeomen, and to a lesser extent husbandmen, do indeed owe more debts – that is, are granted more credit – than labourers, account evidence on residual wealth also demonstrates that this method of calculating inventory wealth would have validity only in reference to the deceased's own lifetime. But a man's credibility dies, if not with him, very soon after. To *add* a man's indebtedness to the value of his estate is somewhat grotesque from the point of view of his widow, to whom his debts signified a very concrete reduction in the level of his estate available for her subsistence, and not a notional asset representing her husband's reputation in the community.

The bulk of accounts represent more the 'middling' than the wage-earning sort, but this varies to some extent according to the court in which the account was filed, and regional variation in the nomenclature of 'middling' is also evident. For example, 'labourers' appear regularly in Lincolnshire accounts, but they are completely absent in West Sussex, where 'husbandmen' are correspondingly poorer in relation to identified yeomen. Accounts make it possible to assess changing social structure, the relation of labourers, husbandmen, and yeomen over time – for example, the number of identified yeomen increases dramatically over the seventeenth century – and the economic fortunes of different groups. Wills were recognised even before inventories as excellent source material for studying the vast majority of the population below the level of the gentry. Wills, however, convey only the testator's intentions, not what actually happened, and there remain suggestions of social bias among testators. Accounts enable for the first time an assessment of previous hypotheses about who made wills and why – that is, whether greater than average wealth or the presence of minor children had anything to do with it – by a comparison of the economic and familial circumstances of testates with those of intestates. Accounts used in conjunction with wills can also explain why it is that a certain child was sometimes not even named in the parent's will, since accounts give details of any settlement made during the deceased's lifetime on that particular child, or the child's inheritance of land, or a marriage portion, or a legacy from a grandparent. Accounts and wills together thus give a more complete picture of

44 John S. Moore, 'Probate inventories', in *Probate records and the local community*, p. 12, and Philips, 'Kendal shoemakers', p. 42.

property division within the family, and accounts on their own provide much-needed evidence of how the law of intestate division was practically applied in cases where the deceased did not leave a will.

IV *Survival patterns*

Finally, there are a few practical points to be considered when working with accounts. First of all, not every single probate account is a mine of fascinating information. Whether all of the types of deductions which I have discussed will appear in the probate accounts nearest you depends largely on the local accounting style. Many accounts are cut-and-dried, but some clerks went so far as to draw up the forms in advance, leaving blank spaces for the names of deceased and accountant, place of residence, and expenses, the latter grouped under general headings of 'funeral', 'debt', and so forth, without room to itemise. This fill-in-the-blank type of account is detectable not only in those cases in which the clerk used a different colour ink for the variables, but also if references to the deceased are to 'he', when the deceased is patently a 'she', or, conversely, if the accountant is referred to as 'she' when in this particular case it happens to be a 'he'. Another limitation occurs in the Dorset accounts, many of which were only ever half-finished and are missing dates.

The contents of accounts, as well as their presentation, varies regionally: Lincolnshire men had relatively few negotiable debts, but frequently specified their social status; Northamptonshire has many accounts (or parts of accounts) in Latin, despite the fact that they all date from after 1665, and very few of them specify social status; Somerset has no Latin, frequent law suits, and rarely gives the disposition of the residual estate. The percentage of all accounts which were filed for women, who were usually widows but sometimes unmarried, also varies in different counties, from 6 per cent in Hampshire to 17 per cent in Dorset.[45] These rates are in general slightly lower than proportions of surviving wills made by women throughout the early modern period, which range in different locations from 13 per cent to 25 per cent,[46] posing the interesting possibility that women were more likely to make a will than men. The gender ratios of probate documents, which seem to

[45] The intermediate ranges are 8 per cent in Taunton, 10 per cent in Lincoln, 11 per cent in Cambridge and Northampton, and 13 per cent in Chichester.

[46] My own statistical calculations are derived from four collections: *Life and death in King's Langley*; *Selby wills*, Yorkshire Archaeological Society Record Series 47 (1912); the Wills Index in WSRO STCI/18; and *Wills and inventories at Chester, 1681–1700*, Lancashire and Cheshire Record Society Series 18 (1888). See also the following estimates: Nesta Evans, 'Inheritance, women, religion and education in early modern society as revealed by wills', in *Probate records and the local community*, pp. 56, 61; Margaret Spufford, *Contrasting communities*, p. 159; Richard Vann, 'Wills and the family in an English town', *Journal of Family History* 4 (1979) p. 366. The lowest figure for female testation is 10 per cent for the Diocese of Ely in the 1560s and 1620s, found by Motoyasu Takahashi, 'Number of wills', in this volume.

vary over time in both wills and accounts, is a line of enquiry which deserves further investigation.

For the purposes of any statistical study, it must be noted that the survival of probate accounts is relatively limited. The Table, p. 286, suggests that only about 30,000 are extant for all of England (they do not appear to exist in other parts of Britain), whereas there are possibly two million wills and a million inventories.[47] Many courts apparently only kept accounts for a short time before discarding them, so their survival is entirely accidental. At York, for instance, over half of the 58 accounts extant for the period before the Civil War are for individuals whose names begin with 'S', so the 'S' file (and the 'N' file and the 'H' file, which were smaller) escaped the cull. In other places, such as Bristol and Winchester, acounts survive in chronological rather than alphabetical clusters (see Table).

The quality and condition of the account collections vary widely. Two record offices will serve to illustrate the variation. In Lincoln, the accounts were long ago bound in volumes, only vaguely in date order and with much overlap, and an index (in the same haphazard order as the volumes) handwritten, listing the deceased's occupation or status and parish. The parish is necessary because if one wishes to find a corresponding inventory for any individual it is necessary to plough through a cardfile index organised by parish, which is also handwritten (by many different people), in no order whatever, and lists many (but not all) probate documents. In contrast, Chichester has recently restored all of its accounts; they are ordered by year, and within year, alphabetically. There is even an index on microfiche, comparable to the ones available for inventories and wills, sorted both alphabetically and parochially. Maidstone is the only office which has microfilmed its probate accounts, and it did so many years ago. On the other hand, in Taunton the accounts are now in such frail condition that microfilming is impossible. Only a thorough restoration project will save them from the mice. It would be a great shame to lose these Somerset accounts as they contain an extraordinary degree of detail on funeral arrangements, unmatched by accounts anywhere else in England.

In conclusion, I highly recommend the perusal of probate accounts, for their proliferation of details on social and economic aspects of ordinary people's lives in early modern England, from midwives' fees, through marriage contracts, to burial ceremonies, and covering most of the essentials – food, clothing, rent, medicine, and inheritance – in between. Thirty thousand is certainly a sufficient number of documents to ask many and varied questions of the source, to learn from accounts all that they can tell us about the people who made them.

47 See above pp. 170 and 187–215 (Eds).

TABLE. Estimated Accounts Survival[48] as of March 1990

Record Office		*Approx. No. Docs*	*Dates*
Aberystwyth		40	C.17
Bristol		100	1611–15 / 1681–9
Bury St Edmunds		30	1726–1781
Cambridge University		340	1561–1823
Chichester		1227	1572–1711
Dorchester		102	1599–1702
Exeter		75	C.14–C.17
Hertford		1000	–
Huntingdon		340	1595–1825
Leicester		145	1667–1672
Leeds		a few	–
Lichfield		600	up to 1680
Lincoln		6000	1524–1853
London	(Lambeth Palace)	21	1628–1710
	(PRO)	1400	1661–1725
	(Guildhall)	some	1660–1740
Maidstone		10000	1568–1740
Northampton		145	1665–1685
Norwich		a few	–
Nottingham		300	–
Oxford	(CRO)	100+	? – post 1732
	(Bodleian)	120	1578–1719
Preston/Chester		200	1660–1708
Reading		1500	–
Taunton		1075	C.16–C.18
Trowbridge		3000	1600–1750
Truro		400	–
Winchester		300	1623–25 / 1661–93
Worcester		300	–
York	(Borthwick)	320	1606–46 / 1660–1800
	Total	*29200*	

48 I am grateful to Peter Spufford for assembling most of the information in this Table as part of the ongoing project to index and analyse probate accounts throughout England, the one-year pilot study for which is funded by the Economic and Social Research Council. The accounts listed here are those currently either catalogued or otherwise accessible. More exist in some record offices, but they are filed with other documents and remain uncatalogued, and so inaccessible at least for the time being.

21. The Genealogist's Use of Probate Records

Anthony J. Camp Society of Genealogists

In the years just prior to the creation of the Public Record Office a well known peerage lawyer who for forty years practised in Copthall Court off Throgmorton Street gave a series of lectures on the Public Records. Drawing on his experiences he published in 1835, *Lectures on the sources from which pedigrees may be traced* (London, 1835). The previous year he had put out a work in which he showed, to his own satisfaction at least, that his family had a better claim to the Principality of Monaco than the then reigning Prince. This was of course, Stacey Grimaldi, who 160 years ago this year published England's first text-book of genealogical research, *Origines genealogicae; or, the sources whence English genealogies may be traced. . .* (London, 1828).

The book still has some value. About probate records as a source for genealogists Grimaldi said:

> They are the principal and often only records by which families in the middling class of life can trace any descent prior to the introduction of parochial records; secondly, the quantity of genealogical information in wills is of great value; the testaments of men of property almost invariably name two and frequently three or four clear descents of pedigree, whilst the limitation of estates, and bequests of legacies, bring to light kindred who could not otherwise have been traced; thirdly, the sanctity belonging to wills in the minds of testators, and the useless wickedness, as far as they can be concerned, of any deception, render them instruments of great authority; and lastly, the description of estates appearing by ancient will to have belonged to a family, and the wardships of children frequently directed by testators before the abolition of the court of wards and liveries, may lead to other documents containing information not to be found in the wills themselves.

Grimaldi was concerned with pure genealogy and the proving of relationships. Others, more recently, like B.C. Jones in 1951, and the speakers at this conference, have shown that probate records, in Jones's words:[1]

1 *Transactions of Historic Society of Lancashire and Cheshire*, vol. 104, 1951.

> are not simply a record of the deceased, his household, his personal possessions and means of livelihood, they are equally a record of the clerk who wrote the will, the executors who were responsible for carrying out its provisions, the doctors and apothecaries who attended the testator in his last sickness, the suppliers of bread and ale, cake and wine and other necessaries for the funeral, the proctors and scriveners of the court, and the servants, neighbours and friends who were called to bear witness.

Both statements are only too true but it would be rash of me, at this late stage in today's proceedings, to attempt to illustrate even what Grimaldi had in mind in any detail. In any case the genealogical value of wills is pretty well known and a fair amount has been published about it. From the genealogical point of view, if there is a will, one looks at it. One does not look at a will in order to solve a particular problem in genealogy, in the way that one would consult a census return to discover a place of birth, but one consults it just for what ever information it may contain. A will may solve almost any problem. A testator may say something about his descendants, his ancestors or his collaterals. He or she may also, of course, mention quite unrelated people and the way in which they are related to each other.

It has thus become a standard procedure when a pedigree cannot be extended further back to search for and read any earlier wills of people of the same surname. If this does not work then some genealogists have realised the importance of reading through and extracting the wills of the people in the area in which the first ancestor appears, or even, in the case of a migrant overseas, all the wills of a given period, in the hope that some mention may be found.

I am therefore going to discuss one or two general points which it might be useful to bear in mind when searching for wills generally, either in connection with one's ancestry or perhaps from the local historian's point of view when looking for the wills relating to a certain area.

I want, first of all, however, to look again at a group of wills for a small open parish in the eighteenth century in an attempt to throw a little more light on the answer to that interesting question 'How many made wills and why?' which Peter Spufford set me thinking about in the early 1960s and which I attempted to answer in the introduction to the 1974 edition of *Wills and their whereabouts*. Much of the research which has been done on this question in the past relates to the sixteenth and seventeenth centuries, but not to the eighteenth century. I have therefore looked at the wills of a group of people in an open parish with a good deal of nonconformity in the eighteenth century.

These are the seventy wills of parishioners of Walkern in Hertfordshire, which I extracted some years ago, made between 1700 and 1812, and all proved in the local court, the Archdeaconry Court of Huntingdon, Hitchin Division. Only eleven per cent of them were made by women, including one spinster. In 1974, after a careful check of the burial registers in the period 1775–1800, I estimated that about ten per cent of the adult males and widows in the parish made wills in that period. This compares with the estimates of Joan Thirsk who, working in Nottinghamshire in the period 1572–1600, thought that over a quarter of adults made wills, a figure which had declined to about a fifth of adults in the later period 1660–1725.[2] Here at Walkern at the end of the century it looks as though only ten per cent made wills. In general in England and Wales by 1800 the figure seems to have been about six per cent. Jane Cox suggests that by the end of the nineteenth century the figure might be five per cent.[3]

In the wider period 1700–1812 some fourteen of the seventy testators were not entered in the burial registers, although from the will of only one of these would one expect a burial in another parish. It seems to indicate a fairly low rate of recording in the registers, and I should add that the bishops transcripts of the parish registers have been checked. Only two of the seventy have surviving monumental inscriptions.

It has often been stated that the making of a will was superstitiously thought to be tempting to death, but from a practical point of view there was little point in going to the expense of making a will if one was going to live and see one's personal and family circumstances change.[4] The period between will making and burial at Walkern in the eighteenth century is therefore interesting. Seven wills (that is ten per cent) were made three or four days prior to the day of burial and thus probably on the death bed; twenty-four were made within two months of death/burial; forty two within two years of death/burial; and the remaining thirteen between three and twelve years of death/burial. William Oliver who made his will in 1749 when 'sick and weak in body' waited twenty three years to die. Timothy Humberstone, on the other hand, made his nuncupative will two days after he was buried in 1702 if we are to believe the statements of his neighbours and the burial register! It is, of course, not a simple matter just to say that the burial register is wrong, as the probate material itself may be incorrectly dated.

The speed with which the great majority of wills was proved is also of interest. That of John Field in 1780 was proved three days before his funeral, that of Edward Chapman in 1743 two days before his funeral, that of the Revd Everard Sturgis on the day of his funeral in 1750, and fourteen within a week thereafter. Altogether half the wills had been proved by the time the month was out, and the remainder were proved within six months of the funeral. The one will, that of Henry Andrews, wheelwright, in 1749, which took fourteen months to prove is clearly an exception, and that perhaps because his only legacy was to be paid twelve months after his death.

Of these seventy testators, thirty had surviving widows, forty-five had named children, and sixteen had named grandchildren. Twenty-six had more distant named relations, brothers and sisters, nephews and nieces, cousins and kinsmen, etc. Elizabeth Brooks in 1746 described the children of her 'kinsmen' as her 'cousins'. Five apparently had no relations living. In only four cases are wills made mentioning widows only, apparently without children, a clear indication perhaps

2 *The Agricultrural History Review*, III, p. 72.

3 *Wills, Inventories and Death Duties*, London, 1988, p.1.

4 See also Christopher Marsh's paper, above, pp. 226–30 for evidence from an earlier period for comparison (Eds).

that wills were made as a hedge against family discord. If the succession were clear then there was, perhaps, little point in making a will or, perhaps I should more correctly say, in proving a will.

George Sherwood, who in 1918 worked his way through every one of the 4,382 wills proved in the Prerogative Court of Canterbury in the one year 1750 (and thus read nine of those enormous register volumes) found when he added up all the names of people mentioned – as only George Sherwood would have done – that there were 40,320 individuals mentioned. That makes an average of very nearly ten persons mentioned in every will.[5] One hardly needs a better indication of the genealogical value of these records.

Sherwood made his search and published his abstracts, *A List of persons named in the P.C.C. wills proved in the year 1750: Register Greenly: (4,382 wills, naming 40,320 persons, arranged in eight groups, topographically)* (London, 1918), in the belief that the list would help solve many a problem as to the origin and relationships of persons and families in the period 'just before the introduction into England of the industrial system' which, as he said, 'caused great migration. Genealogically, the middle of the eighteenth century is one of the msot difficult periods to bridge'. He did so, thinking of the previous publications of this kind – the abstracts of wills in Register Soame (1620) by J.H. Lea of Boston in 1904, chosen because of the early migration to America and New England at that time, and of those in Register Wootton (1658) by William Brigg in 1894–1914, chosen because of the great changes in residence caused by the Civil War. All three volumes, perhaps little known outside genealogical circles, are of considerable interest.

These persons had no particular individual in mind as an object for research when they started their abstracts, but eight years ago Thora Broughton in Essex was trying to discover the place of origin and parentage of one Mary Creffield. She began a search of Essex wills in the area in which she appeared, reading them through and making notes as she went. Seven years later she had read and abstracted 22,000 wills for the period 1721–1858. She had not found her ancestor, but not put off, and having helped many people to find their lost ancestors along the way, she is now tackling the earlier period 1675–1720.[6] One day she will meet Dr Emmison coming the other way! She says that the answer to her problem may lie in the P.C.C.

Perhaps the answer to her problem does lie in the P.C.C. but since the days of George Sherwood no one has been found to make such wide speculative searches, at least not in the eighteenth century records. Late in the last century Samuel Anderson Smith read through every one of the wills proved in the Prerogative Court of Canterbury between 1383 and 1750, a colossal task, and made brief notes in seven volumes now at the Public Record Office of all the testators and family relationships which related to the six western counties of Cornwall, Devon, Dorset, Hampshire, Somerset and Wiltshire. The volumes are apparently not easily found

5 See Peter Spufford's paper, above p. 173, for evidence from an earlier period for comparison (Eds).

6 See *Essex Family Historian*, No. 46. November, 1987.

there, and it would be a splendid thing if someone would type them up or at least pay for duplicates to be made! One or two smaller collections of this kind of abstract will be found mentioned in my article 'The Perils of Preservation' in *The Genealogists' Magazine*, December, 1984.

I have got a little off the track of what I was saying earlier. The proportion of men to women who make wills may be much greater in the local courts than it is in the Prerogative Court of Canterbury where, for instance, of all the 1,533 wills of people called Jones proved between 1750 and 1800, some twenty-three per cent were women (358). I have recently finished checking the Jones entries in connection with volume four of the P.C.C. *Will Index 1750–1800*, covering letters 'H' to 'M', which has just gone to the printers, and thought that it would be an interesting exercise to re-sort the slips in various ways to see what other conclusions could be drawn about the Prerogative Court in the last half of the eighteenth century.

It was Dr Colin Rogers who said that he was always disappointed by the P.C.C. and that in his more cynical moments he thought of it as a court used largely by the rich, south-easterners and sailors.[7] About the sailors he was probably right; of the Joneses some sixteen per cent (247) were described in the calendars as having died in 'Foreign Parts'. Not all were sailors, of course, for those who died or had personal property in Foreign Parts included two esquires and a knight (Sir William Jones who died in 1795) and at least ten others can be identified as having American connections from the lists published by Peter Wilson Coldham.[8] Some seventy are undoubtedly sailors as the names of their ships are given, a practice which seems only to have been regularly observed in the calendars from about 1781 onwards. Six of these sailors were in the East India Company Service and six had 'No ship'. A further seventeen are marked as in 'Service'. Only one was in the army. It is likely that many other wills, particularly for testators who appear in the calendars as of London, Middlesex, Bristol, and Southampton, and probably of Surrey and Kent (which together would cover parts of London south of the Thames), are also those of sailors. Not all sailors were single men, and their often short wills frequently mention wives, fathers and mothers, or brothers and sister, frequently in Ireland or Scotland.

Of course if one takes a name like Jones one is going to find some Welsh wills, and in fact, some nine per cent of the testators (115 men and 32 women) lived in Wales. With such a very frequent Welsh name that is perhaps not a very great number.

It is perfectly true, however, that great numbers of the testators lived in the south-east. London and Middlesex alone provide thirty-seven per cent (577) of the testators, and if one adds Kent, Surrey, Sussex, Hampshire, Berkshire, Oxfordshire, Buckinghamshire, Bedfordshire, Hertfordshire and Essex that accounts for fifty-eight per cent (889) of them.

7 *The Family Tree Detective*, Manchester, 1985, p. 150.

8 *English Estates of American Colonists; American Wills and Administrations in the Prerogative Court of Canterbury 1700–1799*, Baltimore, 1980.

Sailors (or at least Foreign Parts) and the south east thus make up seventy-four per cent, with Wales bringing the figure to eighty-three per cent. That still leaves seventeen per cent for the rest of the country – eight per cent in the West Country (Cornwall, Devon, Somerset, Dorset, Wiltshire, Gloucestershire and Bristol), and nine per cent in the Midlands, East Anglia and the north. It is true to say that in the whole of the Northern Province there are only five Jones entries. There were no entries at all in Cumberland, Westmorland and Durham, and only one each in Nottinghamshire and Northumberland and three in Yorkshire. These figures to a large extent bear out Dr Rogers's cynical thoughts, and yet it would be very unwise not to consult the P.C.C. if the will sought cannot be found locally.

In any case perhaps all I have done, as you are no doubt thinking, is to chart the distribution of the name Jones, and the better class Joneses at that! However, going back to George Sherwood's work on the year 1750 I am glad to see that I have not altogether been wasting my time. From his abstracts it is clear that if you drew a line from Bristol to the Wash (going south of Northamptonshire but including Gloucestershire) you would find that seventy-six per cent of the wills come from the south east of England, only six per cent of these being from the West Country (Devon, Cornwall, Somerset and Dorset). The Foreign Parts entries with Scotland, Wales and Ireland account for twelve per cent. The whole of the rest of England makes up the rest, with only two per cent coming from Durham, Northumberland, Cumberland, Westermorland and Yorkshire. Whatever the distribution of the name Jones outside Wales it thus follows the general distribution of P.C.C. wills in the mid-eighteenth century almost exactly.

I have the impression that this distribution may have been somewhat different in the seventeenth century but the matter is of less importance as such good indexes are widely available, thanks mainly to the work of the British Record Society for the period 1383–1700. In the nineteenth century the position certainly changed. After 1815, if a seaman died with wages totalling less than £20 owing to him, his will was not eligible for probate in the Prerogative Court and would usually be found in the appropriate local court. At the same time, with the general decline of some of the local courts and an uncertainty as to their future, more and more small estates which would normally have been dealt with by the local courts were attracted to the Prerogative Court a process which must have been hastened by the decision of the Bank of England in 1810 to accept no other probate.

Whatever the period, however, the calendars of the Prerogative Court should, as I have said, never be neglected. The problem is, of course, that after 1700 we only have the original calendars to rely on. Peter Coldham may have gone through the Act Books looking for the wills of people who died in America,[9] but since the days of Samuel Anderson Smith there has been surprisingly little use made of the Act Books to prepare indexes to these wills for particular areas, and it would be such a relatively easy thing to do. So far as I know the only local indexes to have been

[9] For his *English Estates of American Colonists [Settlers 1800–1858], 1610–1858*, 3 vols Baltimore, 1980–81.

produced are for Berkshire (to 1870), Cornwall (to 1814 and perhaps incomplete), Dorset (to 1820), Hampshire (to 1749), and Surrey (to 1812 and probably incomplete) all in manuscript at the Society of Genealogists, and Shropshire, printed to 1749 by George Matthews in 1928. For the more northerly counties it would not be a heavy task, and it would save Colin Rogers and many others coming on wasted journeys to the great metropolis!

Not only that, but the resulting list would be a great deal more accurate than any prepared from the original calendars alone. Having spent a good deal of my life working on the calendars from 1750 to 1800 I am only too well aware of what Guy Strutt once told me about them. When preparing the indexes for the period 1694–1700 he reckoned that some ten per cent of the entries did not appear in the original calendars, which had presumably been made up by the clerks at the conclusion of business each day or perhaps at the time of probate, and no doubt often overlooked in the way that such things are. To add confusion these calendars that we see and still use are not the first contemporary ones which the clerks made. They have been recopied at least twice with all the further omissions and errors that would thus be produced. We prepared the slips for the index which we are now publishing for the period 1750–1800 from one set of these calendars. When anything was not clear we checked the entries against the calendars now in the search room at Chancery Lane. It was as though they had been called across a room and no one had bothered to ask 'How is that spelled?'. Quite frequently the spellings did not agree at all. I will give one example. As I have pointed out in the introduction to the volume of H–M, the old calendars did not attempt in any way to differentiate between the initial letters I and J which were interfiled. In addition the strokes of the letters 'i', 'n', 'm' and 'u' are all formed in axactly the same way. It is thus quite impossible to tell any difference whatever between such names of Jugle and Ingle, Junes and Innes, Inster and Juster, and dozens more, and yet if you look them up in the later calendars where the letters are formed differently you will find that someone has put a particular interpretation on them, whether correctly or not I do not know, and that is the interpretation I have followed. Those who have names beginning with 'I' and 'J' and names having 'i's, 'm's, 'u's and 'n's in them should, however, be warned to watch what they are doing and not to trust the calendars. If there is good reason to think that a will existed and may have been proved then one should go to the act books here as one would, perhaps, in the local courts go to the original or register copy wills when no act book exists.

With the transfer of the records of the Prerogative Court from Somerset House to the Public Record Office many more classes of the subsidiary records have become available to the genealogist. As yet little has been published about them other than the standard guide, *Wills, inventories and death duties: the records of the Prerogative Court of Canterbury and the death duty registers* by Jane Cox (London, 1988).

The inventories, which only survive in quantity between 1661 and about 1720, have received some attention and good indexes are now available. Indexes of two groups of inventories 1661–1732 and 1718–82 and part of a third have been printed by the List and Index Society (vols. 149, 85, 86 and 221) but these do not cover all the inventories surviving from those years.[10]

Like any other ecclesiastical court the Prerogative Court heard cases of dispute arising from its ordinary business and whenever the calendar indicates that probate has been granted 'By Decree' or 'By Sentence' then the possibility of further record should be investigated. this is not at all an easy business as Stephen Archer has shown,[11] mainly because the various classes of filed documents are indexed separately. As he points out the suits usually concerned the authenticity of a will or the degree of relationship of an administrator to the deceased. Cases which involved the interpretation of the contents of the will itself usually went to Chancery or another equity court. It was not uncommon for cases to run in parallel in both P.C.C. and Chancery.

Unfortunately, once more the original contemporary calendars cannot be relied on always to say that a will was proved following a Decree of Sentence, and thus the various additional indexes at the Public Record Office should also be searched to see if there was any dispute or problem with the authenticity of the will. Fortunately, there is a valuable typescript list with an index to those Exhibits which contain wills between 1722 and 1858. In the case cited by Stephen Archer the Exhibits were the notes of instructions for a will taken by a solicitor at the bedside of a dying man, a rough draft which he had made and rushed back to read over later that day and the final text which he came back with the next day only to find that his client had died in the night. Another index, both by name of deceased and by place, on cards, covers the inventories in the same class, and a second card index, by deceased and by the name of the case, covers the allegations. Once the year of the action has been determined then the act books can be used to follow its steps and give some indication of what may be found in the other classes of record. The cause papers actually begin in 1642 and the exhibits in 1653, but the indexing is less complete, though there is a card index to the exhibits 1653–1721. The depositions of the witnesses in this court prior to about 1720 (as in other ecclesiastical courts) generally show their places of birth, and as some cases involve whole groups of people in houses, streets and neighbourhoods, with twenty or thirty witnesses being frequently produced, they provide a unique and as yet untapped source of information for genealogists.

Of course many disputed cases went direct to the Court of Arches where disputed causes were treated along with other causes, the wills, administrations and inventories being produced as exhibits or copied into the exhibit or muniment books. Little survives prior to 1661, most of the earlier records being destroyed in the Great Fire of London in 1666, but the splendid volume, edited by Jane Houston, *Index of cases in the records of the Court of Arches at Lambeth Palace Library 1660–1913* (Index Library, vol. 85, London, 1972) provides a very full guide to all that there is. There are indexes by testators, other parties, and places, let alone of courts

10 See also above p. 174 n. 25 (Eds).

11 'Litigation in the Prerogative Court of Canterbury', *Journal of the North West Kent Family History Society* (September, 1985).

of first instance and of subjects. In my search for Hertfordshire references I found fifty-five cases there mentioned. The earlier material, which starts in 1554, is indexed at Lambeth Palace Library.

For those interested in earlier material then the wills in the archiepiscopal Registers at Lambeth Palace should not be overlooked. These registers of the archbishops of Canterbury run almost in parallel with the Prerogative Court (containing, in theory, wills and administrations of those with *bona notabilia* in more than one diocese in the province, as well as wills proved during visitations by the archbishop and others from exempt parishes and peculiars) and they can contain wills from almost anywhere in the British Isles. Fortunately there is again a complete index in *The Genealogist*, New Series, vols. 34 and 35. The recording of wills commenced there in 1312 and goes on to 1637. For Hertfordshire I found forty-five wills therein, all before 1594, including the earliest yet noted, in 1359.

This latter group of wills, like that of the 'Sede Vacante' wills in Canterbury Cathedral Library, is I fear often quite overlooked by genealogists and local historians looking for early wills. When the archbishop died, and at times when vacancies in other sees coincided with his death, wills were proved by the Court of the Prior and Chapter of Christ Church, Canterbury. These 'Sede Vacante' wills start in about 1278 and go on to 1559, but are particularly numerous in the periods following the deaths of Archbishops Morton in 1500 and Deane in 1503, which coincided with vacancies at St Asaph, Chichester, Ely, Lichfield and Norwich. Once more there is a complete index in *Kent Archeological Society Records Branch*, vol. 3 (1914). There is no index of places but from it I again gathered fourteen early Hertfordshire wills.

Perhaps one should, at this stage, add some comment about the wills proved in the other London courts. I do not think that it was until the British Record Society began to publish the indexes of the Commissary and Archdeaconry Courts of London in 1969 that the full extent of their importance was recognised. The registered wills of the Commissary Court antedate those of the P.C.C. by nine years and the testators, in the early years, are not only more numerous than in P.C.C. but they reflect, as Dr Marc Fitch has said, in concentrated fashion, the diverse origins of London inhabitants in a way that is far easier to discern than from a study of the indexes to wills in the Prerogative Court. He thought it safe to add that no other subsidiary court in the country contains so many references external to its jurisdiction. So far three volumes of index have been published covering the period 1374–1625 (Index Library, vols. 82, 86, and 97). In the course of their preparation Mrs Dorothy Clark read through all the wills mentioned (some 2,600 pages for the first volume alone) and made notes of all the subsidiary places in which people held property, were born or gave a legacy, and these places are all indicated in the published indexes. The Bishop of London claimed a spiritual jurisdiction over Englishmen overseas and foreign protestants in London and this accounts for some of the large groups of wills in this court which would normally have gone to the Prerogative Court – the wills, for instance, of two hundred members of the East India Company and many aliens in London.

The same is true to a lesser extent of the Archdeaconry Court of London, where the assiduity of the clerks in laying their hands on testamentary business which did not really lie in their jurisdiction was also strong. In any case, they fortunately had within their jurisdiction the extensive parish of St Botolph Aldgate, for it was to that parish (as well as to St Dunstan Stepney) that mariners, dying abroad, were, by legal fiction, ascribed as residents. Many had very small estates which probably made it easier for the clerks to appropriate the business, and as a result great numbers of such wills appear in the records of the court. Its records, unfortunately, however, have been poorly kept and only survive sporadically from 1393, but there is no doubt that the indexes should be consulted in any general search for wills of any place in England. The index has been printed for the period 1393–1700 (Index Library, vols. 89 and 98).

I want to go back to disputed cases because there was, of course, above the Prerogative Court and the Court of Arches, that court of last resort in disputed probate cases – the High Court of Delegates – which was created by Henry the Eighth in 1533 after the break with Rome stopped any further appeals from the ecclesiastical courts to the pope in Rome. The records are at the Public Record Office in Chancery Lane and again the Muniment Books 1652–1859 contain transcripts of the wills brought into court. An index to these has been published in *The Genealogist*, New Series, vols. 11 and 12. There is no published index to the other records. There are only a relatively small number of wills in this court (two for Hertfordshire) but as the indexes have been printed they are easily checked.

Quite recently I was fascinated to find through a booksellers catalogue, something to which I had not earlier seen any reference, two thick volumes of *Reports of cases argued and determined in the Arches and Prerogative Courts of Canterbury, and in the High Court of Delegates: containing the judgements of the Right Hon Sir George Lee* edited by Joseph Phillmore (London, 1832–3). They cover the period from Hilary Term, 1752, to Michaelmas Term, 1758 (with some others 1724–33), contain every case on which he made a decision, and were published to show that 'justice at that period, was administered, in the Ecclesiastical Courts, purely and promptly, and as compared with other courts, at a very moderate expense'. For seven years these two volumes form an interesting record of the kind of business which came before these courts and of the reasoning of the learned judge before whom it was heard.

The location of wills in the London area, and by that I mean the location of the court in which a particular will was proved, has always been more difficult than the location of wills in the provinces, and it is perhaps for that reason that Londoners have been more interested in the consolidated indexes to practically all wills and administrations which are provided by the Estate or Death Duty Office from 1812 onwards and which became available at the Public Record Office in the 1960s. Of course the volumes of abstracts of wills, which begin for some courts in 1796, are a valuable additional source of information, not yet much used except by professionals in London, which may not give all the details in the will but which may well give extra information about the relationships of beneficiaries, their whereabouts and their dates of death. Ever since the original discussions about the preservation of these records in 1961 the question of the relative completeness or otherwise of the indexes has interested me. Robert Garrett, who made some checks at that time, thought that after 1812 practically every will was indexed there, except perhaps for those of persons who died on active service who were exempt from duty. David Hawkings who checked 308 entries of his surname against the P.C.C.calendars only proved once more that it was the P.C.C. calendars which were deficient, missing three wills which appear in the more carefully compiled Estate Duty indexes, and that of the local wills only two could not be found in the Estate Duty indexes. What he did find, however, was that the series of duplicate abstracts of these wills which were sent to the county record offices at Taunton and Exeter to replace the bombed originals are themselves not complete, and that further Devon, Cornwall and Somerset wills are to be found amongst the bound abstracts.[12] It is the greatest shame that these valuable indexes are now only available on microfilm. I particularly regret that they have not been filmed so that all the letter 'A' entries, for example, fall year after year on the same reel, something which was suggested twenty years ago. I understand, however, that a computerised index to some part of them is shortly to be made available, something which seems to me absolutely necessary unless the original volumes are returned to the open shelves. Even allowing for their known omissions they are undoubtedly more complete than the old calendars of the P.C.C. (though they do not contain the cross-references to the maiden names of married women which sometimes appear in the P.C.C.calendars). They are similarly likely to be more complete than the calendars of other local courts in places where the old originals are still in use, such as at Lichfield and York. They are quicker to use as they are subdivided to the third letter of the surname. They also contain references to wills proved in some of the smaller peculiar courts and lead to abstracts of the wills concerned which do not survive elsewhere.

Another group of records associated with the probate of wills which has recently become available at the Society of Genealogists is the long series of registers presented by the Bank of England and covering the period from 1717 to 1844. Nothing has yet been published about this collection but it contains extracts from the wills of those with money in the public funds, as also of those stockholders who went bankrupt or were declared lunatics. These occasionally provide extra detail: the baptismal certificate of the minor, the burial certificate of a beneficiary, and a variety of comments about the disposition of the funds, which may be invaluable to the searcher. A consolidated index is being prepared but many of the volumes have good comtemporary name indexes.

Finally, at the end of these chapters devoted to the study of wills, I would like to suggest that a will may be one place in which to record one's own genealogy for the use of future generations! I have always been particularly fond of the will of Matthew Humberstone, of Crutched Friars, in St Olave, Hart Street, proved in the P.C.C. in 1709. He had no children but thought it right, as he says in his forty-seven page will, to settle the results of his care and industry on his male heirs who bore his name, his nearest relations by blood being already deceased. He goes on to quote Dugdale's Monasticon, Mr Chauncey's History of Hertfordshire, and the

12 'Estate Duty Wills and Administrations 1786–1857', *Devon Family Historian*, October, 1977.

records of the Herald's Office, giving examples of the antiquity of his name and the place where monuments to it may be found, 'yet by the hand of God, the late civil wars, and the marriage of heiresses, who carried much of the old estates away and in indifferent circumstances'. He therefore put his estate in trust with the Drapers Company and gave instructions that it was to be settled on the most incredible succession of persons bearing his name, the result of a life-long one-name study of Humberstones, ten of whom he had actually 'bred up in learning'. They had to be 'of sound mind, good life and members of the Church of England'. Failing all these named people and their male heirs and 'if it should happen in the course of time that all the male descendants of the Humberstones become extinct', then in a final effort to preserve his name Matthew Humberstone appointed the ministers and churchwardens of the places called Humberstone in Lincolnshire and Leicestershire and of Walkern in Hertfordshire to 'make choice of some virtuous young man to take the name and the coat of arms of Humberstone for him and his heirs male'. One can only say, 'Go thou and do likewise'.

CONFERENCE PROGRAMME

The Commemorative Conference took place in the Inner Temple, London. The main series of lectures took place in the Inner Temple Hall, and the probate lectures on Tuesday, 9 August in the Arbitration Room. Those lectures which appear in this volume have been asterisked.

MONDAY 8 AUGUST

10.15am	*	Opening Address The Rt Hon. The Lord Mackay of Clashfern, The Lord Chancellor Chairman: Dr. G.H. Martin
11.30am	*	Dr G.H. Martin: The Public Records in 1988 Chairman: Dr P. Spufford
12.15pm	*	Dr E.M. Hallam: From Tower Hill to Ruskin Avenue – nine centuries of housing the Public Records Chairman: K.J. Smith
2.15pm	*	R.J.R. Lorimer: Government record keeping – a tale from the Department of Employment Chairman: Mrs M. Banton
3.00pm	*	K.J. Smith: Sampling and selection – Current policies Chairman: Dr E.M. Hallam
4.15pm		Mrs M. Banton: Random relics – some lesser-known kinds of Public Record Chairman: Mrs J.M. Cox
Evening		Conducted tour of the Public Record Office, Kew

TUESDAY 9 AUGUST

10.15am	*	Dr P. Spufford: The British Record Society and probate records (retitled 'A Printed Catalogue of the Names of Testators') Chairman: Dr G.H. Martin

There followed a choice of lecture

11.20am	*	Dr N.G. Cox: The thirty year rule and freedom of information – access to Government Records Chairman: Dr E.J. Higgs
		or
		Mrs J.M. Cox: Hatred pursued beyond the grave – the records of the Prerogative Court of Canterbury Chairman: J.S.W. Gibson
12.10pm	*	Dr E.J. Higgs: The PRO, the historian, and information technology Chairman: Dr E.M. Hallam

	*	Dr M.Spufford and C.W. Marsh: The making of Wills in 16th and 17th centuries (retitled 'In the Name of God? Will Making and Faith in Early Modern England') Chairman: Dr F.G. Emmison
2.30pm		Sir Geoffrey Elton: The PRO and the historical profession Chairman: Dr N.G. Cox
		or
	*	Dr L. Weatherill: Probate Inventories and consumer behaviour Chairman: P.L. Dickinson
3.15pm	*	Miss S. Colwell: A genealogist's view of the Public Records – ideals and reality Chairman: Mrs J.M. Cox
		or
	*	Ms A.L. Erickson: An Introduction to Probate Accounts Chairman: Dr P. Spufford
4.30pm	*	Mrs J.E. Blyth: Records for the Primary School Chairman: Mrs J.M. Cox
		or
	*	A.J. Camp: The genealogist's use of probate records Chairman: C.R. Webb
5.30pm		Sir Geoffrey Elton: The Friends of the PRO
6.00pm		Reception in the Museum of the Public Record Office, Chancery Lane
7.45pm		Tiptoe through the archives – an evening of readings by members of the Bar Theatrical Society (P.L. Dickinson, C. Cartwright and A. Macgregor)

WEDNESDAY 10 AUGUST

10.15am	*	T.R. Padfield: Preservation and Conservation – will our Public Records survive another 150 years? Chairman: Mrs J.M. Cox
11.30am	*	Dr J.B. Post: Record publication at the PRO – past performance and future prospects Chairman: Dr N.G. Cox
12.15pm	*	B.S. Smith: The National Register of Archives and other nationwide finding aids Chairman: Mrs A. Nicol
2.30pm	*	Mrs A. Nicol: Liaison – Public Records held in other Record Offices Chairman: T.R. Padfield
3.15pm	*	M. Roper: The International role of the PRO Chairman: Dr J.B. Post
4.30pm	*	Dr G.H. Martin: Future Developments Chairman: M. Roper
7.30pm. for 8.00pm		Banquet in the Parliament Chamber of the Inner Temple

BRIEF BIOGRAPHIES OF CONTRIBUTORS

MRS JOAN E. BLYTH, M.A., M.A(Ed.). Retired teacher at Grammar School and University, now writing books for teachers of history in primary schools.

MR ANTHONY J. CAMP, B.A., F.S.G (Hon). Director of Society of Genealogists since 1979. Member of Council of British Record Society, Vice-President of AGRA, author of various genealogical guides. Has lectured widely at home and overseas.

MISS STELLA COLWELL, B.A., F.S.G. Professional genealogist formerly at the College of Arms. Sometime Chairman of Executive Committee of Society of Genealogists. Member of councils of British Record Society and Harleian Society. Founder and organiser of first four English Genealogical Congresses. Lecturer in Genealogy for Extra-Mural Boards of Universities of London and Cambridge. Author of two genealogical guides.

DR NICHOLAS G. COX, B.A., Ph.D. Records Administration Officer, Public Record Office. From 1985 to 1988 he was responsible for policy on selection of records for permanent preservation in the Public Record Office.

DR AMY LOUISE ERICKSON, B.A., Ph.D. Research Fellow, Girton College, Cambridge. Has recently completed a Ph.D. thesis with Dr Margaret Spufford on the topic of women and property in early modern England, which she began after graduating from the University of California, Berkeley.

DR ELIZABETH M. HALLAM, B.A., Ph.D., F.S.A., F.R.Hist.S. An Assistant Keeper of Public Records, currently in charge of the Museum, Chancery Lane. Formerly lecturer at Universities of Reading and London, and for the Open University. Author of books on Medieval France and England.

DR EDWARD J. HIGGS, M.A., D.Phil. An Assistant Keeper of Public Records, currently in the Search Department, Chancery Lane. He has recently published a handbook on the Census Returns. Sometime Secretary, then Chairman, of the Local Population Studies Society.

MR R. J. R. LORIMER, J.P. Departmental Record Officer, Health and Safety Officer, and National Transport Officer at the Department of Employment.

THE RT HON. THE LORD MACKAY OF CLASHFERN. The Lord Chancellor. Lord Advocate of Scotland 1979–84. Lord of Appeal in Ordinary 1985–8. Hon. Master of the Bench, Inner Temple, 1979.

MR CHRISTOPHER W. MARSH, M.A. Research Fellow, Churchill College, Cambridge. Currently completing a Ph.D. thesis with Dr Margaret Spufford on the Family of Love in late sixteenth and early seventeenth century England.

DR G. H. MARTIN, C.B.E., M.A., D.Phil., D.Univ., F.S.A., F.R.Hist.S. Keeper of Public Records 1982–8. Previously Professor of History and Pro-Vice Chancellor of the University of Leicester. Member of the Royal Commission on the Historic Monuments of England and Chairman of the British Records Association, and of the Commonwealth Archivists Association 1984–8. Vice-President of the Royal Historical Society 1984–8, and of the British Record Society.

MRS ALEXANDRA NICOL, M.A., B.Litt. A Principal Assistant Keeper of Public Records in Records Administration Division, Kew. Formerly Liaison Officer for the Public Record Office.

MR TIMOTHY R. PADFIELD, M.A. An Assistant Keeper of Public Records, currently in the Search Department, Chancery Lane. Formerly Head of Conservation Department. Sometime Honorary Secretary of the British Records Association. Co-Author, with Mrs Jane Cox, of the genealogical guide to the Public Record Office.

DR J. B. POST, M.A., D.Phil., F.S.A., F.R.Hist.S. A Principal Assistant Keeper of Public Records, and Head of Medieval and Early Modern Records Department, Chancery Lane, formerly Head of Modern Records Department. Sometime member of Council of the British Records Association, and currently honorary editor of the Journal of the Society of Archivists. Author of numerous articles on the legal records of later Medieval England.

MR MICHAEL ROPER, M.A., F.R.Hist.S. Keeper of Public Records since 1988. Deputy Keeper 1985–8. Director of the Ninth International Congress on Archives in London 1980, and since 1988 Secretary General of the International Council on Archives. President of the Society of Archivists and Vice-President of the British Record Society.

MR BRIAN S. SMITH, M.A., F.S.A., F.R.Hist.S. Secretary, Royal Commission on Historical Manuscripts which maintains the National Register of Archives. Formerly Assistant Archivist for Worcestershire, Essex and Gloucestershire, and County Archivist, Gloucestershire, from 1968–79. Chairman of Society of Archivists 1979–80. Author of publications on local history and archives.

MR K. J. SMITH. Principal, Public Record Office, and Head of Repository and Reprographic Department. Part-time lecturer in records management at University College, London, to overseas archivists and record managers, and has worked in setting up records management programmes in developing countries.

DR PETER SPUFFORD, M.A., Ph.D., Litt.D., F.S.A., F.R.Hist.S., F.S.G. Medieval Historian. Fellow of Queens' College, Cambridge and Reader in Economic History in that University, formerly Reader in History at the University of Keele. Chairman, and sometime Secretary, of the British Record Society, and General Editor of its Index Library. Author of books and numerous articles on medieval European economic history.

MR MOTOYASU TAKAHASHI, M.A. Research Student at Churchill College, Cambridge writing a thesis with Dr Margaret Spufford on seventeenth century English rural society, largely based on probate material.

DR LORNA WEATHERILL, M.A., Ph.D. (Econ.). A computing officer in the University of Newcastle upon Tyne. She has been sampling and studying probate inventories and consumer behaviour. The results have recently been published as a book. Has also written two books and numerous articles on the pottery industry in early modern England.

INDEX